Crim

Tony Storey
and
Alan Lidbury

WILLAN
PUBLISHING

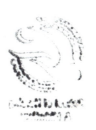

Published by:

Willan Publishing
Culmcott House
Mill Street, Uffculme
Cullompton, Devon
EX15 3AT, UK
Tel: +44(0)1884 840337
Fax: +44(0)1884 840251
e-mail: info@willanpublishing.co.uk

Published simultaneously in the USA and Canada by:

Willan Publishing
c/o ISBS, 5824 N.E. Hassalo St,
Portland, Oregon 97213-3644, USA
Tel: +001(0)503 287 3093
Fax: +001(0)503 280 8832

First published 2001

ISBN 1-903240-25-5

British Library Cataloguing-in-Publication Data
A catalogue record for this book is available from the British Library

12152315

Typesetting and page layout by Willan Publishing. Text set in Times.
Printed and bound by TJ International Ltd, Padstow, Cornwall.

School of Nursing
& Midwifery

Publisher's acknowledgements

We are indebted to the following examination boards for permission to reproduce copyright material:

OCR (Oxford, Cambridge and RSA Examinations): questions from past A-level law examination papers, the AS/A-level law 2001/2002 specimen paper, and the Special Study material for Unit 5, Criminal Law (new AS/A-level Law specification).

AQA (Assessment and Qualifications Alliance): questions from past AEB/AQA A-level law examination papers, and the AQA AS/A-level law 2001/2002 specimen paper.

Advice on possible answers to questions reproduced in this book are provided by the authors, and have not been provided or approved by the boards.

In addition, we are grateful to Sweet & Maxwell Publishers Ltd for permission to reproduce the extracts from *Law Reform and the Law Commission*, by J.H. Farrar, and from the article by Heather Keating on 'The Law Commission's Report on Involuntary Manslaughter: (1) the restoration of a serious crime', in the *Criminal Law Review*, August 1996.

Contents

Part 2 Homicide

Part 3: Offences against the person

Part 4: Offences against property

Part 5: Defences

Part 6 General Principles 2

Part 7 General questions on criminal law

Part 8 Studying criminal law

Introduction

The purpose of this book is to provide a comprehensive review of the general principles of criminal law. It also examines some of the more common offences and the defences that may be available to the accused. It is written mainly for A-level students but will also be a valuable resource for others taking professional examinations at this level, or for undergraduates who are looking for a clear and detailed introduction to criminal law.

For those embarking upon a college or sixth form course, a new approach is being adopted to studies at A-level from 2000. This new approach is designed to encourage flexibility and breadth at 16–18 and offers the student the opportunity to take four or more AS (Advanced Subsidiary) level subjects during their first year, and to then choose at least three A2 (full A-level) subjects during their second year. The detailed study of criminal law normally forms part of the second year of these studies (A2) and follows on from an initial study of the general principles of English law which will have introduced the student to the personnel and structures of the English legal system.

Chapters 23–25 at the end of the book deal with some of the key features that are being introduced under Curriculum 2000, including advice and guidance on synoptic assessment and key skills as well as a chapter that reminds the student that the principles of criminal law must be studied in context and not in isolation. In addition, the source materials intended for use by one of the main examination boards (OCR) as the basis for the synoptic assessment in the years 2002–2003 are reproduced in full, along with explanatory commentary and questions. Students are strongly recommended to familiarise themselves with these new requirements from the start of their course. One of the changes is that the word 'specification' has now replaced 'syllabus' as the correct term to describe the course content.

Two further features of the book are as follows:

- within the text there are boxed questions asking students to consider a variety of moral, ethical and social issues associated with the operation of the criminal law. These provide reminders to think about these kind of issues, and to consider the way in which justice is achieved within the broad context of the society in which we live.

- Examination questions are set at the end of each Part, and in Chapter 23: Additional Questions. The questions at the end of each Part of the book relate predominantly to the subject matter of that particular Part (and are taken from OCR), while the questions in Chapter 23 (taken from AQA) range more broadly across criminal law as a whole. Any student will benefit, however, from tackling either type of question in order to test and improve their understanding of different aspects of criminal law. Answer guidelines for both types of questions are provided at the end of the book so that both students and teachers have the opportunity to test their knowledge against the expectations of the authors, who are both experienced examiners.

As you encounter the various Acts of Parliament and cases that have shaped the rules and principles of law they may at first seem rather like random pieces of a jigsaw. The clear picture is only revealed after some time when the pieces fall into place. This is natural and you should not be put off at the outset by the occasional Latin expression or unfamiliar word.

Indeed, one of the first things the aspiring law student has to grasp is a precise command of words. This is nothing new. Every new student for generations has had to do the same. The sooner you are prepared to open your mind to some new terminology and to understand how and why it has become an important element in the peculiar vocabulary of law, the quicker you will be prepared to address the more important issues which make the study of criminal law so fascinating and attractive. It will become apparent that this special terminology represents the distilled wisdom of Parliament, the courts and academics over a long period. All have played their part in developing the principles of criminal law.

In turn, anyone who studies criminal law will also become familiar with the particular elements that must be established if a successful conviction is to be obtained in an English court of law. They will learn that these elements are no whimsical factors dreamt up on the spur of the moment in the courtroom, but have instead been evolved after careful consideration by judges in previous cases. These are rules and principles of common law, forged and tested over time. The offence of murder is the prime example of a crime which has developed in this way.

Alternatively, the criminal lawyer may encounter, in a new Act, the challenge of fresh concepts and offences devised by Parliament after proper debate and consultation. These may sweep away old rules and replace them with new ones overnight. Such is the authority of the sovereignty of Parliament in our democracy.

However, the beauty and frustration of law is that very often there may be no certain agreement about what the law on a particular topic actually says. Even when an Act of Parliament may appear to be clear and unambiguous, it will require further interpretation by judges before it can be applied with certainty and confidence. This may help to explain why there are so many legal disputes and appeals. If the law was always crystal clear there would be rather less opportunity for professional and academic lawyers to make a living by arguing about it.

For the student this uncertainty need not be a source of worry since very often extremely learned judges in the same court do not agree with each other. From the examiner's point of view it enables questions to be set which allow the student to demonstrate their awareness of these rather 'grey' areas of uncertainty.

Equally, it must be remembered that the adversarial nature of criminal trials typifies the essence of the English legal system. Under our system a person accused of a crime is presumed innocent until proven guilty by the prosecution and the burden of proving that guilt rests upon the Crown Prosecution Service who act on behalf of the State. An accused still has a right to remain silent but normally chooses, through his or her legal representatives, to put forward a defence. Therefore, the student of criminal law must be able to see the possibilities that may exist for both sides of the argument. What offences may a person have committed and what defences may be available to them?

Having read the book you should not only have gained an appreciation and understanding of the principles of criminal law but acquired the necessary knowledge and skills to succeed in your examination. The authors hope that you will also have been encouraged to take your studies further following this introduction to a fascinating and challenging branch of English law.

Table of cases

Table of statutes

Part 1

General principles 1

1   *Actus reus* and *mens rea*

Introduction

The convicted criminal is the object of loathing and fascination in almost equal measure – an outcast, a person with few friends. The hardened, dangerous criminal is liable to be punished by imprisonment or fine. His or her prospects of obtaining or retaining employment and returning to a normal life in society are, in many cases, severely damaged.

So what is it that leads to a criminal conviction? A great deal of detection work? Often, yes. The careful unravelling of clues and evidence that will stand up to careful scrutiny and cross-examination in court? Normally, yes.

Yet it is more than this. It is up to the prosecution (the State, represented by the Crown Prosecution Service) to prove that an accused is guilty (the burden of proof). It involves a court being satisfied that the accused is guilty beyond a reasonable doubt (the standard of proof) following a due process of law. An accused is entitled to a fair trial upon consideration of the relevant facts and the law that relate to their case. A person cannot be convicted upon suspicion alone. Generations of criminal law students have become familiar with the Latin maxim, '*actus non facit reum nisi mens sit rea*'. Do not be afraid of the fact that you 'haven't got the Latin'! Loosely translated, this phrase means that in English law a person cannot be convicted merely upon proof of the fact that they have committed the crime in question (the *actus reus*). It must be established by the prosecution that they also had an accompanying guilty mind (the *mens rea*). The significance of this phrase or maxim is that great importance is attached to the mind of the accused at the time of the offence when determining his or her liability. Therefore, in theory at least, the innocent person is protected from false conviction. Throughout this book a shorthand is used in order to describe the accused person, or defendant, as 'D', while the victim of the defendant's crime is referred to as 'V'.

Actus reus

As stated above, the 'doing part' of any crime is referred to as the *actus reus*. *Actus reus* means the physical elements of the crime. It includes some or all of the following:

- Conduct

- Consequences

- Circumstances

In murder, for example, the *actus reus* could be described as causing the death of another human being under the Queen's Peace. Thus, to be guilty of murder, the defendant (D) must:

- Cause death (this is a consequence)

- Of another human being (this is a circumstance)

- Under the Queen's Peace (this is another circumstance)

In theft, to take another example, the *actus reus* is to appropriate property belonging to another. Thus, to be guilty of theft, D must:

- Appropriate (this is conduct)

- Property (this is a circumstance)

- Belonging to another (this is another circumstance)

You will note that in murder (see Chapter 5) there is no specific conduct requirement, merely that death is caused by the accused. This means that D could (though it is unusual) commit murder by *doing nothing*. Liability for doing nothing will be considered in Chapter 2. In theft, on the other hand, there is no specific consequence required. That is, D does not have to escape with property in order to be guilty; he simply has to 'appropriate' it (this means to assume a right of ownership).

If any one of the *actus reus* elements of a crime are not proven against D, then he cannot be guilty of that offence. D may well cause the death of another human being – but if it was committed during wartime, it would not be 'under the Queen's Peace' and one of the elements of the *actus reus* of murder would be missing. Therefore, D would not be liable. This does not necessarily mean that D will escape liability altogether. There may be other crimes that he has committed. Suppose D administers a slow-acting poison to the V, and V drinks it, but V – coincidentally – drops dead of a heart attack before the poison can take effect. D has tried to commit murder, but he has not done so – he did not 'cause death'. In this case, D is not guilty of murder, but he would be convicted of attempted murder instead. This is, in fact, exactly what happened in *White* (1910).

Causation

As indicated above, to be guilty of murder, D must 'cause death'. This is an example of one aspect of the *actus reus*, 'causation'. Causation must be established for nearly all offences but it so happens that the crime of murder provides the best illustrations of the operation of the principles involved. Whether D's acts or omissions actually caused V's death is always for the jury to decide. The judge should direct them as to the elements of causation, but it is for them to decide if the causal link between D's act and the prohibited consequence has been established. Usually it will be sufficient to direct the jury 'simply that in law the accused's act need not be the sole cause, or even the main cause, of the victim's death, it being enough that his act contributed significantly to that result' (*Pagett* [1983]).

When a problem arises, as occasionally happens, then it is for the judge to direct the jury in accordance with the legal principles which they have to apply. There are two main principles. D may only be convicted of murder, for example, if the jury is satisfied that D's conduct was both:

- a factual cause; and

- a legal cause

of V's death.

Factual causation

D's conduct must be a *factual cause* of the prohibited consequence. This is commonly applied using the '*but for*' test; In other words it must be established that the consequence would not have occurred as and when it did but for D's conduct. If the consequence would have happened anyway, there is no liability (*White* [1910]).

> *White* (1910)
> White put potassium cyanide into his mother's drink with intent to kill her, in order to gain under her will. Later his mother was found dead, sitting on the sofa at her home in Coventry, with the glass full of the poisoned drink beside her. However, medical evidence established that she had died of a heart attack, not poisoning. In any event, White had not used enough cyanide for a fatal dose. White was

acquitted of murder: he had not, in fact, caused her death. (But he was convicted of attempt.)

The mere establishment of a factual connection between D's act and V's death is insufficient. Suppose D invites V to his house for a party. On the way V is run over and killed. Clearly if D had not invited V he would not have died in those circumstances, but (quite apart from lack of *mens rea*) there is no *actus reus*. The missing element is legal causation.

Legal causation

This is closely associated with moral responsibility. The question is whether the result can fairly be said to be the fault of D. In *Dalloway* (1847), D was driving a horse and cart without holding the reins when a child ran in front of the cart, and was run over and killed. D was charged with manslaughter, but was acquitted as the jury believed that D could have done nothing even if holding the reins. Thus, although the child was killed by D's cart, which was being driven negligently, the death would have happened in exactly the same way if he had been driving with all due care.

It is often said that D's act must be a 'substantial' cause of death; this probably states the case too favourably for D. It is sufficient that D's act makes a *more than minimal contribution*. In *Kimsey* (1996), D and a female friend had been involved in a high-speed car chase. Tragically, she lost control of her car at high speed and was killed. It was not absolutely clear what had happened prior to the car going out of control. The Crown case was that it was D's driving which had led her to lose control. The trial judge told the jury that they did not have to be sure that D's driving 'was the principal, or a substantial cause of the death, as long as you are sure that it was a cause and that there was something more than a slight or trifling link'. On appeal, it was argued that it was wrong to say that his driving did not have to be a 'substantial cause'. The Court of Appeal dismissed the appeal; reference to 'substantial cause' was not necessary. Reference to 'more than a slight or trifling link' was perfectly acceptable.

The acceleration principle

D's act will be considered a cause if it has accelerated V's death. It is no defence to say that V was dying of a fatal disease anyway. In *Adams* (1957), D was a doctor charged with the murder of one of his patients, who was terminally ill, by means of an overdose of pain-killers. Devlin J directed the jury that it did not matter that V's days were numbered: 'If her life were cut short by weeks or months it was just as much murder as if it was cut short by years.'

Contributory causes

It is therefore clear that D's act need neither be the sole, nor even the main cause of death. It is sufficient if it is a cause. Other causes may be:

- the actions of third parties, or

- actions of V herself.

Actions of third parties

Suppose D poisons V with a fatal dose but, before she dies E, an escaped lunatic, comes along and stabs her through the heart – then D will not be liable for her death (though he would certainly be liable for an attempt (as in *White*, above). Here, E's act was the sole cause of death. But what is the case where the third party's actions are not quite so unpredictable? The courts tend to take the view that it is only in extreme circumstances that D can avoid liability for causing someone's death by trying to blame someone else. The following case illustrates this:

Pagett (1983)

In this case, several police officers were trying to arrest D for various serious offences. He was hiding in his first-floor flat with his pregnant girlfriend, Gail Kinchen. D armed himself with a shotgun and, against her will, used Gail's body to shield himself as he tried to escape. He fired at two officers, who returned fire; three bullets fired by the officers hit and killed Gail. D was convicted of manslaughter; the Court of Appeal dismissed his appeal. In this case it was said that it was reasonably foreseeable that the police would return fire either in self-defence or in the lawful exercise of their duty.

1. What was the immediate factual cause of death in *Pagett*?
2. Why did the Court of Appeal uphold Pagett's conviction?

Medical treatment

The majority of cases in the area of legal causation involve medical treatment. Where D inflicts an injury on V, typically with a knife or a bullet, which requires medical treatment, will D be held liable for murder or manslaughter if that treatment is improper, or even negligent, such that V eventually dies? The answer, generally speaking, is yes. In *Smith* (1959), Lord Parker CJ said:

If at the time of death the original wound is still an operating cause and a substantial cause, then the death can properly be said to be the result of the wound, albeit that some other cause of death is also operating. Only if it can be said that the original wounding is merely the setting in which another cause operates can it be said that the death did not result from the wound. Putting it another way, only if the second cause is so overwhelming as to make the original wound merely part of the history can it be said that the death does not flow from the wound.

Smith (1959)

Thomas Smith was a soldier stationed in Germany. He stabbed David Creed, a soldier in another regiment, twice with a bayonet during the course of a barrack-room fight. Another soldier carrying C to the medical station twice dropped him. The medical staff were under pressure as two others had been injured in the fight and did not treat him for 45 minutes. As C had been stabbed in the back, they did not immediately realise that one of the wounds had pierced a lung, causing a haemorrhage. Consequently, they gave C treatment which, in the light of this, was described in court as 'thoroughly bad and might well have affected his chances of recovery'. C died, and S was convicted of murder at a court martial in Germany. The Courts Martial Appeal Court dismissed the appeal – the original stab wound was still 'operating' and 'substantial' at the time of death.

A more recent case has shifted the focus slightly, away from the question of whether the wound was still 'operating' to a broader question of whether the death can be attributed to the acts of D. In *Cheshire* (1991), Beldam LJ said that, 'Treatment which falls short of the standard expected of the competent medical practitioner is unfortunately only too frequent in human experience.' Beldam LJ went on to provide a direction that juries should be given in cases involving alleged medical negligence:

It is sufficient for the judge to tell the jury that they must be satisfied that the Crown have proved that the acts of [D] need not be the sole cause or even the main cause of death, it being sufficient that his acts contributed significantly to that result. Even though negligence in the treatment of [V] was the immediate cause of his death, the jury should not regard it as excluding the responsibility of [D] unless the negligent treatment was so independent of his acts, and in itself so potent in causing death, that they regard the contribution made by his acts as insignificant.

Cheshire (1991)

On 9 December, David Cheshire and Trevor Jeffrey were in a fish and chip shop. They got into an argument, and Cheshire produced a handgun. Jeffrey was shot in the stomach. In hospital, he underwent major bowel surgery. This was successful but respiratory problems then ensued, necessitating a tracheotomy (the insertion of a breathing tube into the neck). By 8 February, J was still recovering in hospital, when he began to complain of breathing difficulties. Doctors thought that his respiratory problems were caused by 'anxiety'. In fact his condition deteriorated rapidly on the night of 14 February and he died of a heart attack, as a result of his windpipe becoming obstructed; a side-effect of the tracheotomy. By this time, the gunshot injuries had almost healed and were no longer life-threatening. D's murder conviction was upheld by the Court of Appeal. The court held that it was only in the most extraordinary and unusual case that medical treatment would break the chain of causation.

Using the Smith test of 'operating' cause, would the jury have been able to convict David Cheshire of murder?

The status of *Cheshire* as the appropriate test to use was confirmed by the Court of Appeal in *Mellor* (1996).

Mellor (1996)

V, a 71-year-old man, was attacked by a gang of hooligans, including D, late one winter's evening. He was taken to hospital suffering facial bruising and complaining of chest pain. He died in hospital two days later. D tried to avoid liability by claiming that the hospital had failed to give V sufficient oxygen in time, as a result of which he had developed pneumonia, which was the medical cause of death. But D was convicted of manslaughter and the Court of Appeal upheld the conviction.

Of course, *Smith* has never been overruled, so presumably a judge has the choice when directing the jury. If the wounds are still operating, use *Smith*; if they have healed, fall back on *Cheshire*. Thus, D will be liable of murder or manslaughter if:

- his acts are a more than minimal cause of death; and *either*

- the injuries that he inflicted were still an 'operating' cause at the time of death; *or*

- the injuries inflicted were a 'significant' cause of death.

However, there is one case that supports the proposition that sometimes medical negligence will be so extreme that D will be relieved from liability for his victim's death.

Jordan (1956)
In this case the victim of a stabbing had been taken to hospital and given a drug called terramycin to prevent infection, when he had shown intolerance to a previous injection. Medical experts for the defence described this treatment as 'palpably wrong'. Furthermore, large quantities of liquid had been administered intravenously, which had caused V's lungs to become waterlogged. This was also described as 'wrong' by the defence doctors. As a result of the waterlogging, V developed pneumonia, the medical cause of death. By the time of death, the stab wounds had mainly healed. The Court of Criminal Appeal quashed the conviction: if the jury had heard this evidence, they 'would have felt precluded from saying that they were satisfied that death was caused by the stab wound'. Hallett J said:

We are disposed to accept it as the law that death resulting from any normal treatment employed to deal with a felonious injury may be regarded as caused by the felonious injury.... It is sufficient to point out here that this was not normal treatment.

In *Blaue* (1975), the Court of Appeal described *Jordan* as 'a case decided on its own special facts.' In *Malcherek, Steel* (1981), the Court of Appeal said that *Jordan* was 'very exceptional'. Nevertheless, *Jordan* has never been overruled and, presumably in a future case where medical treatment is found to be 'palpably wrong', a jury will be entitled to find that the chain of causation has been broken. Indeed, in *Blaue*, the Court of Appeal added that *Jordan* was 'probably rightly decided.'

Life-support machines
A particular problem concerns victims who are placed on life-support machines. If there is no prospect of recovery, the doctors may decide to

switch the machinery off. Does this affect D's responsibility? In *Malcherek, Steel* (1981), where two virtually identical cases coincidentally committed at opposite ends of the country were brought before the Court of Appeal together, it was argued that in such cases it was the doctors who had caused death. The Court of Appeal rejected the argument, describing the notion that Malcherek and Steel had not caused death as 'bizarre'.

Malcherek, Steel (1981)

Richard Malcherek had stabbed his wife nine times at her flat in Poole, Dorset. She was admitted to hospital and seemed to be recovering, but then suffered a pulmonary embolism, which stopped her heart. During open-heart surgery, a massive blood clot was removed but severe brain damage had been caused, from which she never recovered. The doctors carried out various tests recommended by the Royal College for establishing 'brain death' and switched off the life support.

Anthony Steel had randomly attacked a woman in a Bradford street. He battered her about the head with a large stone, causing severe head injuries, and left her for dead. She was rushed to hospital and placed on life support immediately. However, she never recovered consciousness, and the support was withdrawn two days later after brain stem tests proved negative.

M and S were both convicted of murder and the Court of Appeal rejected both appeals.

The same principles apply if V is not 'brain dead' but is in a 'persistent vegetative state' (PVS). In *Airedale NHS Trust v Bland* (1993), Lord Goff said that a doctor in discontinuing treatment was 'simply allowing the patient to die in the sense that he [is] desisting from taking a step which might prevent his patient from dying as a result of his pre-existing condition'.

It is clear from the above cases that the courts are extremely reluctant to allow an accused to escape liability by claiming that better medical treatment would have saved the victim's life or reduced the seriousness of their injury. This is sensible public policy. The medical profession and hospital emergency rooms are all too often stretched to the limit at present. In many a town the effects of Saturday night drinking in particular result in violence and a consequent influx of casualties. In such circumstances medical staff do their best to cope, often being verbally or even physically abused in the process. Very rarely mistakes are made or the treatment given is negligent. As far as criminal liability is concerned it would be invidious to hear the attacker, who put that person at risk in hospital, claim, 'so why wasn't the best Harley Street consultant called to attend to my victim?' In all but the most exceptional circumstances the primary liability rests legally, as well as morally, with the original perpetrator.

Actions of the victim

Fright or flight

Where D caused V to apprehend violence, and death occurred while she was trying to escape or otherwise protect herself, then, generally speaking, D remains a legal cause of V's death.. There are limits to this principle, however. Incredibly, the courts have introduced what can only be termed the 'daftness test'! In *Roberts* (1972), Stephenson LJ said that if V does something 'so daft or so unexpected that no reasonable man could be expected to foresee it', then it would break the chain of causation.

In *Williams and Davis* (1992), the Court of Appeal confirmed the 'daftness test'. Stuart-Smith LJ highlighted the key question: whether V's conduct was 'proportionate to the threat, that is to say that it was within the ambit of reasonableness and not so daft as to make it his own voluntary act'.

> *Williams and Davis* (1992),
> Barry Williams and Frank Davis had given a life to a hitchhiker, John Shepherd, who was on his way to the Glastonbury festival. Shortly afterwards, S opened a rear door and jumped out of the moving car. He did not survive the impact. It was the Crown's case that S had jumped clear trying to escape being robbed. Williams and Davis were both convicted of robbery and manslaughter. The Court of Appeal, in quashing their convictions, referred to a lack of any direction by the judge on the question of causation. The jury should have been asked whether S's reaction in jumping from the moving car was 'within the range of responses' which might be expected from a victim placed in such a situation.

In *Corbett* (1996), D head-butted and punched V before the latter ran off with D in pursuit. V fell into the gutter, and was run over and killed by a passing car. The Court of Appeal followed *Roberts*, noted that V's reactions to the attack were not 'daft' but came within a foreseeable range, and upheld D's manslaughter conviction.

The most recent example of the *Roberts* principle is *Marjoram* (1999).

Marjoram (1999)
A gang of people including D had been shouting abuse and kicking V's hostel room door. They forced open the door and burst into the room, at which point V fell, or possibly jumped, from the window. V sustained serious injury in the fall and D was convicted of inflicting grievous bodily harm (see Chapter 8). On appeal, D claimed that V's response was unreasonable but the Court of Appeal upheld the conviction. The reasonable person could have foreseen V's reaction in attempting to escape as a possible consequence of D's actions.

The decision, then, rests with the jury to assess whether the victim's responses to the perceived threat were reasonable and foreseeable in the circumstances, taking into account that V may well have been frightened at the time. This is probably the best compromise that can be achieved since it relies upon jury equity to apply a common-sense conclusion. If they think that the victim's response is 'daft' they will acquit. Otherwise they will convict.

Self-neglect
If V mistreats, or neglects to treat, his own injuries, this will not break the chain of causation. In *Holland* (1841), D cut V on the finger with an iron instrument. The wound became infected, but he ignored medical advice that he should have the finger amputated. The wound caused lockjaw and, although the finger was then amputated, he died. The judge directed the jury that the question was simply whether the wound inflicted by D was the cause of death. The jury convicted. Despite enormous advances in life-saving medical technology, it is still no answer that V refuses medical treatment (*Blaue* [1975], where the Court of Appeal followed *Holland*). In *Dear* (1996), D slashed V with a Stanley knife, severing an artery. V (for reasons that are not entirely clear) failed to do anything to staunch the blood flow. It appears he took the opportunity to commit suicide! The jury convicted of murder and D's appeal was dismissed. The cause of V's death was blood loss which, in turn, was caused by stab wounds inflicted by D. Hence, D caused V's death.

The accused must take the victim as he finds them

D cannot complain if his victim is particularly susceptible to physical injury, for example haemophilia (a condition where the blood does not clot in the normal way). In *Martin* (1832), Parke J said that it was 'perfectly immaterial' that V 'was in a bad state of health'. If D 'was so unfortunate as to accelerate her death, he must answer for it'. In a more modern example,

Mamote-Kulang (1964), the High Court of Australia upheld D's manslaughter conviction, dismissing his appeal that it was his wife's physical condition that was the real cause of her death. D had punched his wife, with considerable force, but on her side. Such a blow would not normally be fatal, but she died soon afterwards. The post-mortem revealed that the blow had ruptured her spleen, which was at the time 'large, soft and mushy'. However, this was no defence. Being punched by D was the sole cause of her death.

The principle that D must take his victim as he finds them is not confined to pre-existing physical or physiological conditions. It has been extended to religious beliefs. In *Blaue* (1975), Lawton LJ said:

> It has long been the policy of the law that those who use violence on other people must take their victim as they find them. This in our judgment means the whole man, not just the physical man. It does not lie in the mouth of the assailant to say that [V's]'s religious beliefs which inhibited her from accepting certain kinds of treatment were unreasonable. The question for decision is what caused her death. The answer is the stab wound. The fact that [V] refused to stop this end coming about did not break the causal connection between the act and death.

Blaue (1975)
Robert Blaue stabbed Jacolyn Woodhead after she refused to have sex with him. One wound penetrated a lung. She was admitted to hospital and told that surgery – and a blood transfusion – were necessary to save her life. Being a Jehovah's Witness, she refused and died soon after. Medical evidence indicated she would have survived had she accepted the transfusion. B was convicted of manslaughter. On appeal, he argued that her refusal was unreasonable and broke the chain of causation. This was rejected (NB D avoided murder liability by pleading diminished responsibility – see Chapter 6).

1. Professor Williams, an academic expert on criminal law, has argued that justice might have been better served by convicting D of the offence of wounding with intent, contrary to s.18 of the Offences Against the Person Act 1861. The sentence would probably have been the same. What do you think?

2. Suppose Blaue had stabbed V in a remote place and she died before medical assistance could reach her. His liability would certainly be

manslaughter (because of the diminished responsibility). So, why should he be allowed to escape a manslaughter conviction on the ground that V was stabbed in a built-up area, near to a hospital, but refused treatment?

Mens rea

Mens rea refers to the mental elements of a crime. *Mens rea* means the mental element, or state of mind, that D must possess at the time of performing whatever conduct requirements are stated in the *actus reus*. Typical examples include:

- Intention

- Recklessness

- Knowledge

- Dishonesty

So, in *murder*, the *mens rea* requirement is called 'malice aforethought' and this, in turn, means intention (either to kill V or to cause really serious injury). In *theft*, the *mens rea* is the dishonest intention to permanently deprive the owner of their property. Again, if one of these elements is missing, D cannot be guilty of the crime. D may well kill another human being – but he is not guilty of murder unless he intended death or really serious injury. D may well appropriate someone else's property, but this is not theft unless he was dishonest and intended never to return it.

With a number of different offences, the *actus reus* is identical, only the *mens rea* is different. For example, the *actus reus* is the same in murder and manslaughter. The *mens rea* of manslaughter is very different from 'malice aforethought', however. Another example is provided by the offences of 'wounding' and 'wounding with intent'. Obviously the *actus reus* of these crimes is identical – the wounding. However, the *mens rea* is different. One crime clearly requires intent. The other does not – it requires recklessness.

Finally, with some crimes the *mens rea* is identical but the *actus reus* is different. The offences of 'battery' and 'assault occasioning actual bodily harm' have different *actus reus* elements. The former can be committed literally by just touching someone. The latter requires 'actual bodily harm' (a consequence), and requires proof of something like a broken nose. But the *mens rea* is the same – intention or recklessness. The meaning of the term 'recklessness' will be explained in Chapter 3; while the meaning of the terms 'intention' and 'malice aforethought' will be explained in Chapter 5.

Coincidence of *actus reus* and *mens rea*

It is not enough that D has the *actus reus* for a crime if he does not have the *mens rea*, or guilty mind, that goes with it. The following case illustrates this.

> *Taaffe* (1983)
> In this case, as D arrived in the UK he told a customs officer that he had nothing to declare. The officer was suspicious and a search revealed several packages containing cannabis resin hidden in D's car. When D was asked what he thought was in the packages he replied, 'money'. He was convicted of being knowingly concerned in the fraudulent evasion of the prohibition on the importation of cannabis. However, the Court of Appeal quashed his conviction and the House of Lords dismissed the prosecution appeal. As D did not 'know' that the packages contained cannabis, he had no *mens rea*.

D actually thought that he was committing an offence. However, importing currency is not illegal. Thus, D's *mens rea*, such as it was, related to a non-existent crime. In the Court of Appeal, Lord Lane CJ described D's actions as 'morally reprehensible', but this did not turn the importation of currency into a criminal offence. D's views on the law as to the importation of currency were irrelevant.

The *mens rea* must coincide in point of time with the act that causes the *actus reus*. Accidentally running over your neighbour, then jumping for joy at the result, does not make you a murderer. Similarly, *mens rea* implies an intention to do a present act, not a future one. Suppose that D is driving to V's house, intent on shooting him. A person runs out in front of D's car, giving D no chance of avoiding the accident. By sheer chance, it is V. D is not guilty of murder.

However, if D does an act with intent thereby to cause the *actus reus*, and does so, it is immaterial that he has repented before the *actus reus* occurs. Thus, in *Jakeman* (1983), D dispatched suitcases which she knew to contain cannabis from Ghana to London. Before they arrived she repented, but was convicted.

A similar principle applies if the very final act is involuntary or accidental. In the Australian case of *Ryan* (1967), D was in the process of tying up a petrol station attendant, whom he had robbed, when she suddenly moved, startling him so that he pulled the trigger of the shotgun he was carrying. His conviction of manslaughter was upheld by the High Court of Australia, despite his argument that the pulling of the trigger was a 'reflex action'.

The continuing act theory

Where the *actus reus* takes the form of a continuing act, it has been held that it is sufficient if D forms *mens rea* at some point during its course. In *Fagan v Metropolitan Police Commissioner* (1969), James J said:

> We think that the crucial question is whether, in this case, the act of the appellant can be said to be complete and spent at the moment of time when the car wheel came to rest on the foot, or whether his act is to be regarded as a continuing act operating until the wheel was removed. In our judgment, a distinction is to be drawn between acts which are complete, though results may continue to flow, and those acts which are continuing... There was an act constituting a battery which at its inception was not criminal because there was no element of intention, but which became criminal from the moment the intention was formed to produce the apprehension which was flowing from the continuing act.

Fagan v Metropolitan Police Commissioner (1969)
Fagan was being directed to park his car by PC David Morris in Fortunegate Road, north London. He drove his car onto the constable's foot. PC Morris said 'Get off, you are on my foot', but Fagan responded, 'F*** you, you can wait', and switched off the engine. PC Morris repeated several times his request for F to move and, eventually, F switched the engine back on and reversed slowly off the officer's foot. F was charged with assault. The magistrates were unsure whether F had deliberately or accidentally driven onto PC Morris's foot; however, they were satisfied that he had 'knowingly, provocatively and unnecessarily allowed the wheel to remain on the foot' afterwards and convicted. The Divisional Court upheld the conviction.

The transaction theory

Where the *actus reus* is itself part of some larger transaction or series of events, it may be sufficient that D forms *mens rea* at some point during that transaction. In a number of cases, D has assaulted or inflicted a wound on V with intent to kill. V has been knocked unconscious, but D, believing him to be dead, disposes of the 'body'. V dies not from the original injuries but from the consequences of being 'disposed of' – typically from drowning or exposure. At the time of the *actus reus* (the disposal) D did not have *mens rea*; at the time of the *mens rea* (the assault or wounding) there was no *actus reus*.

The leading case is the Privy Council decision in *Thabo Meli and Others* (1954).

Thabo Meli and Others (1954)
The appellants, in accordance with a pre-arranged plan, took V to a hut where they plied him with beer so that he was partially intoxicated, then struck him over the head. Believing him to be dead, they rolled his body over a low cliff, making it look like an accident. In fact, V was still alive and eventually died from exposure. They were convicted of murder in South Africa and the conviction was upheld. The Privy Council, which used to hear appeals from South Africa and whose decisions are highly persuasive in English law, said it was 'impossible to divide up what was really one series of acts in this way'.

There is no doubt that the accused set out to do all these acts in order to achieve their plan, and as part of their plan: and it is much too refined a ground of judgment to say that, because they were at a misapprehension at one stage and thought that their guilty purpose was achieved before it was achieved, therefore they are to escape the penalties of the law.

This dictum suggests that the answer might be different if the acts were not part of a pre-arranged plan. However, the Court of Appeal has followed *Thabo Meli*, in several cases where there was no antecedent plan previously arranged. The first of these was *Church* (1965).

Church (1965)
In this case the defendant, Cyril Church, had dumped what he *thought* was the body of a dead woman, Sylvia Nott, into the River Ouse. In fact she was only unconscious – he had punched her during a violent argument concerning his failure to satisfy her sexually and knocked her out – but drowned in the river. The jury convicted him of manslaughter, after a direction that they could do so if they regarded his behaviour 'from the moment he first struck her to the moment when he threw her into the river as a series of acts'. The Court of Criminal Appeal upheld the conviction.

In *Le Brun* (1991), the Court of Appeal again applied the transaction principle. Lord Lane CJ said that:

> Where the unlawful application of force and the eventual act causing death are parts of the same sequence of events, the same transaction, the fact that there is an appreciable interval of time between the two does not serve to exonerate the defendant from liability. That is certainly so where the appellant's subsequent actions which caused death, after the initial unlawful blow, are designed to conceal his commission of the original unlawful assault.

Le Brun (1991)

Le Brun, in a quarrel with his wife on the way home late at night, punched her on the chin and knocked her unconscious. While attempting to drag the 'body' away, probably to avoid detection, he dropped her, so that she hit her head on the kerb and died. The jury was told that they could convict of murder or manslaughter (depending on the intent with which the punch was thrown), if D accidentally dropped V while (i) attempting to move her against her wishes and/or (ii) attempting to dispose of her 'body' or otherwise cover up the assault. He was convicted of manslaughter. The Court of Appeal upheld the conviction.

Mens rea is not the same as motive

Mens rea is the state of mind that D must have had at the moment of committing the *actus reus*. The typical *mens rea* states given above (intention, recklessness, etc.), are all different from D's motivation. For example:

- In murder, D's 'motive' in killing V could be to claim an inheritance, to be rid of an abusive husband, or to earn £20,000 (if D is a professional hired killer). But none of these states have anything to do with *mens rea* (malice aforethought), apart from strengthening a prosecution case.

- In theft, D's 'motive' in stealing food from a shop may be hunger, greed, kleptomania, boredom, or to satisfy a dare. But to be guilty of theft, D must have had the *mens rea* (the dishonest intention to permanently deprive the owner of their property).

Exception: racially aggravated crime

The Crime and Disorder Act 1998 introduced motive into the criminal law, or at least certain aspects of it, for the first time. There are four areas that are affected:

- assaults (including actual bodily harm, grievous bodily harm and wounding) – considered in Chapter 8

- criminal damage – considered in Chapter 13

- public order offences

- harassment

The definition of 'racially aggravated' appears in s.28 of the 1998 Act. The section provides that an offence is racially aggravated if:

- at the time of committing the offence, or immediately before or after doing so, the offender demonstrates towards the victim of the offence hostility based on the victim's membership (or presumed membership) of a racial group; or

- the offence is motivated (wholly or partly) by hostility towards members of a racial group based on their membership of that group.

Prior to the 1998 Act, if D had assaulted V, causing a broken nose, and the offence was 'motivated' by racial hostility, then D would have been convicted of assault occasioning actual bodily harm contrary to s.47 of the Offences Against the Person Act 1861. The *same* liability would have followed even if the offence had *not* been racially motivated. That is, D's motivation would not have affected his liability. Now, however, D commits a different offence: the offence of racially-aggravated assault, contrary to s.29 of the Crime and Disorder Act 1998. His motivation means that he is *guilty of a different offence* and he will be sentenced accordingly.

Transferred malice

If D, with the *mens rea* of one crime, performs the *actus reus* of that crime, then he is guilty. It does not matter if D accidentally performs the *actus reus* in a different way from the one he intended. For example, if D intends to kill someone, but accidentally kills the wrong victim, he is still guilty of murder. Suppose D intends to shoot P, and shoots at a person he believes is P; he hits the person and kills him. The person is, in fact, Q. D is, nevertheless, guilty of murder.

Similarly if D, intending to shoot P, fires at a person who is P, *but misses*, hits and kills Q who is standing nearby, D is guilty of murder. This second situation is an example of the doctrine of transferred malice. Consider the facts of *Attorney-General's Reference (No.3 of 1994)* (1997).

Attorney-General's Reference (No.3 of 1994) (1997)

D had stabbed his girlfriend, P, who was about 23 weeks pregnant. She subsequently made a good recovery from the wound but, some seven weeks later, gave birth prematurely. It was clear the stab wound had penetrated the foetus. D was charged with wounding P with intent, and pleaded guilty. Subsequently, the child, Q, died some four months after birth. D was charged with Q's murder, but was acquitted after the judge held that the facts did not allow for a homicide (murder or manslaughter) conviction against the child. The Court of Appeal, however, held that the trial judge was wrong – a murder conviction was possible because it was unnecessary that the person to whom the malice was transferred, the 'transferee', be in existence at the time of the act causing death. On further reference, however, the Lords decided that, *at most*, manslaughter was possible. The Lords took exception to the Court of Appeal's use of the doctrine. Lord Mustill said that he would not 'overstrain the idea of transferred malice by trying to make it fit the present case'.

Giving judgment in this case, Lord Mustill said:

> The effect of transferred malice... is that the intended victim and the actual victim are treated as if they were one, so that what was intended to happen to the first person (but did not happen) is added to what actually did happen (but was not intended to happen), with the result that what was intended and what happened are married to make a notionally intended and actually consummated crime.

In such a situation, however, it is critical that the (unintentionally killed) human being was in existence at the time of the *actus reus*.

In *Latimer* (1886), Latimer had a quarrel in a public house with P. He took off his belt and swung it at P. The belt glanced off P and struck Q with full force, severely wounding her. The jury found that the injuries to Q were 'purely accidental' and 'not such a consequence of the blow as [Latimer] ought to have expected'. Nevertheless, he was convicted of wounding her.

In *Mitchell* (1983), D was waiting impatiently in a busy post office in Tottenham. He tried to force himself into a queue but he was admonished by a 72-year-old man. D punched the man, causing him to stagger backwards into an 89-year-old woman, who was knocked over; she subsequently died of her injuries. The Court of Appeal used *Latimer* in order to uphold D's manslaughter conviction.

However, if D, with the *mens rea* of one crime, performs the *actus reus* of *another*, *different* crime, he cannot, generally speaking, be convicted of either crime. The *actus reus* and *mens rea* do not coincide. The leading case is *Pembliton* (1874). Here, D committed the *actus reus* of malicious damage (an offence which no longer exists) with the *mens rea* of assault. He was guilty of neither crime.

Pembliton (1874)
Pembliton was involved in a fight outside a pub in Wolverhampton. At about 11pm a crowd of about 40–50 had been turned out of the pub for being disorderly. They began fighting. After a time P separated himself from the group, picked up a large stone and threw it in the direction of the others. The stone missed them and smashed a large window. P was convicted of malicious damage but his conviction was quashed. The jury had found that he intended to throw the stone at the people but did not intend to break the window.

The transferred malice principle is expressly preserved in the Government's draft Offences Against the Person Bill (1998). This draft Bill is considered in more detail in Chapter 9, but for present purposes Clause 17(2) provides that:

A person's intention, or awareness of a risk, that his act will cause a result in relation to a person capable of being the victim of the offence must be treated as an intention or (as the case may be) awareness of a risk that his act will cause that result in relation to any other person affected by his act.

Summary

- *Actus reus* means the physical elements of a crime, things like conduct, consequences, and circumstances.

- *Mens rea* means the mental element that D must possess at the time of performing whatever conduct requirements are stated in the *actus reus*. Different *mens rea* states are intention, recklessness, dishonesty.

- The *actus reus* and *mens rea* elements must all be present. If any are missing, D cannot be guilty of that crime, although he may be guilty of a different offence.

- The *actus reus* and *mens rea* must coincide at the same point in time. If they do not, D cannot be guilty of that offence, although he may be guilty of a different offence.

- Causation is a question of fact and law. Factual causation is tested using the 'but for' test (*White*). Legal causation involves looking at whether there is any break in the chain if causation.

- The chain of causation is not broken if the injuries inflicted by D remain 'operating' and 'substantial' at the time of death (*Smith*).

- Alternatively, D remains liable if the injuries he inflicted 'contributed significantly' to the death (*Cheshire*).

- Medical negligence will very rarely break the chain of causation (*Cheshire*), although it might do if the treatment was 'palpably wrong' (*Jordan*). Doctors switching off life-support machines after brain-death has been diagnosed definitely do not break the chain of causation (*Malcharek, Steel*).

- If D attacks or threatens V who tries to escape and dies in the process, D remains liable unless V's reaction was 'daft' (*Roberts, Williams and Davis, Corbett*).

- D must take his victim as he finds her (*Blaue*).

- Motive is not the same thing as *mens rea*. Normally, motive is irrelevant. However, it does now feature in the crimes of racially motivated assault, racially motivated criminal damage, etc.

- If D, with the *mens rea* of one crime, performs the *actus reus* of that crime, then he is guilty. The fact that he accidentally performs the same *actus reus* but in a different way (e.g. by aiming a gun at P but missing and shooting Q) is irrelevant. This is transferred malice.

- But if D, with the *mens rea* of one crime, performs the *actus reus* of a different crime, then he is not guilty of either crime. He would not have the *actus reus* and *mens rea* of the same crime, as required by the rule that all the elements of the crime must be present and coincide at the same point in time.

Figure 1 Determining causation

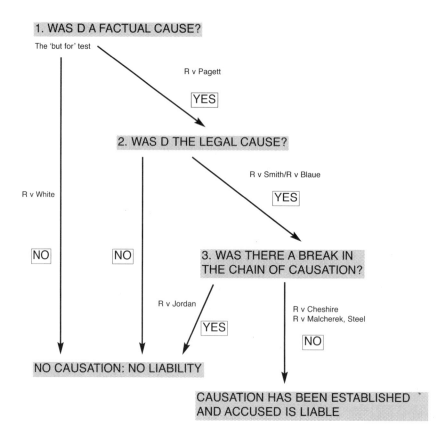

2 Liability for omissions

Introduction

Generally speaking, English law only punishes those who caused a prohibited result by a positive act. There is no general duty to act in order to do good deeds. There may well be a moral obligation on someone to be a 'Good Samaritan', but there is not a legal one. Consider this scenario. A stabs B with a knife, causing serious injuries. If C is standing beside B, he is under no duty to do anything – either to try to stop A, or even to assist B – so, legally, he can simply walk away.

The whole approach to the imposition of criminal liability for failing to act in given situations is influenced by general public policy issues that affect most aspects of criminal law. In particular the balance to be struck between the individual's freedom to do and think as he or she wishes and the individual's responsibility to the rest of society. As with all such issues in criminal law it is up to the courts or Parliament to set the appropriate minimum standards of behaviour that are felt to be acceptable in a civilised society. Since society is a loose affiliation of many disparate groups this is not an easy task. It has become accepted that parents are under duties to care for their children. It is not yet accepted that individuals should be criminally liable for failing to go to the assistance of friends or neighbours who find themselves in distress. Whether there is a moral duty to do so is generally left to the conscience of the individual and Parliament and the courts have been reluctant to intervene.

This is not true in all countries. In France and the Netherlands, for example, there is a so-called 'Good Samaritan' law which makes it an offence in some circumstances not to help somebody in an 'emergency situation' even though they may be a stranger.

Why do you think there is no general duty to act in order to do good deeds?

Consider for example:

* How far it is desirable to encourage 'neighbourliness' in society?

- Could the well-meaning but ignorant 'busybody' do more harm than good, at the scene of an accident, for example?

- Whether the criminal law should ever interfere with questions of morality?

- When to distinguish between allowing a person to die rather than to keep them alive by continuing life preserving medical treatment?

- Is it proper to impose a criminal duty of care upon a person who may not have the social awareness to appreciate the existence or extent of the duty?

- Is it up to a judge or a jury to decide that an accused is under a duty of care?

Nevertheless, English law does punish those who fail to act, in two situations.

- First, there are a large number of crimes that may *only* be committed simply because you do not do something.

- Second, it is possible to be found guilty of crimes that normally require a positive act – such as murder or manslaughter – because you failed to act. However, for this to happen, you must have been under a 'duty of care' at the time. Thus, in the above scenario, if C was related to B – her father or husband, perhaps – or if C was a police officer, then they would be under a duty to act. Any failure to intervene could now lead to criminal liability. Their liability would be for the same offence as if they had used the knife themselves.

Crimes that can only be committed by failing to act

The vast majority of these crimes are statutory and are usually strict liability offences (see Chapter 4). For instance, a motorist who *fails to provide* a police officer with a specimen of breath when required to do so, under s.6 of the Road Traffic Act 1988, commits an offence. Similarly, *failing to stop and provide your name and address* to any person reasonably requiring it when your vehicle has been involved in an accident where there has been injury to another person or damage to another vehicle is an offence under s.170 of the same Act. More seriously, the offence of *failing to disclose information* is an offence under s.18 of the Prevention of Terrorism Act 1989.

However, at least one such offence – misconduct whilst acting as an officer of justice – is a common law offence (*Dytham* [1979]).

Dytham (1979)

PC Dytham, a police officer, was on duty near Cindy's nightclub in St Helens at about 1am. He was standing near a hot dog stand about 30 yards away when a man called Stubbs was ejected from the club by a bouncer. A fight ensued in which a large number of men joined. There was a great deal of shouting and screaming. Three men eventually kicked Stubbs to death in the gutter. All of this was clearly audible and visible to the officer. However, PC Dytham took no steps to intervene, and when the incident was over adjusted his helmet and drove off, telling the owner of the hot dog stand and a bystander that he was going off duty. PC Dytham was convicted. He had wilfully omitted to take any steps to carry out his duty to protect Stubbs or to arrest or otherwise bring to justice his assailants. The Court of Appeal upheld his conviction.

Committing crime by failing to act when under a duty to act

There are two elements that need to be established before liability can be imposed for a failure to act:

- The crime has to be one that is capable of being committed by a failure to act;

- D must have been under a duty to act.

Was the offence capable of 'commission by omission'?

Not all offences are capable of 'commission by omission'. Whether a crime is so capable is a question for the courts. Murder and manslaughter are good examples of crimes that may be committed by omission (see, respectively, *Gibbins and Proctor* (1918) and *Pittwood* (1902), below). Indeed most of the cases concern these two crimes. Some crimes, however, cannot be committed by omission, for example burglary and robbery. There is doubt whether some other offences may be committed by omission; particularly assault and battery. Sometimes the definition of the crime makes it clear a positive act is required. In *Ahmad* (1986), D, a landlord, was charged with 'doing acts calculated to interfere with the peace and comfort of a residential occupier with intent to cause him to give up occupation of the premises', contrary to s.1 of the Protection from Eviction Act 1977. The

Court of Appeal decided that he could not be guilty of this crime by failing to act, as the offence clearly required 'acts'.

One further problem with imposing liability when D fails to act is the requirement of causation (this issue was examined in Chapter 1). Suppose a man sees his young son fall into a canal, but simply stands and watches. There is no doubt that the father is under a duty to save the boy, and deliberate failure to do so could well be regarded as murder. But did the father cause the boy to die? The boy would almost certainly have died in exactly the same way if no-one had been there.

Was the defendant under a duty to act?

The second factor is that D must be under a duty – recognised by the law – to act in the circumstances. In *Khan and Khan* (1998), the Court of Appeal quashed the manslaughter convictions of two drug dealers. They had failed to summon medical assistance after V, a 15-year-old girl, to whom they had supplied heroin, overdosed and died. The men could have helped her; instead they left her to die alone. The court said that, before they could convict, the jury had to be sure that the men stood in such a relationship to V that they were under a duty to act. In the case, the trial judge had not directed the jury in relation to that crucial issue.

The Court of Appeal in *Khan and Khan* did not decide that no duty was owed on the facts, rather that it must be left to the jury to decide whether a duty of care was owed. Specifically, the Court of Appeal said that it was for the trial judge to decide whether, on the facts, a duty of care was *capable* of arising and it was for the jury to decide whether it did, in fact, arise (criminal convictions are sometimes quashed by the Court of Appeal where the judge has misdirected the jury at the original trial. This does not necessarily mean that the Court of Appeal thinks that the accused is entirely innocent, merely that the trial decision is unsafe).

A duty to act may be owed in a variety of situations. Such a duty has been held to exist in the following circumstances.

Duty arising out of contract

Where failure to fulfil a contract is likely to endanger lives, the criminal law will impose a duty to act. This duty will typically be held by the following (this is not an exhaustive list):

- Doctors;

- Members of the emergency services;

- Lifeguards.

In *Adomako* (1994), an anaesthetist was convicted of manslaughter on the basis that he had failed to notice that a vital breathing tube had become disconnected during an eye operation, with the result that the patient suffered loss of oxygen to the brain, massive brain damage and eventual death. This sort of conviction is quite easy to justify – the anaesthetist's (well-paid) job is to ensure that the equipment works because, if it does not, people will be very likely to die or to be injured.

Cases such as *Adomako* and *Pittwood* (1902) demonstrate that the duty is owed to anyone who may be affected by D's breaches of contract, not just the other parties to the contract (that is, D's employers).

Pittwood (1902)
Pittwood was convicted of manslaughter. He was a signalman employed by the railway company to look after a level crossing and ensure the gate was shut when a train was due. He left the gate open and was away from his post, with the result that someone crossing the line was hit and killed. The court rejected his argument that his duty was owed simply to the railway company: he was paid to look after the gate and protect the public.

Why do you think that PC Dytham (above) was charged with misconduct whilst acting as an officer of justice, and not manslaughter based on his duty of care as a police officer?

Duty arising out of a relationship

Though there is little direct authority, it is accepted that:

- parents are under a duty to their children (*Gibbins and Proctor* [1918]);

- spouses (husbands and wives) owe a duty to each other (*Smith* [1979]).

Duty arising from the assumption of care for another

A duty will be owed by anyone who voluntarily undertakes to care for another, whether through age, infirmity, illness, etc. The duty may be express or implied. In *Instan* (1893), D went to live with her elderly aunt, who became ill and, for the last 12 days of her life, was unable to care for herself or summon help. D did not give her any food or seek medical assistance, but continued to live in the house and eat the aunt's food. D was convicted of manslaughter and this was upheld on appeal.

The leading case now is *Stone and Dobinson* (1977).

Stone and Dobinson (1977)
John Stone lived with his mistress, Gwen Dobinson, in South Yorkshire. In 1972, Stone's sister, Fanny, 61, came to live with them. Fanny was suffering from anorexia nervosa and, although initially capable of looking after herself, her condition deteriorated. Eventually she was confined to bed in the small front room. Stone was then 67, partly deaf, nearly blind and of low intelligence. Dobinson was 43 but was described as 'ineffectual' and 'somewhat inadequate'. Both were unable to use a telephone. They tried to find Fanny's doctor but failed. (Fanny refused to tell them, as she believed she would be taken away.) Fanny refused to eat anything other than biscuits, although she used to sneak downstairs to make meals when the others went to the pub (which they did every night). One day, Dobinson and a neighbour tried to give Fanny a bedbath. Shortly afterwards, Fanny died, weighing less than 5 stone. She had two huge, maggot-infested ulcers on her right hip and left knee, with bone clearly visible. The two defendants were convicted of manslaughter, and the Court of Appeal upheld this. They had assumed a duty of care to Fanny, and their pathetically feeble efforts to look after amounted to gross negligence (which is sufficient for a manslaughter conviction – see Chapter 7).

Stone and Dobinson did their best but their best was simply not good enough. Did they deserve to be convicted of manslaughter? Would they have been better off simply ignoring Fanny after she became bedbound?

All of the cases above involved manslaughter. This is because D has assumed a duty of care to someone but has then, for reasons of incompetence or forgetfulness, allowed that person to die. However, a murder conviction is possible if D deliberately fails to assist someone in their care – intending to kill or seriously injure them. This was the case in *Gibbins and Proctor* (1918).

Gibbins and Proctor (1918)

Gibbins was the father of several children including a 7-year-old daughter, Nelly. His wife had left him and he was living with a lover, Proctor. They kept Nelly separate from the other children and deliberately starved her to death. Afterwards they concocted a story about how Nelly had 'gone away'; in fact, Gibbins had buried her in a brickyard. There was evidence that Proctor hated Nelly and had hit her. They were both convicted of murder and the Court of Criminal Appeal upheld the convictions. Gibbins owed Nelly a duty as her father; Proctor was held to have undertaken a duty to her.

Parliament subsequently incorporated parental responsibilities into legislation in the Children and Young Persons Act 1933. In addition, other adult carers such as teachers and guardians now stand '*in loco parentis*' with regard to children in their care.

Duty arising from the creation of a dangerous situation

Where a person inadvertently starts a chain of events – which, if uninterrupted, will result in harm or damage – that person, on becoming aware that he was the cause, is under a duty to take all such steps as lie within his power to prevent or minimise the harm. If he fails to take such steps then he may well be criminally liable for the consequences. In *Miller* (1983), a vagrant who was squatting in a house in Sparkbrook, Birmingham, awoke to find that a cigarette he had been smoking had set fire to the mattress. He did nothing to extinguish the fire but moved to another room and went back to sleep. The fire spread and caused £800 damage. Miller was convicted of arson (see Chapter 13) and the Court of Appeal and House of Lords upheld his conviction.

What do you think James Miller should have done, instead of simply going to sleep in another room?

Should he have tried to extinguish the fire himself?

What if it would be dangerous to tackle the fire personally?

Release from duty

One issue that is still unresolved is whether a duty – once undertaken – may be relinquished. In *Smith* (1979), D's wife had given birth to a still-born child at home. She hated doctors and would not allow D to call one. When she finally gave him permission it was too late and she died. The judge directed the jury to balance the wife's wish to avoid calling a doctor against her capacity to make rational decisions. The jury was unable to agree and D was discharged.

Thus, it would appear that, if V is rational, he may release a relative or carer from their duty of care. In *Airedale NHS Trust v Bland* (1993) – a civil case – the House of Lords provided further guidance on this difficult area. The Trust had applied to the Lords for a declaration that it was lawful for doctors to withdraw life-supporting medical treatment, including artificial feeding, from Tony Bland, a patient in one of its hospitals who was in a persistent vegetative state (PVS) with no prospect of improvement or recovery as a result of being badly crushed in the Hillsborough football stadium disaster in 1989. The House of Lords held that withdrawal of treatment would be lawful. Lord Goff, giving the leading judgment, stated several principles, which should also apply in the criminal law.

- There is no absolute rule that a patient's life has to be prolonged no matter what. The fundamental principle is the sanctity of life, but respect for human dignity demands that the quality of life be considered.

- The principle of self-determination requires that respect be given to the patient's expressed wishes. An adult patient of sound mind could refuse treatment; doctors must to respect that. If a patient is incapable of communicating, an earlier expressed refusal of consent will probably be effective. Where there is no such refusal, that does not mean that life has to be prolonged.

- Treatment may be provided, in the absence of consent, by a patient incapable of giving it, where that treatment is *in the patient's best interests* (see '*Re F [Mental Patient: Sterilisation]*') (1990); conversely, it may be discontinued if this is *in the patient's best interests*.

- Where treatment is futile, there is no obligation on a doctor to provide it – because it would no longer be in the patient's best interests. Any omission to provide treatment would not be unlawful, because there is no breach of duty to the patient. Similar principles apply to the decision to commence treatment in the first place.

Reform

In 1998 the Labour Government published a draft Offences Against the Person Bill. This draft legislation will be given fuller consideration in

Chapter 9 but, for now, it is interesting to note the proposal to create (if it does not presently exist) an offence of assault by omission. Clause 1(2) of the draft Bill states:

> *A person is guilty of an offence if he omits to do an act which he has a duty to do at common law, the omission results in serious injury to another, and he intends the omission to have that result.*

The draft Bill also confirms the application of the *Miller* principle (at least in the context of offences against the person). The relevant provision, clause 16(2), provides that:

> *Where it is an offence under this Act to be at fault in causing a result by an omission and a person lacks the fault required when he makes an omission that may cause or does cause the result, he nevertheless commits the offence if, (a) being aware that he has made the omission and that the result may occur or (as the case may be) has occurred and may continue, and (b) with the fault required, he fails to take reasonable steps to prevent the result occurring or continuing and it does occur or continue.*

Summary

- There is no general duty to act.

- Some (mostly statutory) crimes may only be committed by failing to act (Road Traffic Act).

- Otherwise, the crime must be one that is capable of being committed by an omission (*Ahmad*).

- Murder and manslaughter are capable of commission by omission.

- D must be under a duty to act (*Khan and Khan*).

- A duty to act may be imposed by contract (*Pittwood*).

- A duty to act may be imposed by a relationship with another person (*Gibbins, Smith*).

- A duty to act may be imposed by assuming a responsibility to care for another person (*Instan, Proctor, Stone and Dobinson*).

- A duty to act may be imposed in order to minimize the consequences of a dangerous situation that D created himself (*Miller*).

- A duty to act may be brought to an end, either because the other person requests it (*Smith*) or because it would not be in their best interests (*Bland*).

3   Recklessness

Introduction

Recklessness is a word in everyday use in the English language. When we use the word reckless we probably do not analyse carefully what we mean by its use. For the most part it conveys something that we might also be happy to call dangerous, or very careless or even anti-social. We are not being *that* precise. We read of reckless tackles in football matches; of reckless statements in the press; of reckless drinking in Ibiza, etc. To the law student, however, the words 'reckless', 'recklessly' and 'recklessness' take on a new and special significance. To discover why this should be, one must begin by realising that the word 'reckless' to the lawyer is not a general description of someone or their behaviour. It is a word which refers to a very particular state of mind. It is, indeed, one of those *mens rea* words referred to in Chapter 1.

To a criminal lawyer recklessness involves two things:

- The taking of an unjustifiable risk; and

- An awareness of the risk.

Risk is part of life. Each time we take a car journey there is a risk that we might be injured in a road accident (a small risk of a serious consequence). Each time we place a stake on the National Lottery we risk losing that money (a high risk in return for a potentially high reward). Whether we consciously calculate whether such risks are 'reckless' is doubtful. They simply are part of life and we could probably justify them without serious argument were we asked to do so. Such behaviour by itself is hardly regarded as reckless. On the other hand, the car driver who travels at excessive speed or the single parent who gambles half of their weekly income on the Lottery is likely to be perceived as reckless, whether they themselves think so or not.

The taking of other risks is less easy to justify. Is it 'reckless' to smoke forty cigarettes a day for example? Is it 'reckless' to go mountaineering? What are the risks involved and how do we assess them? Does the individual alone decide? Alternatively, do the family of that individual or the taxpayers, for example, have a legitimate say about the potential medical treatment costs of a lung cancer patient or an injured climber? What about the emotional suffering the risk-taker might cause to others?

It is the question of who must be aware of the consequences of taking serious and unjustifiable risks that has caused all the problems in criminal law.

The taking of an unjustifiable risk

Whether a risk is unjustifiable involves a balancing of the social utility of D's act on one hand, against the seriousness of harm that will result if the risk manifests itself, on the other. Hence:

- Flying a plane with 500 passengers from London to New York. This carries a risk that the plane will crash, killing everyone on board. However, the probability is low and the social utility high, hence the risk is justifiable.

- Stealing a fire engine to go on a high speed joyride. This carries a dual risk (a) that the fire engine will be involved in a crash, causing injury or death and property damage; (b) that if a fire starts somewhere the engine will not be able to attend. The probability of the former risk is high, the latter less so; but the social utility of stealing fire engines is nil, so the risk is unjustifiable.

Subjective 'Cunningham' recklessness

The second issue is awareness of the risk. The law has developed in such a way that there are now two different tests for this. One is known as the 'subjective' test and focuses on the question of whether D foresaw the risks of his conduct; the other test is 'objective' and asks whether the 'ordinary prudent individual' would have foreseen the risk. The only form of recklessness generally recognised prior to 1981 was subjective (gross negligence manslaughter was an exception – see Chapter 7). The leading case was (and is) *Cunningham* (1957). The question for the Court of Appeal was what was meant by 'maliciously' (specifically in s.23 of the Offences Against the Person Act 1861 [OAPA]), but the word appears in many other crimes as well). The judge had directed the jury that it meant 'wickedly'. The Court of Criminal Appeal did not agree. In quashing his conviction, they approved a definition given by Professor Kenny in 1902:

> In any statutory definition of a crime, 'malice' must be taken not in the old vague sense of wickedness in general but as requiring either

(i) an actual intention to do the particular kind of harm that in fact was done; or (ii) recklessness as to whether such harm should occur or not (i.e. the accused has foreseen that the particular kind of harm might be done, and yet has gone on to take the risk of it)....

Cunningham (1957)
Roy Cunningham ripped a gas-meter from the cellar wall of a house in Bradford, in order to steal the money inside. He left a ruptured pipe, leaking gas, which seeped through into the neighbouring house, where Sarah Wade (actually the mother of Cunningham's fiancée) inhaled it. He was convicted of maliciously administering a noxious substance so as to endanger life, contrary to s.23 OAPA, but his conviction was quashed. The crux of the matter was whether D had foreseen the risk; that is, the risk of someone inhaling the gas.

This definition applied throughout the OAPA as well as other statutes containing the word 'malicious', such as the Malicious Damage Act 1861 (MDA). In 1969, the Law Commission was working on proposals to reform the law of property damage. In their final Report in 1970, they recommended the replacement of the MDA with what became the Criminal Damage Act 1971 (CDA). The Law Commission considered that the mental element, as expressed in *Cunningham*, was fine, but that for simplicity and clarity the word 'maliciously' should be replaced with 'intentionally or recklessly'. Unfortunately, the 1971 Act when enacted by Parliament did not define 'reckless' anywhere; it was left to the courts to interpret.

After 1971 the courts initially continued to apply subjective recklessness. In *Stephenson* (1979), D was a schizophrenic tramp. One November night he had decided to shelter in a hollowed-out haystack in a field on the North Yorkshire moors. He was still cold, and so lit a small fire of twigs and straw in order to keep warm. However, the stack caught fire and was damaged, along with various pieces of farming equipment. Some £3,500 worth of damage was caused. He was charged with causing criminal damage 'recklessly'. Evidence was given that schizophrenia could have deprived D of the normal ability to foresee risks.

The judge told the jury that D was reckless if he had closed his mind to the obvious risk of starting a fire in a haystack, and they convicted. The Court of Appeal quashed his conviction. What mattered was whether D had foreseen the risk. This seems to be fair as it is concerned with the state of mind of the accused person, his *mens rea*. Geoffrey Lane LJ said:

A man is reckless when he carries out the deliberate act appreciating that there is a risk that damage to property may result from his act.... We wish to make it clear that the test remains subjective, that the knowledge or appreciation of risk of some damage must have entered the defendant's mind even though he may have suppressed it or driven it out.

Objective 'Caldwell' recklessness

However, two years later the House of Lords in another criminal damage case, *Caldwell* (1982), introduced an objective form of recklessness. Lord Diplock, with whom Lords Keith and Roskill concurred, said:

A person... is 'reckless'... if (1) he does an act which in fact creates an obvious risk... and (2) when he does the act he either has not given any thought to the possibility of there being any such risk or has recognised that there was some risk involved and has nonetheless gone on to do it. That would be a proper direction to the jury; cases in the Court of Appeal which held otherwise should be regarded as overruled.

Caldwell (1982)
James Caldwell, who bore a grudge against his boss, the owner of a hotel, got drunk one night and started a fire in a ground floor room in the hotel. Ten guests were resident at the time. The fire was quickly dealt with, but Caldwell was charged under the Criminal Damage Act with arson (criminal damage by fire), being reckless as to whether life would be endangered. He was convicted and his appeals dismissed by the Court of Appeal and House of Lords.

Later the same day, the House of Lords gave a similar definition to recklessness in the context of the Road Traffic Act 1972. In *Lawrence* (1982), D had killed a pedestrian while riding a motorcycle at high speed along an urban street in Lowestoft. He was convicted of causing death by reckless driving and his appeal was dismissed. Lord Diplock again gave the leading judgment. Basically, he reiterated everything said in *Caldwell*; the only difference being that this time he said that the risk which D created had to be 'obvious and serious', as opposed to merely 'obvious'.

Lord Diplock's definition seems to require that the risk be obvious whether D foresees it or not. This cannot be the case: D who actually foresees a risk and takes it is reckless; it is irrelevant whether or not it was obvious. Indeed the definition refers to D having 'recognised that there was some risk'; and elsewhere in *Caldwell* Lord Diplock said that recklessness includes acting despite existence of 'a risk... that one has recognised' as well as failing to give any thought to an obvious risk.

To whom must the risk be obvious?

There are two possibilities:

- The risk must have been 'obvious' to D, had he thought about the situation;

- The risk must have been 'obvious' to the 'ordinary prudent individual'.

Lord Diplock was not a model of consistency. At one point in *Caldwell* he said of recklessness that it presupposed that, 'if thought were given to the matter *by the doer* before the act was done, it would have been apparent *to him* that there was a real risk of its having the relevant harmful consequences' (emphasis added). This suggests that the former proposition is correct. This would also mean that the decision in *Stephenson* was correct: it is quite possible that, had the tramp thought about the consequences of his act, he would not have been aware of the risk of damage. Caldwell, on the other hand, was rightfully convicted, because (*per* Lord Diplock) the 'risk would have been obvious to him had he been sober'. The rationale for the redefinition of recklessness in *Caldwell* was that a *self-induced* inability to appreciate risks (e.g. through intoxication) should be no defence to crimes requiring recklessness; where the inability is *inherent* then this is something the jury should be entitled to consider.

However, in *Caldwell* Lord Diplock said that, 'cases in the Court of Appeal which held otherwise should be regarded as overruled.' This must include *Stephenson*. Furthermore, in *Lawrence*, he said that recklessness presupposed that there was 'something... that would have drawn the attention of *an ordinary prudent individual* to the possibility that his act was capable of causing... harmful consequences' (emphasis added).

The Queen's Bench Divisional Court (reluctantly) accepted this latter view as being correct in *Elliott v C* (1983). Robert Goff LJ said that he did so 'simply because I believe myself constrained to do so by authority' (that is, *Caldwell*).

Elliott v C (1983)
C was a girl of limited intelligence and in a remedial class at high school. She was aged 14 years and one month at the time she burnt

> down a garden shed and contents worth over £3,000. She had been
> out all night without sleep, and decided to spend the night in the shed.
> To keep herself warm she poured some white spirit on an old carpet
> and lit it, but the fire spread. She was seen running away by a
> milkman and was arrested shortly after. The magistrates acquitted her
> of arson, finding that she had not thought about the risk, but that in
> any case it was not an obvious risk to her. The Crown appealed and
> the Divisional Court directed the magistrates to convict, as the risk
> only had to be obvious to the reasonably prudent person.

In *R (Stephen Malcolm)* (1984), D, a 15-year-old boy, had been convicted
of arson, being reckless whether life would be endangered (exactly the same
crime as *Caldwell*). He and two friends had thrown petrol bombs (milk
bottles containing petrol) towards a neighbour's ground-floor flat. The
bombs smashed against the wall with loud bangs and sent sheets of flame
scorching across a bedroom window. On appeal, it was argued that the
'ordinary prudent individual' should be invested with those characteristics
of D that would affect his ability to appreciate risks – in particular, D's age.
The Court of Appeal rejected the argument, although they seemed to be just
as reluctant as the Divisional Court had been the previous year. Ackner LJ
argued that the perfect opportunity to modify Lord Diplock's test had arisen
in *Elliott v C*, but the House of Lords had refused permission to appeal in
that case. They had not taken it, and Ackner LJ did not see why the Court
of Appeal should take it instead. However, he did say that he had 'difficulty'
in accepting the principle of objective recklessness.

Hence, whether D is young and/or educationally subnormal, or adult but
suffering from a mental illness such as schizophrenia, he is guilty if he
failed to consider a risk that would have been foreseen by a mature, sober,
mentally-normal adult. D is, therefore, judged against a standard that he is
incapable of achieving. This has little to do with justice or indeed *mens rea*.

Where is D's 'guilty mind' in Stephenson or Elliott v C?

There was, of course, no need to give *Caldwell* such a strict interpretation
in *Elliott v C* and *R (Stephen Malcolm)*. In *Caldwell*, Lord Diplock was
concerned with those defendants whose 'mind was affected by rage or
excitement or confused by drink'. This was clear authority to restrict the
ratio of *Caldwell* to self-induced states of mind. Intriguingly, in *Lawrence*,
Lord Diplock said that: 'If satisfied that an obvious and serious risk was

created... the jury are entitled to infer that he was [reckless] and will probably do so; but regard must be given to any explanation he gives as to his state of mind which may displace the inference.'

This was not the view taken in *Elliott v C* and *R (Stephen Malcolm)*, but the House of Lords did raise hopes for a fairer approach in *Reid* (1992), another case of causing death by reckless driving. Lord Keith, although supporting the definition of recklessness in *Lawrence*, said that D should not be considered reckless where he 'acted under some understandable and excusable mistake or where his capacity to appreciate risks was adversely affected by some condition not involving fault on his own part'. Lord Goff also thought there would be no recklessness where a driver was 'afflicted by illness or shock which impairs his capacity to address his mind to the possibility of risk'.

While *Reid* may have been the inspiration for the decision of the House of Lords in *Adomako* (1995) to decide that objective recklessness was not appropriate in manslaughter cases, there is no sign of the position changing in criminal damage cases. In *Coles* (1995), another 15-year-old boy was convicted of arson, being reckless whether life would be endangered, and the Court of Appeal, specifically following *R (Stephen Malcolm)*, upheld the conviction. The court rejected pleas to take into account psychological evidence of D's 'low average range of intellectual functioning'.

Ruling out the risk

The *Caldwell* direction appears to exclude the defendant who stops to think about whether there is a risk, concludes (wrongly) that there is no risk and only then acts – but causes damage, because there was in fact a risk all along. The *Caldwell* direction requires either that:

- D has not given any thought to the possibility of risk which was in fact obvious; or

- that D has recognised that there was some risk involved

Hence, where D thinks about a risk and decides (wrongly) that there is no risk, he is not reckless. This has been described as a 'lacuna' or gap in the law of recklessness. From the point of view of blameworthiness it can be argued that this is fair to the genuine defendant. In practice it may provide a loophole which is capable of exploitation by an accused who is unscrupulous or desperate to escape conviction. In *Chief Constable of Avon and Somerset v Shimmen* (1986), the Divisional Court appeared to accept the lacuna – in theory. However, they pointed out that D is still reckless if he thinks about a risk and recognises that there is one – even if he thinks (rightly or wrongly) that it is a small risk. The lacuna only works if D thinks about a risk and concludes that there is no risk at all.

Chief Constable of Avon and Somerset v Shimmen (1986)

Shimmen held a green belt and a yellow belt in the Korean art of self-defence. He had been out drinking with four friends in Bristol and on the way home they stood outside a shop. He was larking about with one friend, W, deliberately just missing him with kicks and punches. W said that S might one day hurt someone. S assured him that everything was under control, and to prove it aimed a kick at the shop's plate-glass window, thereby demonstrating that he had the necessary skill to avoid breaking it. Predictably, he did break it and was charged with criminal damage. The magistrates acquitted him on the basis that he had thought about the risk and done all he could to minimise it. The Crown appealed and the Queen's Bench Divisional Court directed a conviction. S did not fall into the 'lacuna'. Under cross-examination, S admitted that he 'had eliminated as much risk as possible by missing by two inches instead of two millimetres.' Thus, he had perceived a risk – albeit a small one – and had gone on to take it.

In *Reid* (1992), Lord Ackner and Lord Goff both accepted the existence of the lacuna – again, only in theory. Lord Ackner gave the example of the driver of a left-hand drive car who asks his passenger if the road is clear. The passenger replies yes; but he has misunderstood the question as an inquiry about whether a car is approaching. D pulls out. If charged with reckless driving, Lord Ackner thought D would have a case: he thought there was no risk.

There is much to be said for recognising the lacuna: there is a clear moral difference between someone who does not even think about the risks he might be taking, and one who is convinced there is no risk. On the other hand, the academic Birch, in *The Foresight Saga: The Biggest Mistake of All?* (1988) argued that we cannot afford to acquit appalling drivers 'whose unshakeable faith in their ability to avoid danger displays an arrogance bordering on lunacy'. There has yet to be a single case where a defendant has escaped through the lacuna.

Another problem for D is in convincing a bench of magistrates or a jury that he had, in fact, considered whether there was a risk and decided there was no risk. Furthermore, as the case of *Merrick* (1995) demonstrates, D must have considered whether a risk existed in advance of its occurrence.

Merrick (1995)

Merrick called on various houses and offered to remove old television cabling and equipment. On one occasion he removed a piece of equipment known as a repeater box, which inevitably left live wires exposed. He was convicted of criminal damage, being reckless whether life would be endangered. On appeal, he said that once he realised what he had done, he had concluded that there was no risk to life (the cable was to be exposed for a matter of minutes before D could arrange for the wire to be buried in concrete). The Court of Appeal dismissed his appeal: while the wires were exposed, there was a risk of endangering life. D only considered whether this posed a risk after the event. In order to avoid *Caldwell*, it was necessary to show that D had contemplated the risk and dismissed it before it actually materialised.

Subjectivism *vs* objectivism: the arguments

Lord Diplock in *Caldwell* explained the redefinition of recklessness on several grounds. His arguments have variously been described as 'pathetically inadequate' and 'profoundly regrettable' by Professors Sir John Smith and Glanville Williams, both well known academic authorities.

Recklessness not a 'term of legal art'

According to Lord Diplock in *Caldwell*, the word 'reckless' is 'an ordinary English word', not some 'term of legal art with some more limited esoteric meaning than that which it bore in ordinary speech'. This analysis is undoubtedly *correct*; but given that the words 'intentionally or recklessly' were chosen specifically by the Law Commission to replace 'maliciously', it is arguably *inappropriate*.

Inadvertence to obvious risk as blameworthy as advertence to risk

Lord Diplock thought that someone who failed to realise that there was an obvious risk (i.e. inadvertent) was equally as blameworthy as someone who foresaw a risk but took it anyway (i.e. an advertent person): 'Neither state of mind seems to me to be any less blameworthy than the other.' Admittedly, the argument that someone who fails to consider risks because of intoxication, rage or excitement should be found guilty does have some force. A considerable body of case law has built up concerning intoxicated defendants (see Chapter 14).

In *Reid* (1992), the House of Lords confirmed Lord Diplock's view and extended it. Lord Goff said that 'recklessness' should be taken to include cases where:

- D's perception was impaired by drink, rage or some other excitement;

- D does not care less whether a risk exists or not;

- D deliberately closes his mind to the possibility of risk (wilful blindness); and

- D simply does not think about the matter at all, perhaps because he is 'acting impetuously on the spur of the moment without addressing his mind to the possibility of risk'.

Reid (1992)
John Reid was driving east along the inside lane of Kensington Road, West London – a dual carriageway. The traffic was heavy. Further down the road a taxi-drivers' hut protruded a distance of six feet into the lane. Lines were painted on the road to show that it was necessary to pull out to avoid it. Reid accelerated, trying to undertake, but drove into the hut and killed his passenger. He was convicted of causing death by reckless driving (the same offence as in *Lawrence*). The Court of Appeal dismissed the appeal, but certified a question to the House of Lords about the appropriateness of the *Caldwell/Lawrence* test. The Lords confirmed the test was to be used.

Simplifies task for juries

Having stated that there was no difference between advertent and inadvertent risk-taking in terms of blameworthiness, Lord Diplock continued by saying that he could see 'no reason' why Parliament, in enacting the Criminal Damage Act in 1971, should have 'gone out of its way to perpetuate fine and impracticable distinctions such as these, between one mental state and another. One would think that the sooner they were got rid of, the better.' He also said that the subjective *Cunningham* test required the jury to undertake a 'meticulous analysis... of the thoughts that passed through the mind of the accused'.

But what is so objectionable about that? The jury does this whenever they consider the *mens rea* state of intention (which is required in every murder and theft case, for example) and, prior to *Caldwell* they used the *Cunningham* test with no obvious difficulties.

To which crimes do the different tests apply?

In *Seymour* (1982), a manslaughter case, Lord Roskill said that the word 'reckless' should 'be given the same meaning in relation to all offences which involve 'recklessness' as one of the elements unless Parliament has otherwise ordained.' This clearly *obiter* statement was seized on quite enthusiastically in the early-to-mid-1980s and indeed extended into the major offences against person. In *Kong Cheuk Kwan* (1985), for example, the Privy Council had no reservations about applying *Caldwell* to the common law offence of manslaughter. Since then the position has changed dramatically. Indeed, in *Adomako* (1995) the House of Lords overruled *Seymour* and stated that the offence of reckless manslaughter no longer existed. Their Lordships appear to have held the view that reckless manslaughter could now be subsumed within the offence of gross negligence manslaughter. Some academics argue that while the *Caldwell* test is inappropriate for manslaughter *Cunningham* subjective reckless manslaughter ought still to exist. This has merit, since not only would it be in line with the non-fatal offences against the person, it would also reflect the proposals of the Law Commission on involuntary manslaughter. Indeed, it is clearly justifiable to convict of manslaughter where the accused has proceeded to run a conscious risk of causing death or serious harm to his victim (see Chapter 7 for further discussion).

The Cunningham test

The *Cunningham* test certainly applies wherever a statute uses the word 'maliciously'. In *DPP v Parmenter* (1991), a case of inflicting grievous bodily harm contrary to s.20 of the Offences Against the Person Act 1861 (OAPA), Lord Ackner, giving the unanimous decision of the House of Lords, concluded that 'in order to establish an offence under s.20 the prosecution must prove either that [D] intended or that he actually foresaw that his act would cause harm.'

But it has a wider application than that. In *DPP v K*, the Divisional Court applied *Caldwell* to s.47 of the OAPA (which does not use the word 'maliciously') but, in *Spratt* (1990), the Court of Appeal declared that *DPP v K* was wrongly decided. They said:

> The history of the interpretation of [OAPA] shows that, whether or not the word 'maliciously' appears in the section in question, the courts have consistently held that the *mens rea* of every type of offence against the person covers both intent and recklessness, in the sense of taking the risk of harm ensuing with foresight that it might happen.

Subjective recklessness is also the appropriate test in cases of rape (*Satnam and Kewall* [1983]) and offences such as indecent assault (*Kimber* [1983]), although, in sexual offences, the courts are also prepared to adopt the slightly wider concept of recklessness in the sense that D is guilty if he could not care less. In *Kimber*, for example, Lawton LJ referred to D's state of mind by the colloquial expression, 'couldn't care less'. In law this is recklessness. This is because in sex crimes the courts are concerned with whether D appreciated a risk that V was not consenting.

Caldwell

Caldwell does remain the appropriate test in criminal damage and arson. Although the Lords in *Reid* (1992) confirmed the objective test for reckless driving offences, as established in *Lawrence*, the *mens rea* element in such offences has since been replaced by 'dangerousness' (s.1 Road Traffic Act 1991). With the overruling in *Adomako* (1995) of *Seymour*, the objective form of recklessness does not apply in manslaughter either.

The only other mainstream criminal offence in which *Caldwell* recklessness has any role is in constructive manslaughter, where D may be convicted if he kills, having committed an unlawful and dangerous act (see Chapter 7). If D's unlawful and dangerous act was criminal damage or arson, then the prosecution must prove that D committed the offence with the appropriate *mens rea* which, in this context, would mean objective recklessness (*Goodfellow* [1986]).

Reform

The Law Commission's Criminal Code Bill (1989), Criminal Law Bill (1993) and the more recent Government Offences Against the Person Bill (1998) all contain definitions of 'recklessness' that clearly confirm subjective recklessness. The 1998 Bill's definition provides that:

A person acts recklessly with respect to a result if he is aware of a risk that it will occur and it is unreasonable to take that risk having regard to the circumstances as he knows or believes them to be.

Of course this Bill, if enacted, would only apply to offences against the person, which are already subject to the subjective test. In that respect the Law Commission's 1989 proposals are more significant in that they adopt a subjective standard across the board, including criminal damage.

Summary

- Recklessness involves two things: the taking of an unjustifiable risk; *and* an awareness of the risk.

- There are two tests for establishing whether D had foresight of a risk: *Cunningham* and *Caldwell*.

- *Cunningham* is a subjective concept, that is, it focuses on what D, himself, foresaw. *Caldwell* is an objective concept, that is, it focuses on what the ordinary prudent individual would have foreseen.

- Under the *Caldwell* test, D is reckless if he failed to consider a risk that the ordinary prudent individual would have foreseen as obvious and serious.

- The ordinary prudent individual is characterless. This person does not share any of D's individual characteristics, including age (*R [Stephen Malcolm]*, *Coles*) or mental subnormality (*Elliott v C*).

- There is a 'lacuna' in *Caldwell* recklessness, which occurs if D considers whether a risk exists and concludes (wrongly) that it does not (*Shimmen*, *Reid*). However, it has never been argued successfully and remains theoretical.

- *Cunningham* recklessness applies to all non-fatal offences against the person (assault, battery, wounding, grievous bodily harm). A modified, slightly wider form of subjective recklessness applies in rape and other sex crimes. *Caldwell* recklessness applies to criminal damage and arson.

Figure 2 Table comparing Cunningham and Caldwell recklessness

Cunningham – subjective type	Caldwell - objective type
Origin – *R v Cunningham* (1957 CA)	**Origin** – *R v Caldwell* (1982 HL)
Offence – S.23 Offences against the Person Act 1861: '*maliciously*' administering a noxious substance.	**Offence** - S.1(2) Criminal Damage Act 1981 arson (criminal damage by fire), being 'reckless' as to whether life would be endangered.
Short definition: 'conscious risk taking'	**Short definition**: 'obvious risk taking'
Long definition: The accused is aware of the risk of the consequence of his actions but goes on to take the risk of it occurring.	**Long definition**: Where the prohibited consequence arises out of the defendant's failure to consider a risk which would have been obvious to the ordinary prudent person.
• Foresight of the consequences required	• Foresight of the consequences not required
• Accused is convicted on consequences of which he was aware	• Accused may be convicted on the basis of 'thoughtlessness'
• Easily justifiable as blameworthy	• More difficult to justify other than on public policy grounds, e.g. *Elliott v C* (1983)
Potentially fair	Potentially unfair
Application Non-fatal offences against the person; rape. Arguably manslaughter?	**Application** Criminal damage only

The 'Lacuna'
Shimmen; *Reid*; *Merrick*
Accused recognises the risk, decides there is none, and goes ahead on that premise.

4 Strict liability

Introduction

As we have seen, the prosecution will normally have to establish that an accused has carried out the prohibited criminal act (*actus reus*) with the accompanying 'guilty mind' (*mens rea*). This sounds fair enough. After all it is essentially the state of mind of an accused that marks his behaviour out as 'criminal' and is reflected appropriately in the sentence. For example, intentionally causing serious harm is a far more serious offence than recklessly (maliciously) causing serious harm since the harm is actually intended rather than simply being risked. The convicted criminal is likely to be given a heavier sentence as a result and we can see that this can be justified. It will, however, come as little surprise to learn that there are one or two exceptions to this general rule.

Crimes which do not require proof of *mens rea* – intention, recklessness or even negligence – as to one or more elements of the *actus reus* are known as offences of *strict liability*. D will have no excuse, no matter how careful he has been. Simply causing the prohibited consequence will be sufficient to convict. This was demonstrated in the case of *Callow v Tillstone* (1900).

> *Callow v Tillstone* (1900)
> D, a butcher, asked a vet to examine a carcass to check that it was fit for human consumption. On receiving the vet's recommendation that it was fit, he offered it for sale. But the vet had been negligent, and the meat was not fit. D was convicted of exposing unsound meat for sale, even though he had exercised due care and taken reasonable steps to avoid committing the offence.

Short of not selling the meat, there was no way D could avoid liability. This, of course, scarcely seems fair to the individual. Similarly, D will be liable for driving while unfit through drink (s.4, Road Traffic Act 1988) or driving with a level of alcohol in his blood, breath or urine above prescribed limits (s.5 RTA) even if he was unaware of his condition and not responsible for it, for example where his soft drink has been surreptitiously spiked with alcohol. So how can this be justified?

The answer is that Parliament, and in rare cases the courts, have been prepared to surrender the traditional insistence upon proof of a guilty mind where there is a greater benefit to be obtained to the public as a whole. Typically strict liability offences are the less serious, regulatory offences involving road safety, pollution or food hygiene. In cases of doubt the courts maintain a vigilant attitude wherever possible so as to protect an individual against unjust conviction. This they do by asserting that they will normally require the prosecution to prove *mens rea* unless convinced by the wording of an enactment that Parliament has clearly intended otherwise. In any case of ambiguity the benefit of doubt goes to the accused.

While liability may be strict in respect of one element of the *actus reus*, other elements of the *actus reus* may require intention, recklessness or negligence. Consider the offence under s.55 of the Offences Against the Person Act 1861, taking an unmarried girl under the age of 16 out of the possession of her father against his will (now in s.20 of the Sexual Offences Act 1956). In *Prince* (1875), D was convicted – despite his defence that he reasonably believed the girl was 18 – because the court held that liability with respect to the age of the girl (who was in fact 15) was strict. However, in *Hibbert* (1869), D was acquitted – it was not proved that he knew the girl was in the possession of her father – because liability with respect to this aspect of the offence was not strict.

Contrast with absolute liability

Where an offence is one of *strict* liability, the prosecution must still prove that D committed the *actus reus*; if D acted involuntarily then there is no *actus reus* and so D cannot be held liable. Hence, D has a defence of automatism to driving offences if it is not proven that D was actually 'driving' (see Chapter 16). On the other hand, if an offence is one of *absolute* liability, even the lack of a voluntary act by D will not allow him to avoid liability (*Larsonneur* [1933], *Winzar v Chief Constable of Kent* [1983]).

Common law offences

There are few common law offences of strict liability since the courts have always been opposed to the notion. Criminal and/or blasphemous libel are often cited as examples.

Criminal libel

Hence a newspaper editor may be liable for libels (written statements about a person that would tend to lower the reputation of that person among other members of society) published with or without his consent.

Blasphemous libel

This had fallen into disuse, but was resurrected thanks largely to the efforts of the well-known moral campaigner Mary Whitehouse in *Lemon and Gay News Ltd* (1979).

Lemon and Gay News Ltd (1979)
Denis Lemon was the editor and Gay News Ltd the publishers of the *Gay News* newspaper. One issue contained an illustrated poem, which described, in detail, acts of sodomy and fellatio on Christ's body immediately after the crucifixion; it also suggested that Christ had previously enjoyed homosexual relationships with the Apostles. Mrs Whitehouse brought a private prosecution. They were convicted and appealed on the basis that a subjective intent to shock and arouse resentment among Christians had to be proved. However, the House of Lords held that an intention to publish the words would suffice. Liability as to whether the words were blasphemous was strict.

Criminal contempt of court

When Parliament passed the Contempt of Court Act 1981, s.1 expressly affirmed 'the strict liability rule' for the offence of contempt, which continues to be a common law offence, albeit modified by the Act.

Statutory offences

The vast majority of strict liability offences are statutory. They have their origins in eighteenth- and nineteenth-century regulatory statutes relating to the adulteration of tobacco and foodstuffs, alongside legislation concerning liquor, factories, pollution and other public welfare matters. Faced with a welter of legislation, the courts abandoned the requirements of *mens rea* in many cases where there were no express words in the statute requiring proof of fault.

Strict liability has survived its Industrial Revolution origins and new offences may still be created (see *Harrow LBC v Shah & Shah* [1999], below, for a very recent example). Indeed it is now accepted that the ordering of a complex modern society is simply not possible without the existence of such offences. The House of Lords has upheld the principle of strict liability on many occasions, the first being *Warner v MPC* (1969). In that case the Lords held that the offence of unauthorised possession of drugs, contrary to s.1 of the Drugs (Prevention of Misuse) Act 1964, amounted to a crime of strict liability.

Identifying offences of strict liability

The presumption of *mens rea*

There could, in theory, never be any doubt whether *mens rea* is required or not. It can be expressly stated in a statute that *mens rea* is required by using a word like 'intentionally', 'recklessly' or 'knowingly', or it can be stated that no *mens rea* is required (as in s.1 of the Contempt of Court Act 1981). However, many statutory offences remain silent, and the courts must resort to statutory interpretation.

The overriding principle is the presumption of *mens rea*. Judges have recognised that the starting point in interpreting a statutory offence is that Parliament intended the offence to be one of *mens rea*. The presumption must therefore be displaced. The mere absence of words imposing *mens rea* is *not* conclusive that the offence is one of strict liability. In *Sherras v De Rutzen* (1895), Wright J said that there was 'a presumption that *mens rea*, or evil intention, or knowledge of the wrongfulness of the act, is an essential ingredient of every offence'. In *Sweet v Parsley* (1970), the Lords affirmed the presumption. Where Parliament expressly provided that an offence was strict, the courts must follow that. But, in other cases, the courts would assume that 'Parliament did not intend to make criminals of persons who were in no way blameworthy'. Thus, said Lord Reid, 'whenever a section is silent as to *mens rea* there is a presumption that... we must read in words appropriate to require *mens rea*...'

> *Sweet v Parsley* (1970),
> Stephanie Sweet, a school teacher, had rented a farmhouse near Oxford intending to live in it. However, this proved impracticable and instead she sub-let rooms to students. She did retain one room for her own use on the occasions when she visited the property to collect rent and see that everything was in order. Sometimes she stayed overnight. Apart from those visits the students had the property to themselves. The students were all using cannabis and LSD, though it appeared Ms Sweet had no knowledge whatsoever that this was going on. Nevertheless, she was convicted of being concerned in the management of premises, which were used for the purpose of smoking cannabis, contrary to s.5 of the Dangerous Drugs Act 1965. The Divisional Court upheld her conviction but the Lords allowed her appeal. Knowledge that the premises were being used for the prohibited purpose was required.

NB s.8 of the Misuse of Drugs Act 1971, which replaced s.5 of the 1965 Act, expressly provides that knowledge is required.

At the time of writing, it is still too early to assess the impact of the House of Lords judgment in the following case. However, *B v DPP* (2000) may be the most significant ruling on the application of strict liability since *Sweet* – if not ever. B, aged 15, was convicted of inciting a child under the age of 14 to commit an act of gross indecency with him, contrary to s.1 of the Indecency with Children Act 1960. He had persistently, but unsuccessfully, asked a 13-year-old girl to perform oral sex on him. When charged he claimed that he thought she was older, at least 14. The magistrates ruled that the offence was one of strict liability and therefore, even in the event that B had a genuine belief that the girl was over 14, he would be guilty. The Divisional Court rejected B's appeal but, on further appeal, the House of Lords quashed the conviction. The Lords decided that the offence required *mens rea* as to the age of the child, namely, either, an intent to incite a child under 14, or recklessness as to whether the child was under 14.

B v DPP is a landmark case because no court has ever ruled that *mens rea* is required to be proven as to age in such offences. The case of *Prince* (1875), above – which decided that D was guilty despite believing that the girl was older than she was – is certainly much weakened as an authority. All offences where age is an element are now, potentially, under threat. These include the following, all under the Sexual Offences Act 1956:

- Unlawful sexual intercourse with a girl under 13 (s.5);

- Unlawful sexual intercourse with a girl under 16 (s.6);

- Taking an unmarried girl under the age of 18 out of the possession of her parent or guardian with the intention of having unlawful sexual intercourse (s.19);

- Taking an unmarried girl under the age of 16 out of the possession of her parent or guardian (s.20).

However, there are special considerations that apply to some (but not all) of these. For instance, s.6 of the 1956 Act includes the so-called 'young man's defence'. S.6(3) provides that 'A man is not guilty of an offence under this section… if he is under the age of 24 and… believes [the girl] to be of the age of 16 or over and has reasonable cause for the belief.' The imposition of this defence based on belief specifically for men under 24 strongly suggests that liability is strict for men aged 24 or over.

Rebutting the presumption
In *Gammon (HK) Ltd v A-G of Hong Kong* (1985), part of a temporary support on a building site had collapsed. Various parties involved in the

building works were charged with deviating in a 'material' way from work shown on an approved plan. The question was whether the parties had to *know* their deviance was material, or whether liability was strict. The Privy Council held liability was strict. Lord Scarman indicated the matters that a court should consider to determine whether the presumption has been rebutted:

- there is a presumption of law that *mens rea* is required before a person can be held guilty of a criminal offence;

- the presumption is particularly strong where the offence is 'truly criminal' in character;

- the presumption applies to statutory offences, and can be displaced only if it is clearly or by necessary implication the effect of the statute;

- the only situation in which the presumption can be displaced is where the statute is concerned with an issue of social concern;

- even where a statute is concerned with such an issue, the presumption of *mens rea* stands unless it can also be shown that creation of strict liability will be effective in promoting the objects of the statute by encouraging greater vigilance to prevent the commission of the prohibited act.

In *Blake* (1997), the Court of Appeal specifically referred to Lord Scarman's five-point test in determining whether the offence in s.1 of the Wireless Telegraphy Act 1949, using a radio station without a licence, was one of strict liability (they decided that it was). In considering whether the presumption has been rebutted, the following factors may be considered.

Statutory language
There are many words in statutes which strongly imply that *mens rea* is required, while many other statutes, or even different sections of the same statute, do not have such words. Where Parliament has failed to include any word that might imply *mens rea*, it can be argued that it deliberately left them out, indicating a desire to create an offence of strict liability. However, even where no such words are used, it is not necessarily decisive (as in *Sweet v Parsley* above).

Verbs
Some verbs imply a mental element. Other verbs are less clear. What about 'permitting'? It is an offence under the Motor Vehicles (Construction and Use) Regulations 1951 if D 'uses or causes or permits to be used' on the

road a motor vehicle with defective brakes. In fact, this creates three separate offences. In *James & Son Ltd. v Smee* (1955), the Divisional Court held that *using* a motor vehicle with defective brakes was an offence of strict liability; but the defendant company had been charged with *permitting the use* of the vehicle in question, and this offence was one which 'imports a state of mind'.

Adverbs

The use of adverbs makes it clear that *mens rea* is required. Clearly offences which may only be committed 'maliciously' or 'recklessly' cannot be strict liability. The clearest of all is 'knowingly' – it would surely be impossible for a court to interpret an offence requiring that D act 'knowingly' as one not requiring *mens rea*! The position of 'wilfully' is less clear. The case law is inconsistent, but the leading authority is *Sheppard and Sheppard* (1980), decided in the House of Lords. D was not guilty of 'wilfully neglecting' a child in a manner likely to cause it unnecessary suffering or injury to its health, contrary to s.1 of the Children and Young Persons Act 1933, by simply refraining from getting medical aid and allowing it to die.

> *Sheppard and Sheppard* (1980)
> James and Jennifer Sheppard had a young son. They were themselves a young couple in their early twenties. The child died, aged 16 months, of hypothermia associated with malnutrition. The couple, who were of low intelligence and on a meagre income, denied 'wilfully neglecting' the boy in the weeks preceding his death. Although they were convicted the House of Lords allowed their appeal. The court ruled that a conviction could only be imposed where (a) D knew that there was a risk that the child's health would suffer or, (b) where he was unaware of the risk, if he did not care whether the child might be in need of medical care or not. Lord Diplock accepted their version of events: that they did not realise that the boy was ill enough to need a doctor; they genuinely thought his loss of appetite and failure to keep down his food was due to 'some passing minor upset'.

The statutory context

Assistance may come from *other* sections of the same Act. If *mens rea* words are used in some sections, but not in others, this suggests that Parliament deliberately created offences of strict liability in the latter sections. In *Cundy v Le Cocq* (1884), D, a publican, was convicted of selling intoxicating liquor to a person who was already drunk, contrary to s.13 of the Licensing Act 1872. Despite the fact that D did not know that the man was drunk, his conviction was upheld, after the Divisional Court examined the *other* sections of the 1872 Act. Some sections contained the word 'knowingly' while s.13 did not.

Similarly, in *Pharmaceutical Society of Great Britain v Storkwain Ltd* (1986), the defendant company supplied specified drugs on prescriptions, purportedly signed by a Dr Irani. The prescriptions were forged. The company was charged under s.58 of the Medicines Act 1968, which provides that no person shall sell by retail prescription-only medicines except in accordance with a prescription given by an appropriate medical practitioner. There was no suggestion that the company had acted intentionally, recklessly, or even negligently – the forgery was a very good one. But the House of Lords held that the offence was one of strict liability. The presence of words requiring *mens rea* in other parts of the 1968 Act helped the House of Lords to this conclusion.

This test is not, however, decisive. In *Sweet v Parsley*, Lord Reid said that 'the fact that other sections of the Act expressly require *mens rea*... is not itself sufficient to justify a decision that a section which is silent as to *mens rea*' creates a strict liability offence. An example of this occurred in *Sherras v De Rutzen* (1895). D, a publican, was convicted under s.16(2) of the Licensing Act 1872, unlawfully supplying liquor to a policeman on duty. D regularly served officers in uniform if they were off-duty, which was indicated by the officer not wearing an armlet. On the day in question, an officer was in D's bar without an armlet, so D assumed – on this occasion, wrongly – that he was off-duty. The Divisional Court noted that s.16(1) made it an offence for a licensee to 'knowingly' harbour or suffer to remain on his premises any constable on duty. The court therefore imported a similar requirement into s.16(2), despite the absence of any *mens rea* word in that subsection, and quashed D's conviction.

> Is it possible to reconcile the decisions in Sherras v De Rutzen and Storkwain in terms of fault? The accused in both cases could be regarded as the victims of deception.

'True' crimes and 'quasi' crimes

The courts have drawn a distinction between 'real' or 'true' crimes, on one hand, and 'quasi' crimes, on the other. In *Gammon (HK) Ltd v A-G of Hong Kong* (1985), Lord Scarman, giving the opinion of the Privy Council, said that the presumption of *mens rea* was particularly strong where the offence was 'truly' criminal. In *Wings Ltd v Ellis* (1985), Lord Scarman again said of the Trade Descriptions Act 1968 (which creates various criminal offences that are designed to regulate trading and to protect the consumer) that the entire statute 'belongs to that class of legislation which prohibits acts which are not criminal in any real sense'. These are often referred to as 'quasi-crimes'.

So what distinguishes a 'true' crime (requiring *mens rea*) from a 'quasi' crime (strict liability)? The former category includes offences that could be (very loosely) described as immoral (murder, rape, assault, theft, etc.). The latter are those which involve a technical breach of the law, but it is a breach to which no social stigma, no 'disgrace of criminality', attaches. Most offences of strict liability – relating to driving, food hygiene and public safety – are not inherently immoral. There is nothing inherently *immoral* in driving at 70.1 mph, as opposed to 69.9 mph, but Parliament has made it an offence, in the interests of public safety. Those who break such laws are punished in order to encourage them, and others, to follow the laws for their own safety. But such people are not really regarded as 'criminals'.

The recent case of *Harrow London Borough Council v Shah and Shah* (1999) helps to demonstrate this issue. The National Lottery Regulations 1994 provide that 'No National Lottery ticket shall be sold by or to a person who has not attained the age of 16 years'. One day H, who worked at the defendants' newsagent's shop in Harrow, sold a national lottery ticket to a 13-year-old boy. H thought, reasonably, that the boy was at least 16. The Queen's Bench Divisional Court directed a conviction: the offence was one of strict liability. The court said that the offence was 'plainly' not truly criminal.

Of course, strict liability is not confined to 'quasi' crimes. This test, like all of the tests in this section, provides guidance but is never decisive and must be considered alongside the other tests.

General or specific application?

The judges' perceptions of public policy considerations have greatly influenced the application of strict liability offences in particular situations. If an offence applies only to a specific class of persons, who are engaged in a particular activity, trade or profession, such as food and drugs, liquor, particular industries, etc., the courts are more likely to find that it is strict liability. If it applies to society as a whole, it is more likely to be a 'real' crime (although driving is an exception). This helps to explain cases such as *Storkwain*, above – the prohibition was particular to pharmacists.

Degree of social danger

The greater the social danger, i.e. the more people likely to be affected by commission of the offence, the more likely the presumption of *mens rea* will be rebutted. Hence many strict liability offences relate to industrial activities, pollution, and food hygiene. Crucially, it also explains why driving offences are strict liability even though the vast majority of citizens partake of the activity. In *Alphacell Ltd v Woodward* (1972), which concerned the offence of causing polluting matter to enter a river, contrary to s.2 of the Rivers (Prevention of Pollution) Act 1951, Lord Salmon said, 'It is of the utmost public importance that rivers should not be polluted.'

Alphacell Ltd v Woodward (1972)

Alphacell Ltd had a factory on the banks of a river where they produced manilla fibres, a raw material for paper. Part of the process involved washing the fibres. The dirty water was then piped down to two 'settling tanks' on the riverbank, where the water would be cleaned. The tanks were equipped with pumps, designed to prevent overflow into the river. If the pumps failed to work, the tanks would overflow, so every weekend a man was supposed to inspect the pumps. However, over a period of time a quantity of brambles, ferns and leaves were allowed to clog up the pumps until eventually the tanks overflowed and dirty water was released directly into the river. The company was convicted of causing polluting matter to enter a river, contrary to the 1951 Act – despite the presence of the pumps and the man whose job it was to inspect them.

A more recent decision of the House of Lords, *Empress Car Company v National Rivers Authority* (1998), also imposed strict liability on the offence of causing polluting matter to enter controlled waters, contrary to the Water Resources Act 1991. Thus the defendant company was liable for pollution caused by oil escaping into a river – even though an unknown person had opened a tap on a diesel tank. The Lords said that the company was responsible for matters of ordinary occurrence, such as vandalism, but would not be held liable for extraordinary events such as terrorist attack.

In a similar vein, in *Wings Ltd v Ellis* (1985), Lord Scarman decided to construe the offence, in s.14 of the Trade Descriptions Act 1968, for any person in the course of trade or business to 'make a statement which he knows to be false' as one of strict liability. The company had published a holiday brochure in which it was stated, innocently but incorrectly, that a room at the Seashells Hotel in Sri Lanka was air-conditioned. A couple from Plymouth booked a holiday in reliance upon the brochure – and duly suffered the consequences of a holiday in a non-air-conditioned room in sweltering heat and humidity. They complained to trading standards officers on their return, and they brought a prosecution. The House of Lords held that the company was liable. Lord Scarman described the 1968 Act as 'plainly a very important safeguard for those members of the public (and they run into millions) who choose their holidays in this way'.

In *Blake* (1997), the Court of Appeal decided that the offence of operating a radio station without a licence, contrary to s.1 of the Wireless Telegraphy Act 1949, was one of strict liability. Unlicensed radio transmissions were dangerous because they could interfere with radio systems employed by the emergency services and air traffic controllers. And in *Harrow LBC v Shah* (1999), the Divisional Court held that the offence of selling national lottery tickets to minors was strict liability. The National Lottery Regulations 1994 dealt with an issue of social concern, namely, the problem of young people gambling.

Severity of punishment

The courts' approach here reveals no consistency. A low maximum penalty in a statute may indicate that an offence is not 'truly' criminal, and hence liability should be strict. Conversely, a severe penalty, particularly imprisonment, may suggest that the offence deals with a matter of grave social danger, and so liability should be strict. Hence, in *Storkwain*, the maximum penalty of two years' imprisonment did not prevent the House of Lords deciding that liability was strict. Similarly, in *Gammon*, the maximum penalties were a HK$250,000 fine and/or three years' imprisonment. The Privy Council thought this indicated the 'seriousness with which the legislature viewed the offence' – it did not prevent the imposition of strict liability. The most extreme example is *Howells* (1977), where D was charged with possession of a firearm without a certificate contrary to s.1 of the Firearms Act 1968. The Court of Appeal held that the maximum prison term of five years did not preclude strict liability. Other factors, in particular the danger to the community arising from unregistered possession of lethal weapons, justified the decision.

Promotion of standards and law enforcement

The mere fact a statute deals with an issue of social concern will not displace the presumption of *mens rea*. Strict liability must be effective in encouraging vigilance and observance of the law, and promoting standards generally. If it would not have this effect, the offence is probably not strict liability. In *Reynolds v G H Austin and Sons Ltd* (1951), Devlin J said that to punish a private-hire coach company for breaches of the Road Traffic Act 1934 caused by the acts of the trip organiser, over whom the company had no influence or control, would engage the law 'not in punishing thoughtlessness or inefficiency, and thereby promoting the welfare of the community, but in pouncing on the most convenient victim'.

Similarly, in *Lim Chin Aik* (1963), D had been convicted under s.6(2) of the Immigration Ordinance 1952 of remaining in Singapore after having been denied entry. He had not known about the prohibition, which had not even been published. The Privy Council quashed his conviction.

However, the theory that making offences strict liability encourages better standards has been queried. In *City of Saulte Ste Marie* (1978), the Supreme Court of Canada, observed that:

> If a person is already taking every reasonable precautionary measure, is he likely to take additional measures, knowing that however much care he takes, it will not serve as a defence in the event of breach? If he has exercised care and skill, will conviction have a deterrent effect upon him or others?

A glaring example of the courts imposing strict liability, in a case where it is difficult to see how D could have done much more, is *Smedleys Ltd v Breed* (1974). A Dorset housewife bought a tin of peas from a supermarket. The tin of peas was one of 3.5 million tins that had been tinned by Smedley's that year. When the woman opened the tin she found a dead Hawk Moth caterpillar inside. The caterpillar being small, round in shape, green in colour – in fact, looking exactly like a pea – had passed through the tinning process undetected. A prosecution was brought under s.2 of the Food and Drugs Act 1955. The magistrates, although finding that Smedley's had exercised all reasonable care, were nevertheless guilty of the offence, because it was one of strict liability. Appeals to the Divisional Court and House of Lords were unsuccessful.

Pros and cons of strict liability

One of the main justifications for imposing liability without fault is the *ease of conviction*. Convictions, especially for regulatory offences, may be difficult to secure if *mens rea* had to be proved. Making an offence strict liability makes for efficient law enforcement and administration of the judicial process. It is only necessary to prove the *actus reus* was carried out; there is no need to prove *mens rea*, which is also more difficult to do and easy to deny.

While this is true, making such offences strict is not *necessary* for conviction. Legislation *could* be interpreted to involve a reversal of the burden of proof, imposing a presumption of negligence, so that D would be convicted unless he proved he had not been at fault, i.e. a 'no fault' or 'due diligence' defence could be utilised (see below). If this had been adopted when strict liability was in its infancy it may well have stuck, but whether the position will change now is questionable.

Baroness Wootton, in her book *Crime and the Criminal Law* in 1981, argued for the extension of strict liability to all crimes. She wrote that, 'If...

the primary function of the courts is conceived as the prevention of forbidden acts, there is little cause to be disturbed by the multiplication of offences of strict liability.' Of course, what is a 'forbidden act'? If, in murder, it is causing death, a boxer could be liable if his opponent suffers brain damage and dies; a surgeon could be liable if the life-saving heart transplant is successful but complications set in and the patient dies.

This would curtail much human activity – would any surgeons undertake operations carrying any risk of death? Such a law would jeopardise society, not protect it. Leaving it up to the judge to correct this in sentencing does not prevent the fact that the surgeon was convicted of murder. The courts would also be cluttered with blameless people who had caused various 'forbidden acts' but who would end up with an absolute discharge.

One purpose of the criminal law is to deter harmful conduct, but it only makes sense to deter intentional, reckless or negligent behaviour; if the harm occurs even if D takes reasonable care, imposing liability for it will only prevent its occurrence in the future if no-one does the act at all. That would mean no-one driving, operating factories, selling food, etc. – which is ridiculous. The law should encourage care on the part of the people undertaking these activities, but should not discourage them altogether.

In *Storkwain*, Lord Salmon said that strict liability would encourage those who might be potential polluters 'not only to take reasonable steps to prevent pollution but to do everything possible to ensure that they do not cause it'. This is fanciful to say the least.

Why should a firm take hugely expensive precautions when they are going to be punished if they nevertheless accidentally pollute a river? Would it not make more sense for companies to scrap all precautions and save money to pay any fines imposed?

Sentencing

Another problem with extending strict liability is that it would make sentencing very difficult. The person who *deliberately* pollutes a river is deserving of much harsher punishment than someone who *inadvertently* pollutes a river despite taking the most elaborate and expensive precautions possible. Yet, if the prosecution only have to prove the *actus reus*, mitigating evidence would not come out before the court.

Due diligence defences

A defence of due diligence, or no-negligence, may be available in certain situations. The burden of proof is on D to establish the defence. Due diligence defences appear in many statutes, such as s.24 of the Trade Descriptions Act 1968. In some cases the defence is combined with a third-party defence requiring D to prove both that he exercised due diligence, and the offence was due to the act or default of a third party. S.24 is an example. It provides that it is a defence for the person charged to prove:

- that the commission of the offence was due to a mistake or to reliance on information supplied to him or to the act or default of another person, an accident or some other cause beyond his control; and

- that he took all reasonable precautions and exercised all due diligence to avoid the commission of such an offence....

The defence was relied upon in *Tesco Ltd v Nattrass* (1972). The supermarket chain was accused of the offence under s.11 of the 1968 Act (giving an indication that goods are on sale at a lower price than that at which they are, in fact, on sale). 'Radiant' washing powder had been advertised as on sale at the company's Northwich branch for about 14p whereas the true price was nearer 19p. The company relied upon s.24(1); specifically, they blamed the store manager, a Mr Clement, for not checking the shelves thoroughly. The House of Lords held that the company was entitled to rely upon the defence.

Due diligence defences have been developed by the courts at common law in Australia, Canada and New Zealand. These have general application: that is, they apply to every strict liability offence notwithstanding lack of a statutory defence. According to the Supreme Court of Canada in *City of Sault Ste Marie*: 'The defence will be available if [D] reasonably believed in a mistaken set of facts which, if true, would render the act or omission innocent, or if he took all reasonable steps to avoid the particular event.' Despite the notion of strict liability itself being a common law invention, no court in England has followed these leads. One problem would be in deciding exactly how to structure such a defence.

> A due diligence defence of general application (that is, it would apply to every strict liability offence notwithstanding lack of a statutory defence) could take any one of the several forms. Which of the following (if any) would you adopt?

- D must *prove*, on the balance of probabilities, that he honestly believed in a state of facts which, had they existed, would have made his act innocent;

- As above, but D must *also* prove that his belief was *reasonably held*;

- D must *produce evidence* that he honestly believed in a state of facts which, had they existed, would have made his act innocent, in which case the Crown must prove beyond reasonable doubt that he had no such belief;

- As above, but D must *also* produce evidence that his belief was *reasonably held*, while the Crown may seek to prove beyond reasonable *that his belief was unreasonable.*

Summary

- Crimes of strict liability are those which do not require *mens rea* – intention, recklessness or even negligence – as to one or more elements of the *actus reus.*

- D will have no excuse, no matter how careful he has been (*Callow v Tillstone, Smedleys Ltd v Breed*).

- The vast majority of these crimes are statutory, but some are common law, e.g. criminal or blasphemous libel (*Lemon and Gay News Ltd*).

- Strict liability was first used in the nineteenth century but even today courts are prepared to hold that recent statutory provisions impose strict liability (*Harrow LBC v Shah and Shah*).

- There is a presumption of *mens rea* (*Sherras v De Rutzen, Sweet v Parsley, B v DPP*).

- But the presumption may be rebutted (*Gammon [HK] Ltd v A-G of Hong Kong*).

- The courts will look at a number of factors in deciding whether the presumption has been rebutted – none of which is decisive. These factors include:

  - The statutory language. Certain words are suggestive of *mens rea* (*Sheppard and Sheppard*).

  - The statutory context (*Cundy v Le Cocq, Pharmaceutical Society of Great Britain v Storkwain Ltd, Sherras v De Reutzen*).

- Whether the offence was a 'true' or 'quasi' crime; true crimes require *mens rea* (*Wings Ltd v Ellis, Harrow LBC v Shah & Shah*).

- Whether the offence was of general or specific application. Offences of specific application may not need *mens rea*.

- The degree of social danger. The more dangerous the activity, the more likely strict liability will be imposed (*Alphacell Ltd v Woodward, Wings Ltd v Ellis*).

- The severity of punishment. Low statutory penalties suggest strict liability, but this is not decisive (*Howells*).

- Whether the imposition of strict liability would promote higher standards and/or law enforcement (*Reynolds v G H Austin and Sons Ltd, Lim Chin Aik*).

- Certain statutes contain due diligence defences (*Tesco Ltd v Nattrass*) but there is no common law due diligence defence of general application.

Questions on Part I General Principles I

1 Explain what is meant by the term 'causation' in criminal law and assess how the courts have interpreted its significance in determining liability.

(OCR 2000)

2 'In general, the criminal law prohibits the doing of harm but does not impose criminal liability for a failure to do good.' Assess the truth of this statement by reference to the situations where a person may incur criminal liability by reason of a failure or omission to act and the arguments used to justify it.

(OCR 1999)

3 'The Caldwell test fails to make a distinction which should be made between the person who knowingly takes a risk and the person who gives no thought to whether there is a risk or not.' – Smith and Hogan, 1992. Consider the meanings of 'recklessness' in criminal law which gave rise to this criticism, indicating to what extent you agree with it.

(OCR 1998)

4 'Strict liability offences are contrary to fundamental legal principle. The imposition of criminal liability without reference to the state of mind of an accused can never be justified.' Consider why and in what circumstances the courts recognise the existence of crimes of strict and absolute liability.

(OCR 2000)

Part 2

Homicide

5   Murder

Introduction

The offence of murder is the most serious of criminal offences and attracts a mandatory life sentence upon conviction. It is associated with some of the most notorious names in the annals of crime: Dr Crippen, Peter Sutcliffe, Dennis Nielsen and Dr James Shipman to name but a few. It may, therefore, seem odd that murder is still defined through a whole series of common law decisions that have occurred over the years. There is, for example, no Murder Act in this country. Contrary to popular misconception, s.1 of the Homicide Act 1957 does *not* define murder. The Act mainly deals with a number of special defences that can be pleaded to the charge. To discover the law of murder you have to trace its evolution through a series of important judgments in decided cases since the seventeenth century, culminating in the House of Lords decision in *Woollin* (1998). As with other offences it is essential to appreciate the elements of *actus reus* and *mens rea* that constitute the offence.

Actus reus

The *actus reus* of murder – which is exactly the same for manslaughter – comprises the following four elements:

- Causing the death

- Of another human being

- Under the Queen's Peace

- Within any country of the realm

All of these must be present. If any one of them is missing, there cannot be liability for murder under English law. There used to be a fifth element:

- Within a year and a day

However, this element was deemed surplus to requirements and was abolished in 1996.

Mens rea

The *mens rea* of murder is 'malice aforethought'. This means one of two things:

- An intention to kill (express malice aforethought)

or

- An intention to cause grievous bodily harm (implied malice aforethought).

Either of these states of mind will be sufficient for a conviction. If both are missing, the defendant cannot be convicted of murder – but may well be facing liability for involuntary manslaughter (see Chapter 7).

Causing death

When D is charged with murder (or manslaughter) it is necessary to prove that D, by his acts or omissions, caused V's death. If V dies because of some other cause then the offence has not been committed even though all the other elements of the offence, including the *mens rea*, are present. D may of course be liable for attempt instead (*White* [1910]). The vast majority of reported cases on causation involve homicide (see Chapter 1), but the principles of causation apply equally to any result crime (e.g. criminal damage, various assaults). It does not matter how the death is caused (by shooting, stabbing, drowning, strangling, poisoning, etc.) so long as it is caused by the conduct of the accused.

Another human being

Only human beings can be the victims of murder. This sounds obvious – but there are potential problems with people just beginning, or nearing the end of, their lives. For example, a foetus that is killed in the womb cannot be a victim of murder, though there are other offences: procuring a miscarriage and child destruction.

A person who is already dead obviously cannot be the victim of murder (although the person who shoots a corpse lying under bedclothes, without realising the intended victim is already dead from natural causes, could theoretically be convicted of *attempted* murder – see Chapter 21). However, the correct definition of death has proved elusive. There is conventional death, when the heartbeat and breathing stop. But there is also brain death, when through artificial means the heart continues to beat and air circulates the lungs. Brain death is recognised by the British Medical Association and is the point when life-support machinery will be switched off. In *Malcharek, Steel* (1981), the Court of Appeal referred to this test although they did not have to decide the point. It is likely that if the question arose squarely that the courts would adopt the brain death test (or strictly *tests* as there are six of them). Thus, if D stabs V who has been certified brain dead but whose functions are being maintained on a ventilating machine, it is likely that he would be acquitted of murder but convicted of the attempt.

The Queen's Peace

This only serves to exclude from homicide cases when enemy soldiers are killed in the course of war.

Within any country of the realm

The limitations in this phrase have now all but disappeared. Murder and manslaughter are exceptional from a jurisdictional point of view in that they are triable in England even if the offence is perpetrated abroad, provided D is a British citizen.

The year-and-a-day rule

There used to be a rule that death had to occur within a year and a day of the original stabbing, strangling, etc. This rule was justified because of the difficulty in establishing causation where there was a long interval between the original wound and V's death. The net result was that if D stabbed or shot someone, but V was kept alive for 367 days before death, D could not be guilty of homicide.

Medical science developed to such an extent that the original justification was no longer valid. The Law Commission recommended the abolition of the rule and in 1996 the Law Reform (Year-and-a-Day Rule) Act 1996 came into force, abolishing the rule (s.1). The reform applies to any 'fatal offence', defined as including murder, manslaughter, infanticide and 'any other offence' of which one of the elements is causing a person's death. The Law Commission recognised the undesirability of an unqualified abolition of the rule in two circumstances (s.2(2)).

- If a very long time had passed since the original incident, it would be undesirable to have the history of the case trawled over again in a homicide trial. It could mean D having to live for years with the threat of a murder charge hanging over him. It makes more sense to prosecute for an assault or wounding charge now, rather than wait for years to see whether V dies or not. Hence, if the injury alleged to cause death was sustained *more than three years* before the death occurred, then homicide proceedings may not be brought except by or with the consent of the Attorney-General.

- If D has already been convicted of a non-fatal offence, or attempt, on the same set of facts, the consent of the Attorney-General is also required.

'Malice aforethought'

The *mens rea* of murder is malice aforethought. This is a technical term which implies neither ill-will nor premeditation. A person who kills out of compassion to alleviate suffering (a so-called 'mercy killing') almost certainly acts with malice aforethought. The term means that D either:

- intended to kill (*express malice*); or

- intended to cause grievous bodily harm (GBH) (*implied malice*).

This was not always entirely clear; but the House of Lords in *Moloney* (1985) confirmed that 'malice aforethought' means an intention to kill or an intention to cause GBH. Thus, it is possible for D to be convicted of murder when he intended some serious injury but did not even contemplate that V's life be endangered.

Intention

In many offences, the *mens rea* required is an 'intention' to cause a particular result. In murder, the *mens rea* is an intention to kill or cause GBH. Other crimes requiring intent include causing grievous bodily harm with intent to do so (see Chapter 8) and theft, where the intent is to permanently deprive the owner of their property (see Chapter 10). However, it is in the context of murder that the vast majority of intent cases have arisen, so it makes more sense to examine the topic here.

There are two forms of intent:

- Direct intent – this is what D desires;

- Indirect or oblique intent – this is not necessarily what D desires but what he foresees will almost certainly happen.

Direct intention

The dictionary definition of intention is to have something as one's aim or purpose. This form of intention is called direct intention. Suppose that D stands to gain under an insurance policy on V's life. He decides to kill V in order to gain the cash. Thus his desire is to kill V; his motive is to get rich. D points a gun at V's head and pulls the trigger. Clearly here D intends V's death. The consequence (death) was actually desired.

This is so even though V is far away, it is dark, D's aim is poor, and D believes that the chances of him hitting V are slim. If – despite the odds! – D succeeds in putting a bullet in V's brain, he will still be guilty as it was his desire and therefore also his intention to kill.

Now suppose that D sees V sitting in his car and shoots at his head. D realises that the bullet will pass through the car windscreen first. It may be said that D also intends to break the window, as it is a *necessary precondition* to killing V. Although V's death remains D's direct intention, he is prepared to accept the criminal damage and therefore also intends to break the windscreen. It is irrelevant that D does not want to break the windscreen.

Oblique intention

Now suppose that D places a bomb under V's airplane seat designed to explode when the plane is 30,000ft up over the mid-Atlantic. The consequence which D desires remains V's death – but what of the other passengers and crew? The other deaths are not a necessary precondition to killing V, but are an *almost inevitable consequence*. If D bothered to think about it, he would conclude that the deaths are practically certain. Thus he *may* be said to have intended their deaths too. This form of intention is described as *oblique intention*.

However, this scenario invites problems. What degree of probability is required before an undesired consequence, but which D has foreseen, can be said to have been intended? Some would argue none – that once one steps away from foresight of something as 100 per cent *certain to happen* then one is dealing with *risk*, and that means *recklessness*, not intent. Others would argue that very high probability would suffice.

The leading case is now that of the House of Lords in *Woollin* (1998). It is the culmination of several House of Lords and Court of Appeal decisions, dating back to the early 1970s. Various formulae have been proposed, adopted, criticised and dropped again as the courts have struggled to come up with a direction to juries that conveys the correct message. In *Woollin*, Lord Steyn (with whom the other Law Lords agreed) laid down a model direction, for trial judges to use in cases where D's intention is unclear, as follows:

The jury should be directed that they are not entitled [to find] the necessary intention, unless they feel sure that death or serious bodily harm was a virtual certainty (barring some unforeseen intervention) as a result of [D]'s actions and that [D] appreciated that such was the case.

Woollin (1998)

Stephen Woollin had killed his three-month-old son, Carl Roper, by throwing him against a wall, fracturing his skull. W did not deny doing this, but claimed that he did not have the *mens rea* for murder. He claimed that he had picked the child up after he began to choke and shake him, then, in a fit of rage or frustration, had thrown him with some considerable force towards a pram four or five feet away. The trial judge directed the jury that they might infer intention if satisfied that when W threw the child he had appreciated that there was a 'substantial risk' that he would cause serious harm to the child. W was convicted of murder and appealed on the basis that the phrase 'substantial risk' was a test of recklessness, not of intent, and that the judge should have used 'virtual certainty'. The Court of Appeal dismissed the appeal but the House of Lords unanimously reversed that Court's decision, quashed W's murder conviction and substituted one of manslaughter.

The reason that the trial judge directed the jury to 'infer' intention is due to s.8 of the Criminal Justice Act 1967. This states that, 'A court or jury in determining whether a person has committed an offence... shall decide whether he did intend... that result by reference to all the evidence, drawing such inferences from the facts as appear proper in the circumstances.' The statute therefore requires that juries must 'infer' intent. Trial judges across the country used this word faithfully for the next 30 years – but in *Woollin*, the Lords decided that the word 'find' got the point across more clearly.

The model jury direction in *Woollin* was first laid down by Lord Lane CJ in *Nedrick* (1986). That case provides a useful illustration of when D may be said to have an 'oblique' intent. D had a grudge against a woman. In the early hours the morning, he poured paraffin through the letterbox of her house and set it alight. She survived but her 12-year-old son Lloyd died in the fire. D claimed that he had not intended to harm anyone, merely to wake the woman and frighten her. In the Court of Appeal, D's murder conviction was quashed and one of manslaughter substituted – like *Woollin*, the jury had not been directed properly. However, it is possible that, had the jury been given the model direction, they may well have decided that D foresaw it as 'virtually certain' that someone – not necessarily Lloyd – would be killed or at least seriously injured, and so convicted D of murder. Many convictions are quashed in the Court of Appeal for technical legal reasons. Students should not be confused that this means that the Court is stating that in their view an accused is completely innocent and sometimes a re-trial is ordered.

An illustration of the sort of case where references to 'oblique' intent should be avoided altogether is *Moloney* (1985). D and his stepfather, V, had been drinking heavily into the early hours of the morning. The two men were heard talking and laughing until 4am when a shot rang out. D phoned the police to say, 'I've just murdered my father.' He said that they had a disagreement over who could load and fire a shotgun the fastest. He had fetched two guns and cartridges. D loaded first, at which point V goaded him to pull the trigger. D did so, apparently without aiming, but shot V in the head. D told the police, 'I just pulled the trigger and he was dead.' The trial judge directed the jury in terms of oblique intent and they convicted of murder. However, on appeal, a manslaughter conviction was substituted. Lord Bridge in the House of Lords stated that:

> The golden rule should be that, when directing a jury... the judge should avoid any elaboration or paraphrase of what is meant by intent, and leave it to the jury's good sense to decide whether the accused acted with the necessary intent, unless the judge is convinced that, on the facts and having regard to the way that case has been presented... some further explanation or elaboration is strictly necessary to avoid misunderstanding....

In *Moloney*, the trial judge's direction created unnecessary confusion. The question for the jury was essentially factual. If D knew the gun was pointing at V's head, the jury was surely bound to convict him of murder, on the basis that he must have wanted to shoot V in the head. But, if they thought that D had not realised that the gun was pointing at V's head (given his tired and drunken condition), they should have convicted him of manslaughter (either on the basis that he had committed an unlawful and dangerous act or that he had been grossly negligent – see Chapter 7). Either D had the direct intent to kill, or he had no intent at all other than pulling the trigger. Oblique intent simply did not come into it.

However, *Woollin* does not completely clear up the confusion. Lord Steyn said that, if the jury are satisfied that D foresaw death (or really serious injury) as virtually certain to occur, then they are 'entitled to find' that he intended it. That is, the jury do not *have* to do so – they do not *have* to convict of murder. *Woollin* tells the jury nothing about what factors, if any, to take into account in deciding whether 'to find' intention, once they are sure that D foresaw death or really serious injury.

Intriguingly, in *Woollin*, Lord Steyn also said, at one point, that 'a result foreseen as virtually certain is an intended result.' However, that comment did not form part of the *ratio* of the case. Professor Sir John Smith says that that 'is what the law should be', but it is not – yet. The law remains that foresight of a virtually certain consequence is not the same thing as intent, and that juries must be left to decide whether D intended a consequence. In *Scalley* (1995), a case which was almost factually identical to *Nedrick*, a jury was directed to convict of murder if they found that D had foreseen death as a virtually certain consequence, which they did. But the Court of Appeal quashed the conviction. The jury should have been told that if they found D had the necessary foresight then they could convict him of murder *but they did not have to.*

The following propositions can be made about indirect/oblique intention, as follows:

- Intention is a subjective concept. That is, it is entirely dependent on what was going through D's mind at the time he killed V.

- Unless dealing with direct intent, reference *must* be made to what D foresaw would happen as the result of his actions.

- It is only if D foresaw death or really serious injury as 'virtually certain' to happen, that a jury are 'entitled' to find that he intended it to happen.

- Other phrases, such as 'highly probable' or even 'very highly probable', do not satisfy this standard.

- It may be helpful to visualise degrees of foresight in relation to oblique intent where, remember, the accused does not desire the death but foresees the risk of it occurring, as follows:-

Figure 3 Degrees of foresight

D foresees death or serious harm as:

Impossible	Unlikely	Possible	Probable	Highly probable	Virtually certain	Certain
↓	↓	↓	↓	↓	↓	↓
	Manslaughter D is arguably subjectively reckless				Jury can find intent *Woollin*	Murder D has intention

'Grievous bodily harm'

What does 'grievous bodily harm' (GBH) mean? In *DPP v Smith* (1961), Viscount Kilmuir, with whom the rest of the Lords agreed, held that there was no reason to give the words any special meaning: '"Bodily harm" needs no explanation and "grievous" means no more and no less than "really serious"'. In *Saunders* (1985), D was charged with inflicting GBH contrary to s.20 of the Offences Against the Person Act 1861 after punching a stranger in the face, breaking his nose. He was convicted after the jury was directed that GBH meant 'serious injury'. The Court of Appeal dismissed the appeal, holding that the omission of 'really' was not significant. This was confirmed in *Janjua and Choudury* (1998). The Court of Appeal held that a trial judge has discretion when directing the jury whether or not to use the word 'really' before the words 'serious bodily harm'.

Reform

Generally

The Law Commission has recommended a refinement to the meaning of implied malice. Clause 54 of the Criminal Code Bill (1989) provides:

(1) A person is guilty of murder if he causes the death of another –

(a) intending to cause death; or

(b) intending to cause serious personal harm and being aware that he may cause death....

The Report of the Select Committee of the House of Lords on Murder and Life Imprisonment (1989) supported this recommendation, stating that 'unforeseen... killings are properly left to the law of manslaughter'.

Intention

Clause 18 (b) of the Criminal Code Bill (1989) defines intention, by stating that 'a person acts... (b) intentionally with respect to... (ii) a result when he acts either in order to bring it about or being aware that it will occur in the ordinary course of events.' In the Commentary on the draft code, the Law Commission state that:

A definition of intention for criminal law purposes must refer... to 'the means as well the end and the inseparable consequences of the end as well as the means'... A person's awareness of any degree of probability (short of virtual certainty) that a particular result will follow from his acts ought not, we believe, to be classed as intention to cause that result.

In the Government's draft Offences Against the Person Bill (1998), 'intention' is defined in similar terms, i.e. D acts intentionally if a result was (a) his purpose or (b) where it was not his purpose, he knew that it would occur in the ordinary course of events if he were to succeed in his purpose of causing some other result. Although this proposal has no bearing for the law of homicide, it does support the Law Commission's view that both direct and oblique intent should continue to satisfy the legal requirement of 'intention'.

There have, however, been contrary views that intention should be limited to direct intention, i.e. aim or purpose. This would make the legal definition fit with the word's everyday dictionary meaning. In *Steane* (1947), this approach was adopted by the Court of Criminal Appeal. D was charged with doing acts likely to assist the enemy with intent to assist the enemy, contrary to the Defence (General) Regulations 1939. He was a British film actor resident in Germany prior to World War II who had been arrested when the war broke out and forced, extremely reluctantly, to broadcast propaganda on German radio. Threats had been made to place his wife and children in a concentration camp if he did not comply. The Court quashed his conviction, because of his lack of intent.

Such reform would also provide a clear distinction between intention and recklessness. How is it possible to distinguish a consequence foreseen as 'virtually certain' (which is intended) from one foreseen as 'highly probable' (where D is reckless)? There is no obvious cut-off.

Do you agree that some clear, legal and/or moral distinction should be drawn between the following:

- D1, who causes V's death because that is what he wants to happen, and

- D2 who (in seeking to achieve some other purpose) foresees that V's death is virtually certain to happen, although he desperately hopes that it will not happen.

The approach of the American Law Institute's *Model Penal Code* (similar to the Law Commission's Criminal Code Bill – the difference is that several American states have adopted at least part of the Code into legislation) is to distinguish between 'intention' and 'knowledge'. Thus, the *Code* states that 'a person acts intentionally... when... it is his conscious object to... cause such a result' and that 'a person acts knowingly... when... he is aware that it is practically certain that his conduct will cause such a result.'

One state that has adopted the *Code* is Alaska, where it is first-degree murder to kill 'with intent to cause the death of another person', but second-degree murder for a person to kill 'knowing that his conduct is substantially certain to cause death'. The state of New Hampshire, however, distinguishes between 'purposely' killing and 'knowingly' killing.

Murder in the first degree

In the United States, and some other countries including Canada, many crimes are divided into 'degrees'. Hence, for example, the expression 'first-degree murder'. What does it mean and should it be considered for adoption into English law? First-degree murder is distinguished from second-degree murder by the presence of three factors, as follows:

- premeditation (conception of a plan to kill);

- deliberation (consideration of that plan); and

- wilfulness (the intentional execution of the plan)

An intentional, but more spontaneous, killing is second-degree murder. In England, no distinction is made between first- and second-degree murder; any intentional killing is murder and carries the same sentence, mandatory life imprisonment. Of course, life rarely means life and the trial judge will recommend a minimum period of time before the killer should be considered for parole. In the United States, on the other hand, a majority of states have retained or restored the death penalty, principally but not exclusively for murder. When a sentence of death may be imposed following first-degree but not second-degree murder, it is apparent that a distinction between the two is fundamentally important. As long as England does not restore the death penalty (and it would be extremely unlikely, given the Labour Government's decision to ratify the Sixth Protocol to the European Convention on Human Rights), the distinction between premeditated and deliberate murder and 'other' murders does not bear such a heavy weight.

Summary

- To be liable for murder, D must cause the death of another human being, under the Queen's Peace, within any country of the realm, with malice aforethought.

- The requirement that death occur within 'a year and a day' was abolished in 1996.

- Malice aforethought means an intention to kill or cause grievous bodily harm (*Moloney*).

- 'Grievous' bodily harm means 'really serious' bodily harm (*DPP v Smith*).

- If there is proof that D wanted or desired death or really serious injury then he intended it. This is 'direct' intent.

- If there is proof that D foresaw death or really serious injury as virtually certain to happen without necessarily wanting or desiring it, then the jury is 'entitled to find' that he intended it (*Woollin*). This is 'indirect' or 'oblique' intent. Foresight of a virtually certain consequence is not the same thing as intent (*Scalley*) – the jury must be left to 'find' intent.

Figure 4 Unlawful homicide

Unlawful homicide is essentially either murder or manslaughter and can be broadly classified as follows:

1. Murder

Unlawful killing of a human being under the Queen's Peace with malice aforethought (*Moloney 1985 HL/Woollin 1998 HL* – note this is *not* a statutory definition).

Malice aforethought – intention to kill or cause the victim serious bodily harm.

2. Manslaughter

There are two categories of manslaughter:

(a) VOLUNTARY and (b) INVOLUNTARY, each of which can be further subdivided:

Although malice aforethought is present the accused successfully pleads a special and partial defence under the Homicide Act 1957.

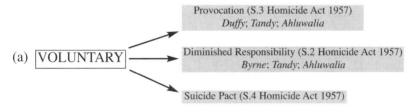

(a) [VOLUNTARY]

    Provocation (S.3 Homicide Act 1957)
    Duffy; Tandy; Ahluwalia

    Diminished Responsibility (S.2 Homicide Act 1957)
    Byrne; Tandy; Ahluwalia

    Suicide Pact (S.4 Homicide Act 1957)

(b) [INVOLUNTARY]

    The unlawful killing of a human being under the Queen's Peace without malice aforethought

- Killing by an unlawful and dangerous act (constructive manslaughter) *Church; Newbury and Jones; A-G's Ref No. 3 of 1994*

- Gross negligence manslaughter *(Stone and Dobinson; Adomako)*

Be sure you understand this classification and that murder requires a *specific intent* to kill or do serious harm whereas involuntary manslaughter is a crime of *basic intent*. This will be significant when related to the defence of intoxication.

6   Voluntary manslaughter

General introduction

The verdict of voluntary manslaughter is unique. Firstly it is not a specific charge in itself but rather arises from a charge of murder to which a special and partial defence has been pleaded. These special and partial defences will be considered below but are called *special* since they may only be pleaded in defence to murder and *partial* because a successful plea results, not in acquittal but in a conviction for manslaughter. This allows the judge to exercise discretion in choosing the appropriate sentence depending upon all the circumstances of the individual case.

The defences are contained in the Homicide Act 1957, which was passed at a time when capital punishment was the mandatory sentence for murder. It was acknowledged that many murders were spontaneous rather than planned and that most occurred within close relationships. Consequently the defences of provocation, suicide pact and infanticide were justifiable insofar as they mitigated the otherwise harsh consequences of a murder conviction. The defence of diminished responsibility was introduced partially as an admission that the law relating to mental abnormality was inadequate and outdated. Those who were accused of murder and suffered from certain mental conditions, for example psychopaths, did not fall within the rules relating to insanity and were liable to conviction and would be hanged; this despite the fact that they had been diagnosed as unable to control their actions due to their mental condition.

A   Provocation

Introduction

Provocation is only a defence to murder. Even when D successfully pleads provocation as a defence to murder, it only reduces liability to manslaughter. Provocation existed – indeed still exists – at common law. The common law rule has been *modified* but *not replaced* by s.3 of the Homicide Act 1957.

Homicide Act 1957
3. Where on a charge of murder there is evidence on which the jury
can find that the person charged was provoked (whether by things
done or by things said or by both together) to lose his self-control, the
question whether the provocation was enough to make a reasonable
man do as he did shall be left to the jury; and in determining that
question the jury shall take into account everything both done and
said according to the effect it would have on a reasonable man.

Provocation therefore consists of two questions:

- Did D lose his self-control? (a subjective question)

- Would the reasonable man have lost his self-control? (an objective question)

Before tackling those questions, which are both for a jury alone, there is a preliminary question, which is for the judge alone – was there enough evidence of provocation for the defence to be left to the jury to consider?

What can amount to provocation?

Under the 1957 Act, provocation need not be something illegal, or wrongful. It simply has to be something 'done' or 'said'. In *Doughty* (1986), D's murder conviction was quashed on the ground that provocation should have been left to the jury. He had killed his 19-day-old son after the child would not stop crying. The Court of Appeal held that it should have been left to the jury to decide whether the baby's crying was provocation by 'things done'.

Provocation may *come from* or be *be directed at* third parties. In the following cases the Court of Appeal held that the trial judge had wrongly denied D the defence even though:

- *Davies* (1975) – D was provoked by his wife's lover into shooting her;

- *Pearson* (1992) – D was provoked by his father's abusive treatment of D's brother into killing the father with a sledgehammer.

The subjective question

The first question for the jury is: was D provoked to lose his self-control? If he kept his cool, then it is unnecessary to consider the objective question. If

D is unusually phlegmatic or emotionless and retains his cool (even when the reasonable man would have lost his), then the defence is not available.

A 'sudden and temporary loss of self-control'

In *Ibrams and Gregory* (1981) and *Thornton (No.1)* (1992), the Court of Appeal approved the classic test of Devlin J in *Duffy* (1949) that there must be 'a sudden and temporary loss of self-control, rendering the accused so subject to passion as to make him or her for the moment not the master of his mind'. In *Ibrams and Gregory*, Lawton LJ said:

> Indeed, circumstances which induce a desire for revenge are inconsistent with provocation, since the conscious formulation of a desire for revenge means that a person has had time to think, to reflect, and that would negative a sudden temporary loss of self-control, which is the essence of provocation.

Ibrams and Gregory (1981)
Ibrams was sharing a flat with his fiancée, Laura. An ex-boyfriend of hers, John Monk, regularly visited the flat and terrorised them. The police were contacted on 7 October, but did nothing. Thus, on 10 October, Ibrams, Laura and a friend called Gregory met and agreed a plan for dealing with Monk. The plan was to get him drunk and encourage him to go to bed with Laura. The two men would then burst in and attack Monk while he was in bed. The plan was carried out on 12 October and Monk was killed. The Court of Appeal upheld their murder convictions. There was no evidence that Monk had done anything after 7 October to provoke them. The interval of time between the last act of provocation, combined with the pre-formulated plan, negatived their claims of loss of self-control.

In *Baille* (1995), the Court of Appeal stressed that the question whether D had lost his self-control at the time of the killing was one for the *jury*. The judge's task was simply whether there was *evidence* that D had lost his self-control. D had learnt from his son that a drug dealer, M, had threatened his son with violence. D armed himself with a shotgun and drove around to M's house. There was an altercation, which resulted in D shooting and killing him. D pleaded provocation, partly based on being told of the threats by his son. The judge directed the jury to ignore the possible provoking effect of the threats, because any loss of self-control induced earlier *must have ceased* by the time of the shooting. The Court of Appeal allowed D's appeal: there was evidence of provocation, it was then for the jury to determine whether D had lost self-control at the time of the shooting.

Cumulative provocation

Evidence of provocation is not confined to the last act or word before the killing. There may have been previous acts or words which, when added together, cause D to lose self-control, even though the last act on its own may have been 'relatively unprovocative if taken in isolation', according to Lord Goff in *Luc Thiet Thuan* (1997). All the evidence of provocation must be left to the jury to consider (*Humphreys* [1995]).

'Slow burn'

The defence of provocation developed from traditional, male ideas of reacting instantly to violence with further violence. Consequently, the defence struggles to cope when it is a woman who kills. It has been argued that, in domestic violence cases, the 'sudden and temporary loss of self-control' test is inappropriate. Where a woman who has suffered years of violence and abuse finally seizes her opportunity when the husband is asleep or drunk or both, and kills him, she may not be reacting to any particular act or incident, but rather the accumulation of years of abuse. Although the situation does call for mitigation, the courts in such cases have consistently upheld the *Duffy* test. Consequently, battered women who kill face life sentences for murder. The leading cases are *Thornton (No.1)* (1992) and *Ahluwalia* (1992).

Thornton (No.1)
Sara and Malcolm Thornton's marriage quickly degenerated, Sara suffering physical abuse from Malcolm, who was jealous and possessive and a heavy drinker. One night, Sara returned home to find her husband lying on the sofa. He called her a 'whore'. She went into the kitchen, found a bread-knife, sharpened it, and returned to the living room. Malcolm said that he would kill Sara when she was asleep. She replied she would kill him first, and stabbed him in the stomach. Sara was convicted of murder and her appeal was dismissed. Her years of provocation were ignored; at the crucial time she was not suffering a 'sudden temporary loss of self-control'. The fact she had gone to the kitchen to fetch, and sharpen, the knife, were crucial factors.

In *Ahluwalia*, D was also the long-term victim of an abusive and violent marriage. One night, her husband threatened her with violence the next day unless she paid a bill; he then went to bed and fell asleep. Later, D doused him in petrol and set him alight. He died six days later. D was convicted of murder but, on appeal, argued that the *Duffy* test was inappropriate in battered woman cases. However, the Court of Appeal rejected her appeal on this ground. The court did stress that the requirement was that D's reaction had to be 'sudden' as opposed to 'immediate', but pointed out that 'the longer the delay and the stronger the evidence of deliberation on the part of the accused, the more likely it will be that the prosecution will negative provocation.'

The objective question

The jury must be satisfied that the reasonable man would – or might – also have lost self-control if subjected to the same provocation.

Who is the reasonable man?

Before the Homicide Act 1957, judges consistently held that the reasonable man was an adult with normal physical and mental attributes. This led to some very harsh decisions. In *Bedder v DPP* (1954), a prostitute taunted D about his impotence – something he was, unsurprisingly, very sensitive about – with the result that he stabbed her to death, the House of Lords upheld his murder conviction. The Lords approved a jury direction that they had to consider what effect the provocation would have had on the ordinary person with no sexual hang-ups (presumably, very little).

This decision was not reversed until *Camplin* (1978). The House of Lords held that *Bedder* had, in fact, been overruled by s.3 of the 1957 Act. Lord Diplock, giving a model direction with which the rest of the House concurred, concluded that:

> A proper direction to a jury... should state... that the reasonable man... is a person having the power of self-control to be expected of an ordinary person of the sex and age of the accused, but in other respects sharing such of the accused's characteristics as they think would affect the gravity of the provocation to him; and that the question is not merely whether such a person would in like circumstances be provoked to lose his self-control but also whether he would react to the provocation as the accused did.

DPP v Camplin (1978)
Mohammed Khan, a middle-aged man, had sexually abused Paul Camplin, a 15-year-old boy, and then laughed at him. At this, C hit K over the head with a chapati-pan and killed him. The judge directed

the jury to consider the effect K's provocation would have had on an ordinary *man*. The jury convicted but the Court of Appeal quashed the murder conviction by *distinguishing* Bedder on the ground that youth was a normal state, not an abnormality like impotence. The House of Lords went further and *overruled* Bedder. The jury should have been told to assess the impact of the provocation on a reasonable *15-year-old boy*.

The relevance of D's characteristics

Thus, *Camplin* allows juries to take account of D's characteristics when deciding whether the reasonable man would have lost self-control. Lord Diplock's direction appears to divide the objective question into two separate and distinct issues.

- The gravity of the provocation

- The power of self-control

This was certainly the view of a majority of the Privy Council in *Luc Thiet Thuan* (1997). Their decision was that while characteristics were admissible in assessing the gravity of the provocation, they had no role to play when assessing the power of self-control to be expected. In *Luc*, D had been charged with the murder of Candy Shukman, a former girlfriend, after stabbing her in a rage triggered by her comparing him unfavourably to another man. He was convicted and appealed on the basis that he had previously suffered a head injury caused by a fall and that this left him susceptible to uncontrolled, explosive acts. This, he argued, constituted a characteristic that should be attributed to the reasonable man, but the trial judge had refused to direct the jury as D had hoped. However, the Privy Council dismissed his appeal. This view of the law was also adopted by the Supreme Court of Canada (*Hill* [1986]) and the High Court of Australia (*Stingel* [1990]).

In *Luc*, however, Lord Steyn delivered a dissenting opinion (which is very unusual for the Privy Council, who nearly always deliver unanimous judgments). He decided that it would not be proper in such a case 'to ask the jury to ignore the defendant's brain damage'. Subsequently, Lord Steyn's dissenting view has come to be accepted as correct: it was specifically relied upon by the Court of Appeal in *Campbell (No.2)* and *Parker* (both 1997). Now, in *Smith* (2000), the House of Lords has confirmed that the objective test cannot be divided up in the way that the Privy Council had done.

Smith (2000)
Morgan Smith suffered a severe depressive illness. One day he got into a heated argument with an old friend of his, James McCullagh, and eventually stabbed him through the heart. Smith was charged with murder, and pleaded various defences: lack of intent, diminished responsibility, and provocation. As to the latter defence, the trial judge directed the jury that while D's depressive illness was a characteristic that was relevant to the gravity of the provocation, it was *not* relevant to the standard of self-control to be expected of the reasonable man. The jury rejected all of D's defences and he was convicted of murder. However, the Court of Appeal quashed the conviction and substituted one of manslaughter. The House of Lords (albeit by 3:2) dismissed the prosecution's appeal.

Which characteristics are relevant?

Even following *Smith*, the position remains that the question of characteristics is most relevant when assessing the gravity of the provocation. As the old and discredited case of *Bedder* demonstrates, if D's characteristics are ignored, taunts and insults may become totally meaningless and the provocation defence is almost bound to fail. The gravity of an insult can only be measured accurately if put into context. That is not to say that *all* of D's characteristics must automatically be taken into account! As Lord Taylor CJ pointed out in *Dryden* (1995), if all of D's characteristics are attributed to the reasonable man, the reasonable man becomes D.

Some – probably most – characteristics have simply no relevance. As a judge of the Supreme Court of Canada stated in *Hill* (1986), 'the race of a person will be irrelevant if the provocation involves an insult regarding a physical disability. Similarly, the sex of an accused will be irrelevant if the provocation relates to a racial insult… the central criterion is the relevance of the particular feature to the provocation in question.'

Furthermore, certain characteristics are, by their very nature, *not* characteristics of the *reasonable* man. In *Camplin*, Lord Simon stated that the judge may tell a jury that D is not entitled to rely on any of the following:

- exceptional exciteability (whether idiosyncratic or by cultural environment or ethnic origin);

- pugnacity;

- ill-temper;

- drunkenness.

However, any other characteristic that could affect the gravity of the provocation may potentially be attributed to the reasonable person. Age and sex may well be relevant when determining the gravity of the provocation. For example, if the abuse directed at D is that she is called an 'old slapper', it is relevant to the gravity of the provocation that she is not a young woman.

Is there a requirement of a connection?

In *Newell* (1980), D, an alcoholic, was upset after his girlfriend had left him. He had taken a drug overdose in a failed suicide bid. One night he and a friend had consumed a considerable quantity of alcohol before returning to D's flat. The friend made derogatory remarks about the girlfriend, then suggested that D sleep with him instead. At this D flew into a rage and battered him to death with an ashtray. He pleaded provocation but was convicted of murder. The Court of Appeal, dismissing the appeal, considered that the only potential relevant characteristic was D's alcoholism. However, the Court concluded that there was no connection between D's alcoholism and the provocation; consequently, they did not have to decide whether alcoholism could actually be a characteristic. The court stated that:

> There must be some real connection between the nature of the provocation and the particular characteristic of the offender by which it is sought to modify the ordinary man test. The words or conduct must have been exclusively or particularly provocative to the individual because, and only because, of the characteristic.

However, this statement no longer represents the law. In *Ahluwalia* (1992), considered above, the Court of Appeal said that the law would be 'unjustifiably aggravated' by a requirement that provocation be directed at a particular characteristic. Similarly, in *Luc Thiet Thuan* (1997), the Privy Council pointed out that while 'in the great majority of cases' the provocation will in fact have been directed at some particular characteristic, 'this need not always be so.'

Thus, in *Ahluwalia*, the Court of Appeal accepted that *if* D had been suffering Battered Woman Syndrome, this *could* have been relevant because a battered woman might well perceive threats of violence more seriously than a woman who had never suffered physical violence before. Similarly, in *Dryden* (1995), D's eccentricity or obsessiveness could well have exacerbated the provocative behaviour of the council officials who were trying to demolish a bungalow that D had built without planning permission. In *Humphreys* (1995), while some of the provocation was clearly addressed at one of D's characteristics – her attention-seeking – the Court of Appeal stated that her immaturity was also relevant. In any event, if physical age is regarded as relevant, then surely mental age should also be relevant. These cases will be returned to shortly.

Temporary characteristics

Transient states of mind such as intoxication, and depression, have generally been held *not* to be 'characteristics'. Hence, in *Newell*, the Court refused to consider D's drunkenness as a possible characteristic. It was not a permanent feature of character. However, the decision of the House of Lords in *Morhall* (1996) makes it clear that characteristics should be given a more flexible quality. Lord Goff said that, in an appropriate case, it might be necessary to refer to other circumstances, which might affect the gravity of the provocation to D, but which could not properly be described as 'characteristics'. This could include D's history, or the circumstances in which he found himself at the time. In such a case, the judge was entitled to direct the jury to take into account the 'entire factual situation' when considering the gravity of the provocation. (*NB* this part of Lord Goff's judgment was *obiter* as *Morhall* considered a characteristic which *was* more than transient.)

Self-induced characteristics

It is clear that characteristics may *not* be withdrawn from the jury's consideration simply because they were self-induced, such as alcoholism. This point was made by the Court of Appeal in *Newell* (above) and confirmed by the House of Lords in *Morhall* (1996), which involved an addiction to sniffing glue.

Morhall (1996)

Alan Morhall was addicted to glue-sniffing. One night, after a day spent arguing and fighting with his friend, Stephen Denton, about M's condition, Morhall stabbed him to death with a dagger. At his murder trial the sole question was provocation. The trial judge directed the jury that addiction to glue-sniffing *could* be taken into account, especially as it was M's glue-sniffing that was the subject of the 'provocative' words uttered. The jury rejected the defence and convicted; the Court of Appeal dismissed his appeal. The court said that the judge's direction was, if anything, *over generous*. A 'self-induced addiction' such as glue-sniffing was 'inconsistent with the concept of the reasonable man and would allow indulgence for all kinds of abuse'. However, the House of Lords allowed Morhall's appeal and substituted a conviction of manslaughter. Lord Goff, with whom the rest of the House agreed, said that the reasonable man shared *whatever* of D's characteristics as might affect the gravity of the provocation. This might include addiction to glue-sniffing.

Mental characteristics

There has been some dispute in the past about whether mental characteristics should be considered under the provocation defence. The argument is that such conditions as mental illness should be dealt with under the diminished responsibility defence, and not under provocation at all (this was the firm view of the majority of the Privy Council in *Luc* [1997]). However, it seems to be settled now that mental characteristics are, where relevant, admissible as characteristics of the reasonable man under the objective limb of the provocation defence. In *Ahluwalia* (1992), it was argued on appeal that the trial judge had omitted to mention the fact that D was suffering from Battered Women's Syndrome (BWS) when describing the reasonable woman to the jury. The Court of Appeal accepted that this factor *could* be relevant but that, on the facts, there was no evidence that D was actually suffering the condition.

In *Dryden* (1995), the Court of Appeal accepted that D's eccentricity and obsessiveness were features of his character 'which fell into the category of mental characteristics and which ought to have been left to the jury.' In *Humphreys* (1995), the Court of Appeal was prepared to accept that D's immaturity and exhibitionism were relevant characteristics. D, a 17-year-old prostitute, had killed her 33-year-old partner and pimp. On the night in question, she had slashed her wrists while he was out. On his return he jeeringly told her that she had not made a very good job of it, whereupon she took a knife and stabbed him to death. She was convicted of murder in 1984, but brought an appeal after the Court of Appeal in *Ahluwalia* allowed for the possibility of mental characteristics. Her conviction was quashed.

Other recent cases allowing mental characteristics to be attributed to the reasonable man include *Thornton (No.2)* (1996) – obsessive personality disorder; *Campbell* (No.2) and *Parker* (both 1997) – chronic alcoholism with some brain damage; and now, of course, *Smith* (2000) – depressive illness.

Would the reasonable man have lost self-control and done as the defendant did?

Under s.3 of the Homicide Act 1957, it is a question – for the jury alone – to consider whether the reasonable man, having lost his self-control, would have done as D did. The jury should consider all of D's behaviour, not just the immediate act of killing.

In *Clarke* (1991), D head-butted and strangled his girlfriend, V, after she told him that she was pregnant but thinking of having an abortion. She may have still been alive at this point but D, panicking, electrocuted her as well by placing wires from a lamp into her mouth and switching it on. At his trial for murder, the judge refused D's submission that the jury should be told to confine their consideration of what the reasonable man might have done to the head-butting and strangling only. Unsurprisingly, the jury convicted and the Court of Appeal dismissed his application of leave to appeal. The court was satisfied that the Homicide Act required the jury to take into account everything that D did, apart from those acts that were 'too remote', such as disposal of a body. On the facts, the electrocution followed very soon after the strangulation and it would have been artificial to ask the jury to divide up D's acts.

Procedure

If D wishes to rely on the defence, he must provide evidence of provocation. The onus is then on the prosecution to prove that D was *not* provoked. If there is evidence of provocation, the judge must direct the jury to consider it. Often, the defence will raise self-defence only, a tactical move, hoping for an acquittal. (While provocation only reduces murder to manslaughter; self-defence leads to a complete acquittal – see Chapter 19.) Where this happens, the judge remains obliged to direct the jury on provocation regardless of what the defence wants.

In *Rossiter* (1994), D stabbed her husband to death. She had been exposed to a great degree of verbal abuse and physical violence from him on the day in question but she refused to admit that she had deliberately stabbed him, maintaining that it was self-defence. The Court of Appeal quashed her murder conviction and substituted manslaughter. There was evidence, particularly the number of stab wounds (over 20), from which the jury could have concluded that she had lost her self-control. The judge should have left the defence to them.

Nevertheless there *must* be *some* evidence of provocation to bring the judge's duty into play. If there is no evidence of provocation, it is not up to the judge to direct the jury on what would be a hypothetical, speculative possibility. In *Acott* (1997), D was charged with the murder of his elderly mother. He claimed that she had fallen and her injuries were the result of this plus his desperate efforts to resuscitate her. However, he was convicted of murder. On appeal, he argued that the judge should have directed the jury on provocation. However, both the Court of Appeal and the House of Lords rejected his appeal. There was simply *no evidence* of provocation.

Summary

- Provocation is a common law defence but it is regulated by s.3 of the Homicide Act 1957.

- It is a defence only to murder and reduces D's liability to manslaughter.

- There must be some evidence of provocation (which is a question of law) before the defence can be left to the jury (*Acott*). It is then up to the prosecution to disprove the defence.

- Provocation may be by things done, or things said, or both. There are no limitations on these concepts. The provocation does not necessarily have to come from V (*Davies*), nor does it need to have been directed at D (*Pearson*).

- There is a subjective element and an objective element – both must be disproven by the Crown.

- The subjective element – was D provoked to lose his self-control? – requires that D must have undergone 'a sudden and temporary loss of self-control' (*Duffy*; *Ibrams and Gregory*, *Ahluwalia*, *Thornton [No.1]*)

- But 'sudden' does not mean 'instant' and in cases, particularly those involving domestic violence characterised by 'slow burn' reactions, the defence may be available despite a lengthy time delay (*Ahluwalia*).

- The courts recognise cumulative provocation (*Humphreys*).

- The objective requirement means that the jury must be satisfied that the reasonable man might also have lost self-control.

- The reasonable man shares whichever of D's characteristics as would affect the gravity of the provocation to him (*DPP v Camplin* [1978]). This does not necessarily mean all of D's characteristics (*Dryden* [1995]).

- When assessing the power of self-control to be expected of the reasonable man, any of the defendant's characteristics which affect his power of self-control may (subject to the point below) be attributed to the reasonable man (*Smith*).

91

- Certain characteristics are *always* excluded, e.g. bad temper and exciteability, because they are contradictory to the concept of the 'reasonable man' (*DPP v Camplin, Smith*).

- There is no requirement that the provocation has to be connected to or directed at the characteristic (*Ahluwalia, Dryden, Luc*).

- Characteristics may be self-induced (*Morhall*).

- Temporary characteristics may be relevant (*Morhall*).

- Mental characteristics are as relevant as physical ones – provided that they affect the gravity of the provocation (*Ahluwalia, Dryden, Humphreys, Thornton [No.2]*).

B   Diminished responsibility

Introduction

The defence of diminished responsibility (DR) evolved in the courts of Scotland as a common law defence. However, it was only introduced into English law by s.2 of the Homicide Act 1957.

Homicide Act 1957

2 (1) Where a person kills or is party to a killing of another, he shall not be convicted of murder if he was suffering from such abnormality of mind (whether arising from a condition of arrested or retarded development of mind or any inherent causes or induced by disease or injury) as substantially impaired his mental responsibility for his acts and omissions in doing or being party to the killing.

(2) On a charge of murder, it shall be for the defence to prove that the person charged is by virtue of this section not liable to be convicted of murder.

DR operates as a limited defence, in two ways. First, it may only be pleaded to a charge of murder. Second, it only reduces liability from murder to manslaughter. However, this allows the judge full discretion on sentencing. Some defendants may receive an absolute discharge, others probationary or suspended sentences, while in appropriate circumstances some will receive hospital or guardianship orders under the Mental Health Act 1983. Others may still face imprisonment, with some receiving life sentences for manslaughter (about 15 per cent of cases).

S.2(1) breaks down into three components:

- An abnormality of mind;

- Arising from certain specified causes;

- Which substantially impairs mental responsibility.

The defence must establish all three elements before D can avoid a murder conviction. But there are no further requirements. For instance, the fact that a killing was premeditated does not destroy a plea of DR (*Byrne* [1960]).

'Abnormality of mind'

Although medical evidence is important, the decision whether D was suffering such an abnormality is one for the jury. In *Byrne* (1960), D was a sexual psychopath who suffered violent, perverted sexual desires, which he found difficult, if not impossible, to control. He strangled a girl in a YWCA hostel in Birmingham and then mutilated the body. He was convicted of murder, but the Court of Criminal Appeal reduced his conviction to manslaughter. Lord Parker CJ said that 'Abnormality of mind... means a state of mind so different from that of ordinary human beings that the reasonable man would term it abnormal.'

The definition is much wider than that of insanity under the M'Naghten Rules (see Chapter 15). Crucially, for psychopathic defendants like Byrne, DR recognises the so-called 'irresistible impulse' defence, a plea that D should be excused liability because of an inability, or even difficulty, to control impulses. This has never been allowed as part of the insanity defence but, since *Byrne*, is at least a defence to murder. In fact, the impulse need not be *irresistible*; it is sufficient that D's difficulty in controlling his impulses is *substantially greater than normal*.

The Court of Criminal Appeal approved the medical witnesses' description of Byrne's condition as amounting to 'partial insanity'. Earlier cases had used expressions such as 'not quite mad but a borderline case'. Unsurprisingly, such directions created a risk of confusion with the insanity defence. The position was only resolved in *Seers* (1984), where the judge had directed the jury that DR was only available to those who were 'partially insane' or 'on the borderline of insanity'. D, who suffered a depressive illness, was convicted of murder, but the Court of Appeal substituted manslaughter. While a depressive illness could amount to an

93

abnormality of mind, few people would consider it to be on the 'borderline of insanity.' In future, judges should keep to Lord Parker CJ's direction in *Byrne* and avoided references to 'insanity' altogether.

The specified causes

Although there is nothing in s.2 to rule out any other causes, D's abnormality of mind should be attributable to one of the causes listed in s.2:

- a condition of arrested or retarded development of mind; or

- any inherent cause; or

- induced by disease; or

- induced by injury.

The judge should attempt to tailor the direction to fit the facts of the case. In most cases it would not be particularly unhelpful for the judge to direct the jury by simply reading out s.2 in full; he should only mention those causes that could be relevant.

The courts have generally been prepared to allow a wide range of mental conditions to provide a basis for DR pleas. The abnormality of mind does not have to have any degree of permanence, provided that it existed at the time of the killing and that it substantially diminished D's responsibility. Factors such as jealousy and rage have been used to support the defence. Mercy killers not infrequently receive verdicts of not guilty to murder on grounds of DR.

'A condition of arrested or retarded development of mind'

Mental deficiency was accepted as an 'abnormality of mind' in *Speake* (1957).

'Any inherent cause'

The words 'any inherent cause' clearly have a wide scope. The word 'inherent' in s.2 does *not* require that the condition be an inherited one. Nor need it have been present from birth (*Gomez* [1964]). The following have all been accepted as inherent causes:

- psychopathy;

- paranoia;

- epilepsy;

- depression;

- pre-menstrual tension.

'Induced by disease'

'Disease' is wide enough to cover mental, as well as physical, diseases. In *Sanderson* (1993), S was convicted of murder after the judge's direction to the jury to the effect that the defence had to show injury to the brain. On appeal, the Court of Appeal accepted that the defence did *not* have to show some physical injury. The physical condition of the brain, though not irrelevant, was a question for evidence only. In any event, 'any inherent cause' would cover functional mental illness.

The courts in England were slow to accept Battered Woman Syndrome, despite its recognition as a psychological condition, especially in the United States, as providing a basis for a successful defence of DR. However, in *Ahluwalia* (1993) – considered above under provocation – the Court of Appeal actually allowed her appeal against a murder conviction on the basis of such a condition.

'Induced by injury'

This would include physical blows to the head, for example, that left D suffering brain damage.

> Is physical violence essential before someone can be said to have suffered an 'injury'? What else could cause an 'injury'?

Other factors

The basic position here is that if D pleads DR he may not support this plea with any evidence of abnormality derived from factors not listed in s.2. Where the evidence suggests that D suffered from one of the causes within s.2, *plus* another factor which falls outside of s.2, then the judge should direct the jury to ignore the effects of the inadmissible cause. This unfortunately means that the jury must answer a hypothetical question. This problem raises itself most often when D claims that he was intoxicated *and* had an abnormality of mind due to a specified cause (see below).

'Substantially impaired... mental responsibility'

The expression 'diminished responsibility' does not actually appear in s.2 itself; rather it is used in a marginal note in the Homicide Act. Instead, s.2 uses the phrase 'substantially impaired... mental responsibility'. In *Byrne*, the Court of Criminal Appeal said that the question of whether D's impairment could be described as 'substantial' was a question of degree and, hence, although medical evidence was not irrelevant, one for the jury. In *Lloyd* (1967), the trial judge, Ashworth J, directed the jury as follows:

> Substantial does not mean total, that is to say, the mental responsibility need not be totally impaired, so to speak, destroyed altogether. At the other end of the scale substantial does not mean trivial or minimal. It is something in between and Parliament has left it to you and other juries to say on the evidence, was the mental responsibility impaired and if so, was it substantially impaired?

The effect of intoxication

This is a tricky area of law. There is often conflicting medical evidence, which can create confusion in the mind of the jury – and sometimes the judge! The case of *Sanderson* (1993) illustrates some of the difficulties in this area. D was a regular user of cocaine and heroin. He admitted killing his girlfriend with a hockey stick. The only issue was whether he was guilty of murder or manslaughter. The prosecution and defence psychiatrists disagreed:

- *Defence*: D was suffering *paranoid psychosis* – a mental illness – which was already present, irrespective of his drug abuse. It was an 'inherent cause' and, although exacerbated by cocaine abuse, was an abnormality of mind in its own right.

- *Prosecution*: D was suffering from paranoia caused purely by his *cocaine abuse*. There was no 'disease'. Furthermore, cocaine or heroin abuse could not damage the physical structure of the brain in the way that alcohol could; hence, there was no 'injury'.

D was convicted of murder and appealed. The Court of Appeal quashed the conviction because of contradictions in the judge's summing-up which might have confused the jury. However, it is not difficult to see how the jury would have struggled to reach a verdict in this case, with so much conflicting evidence presented to them.

There are two distinct situations to consider:

- D killed whilst intoxicated *and* whilst suffering some unrelated 'abnormality of mind'.

- D killed whilst some suffering an 'abnormality of mind' *caused by* intoxication.

The defendant was intoxicated and was also suffering some unrelated 'abnormality of mind'

A plea of DR may not be supported with evidence of intoxication. In *Fenton* (1975), Lord Widgery CJ said, 'we do not see how self-induced intoxication can of itself produce an abnormality of mind due to inherent causes'. In *Gittens* (1985), D suffered from depression for which he sought and received medical treatment. One night he consumed a large amount of drink and anti-depressant pills. In this state he clubbed his wife to death and then strangled his stepdaughter. The Court of Appeal quashed his murder conviction and substituted one of manslaughter because of a misdirection to the jury about the role of intoxicants. Lord Lane CJ said the jury should be directed to disregard the effect of the alcohol or drugs. Then the jury should consider whether D, had he been sober, would have been suffering from such abnormality of mind as substantially impaired his mental responsibility.

In *Egan* (1992), there was evidence that D was mentally abnormal. One day he drank fifteen pints of beer plus some gin and tonics, then bludgeoned an elderly woman to death. The Court of Appeal, agreeing with the trial judge's direction, said that 'the vital question' for the jury was whether D's abnormality of mind was such 'that he would have been under diminished responsibility, drink or no drink?'

The defendant was suffering an 'abnormality of mind' caused by intoxication

This may happen in two situations:

'*Injury*'

First, where D's long-term alcohol and/or drug abuse has actually led to brain damage or psychosis, this would almost certainly be held to amount to an 'injury' within s.2. The leading case is *Tandy* (1989). Watkins LJ said that 'If… alcoholism had reached the level at which her brain had been injured by the repeated insult from intoxicants so that there was gross impairment of… judgment and emotional responses, then the defence was available.'

For obvious reasons, the *immediate* effects of taking alcohol or drugs cannot be classed as an 'injury'. In *Di Duca* (1959), it was unsuccessfully argued that the toxic effect of alcohol on the brain was an 'injury' for the purposes of s.2. This decision was recently confirmed in *O'Connell* (1997) concerning the effect on D's brain of sleeping pills.

'*Disease*'

Alcoholism and/or drug addiction may amount to a 'disease'. However, the courts have been reluctant to accept that simply being an alcoholic suffices and have imposed further conditions. In *Tandy* (1989), Watkins LJ said that if D were able to establish that the alcoholism had reached the level where her drinking had become involuntary, so that she was no longer able to resist the impulse to drink, then DR would be available. Thus, as well as simply being an alcoholic, D must also have a craving for drink or drugs to the extent that drinking becomes 'involuntary'.

> *Tandy* (1989)
>
> Linda Tandy was an alcoholic and had been for a number of years. She usually drank only barley wine or *Cinzano*. However, over the course of one day she drank 90 per cent of a bottle of vodka, a beverage that she had not drunk before but which is significantly stronger than either barley wine or *Cinzano*. That evening she strangled her 11-year-old daughter, after she told her mother that Tandy's second husband had sexually interfered with her. The judge directed the jury to decide was whether Tandy was suffering from an abnormality of mind, as a direct result of her alcoholism, or whether she was simply drunk. She was convicted of murder. The Court of Appeal dismissed the appeal. Tandy had not shown that her brain had actually been injured, nor had she proven that her drinking was 'involuntary'.

Despite criticism of this decision, the Court of Appeal followed *Tandy* in *Inseal* (1992). D suffered from 'alcohol dependence syndrome'. One night in bed he strangled his girlfriend. Despite expert medical witness testimony to the effect that the syndrome was an abnormality of mind, the jury convicted of murder after being directed to focus on the question of whether D's drinking had become involuntary. The Court of Appeal dismissed the appeal. The jury must have been satisfied that D could have resisted the temptation to take the first and subsequent drinks, and that 'accordingly' any abnormality of mind was not induced by alcoholism.

Tandy raises questions about the nature of alcoholism, and how the courts should view it. If alcoholism is a disease, it deserves to be treated as such. That would entail the totality of its symptoms being weighed up, instead of just the craving for drink, on which the Court of Appeal has focussed. The Court of Appeal has tended to view alcoholism as black and white; either D was able to resist her first drink (guilty of murder) or she was incapable of doing so (not guilty of murder). In *Tandy*, the Court of Appeal approved the judge's direction, which was to the effect that the jury should not concern themselves with the question of whether or not alcoholism was a 'disease'. This allowed them to focus on only one symptom, the craving for alcohol. Having decided that her craving was not overwhelming, it was then easy to conclude that she was not suffering an abnormality of mind. Yet what of the other symptoms of the disease? These were ignored.

Procedure

Initially, it was thought that the judge's task was simply to read s.2 and leave it up to the jury. However, it has since been made clear that trial judges must direct the jury as to the meaning of s.2. As with insanity, D bears the burden of proving the defence, on the balance of probabilities. If the defence rely on another defence that puts D's abnormality of mind in issue, like automatism, then it would seem the prosecution can seek to show this is DR. But the prosecution may not seek to raise DR or insanity unless the defence has first put D's state of mind in issue.

Originally the courts took the view that DR had to be proved to the jury, and could not be accepted by a trial judge. Again the position has since changed. Now D may plead guilty to manslaughter on the ground of DR. The judge has to decide whether to accept the plea. The judge should do so only where medical evidence is clear. A plea of guilty to manslaughter was correctly refused in *Ahmed Din* (1962). Din had stabbed his lodger seven times with a hacksaw and then cut off the man's penis. D pleaded guilty to manslaughter, based on paranoia, but the judge thought that there was insufficient evidence of an abnormality of mind and left the defence to the jury, who returned a verdict of guilty of murder. The Court of Criminal Appeal dismissed the appeal.

According to research by Dell, *Diminished Responsibility Reconsidered* (1982), in practice 80 per cent of pleas of guilty to manslaughter are accepted. Of all pleas refused, most are because the prosecution's medical experts disputed the application of the defence. Where the case does go to trial, there is about a 60 per cent chance of conviction for murder. Thus the overall failure rate of the defence is quite small, around 10 per cent.

Where D pleads DR but it is rejected by the jury, the Court of Appeal may, if it believes the murder conviction to be unsupported by the evidence, quash it and substitute one of manslaughter. In *Matheson* (1958), the medical experts agreed that D was suffering an abnormality of mind but the jury rejected the defence. The Court of Criminal Appeal quashed the murder conviction. Where there was 'unchallenged' evidence of abnormality of mind and substantial impairment of mental responsibility, and 'no facts or circumstances appear that can displace or throw doubt on that evidence' then the court was 'bound' to say that the conviction was unsafe.

Importance of medical evidence
Medical evidence is crucial to the success of the defence. In *Byrne* (1960), it was said that while there is no statutory requirement that a plea be supported

by medical evidence, the question of what actually caused the abnormality of mind did, however, 'seem to be a matter to be determined on expert evidence'. This view has been supported ever since.

Where D was suffering a condition that was not, at the time of the trial, regarded by psychiatrists as a mental condition the defence will be unavailable but, if the condition subsequently becomes so regarded, a conviction may be quashed. In *Hobson* (1998), D was tried for the murder of her abusive partner in 1992. The trial judge refused to leave DR to the jury and they convicted. However, in 1997 she appealed, claiming that the evidence at trial supported a DR defence, namely Battered Women's Syndrome (BWS). The Court of Appeal, allowing the appeal and ordering a retrial, noted that BWS was not recognised as a mental disease until 1994, two years after her trial.

Reform

Both the Butler Committee and the Criminal Law Revision Committee (CLRC) have recommended that DR be revised. The Butler Committee's preferred solution was to abolish the mandatory life sentence for murder, and so leave it entirely to the judge to reflect D's (lack of) culpability in sentence. The CLRC objected to this on two grounds:

- Murder would then effectively cover the entire gamut of unlawful homicides, from cases of gross negligence manslaughter to pre-meditated executions. The appropriate penalties for these offences would vary enormously, but a simple jury verdict of 'guilty to murder' would give no guidance to the judge on his sentencing decision.

- Juries might be reluctant to convict of murder, where before they would have been happy to convict of manslaughter on the ground of DR, and acquit instead.

The *Butler Committee* was aware of these problems, and so suggested a revised version of s.2:

> Where a person kills or is party to a killing of another, he shall not be convicted of murder if there is medical or other evidence that he was suffering from a form of mental disorder as defined in (the Mental Health legislation) and if, in the opinion of the jury, the mental disorder was such as to be an extenuating circumstance which ought to reduce the offence to manslaughter.

This was largely accepted by the CLRC, who made minor amendments (as well as recommending that the defence also apply to a charge of attempted murder).

The Draft Criminal Code Bill (1989)

This revised formula appears in the Draft Criminal Code Bill (1989), which provides:

Clause 56

(1) A person who, but for this section, would be guilty of murder is not guilty of murder if, at the time of his act, he is suffering from such mental abnormality as is a substantial enough reason to reduce his offence to manslaughter...

(2) ...'mental abnormality' means mental illness, arrested or incomplete development of mind, psychopathic disorder, and any other disorder or disability of mind, except intoxication....

(3) Where a person suffering from mental abnormality is also intoxicated, this section applies only where it would apply if he were not intoxicated.

Points to note: the burden of proof would be transferred from defence to prosecution, although evidence must be provided first; there is no longer any requirement that the mental abnormality stem from any specified cause; the new definition makes clear that it is the jury's task to determine whether D's mental abnormality was 'substantial'.

Summary

- Diminished responsibility is a limited defence. It is available only to murder and reduces liability only to manslaughter. The burden of proving the defence rests with the defence, on the balance of probabilities.

- It is a statutory defence, introduced by s.2 of the Homicide Act 1957.

- The defence must prove that D was suffering an abnormality of mind, arising from certain specified causes, which substantially impaired his mental responsibility.

- A plea of guilty to manslaughter based on the defence may be accepted but only where the evidence is plain.

- Where the defence goes to the jury, medical evidence is crucial (*Byrne*). If there is strong medical support for the defence but the jury ignores it, the Court of Appeal may quash a murder conviction and substitute one of manslaughter (*Matheson*).

- 'Abnormality of mind' means a 'state of mind so different from that of ordinary human beings that the reasonable man would term it abnormal' (*Byrne*).

- The abnormality of mind should be the result of a condition of arrested or retarded development of mind or any inherent cause, or be induced by disease or injury.

- Substantial does not mean total, nor does it mean trivial or minimal (*Lloyd*).

- Intoxication is irrelevant to the defence. Juries should be directed to ignore the effect of alcohol or drugs when considering whether D has an abnormality of mind (*Fenton, Gittens, Egan*).

- Alcoholism may support the defence, but only if D's 'brain had been injured' and/or where D's 'drinking had become involuntary' (*Tandy, Inseal*).

C   Suicide pact

S.4(1) of the Homicide Act 1957 provides a defence to the survivor of a suicide pact. Again it is a partial defence, available in murder cases only and reducing the liability to one of manslaughter. 'Suicide pact' is defined in s.4(3) of the Act as 'a common agreement between two or more persons having for its object the death of all of them'. As with diminished responsibility, the burden of proof is on the defence and the standard of proof is on the balance of probabilities.

7   Involuntary manslaughter

General introduction

The term involuntary manslaughter encompasses a variety of situations where death has occurred as a result of the conduct of the accused and in circumstances where it has been deemed appropriate to find the accused criminally responsible for that death. However, it should never be confused with the verdict of voluntary manslaughter since the accused will not have intended to kill or cause grievous bodily harm.

The student must appreciate that the offence of involuntary manslaughter covers a diversity of circumstances. At one end of the spectrum is very blameworthy behaviour involving a high risk of death or serious injury, but falling short of murder because the element of intention is lacking. At the other extreme the death may verge upon careless conduct which is nevertheless so blameworthy as to be considered criminal.

The maximum sentence for the offence is life imprisonment and the judge has discretion in handing out the appropriate type and length of sentence up to that maximum. It is not unknown for a non-custodial sentence to be given for an involuntary manslaughter conviction.

There have been many proposals for the reform of involuntary manslaughter through legislation, most recently in relation to so-called corporate manslaughter. The debate has been given fresh impetus following the disastrous train crash at Ladbroke Grove, just outside Paddington Station, in 1999. This chapter will deal with these proposals for reform, although at the time of writing there is little firm indication that they will be implemented by Parliament in the near future.

A   Constructive manslaughter

Introduction

D will be guilty of constructive manslaughter if he kills by doing an act that is both 'unlawful' and 'dangerous'. It is called constructive manslaughter because the liability for death is built or 'constructed' from the unlawful and dangerous act from which the death has flowed, even though the risk of death may never have been contemplated by the accused. For this reason the offence has often been criticised for being potentially harsh. On the other hand the death of an innocent victim has been caused by the unlawful and dangerous actions of the accused. The degree of blameworthiness will be reflected in the sentence.

The *actus reus* of constructive manslaughter

The *actus reus* is virtually exactly the same as for murder. It still requires D to cause the death of another human being.

In *Dalby* (1982), Waller LJ said, *obiter*, that, 'where the charge of manslaughter is based on an unlawful and dangerous act, it must be an act directed at the victim and likely to cause immediate injury, however slight.' This dictum, particularly the reference to 'an act directed at the victim' is notoriously ambiguous. However, it has subsequently been held that Waller LJ was not imposing some extra, special requirement. Instead, he was simply confirming that D's act must cause V's death. In the constructive manslaughter case of *Mitchell* (1983), which was considered in Chapter 1, Staughton J said that, 'Although there was no direct contact between [D] and [V], she was injured as a direct and immediate result of his act.... The only question was one of causation: whether her death was caused by [D]'s acts. It was open to the jury to conclude that it was so caused.'

In *Goodfellow* (1986), the Court of Appeal confirmed that all Waller LJ was intending to say was that 'there must be no fresh intervening cause between the act and death.'

> *Goodfellow* (1986)
> Goodfellow wanted to be moved from his council house in Sunderland. There was little chance of the council moving him as he was some £300 in rent arrears. He therefore planned to set the house on fire in such a way that it would look like a petrol bomb attack. He poured petrol over the sideboard, chair and walls of the living room, then set it alight. The fire got out of control and his wife, son and another woman all died. The court of appeal upheld his manslaughter conviction. They rejected his argument that, because he had not desired their deaths, his acts were not 'directed at' the victims.

D must commit an unlawful 'act'

There is one crucial difference between the *actus reus* of murder and that of constructive manslaughter. Given that constructive manslaughter requires an unlawful and dangerous *act*, it follows that, if D *omits* to act, he cannot be guilty of this form of manslaughter. In *Lowe* (1973), D was convicted of both neglecting his child and manslaughter. The trial judge had directed the jury that if they found Lowe guilty of the neglect offence they had to find him also guilty of manslaughter. The Court of Appeal quashed his manslaughter conviction.

D must commit an 'unlawful' act

D must commit an 'unlawful' act to be found guilty of the offence of constructive manslaughter. Indeed, this is where the expression 'constructive' manslaughter comes from – D's liability is 'constructed' by adding together various elements, as follows:

Unlawful act + dangerousness + death = constructive manslaughter

The unlawful act must be a crime (as opposed to a civil wrong or tort). In *Lamb* (1967), D's manslaughter conviction was based on the unlawful act of assault. This offence will be considered in Chapter 8 but, briefly, it requires that D do or say something to cause V to apprehend immediate unlawful violence. The Court of Appeal quashed D's conviction because there was no evidence that V had been put in fear. Sachs LJ said that D's act was not 'unlawful in the criminal sense of the word.'

> *Lamb* (1967),
> Terry Lamb had shot his best friend with a revolver. The shooting was completely accidental. Although Lamb knew that the gun was loaded, and had pulled the trigger whilst pointing it at his friend, both men thought – wrongly – that it would not fire. There were two bullets in the five-chamber cylinder, but no bullets in the chamber opposite the barrel. Both men failed to appreciate that the cylinder revolved *before* the hammer struck the back of the mechanism.

The unlawful/criminal act will, typically, be a battery – defined as the intentional or reckless application of unlawful force to another person (see Chapter 8). In *Larkin* (1943), a constructive manslaughter conviction based upon the crime of assault was upheld. D had threatened another man at a party with a razor. D's somewhat dubious account of what happened next was that a drunken woman swayed against him and cut her throat by accident! He was charged with the manslaughter of the woman. The trial judge directed the jury that threatening a man with a naked razor in order to scare him was an unlawful act and the jury convicted.

Possibly the classic case of constructive manslaughter occurs during a fight when D punches V, who falls backwards and bangs his head on the pavement, with fatal results. Inevitably, the case law has thrown up less obvious examples. These include:

- administering a noxious substance (drugs), contrary to s.23 of the Offences Against the Person Act 1861 – *Cato* (1976), *Kennedy* (1999);

- arson – *Goodfellow* (1986);

- burglary – *Watson* (1989);

- criminal damage – *DPP v Newbury and Jones* (1977);

- robbery – *Dawson and Others* (1985)

In *DPP v Newbury and Jones*, two 15-year-old boys pushed a paving stone from a bridge onto the cab of a train, which smashed through the cab window, hit a guard and killed him. The House of Lords upheld their convictions – without specifying upon what offence this was based. The most obvious is criminal damage.

The *mens rea* of constructive manslaughter

The *mens rea* of constructive manslaughter has two elements, both of which must be present:

- the fault required to render his act unlawful;

- dangerousness.

Unlawfulness
In order to be guilty of constructive manslaughter, D must commit an unlawful act, which must be a crime – so D must have the required *mens rea* for that crime. If the offence is assault or battery, D must have acted intentionally or recklessly. This was another reason for quashing D's conviction in *Lamb* (1969). As D did not think that the gun would fire when he pulled the trigger, he had not been reckless as to whether his friend would be harmed, still less had he intended it; therefore there was no *mens rea* for assault.

'Dangerousness'
In *Church* (1965) – the facts of which appear in Chapter 1 – the Court of Criminal Appeal laid down test an objective test for dangerousness:

An unlawful act causing the death of another cannot, simply because it is an unlawful act, render a manslaughter verdict inevitable. For such a verdict inexorably to follow, the unlawful act must be such as all sober and reasonable people would inevitably recognise must subject the other person to, at least, the risk of some harm resulting therefrom, albeit not serious harm.

All the circumstances are relevant to the *Church* test. This includes those known to D, as well as those that would have been known by the hypothetical 'sober and reasonable' person, had he been present. In *Watson* (1989), D burgled the house of a frail, 87-year-old man, Harold Moyler. When Harold came to investigate he was abused verbally. However, Harold was so distressed by what had happened that he died of a heart attack 90 minutes later. D was convicted of manslaughter. Although the Court of Appeal quashed his conviction (on the basis that the heart attack may have been caused by all the subsequent commotion), they upheld the jury's finding that the burglary was 'dangerous' – or at least it *became* dangerous as soon as Harold's age and condition would have become apparent to the reasonable man.

However, in *Dawson and Others* (1985), manslaughter convictions were quashed because the Court of Appeal decided that an attempted armed robbery was not 'dangerous'. When the three defendants arrived at a petrol station, masked and armed with pickaxe handles and replica guns, the attendant – who had a heart condition – managed to sound the alarm but then promptly dropped dead from a heart attack. The Court of Appeal held this was not manslaughter – the reasonable person could not have been aware of the attendant's 'bad heart'.

According to the *Church* test, V must be subjected to 'the risk of some harm'. What does this mean? Will a shock or a fright suffice? In *Dawson and Others*, the Court of Appeal thought that 'harm' included 'injury to the person through the operation of shock emanating from fright'. What does this mean exactly?

Reform

In 1994, the Law Commission provisionally recommended the abolition of constructive manslaughter in a consultation paper, *Involuntary Manslaughter*:

> It... is inappropriate to convict a defendant for an offence of homicide where the most that can be said is that he or she ought to have realised that there was a risk of some, albeit not serious, harm to another resulting from his or her commission of an unlawful act.

The Law Commission's proposals will be considered further at the end of the next section on 'gross negligence' manslaughter.

Summary

- D will be guilty of constructive manslaughter if he kills by doing an act that is both 'unlawful' and 'dangerous'.

- Constructive manslaughter requires an unlawful and dangerous *act* – thus, if D *omits* to act, he cannot be guilty (*Lowe*).

- The unlawful act must be a criminal offence, typically battery or assault, but it could be arson, burglary, robbery or – probably – criminal damage.

- D must have both the *actus reus* and *mens rea* of that criminal offence. If he does not, there can be no conviction of constructive manslaughter (*Lamb*).

- The act must be 'dangerous', which means doing an act that the reasonable person would inevitably recognise must subject V to the risk of some harm (*Church*).

- 'Harm' includes 'injury to the person through the operation of shock emanating from fright' (*Dawson and Others*) so long as the risk of the harm was apparent to the accused or the reasonable person (*Watson*).

B   Gross negligence manslaughter

Introduction

According to the leading case, *Adomako* (1995), the elements of this form of involuntary manslaughter, are:

- the existence of a duty of care;

- breach of that duty causing death;

- gross negligence which the jury consider justifies criminal conviction.

In *Watts* (1998), the Court of Appeal decided that, whenever manslaughter by gross negligence is raised, then the judge *must* direct the jury in accordance with the principles established in *Adomako*.

Duty of care

The criminal law recognises certain duty situations – see Chapter 2. *Adomako* itself involved a breach of duty owed by a hospital anaesthetist towards a patient – imposed under a *contract of employment*. In *Adomako*, the House of Lords approved *Stone and Dobinson* (1977) – where the defendants had undertaken a duty of care.

So is the ambit of the offence limited to those who, for whatever reason, have either undertaken or had a duty imposed upon them – or should it be wider? In *Adomako*, Lord Mackay LC actually said that the 'ordinary principles of law of negligence apply to ascertain whether or not D has been in breach of a duty of care towards the victim.' That being so, it logically follows that those same principles should apply in determining those persons to whom a duty is owed. These principles are to be found in the leading negligence case of *Donoghue v Stevenson* (1932), where Lord Atkin in the House of Lords said:

> You must take reasonable care to avoid acts or omissions which you can reasonably foresee would be likely to injure your neighbour. Who then is my neighbour? The answer seems to be – persons who are so closely and directly affected by my act that I ought reasonably to have them in contemplation as being so affected when I am directing my mind to the acts or omissions which are called into question.

This clearly goes much further than the traditional duty situations identified in Chapter 2. If this analysis is correct, then this form of manslaughter has a very wide scope indeed.

Breach of duty

The next issue is at what point D breaks that duty. In civil law, D is judged against the standard of the reasonable person performing the activity involved. If D is driving a car, for example, he must reach the standard of the reasonable driver. If D is a doctor, he is judged against the standard of the reasonably competent doctor – no more, no less.

Gross negligence

Simply proving that D has been in breach of a duty owed to another person and caused that person's death will not lead inevitably to liability for gross negligence manslaughter. Something more is required. In *Adomako*, the House of Lords confirmed that the correct test for this extra element was 'gross negligence'. This confirmed a line of case law dating back to the nineteenth century, but which was (like many other areas of the criminal law) thrown into turmoil and confusion by the appearance of objective recklessness in 1981.

In *Bateman* (1925), which involved negligent treatment by a doctor which caused the patient to die, Lord Hewart LCJ explained that, in order to establish criminal liability for gross negligence, 'the negligence of the accused went beyond a mere matter of compensation between subjects and showed such disregard for the life and safety of others as to amount to a crime against the state and conduct deserving punishment.'

This passage may be criticised for being somewhat vague: it tells the jury to convict if they think that D's negligence was bad enough to amount to the crime. However, the *Bateman* test received approval from the House of Lords in *Andrews v DPP* (1937), which involved death caused by extremely negligent driving (sometimes loosely referred to as 'motor manslaughter'). In *Adomako* (1995), Lord Mackay LC affirmed the continuing authority of the *Bateman* test, stating that it was for the jury 'to consider whether the extent to which [D's] conduct departed from the proper standard of care incumbent on him... was such that it should be judged criminal'. The Lord Chancellor acknowledged that the test 'involves an element of circularity', but was adamant that the matter had to be left to the jury: 'an attempt to specify that degree [of badness] more closely is I think likely to achieve only a spurious precision'.

In *Andrews*, Lord Atkin at least offered some guidance on exactly how 'bad' D's negligence has to be. He said that 'a very high degree of negligence is required to be proved'. He added that 'mere inadvertence' by D would never suffice for criminal liability; D must have had 'criminal disregard' for others' safety, or 'the grossest ignorance or the most criminal inattention'.

What states of mind will amount to 'gross negligence'?

This is obviously a question of crucial importance, and it has caused the courts considerable difficulty over the years. When *Adomako* was heard in the Court of Appeal in 1993, Lord Taylor CJ attempted to prove a list of what states of mind could be considered to be 'grossly negligent'. He acknowledged that it was not possible to prescribe a standard jury direction, because of the wide variety of possible duties and breaches. However, 'in accordance with the authorities' (by which he meant he had collated various statements from *Bateman, Andrews* and *Stone and Dobinson*) albeit 'without purporting to give an exhaustive definition', he suggested that the following states of mind may justify a jury deciding D had been grossly negligent:

- Indifference to an obvious risk;

- Actual foresight of a risk, coupled with a determination nevertheless to run it;

- An appreciation of a risk, coupled with an intention to avoid it, but also coupled with such a high degree of negligence in its attempted avoidance as the jury thinks justifies conviction;

- Inattention or failure to advert to a serious risk, which went beyond 'mere inadvertence'.

'Actual foresight of risk coupled with a determination nevertheless to run it', of course, is what we know of as subjective, *Cunningham* recklessness; 'failure to advert to a serious risk' is objective, *Caldwell* recklessness. Thus, gross negligence *includes* both forms of recklessness. Yet, it goes further than that: according to Lord Taylor CJ, it *also includes* 'a high degree of negligence' in the attempted avoidance of a known risk, and 'indifference to an obvious risk'.

However, when the case reached the Lords, Lord Mackay rejected Lord Taylor's proposals to list the different states of mind. The Lord Chancellor said that 'the circumstances to which a charge of [gross negligence] manslaughter may apply are so various that it is unwise to attempt to categorise or detail specimen directions'. Lord Mackay LC did say that, depending on the circumstances of the case, it might be 'perfectly appropriate' to use the word 'reckless' when directing a jury – but in the 'ordinary connotation of that word.' This harks back to what Lord Atkin said in *Andrews v DPP* (1937) – 15 years before *Cunningham* and 54 years before *Caldwell* – when he offered this explanation of 'gross negligence':

> Probably of all the epithets that can be applied 'reckless' most nearly covers the case... but it is not all-embracing, for 'reckless' suggests an indifference to risk, whereas the accused may have appreciated the risk, and intended to avoid it, and yet shown in the means adopted to avoid the risk such a high degree of negligence as would justify a conviction.

The foregoing may have suggested that there has been an unbroken line of gross negligence cases from *Bateman* and *Andrews* in the early years of the century to *Adomako* in 1995. This is, in fact, not the case. During the 1980s and early 1990s gross negligence seemed to have been permanently supplanted by objective, *Caldwell* recklessness. This was caused by the House of Lords decision in *Lawrence* (1982) – like *Andrews*, a motor manslaughter case – to apply the *Caldwell* test. However, in *Adomako* the House of Lords overruled Lawrence and firmly re-established gross negligence as the correct test.

Adomako (1995)

V was a patient undergoing an operation for a detached retina. He was totally paralysed, and the only part of his body visible was his eyes. Oxygen was supplied through a tube. An array of machines monitor the patient's condition. It was the job of D, an anaesthetist, to watch the machines while the surgeons operated. After the tube accidentally became disconnected, D failed to notice anything wrong for several minutes, until V went into cardiac arrest and the ECG display (which monitors the patient's heartbeat) showed a flat line. He eventually died six months later from hypoxia (lack of oxygen to the brain). D was charged with manslaughter. The prosecution called two witnesses who described D's failure to react as 'abysmal' and said that a competent anaesthetist would have recognised the problem 'within 15 seconds'. The jury was given a direction based on gross negligence and convicted. The Court of Appeal and House of Lords thought this correct.

The Lords' decision may have been expected to lead to a rush of appeals. This has not proven to be the case. It actually took over three years before another gross negligence case reached the Court of Appeal. In *Litchfield* (1998), D was the master of a sailing ship that had foundered on rocks and broken up, killing three crew members. He was charged with manslaughter on the basis that, in sailing on – when he knew that the engines might fail through fuel contamination – he had been in breach of duty serious enough to amount to gross negligence. He was found guilty by the jury and the Court of Appeal, applying *Adomako*, upheld the conviction.

Most recently, in *Attorney-General's Reference (No.2 of 1999)* (2000), the Court of Appeal held that a jury could properly convict D of gross negligence manslaughter in the absence of *any* evidence as to his state of mind. Obviously, in deciding whether D's conduct fell so far below the standards of the reasonable man that it became criminal conduct, an assessment of what D was thinking at the time is very helpful to the jury. But, the Court of Appeal has decided, it is not essential. This will assist future juries to return guilty verdicts in 'corporate manslaughter' cases, of which this was one.

Attorney-General's Reference (No.2 of 1999) (2000)

In September 1997 a passenger train crashed into a freight train at Southall in London, killing seven people. Manslaughter prosecutions were brought against the train company responsible for the passenger train, but the trial judge decided it was a prerequisite for conviction in such a case that a guilty mind be established against an identifiable human being. The manslaughter prosecutions collapsed at that point and the train company instead pleaded guilty to an offence under the Health and Safety at Work Act 1974. However, the Court of Appeal decided that the trial judge had made a mistake as to the law.

What must the risk involve?

In *Adomako*, Lord Mackay LC confirmed that it was appropriate for a judge to refer to 'recklessness' in the ordinary sense of the word when explaining gross negligence to a jury. However, one thing that has never been made entirely clear is *what* must actually be risked. Lord Mackay twice referred to the risk being of *death*. This is consistent with *Bateman*, where it was said that D's negligence had to display a 'disregard for life and safety' in order to found liability for manslaughter. In *Singh* (1999), the trial judge directed the jury that 'the circumstances must be such that a reasonably prudent person would have foreseen a serious and obvious risk not merely of injury or even of serious injury but of death.' However, in *Adomako*, Lord Mackay also approved directions on recklessness in *Stone and Dobinson* (1977). In that case, Lane LJ referred to a risk *to the health and welfare of the infirm person*.

Perhaps Lord Mackay LC meant to draw a distinction based on D's attitude. He may have meant that mere *inadvertence* to a risk will only found liability where the risk was of death, whereas if D had a couldn't-care-less attitude (*indifference*) to an obvious risk to V's health and welfare, he may be found liable. The law is less than clear at the moment, and further case law will be required to establish exactly what must be risked, and what D's attitude towards it may be.

Corporate manslaughter

As mentioned above, there has been much discussion in recent years about the difficulty of sustaining successful actions based upon corporate manslaughter. Part of the problem arises from the gravity of a manslaughter conviction, which attributes blame for causing a death. For lesser crimes, it has become accepted that it is right that a company should pick up the 'bill', for example, for polluting the environment. Thus, in *Alphacell Ltd v Woodward* the defendant company were convicted of a strict liability offence under the Rivers (Prevention of Pollution) Act 1951 when it had been impossible to show which particular employee had been responsible for causing a river to become polluted (see Chapter 4). This is easily justifiable in public policy terms since the 'costs' of the fine are met by the company rather than an individual. This encourages the company to develop systems and procedures that will minimise risk to the public.

For crimes requiring proof of *mens rea* (as opposed to strict liability offences) there is a technical difficulty. A 'company' in law is recognised for most purposes as a separate legal entity. As such it enjoys a status separate from the individual directors, employees or members, who may from time to time be employed by 'the company' or, in the case of members, own shares in it. Nevertheless, the courts have established that, in certain circumstances, a company may incur criminal liability for the acts of its senior officials. The principle applied to such circumstances is known as 'identification'.

Since the separate legal status of a company is an artificial legal concept, the acts of a company are in reality carried out by individuals who act as the human agents of the company. However, the truth is that corporate decisions are undertaken by directors and senior managers of the company who may be *identified* as the 'mind' of the company. Lord Reid confirmed this in *Tesco v Nattrass* (1972) where he said that a senior person in a company is 'the embodiment of the company... and his mind is the mind of the company. If it is a guilty mind then that guilt is the guilt of the company'. In the past, the courts have made a distinction between levels of employees by declaring that directors and senior employees may be perceived as the 'brains' of the company whereas the ordinary employees are merely the 'hands'.

The simplest illustration of the identification principle can be found in *Kite v OLL Ltd* (1994). Peter Kite was managing director of an outdoor pursuits centre. His staff (some of whom were unqualified) had told him that they were concerned about safety measures in relation to canoeing expeditions that were often undertaken in Lyme Bay, but he had done nothing about it. Four sixth-formers from a school in Plymouth were drowned when their canoes capsized in heavy seas. Both Peter Kite himself and the company OLL Ltd were convicted of manslaughter. In this case it was easy to identify Peter Kite as the controlling mind of OLL Ltd since the organisation was so small. He was clearly responsible for all decisions taken in relation to safety. They were essentially the company decisions as well as his own personal decisions.

In larger organisations it has been more difficult for courts to accept the 'identification' principle. In *Tesco Supermarkets v Nattrass*, Tesco itself was found not liable for an offence under the Trade Descriptions Act 1968 where one of its branch managers had wrongly marketed goods contrary to the requirements of the Act. It was held that the acts were those of 'another person' rather than Tesco itself which had apparently exercised all 'due diligence' in training and supervising its staff. The branch manager was not considered sufficiently senior to be regarded as the 'brains' of Tesco.

This hardly seems satisfactory since the larger the organisation, the more likely it is to have sophisticated systems of 'middle management' behind which it appears possible for senior management to 'hide'. The gravity of a potential manslaughter charge makes a court even more reluctant to apply the 'identification' principle and yet the harm done may be very great.

The courts have traditionally tended to place manslaughter in a different category from the more 'regulatory' offences. It appears that judges are constrained by the fact that crimes of violence in general are obviously committed by individuals rather than artificial legal entities. The employee who intentionally causes serious harm in the course of his employment rightly incurs personal liability. It would be absurd to hold the company responsible unless it could be demonstrated that the employee's actions had been authorised by the company.

Recently, however, public confidence in the entire criminal justice system has been undermined by the lack of convictions for corporate manslaughter, despite evidence that a company has caused deaths by acting in serious disregard of health and safety requirements. Even a substantial fine is seen to be wholly inadequate in such circumstances.

In response to this disquiet, it was accepted as a matter of principle in the Zeebrugge disaster trial that a corporate body could be indicted for manslaughter, and this was affirmed in *Kite v OLL* (above). Unfortunately, the case against P&O Ferries Ltd (who owned the ill-fated *Herald of Free Enterprise* which capsized off Zeebrugge, killing 187 passengers) collapsed due to lack of firm evidence that the board of directors knew about or had approved the unsatisfactory safety systems on board.

The immediate cause of the disaster was that the cross-channel ferry, *Herald of Free Enterprise*, had left port, contrary to regulations, with its bow doors open. The responsibility for closing the bow doors lay with the assistant-bosun who was asleep at the time. The responsibility for setting sail lay with the captain who was apparently unaware that the bow doors had not been properly closed. The Crown Prosecution Service exercised its discretion not to prosecute these two employees for manslaughter on the grounds that it would not be in the public interest to make them 'scapegoats' for a more serious failure of safety procedures which more properly were the responsibility of P&O Ltd at management level. There was, for example, evidence that ships had previously left port without their bow doors closed and that the risk of doing so had been brought to the attention of senior officers on board other P&O ferries. These concerns had apparently never been acted upon. There were also suggestions that the competitive nature of the cross-channel ferry trade had led P&O to introduce extremely short 'turn around' targets for their crews whenever they arrived in port. This in turn led to criticisms of the 'profit motive' versus safety considerations.

The problem confronting the court in this case was familiar. How could you 'identify' the criminal 'mind' of the company? It has been suggested that somehow the acts, omissions and mental states of more than one person within the company could be combined to satisfy an overall concept of criminal liability. Whilst such a suggestion seems attractive from the point of view of justice it is not appropriate as a way of attributing liability. The 'hands on' employee could be innocent with regard to lack of intention, recklessness or other mental attitude or have a defence such as mistake or automatism; but so the senior manager, in his or her individual capacity as the 'brains' of the company could also claim, a lack of knowledge or relevant *mens rea*. Could it really be logical to aggregate the minds of both to impose liability for a serious offence?

In the relatively narrow field of corporate manslaughter, the Law Commission has proposed the new offence of *corporate killing*. In their 1996 Report no. 237 they referred to a series of high profile disasters such as Zeebrugge, the King's Cross underground station fire in London which caused 31 deaths, the Piper Alpha oil platform disaster in which there were 167 fatalities and the Clapham rail crash in which 35 people died. Since the Report was issued there have been further fatal rail disasters at Southall and Ladbroke Grove, which have heightened the clamour for reform.

The Law Commission report stresses that liability should be based upon '*gross* carelessness' rather than mere carelessness, and that this should be broadly based upon 'management failure' resulting in a person's death in circumstances where the management failure falls far below what can be reasonably expected of a corporation in the circumstances. The sanctions recommended are an unlimited fine and a remedy for the cause of death. Presumably, this latter punishment would be enforced by measures over and above those already available to the Health and Safety Executive. It is worthy of note that the Health and Safety Executive has since endorsed the Law Commission's Report, and indeed gone further, in recommending that a custodial sentence is appropriate as an option for those found guilty of such an offence in their capacity as 'management'. This view is opposed by employer organisations who argue that it could be unfair to pin the entire blame on one individual. The Home Office are currently consulting and have suggested that large companies should appoint a 'Safety Director' who would become the person responsible, thus solving the 'identification' problem.

At the time of writing, it remains to be seen when, if at all, these proposals are introduced in the form of legislation. It is probably true to say that, in the area of corporate manslaughter, more than many other offences, there is an opportunity to frame a law which could have real deterrent value.

It could persuade companies to take proper measures that could effectively prevent death and serious injury from occurring in the first place. Such an outcome would do a great deal to protect society from indifferent exposure to the risk of death by corporations. It would also serve to satisfy the public that those responsible were properly brought to account for their grossly careless acts or omissions.

Reform

The inherent vagueness and circularity of the gross negligence test, leaving the jury to decide the ambit of a (very serious) offence such as manslaughter, suggests that reform may be necessary. One option would be to have a test based on subjective recklessness. This is already part of gross negligence, but the extent to which the *Adomako* test goes beyond subjective recklessness is the cause of the uncertainty. A test based purely on what D actually foresaw would be easier for juries to apply and would promote consistency.

It would also promote fairness. Suppose the patient in *Adomako* had survived, but had been permanently brain-damaged through hypoxia. If D had been charged with, say, inflicting grievous bodily harm under s.20 of the Offences Against the Person Act 1861, it would have been necessary to prove that, *at the very least*, he foresaw a risk of some physical injury to the patient. Negligence – of whatever degree – is insufficient for liability for any non-fatal offence. That is to say, the standard of liability in a manslaughter case (where the maximum penalty is life imprisonment) is *lower* than that in a case of a non-fatal offence (where the maximum penalty is five years' imprisonment)! Yet, in either case, D is equally culpable. It is the chance consequence of death, something entirely outside D's control, which results in liability for manslaughter.

As indicated above, a key question remains unanswered about what D must be proven to have foreseen, or not foreseen, or been indifferent about. There are various possibilities, depending on (a) the degree of risk and (b) the consequence.

Should D be liable of manslaughter if there is proof that he foresaw any, or just some, of the following, but decided to take that risk anyway?

- a serious risk of death;

- a serious risk of serious physical injury;

- a serious risk of any physical injury;

- any risk of death;

- any risk of serious physical injury;

- any risk of any physical injury.

If you think just some, which one(s) would you exclude? The first illustration appears too narrow; the last too broad. Perhaps foresight by D of either a serious risk of serious physical injury, or any risk of death should suffice?

Now go through the list again, but this time ask yourself:

Should D be liable of manslaughter if there is proof that he failed to consider any, or just some, of the risks?

Now go through the list again, and this time ask yourself:

Should D be liable for manslaughter if there is proof that he was indifferent (that is, he had a 'couldn't care-less' attitude) to any, or just some, of the factors above?

The Law Commission proposals

The Law Commission have provisionally recommended the creation of an offence of manslaughter by subjective recklessness, to fit immediately below murder, and to cover cases where death or serious injury was foreseen as probable, as opposed to virtually certain, which would be murder (*Involuntary Manslaughter* [1994]). The Law Commission recommend the abolition of constructive manslaughter but the retention of gross negligence manslaughter, to cover some situations presently under the scope of constructive manslaughter, stating:

> *If it continues to be thought appropriate on policy grounds that the law should retain the capability of imposing punishment to mark the serious factual occurrence of the accused having caused death, even where he or she neither foresaw nor intended that death, then our provisional view is that [the] possibility should be pursued through... manslaughter by gross negligence.*

This would, however, be seen as a last resort to be used 'only when other sanctions which already exist against the behaviour complained of seem inappropriate'. It would 'apply only to behaviour which is seriously at fault'

The jury would, as at present, be responsible for deciding whether 'conduct, although not involving intentional wrongdoing, is so bad in every other respect that society thinks it must be punished'. Because the offence would be a 'crime of last resort, it cannot of its very nature be too closely tied down by definitional rules'.

The Law Commission does, however, suggest some limits, to reflect the fact that manslaughter is a crime of homicide. Consequently, indifference or negligence as to risks less than death (or perhaps serious personal injury) should *not* be sufficient. The Commission suggests the following:

- The accused ought reasonably to have been aware of a significant risk that his conduct could result in death or serious injury.

- His conduct fell seriously and significantly below what could reasonably have been demanded of him in preventing that risk or in preventing the risk, once in being, from resulting in the prohibited harm.

For those situations which would cease to be manslaughter were the constructive form to be abolished, the Commission suggests the creation of a new offence, 'causing death'. This would require at least advertence to the risk of injury: 'A person is guilty of an offence if he causes the death of another, intending to cause injury to another or being reckless as to whether injury is caused.'

Summary ·

- There are three elements to this form of involuntary manslaughter: the existence of a duty of care; breach of that duty causing death; gross negligence which the jury consider justifies criminal conviction.

- A duty of care will certainly be held to exist in doctor/patient situations (*Bateman, Adomako*) and in situations where D had or assumed responsibility for the welfare of another person (*Litchfield, Stone and Dobinson*).

- Duties may, however, be owed in other situations, e.g. motorists owe a duty to other road users (*Andrews*).

- Breach of duty is the same as in civil law, that is, falling below the standard to be expected of the reasonable person (*Adomako*).

- Liability will only be imposed where D was 'grossly negligent' – this is a question for the jury to decide (*Andrews; Adomako*).

- Gross negligence includes, but is not limited to: deliberate risk-taking, inadvertence to serious risks, indifference.

- It is not clear exactly what the risk must be of: whether it must be death, or serious injury, or merely health and comfort.

Questions on Part 2 Homicide

1 Rupert, a famous businessman, who is very heavily in debt, is being threatened with insolvency proceedings by his creditors. Without telling his family, he insures his own life to the maximum. He then places a bomb in his briefcase, which is not detected at airport security, and boards a passenger plane at Heathrow bound for New York. The bomb is set to detonate over the Atlantic, two hours into the flight. The plane develops engine trouble shortly after take-off and is forced to return to Heathrow one hour after take-off. The passengers disembark and whilst they are awaiting the arrival of the maintenance crew, Patrick, a cleaner, boards the aeroplane. Rupert leaves his briefcase on board but says nothing about his plan. The bomb explodes and Patrick is killed. Rupert has now been charged with murder. Discuss.

(OCR 2000)

2 Peter and Sandra have been married for several years and have two young children. In the past few years they have had frequent quarrels during the course of which Peter has often hit Sandra. She has become very depressed and has been placed on medication by her doctor after telling the doctor how she feels 'trapped' in the relationship. One evening Peter returns home from the pub rather drunk. They begin an argument and Peter tells Sandra that she has always been a hopeless wife and an inadequate mother. Sandra begins to cry. Peter slaps her face and tells her to pull herself together. Enraged, Sandra grabs a marble statuette from the mantle shelf next to her and smashes it over Peter's head, killing him instantly.
Advise Sandra, who is charged with the murder of Peter.

Would it make any difference to your advice if Sandra had waited until Peter had fallen asleep in his chair and then killed him with the statuette?

(OCR 2000)

3 Discuss how successful the courts have been in defining the concept of intention.

(OCR 1999)

4 Dennis was throwing stones at passing cars. One stone hit the windscreen of Angela's car causing her to lose control. The car swerved on to the pavement running over Sarah, a 9-year-old child, who had just left home on her way to school. Mary, Sarah's mother, who had a weak heart, witnessed the accident, suffered a heart attack and died. Sarah was badly injured and was rushed to hospital for treatment.

After two weeks in an intensive care unit Sarah was being transferred to a normal recovery ward when her intravenous drip tube became dislodged from her arm when a hospital porter negligently pushed past her trolley in the corridor. This problem was not observed until the next morning when it was discovered that Sarah had lapsed into a coma as a result of the drip having been dislodged. She did not regain consciousness and three days later Sarah died.

Consider Dennis' liability for the deaths of Sarah and Mary.

(OCR 1999)

5   'In struggling to define the boundaries of involuntary manslaughter the courts have encountered considerable difficulties and the resulting muddle is not a credit to English law'.

Discuss whether this criticism is justified.

(OCR 2000)

Part 3

Offences against the person

8 Non-fatal offences against the person

Introduction

There are a number of offences against the person, with distinctions made according to the seriousness of the injuries caused and D's mental state at the time of causing them (intent or recklessness). The offences are, in ascending order of seriousness:

- Assault – contrary to s.39 of the Criminal Justice Act 1988 (CJA);

- Battery – also contrary to s.39 CJA;

- Assault occasioning actual bodily harm – contrary to S.47 of the Offences Against the Person Act 1861 (OAPA);

- Inflicting grievous bodily harm – contrary to s.20 OAPA

- Wounding – also contrary to s.20 OAPA

- Causing grievous bodily harm with intent to do so or with intent to resist arrest – contrary to s.18 OAPA

- Wounding with intent to do grievous bodily harm or with intent to resist arrest – also contrary to s.18 OAPA

Note that there is no offence of 'wounding with intent to wound'. It may also strike you as odd that the relevant sections in the statute are 18, 20 and 47. This is because the OAPA was a 'consolidating' statute, one that drew together a wide range of non-fatal offences contained in older legislation into one new statute (sections 23 and 24 deal with poisoning, for example).

Assault and battery are summary offences and can only be tried in the magistrates' court with a maximum sentence of six months' imprisonment. The offences under s.47 and s.20 are 'either way' and so can be tried either in the magistrates' court or the Crown Court; if tried 'on indictment' in the Crown Court the maximum penalty is five years' imprisonment. The offences under s.18 are the most serious and must be tried in the Crown Court; the maximum sentence is life imprisonment.

For convenience, the following abbreviations will be used throughout this Chapter:

- ABH = actual bodily harm

- GBH = grievous bodily harm

- OAPA = Offences Against the Person Act 1861

- CJA = Criminal Justice Act 1988

Assault and battery

Assault and battery are separate crimes, under s.39 of the Criminal Justice Act 1988. This was confirmed in *DPP v Little* (1992), where a single charge alleging that D 'did unlawfully assault and batter' V was held to charge two offences and was therefore bad for 'duplicity' (different offences have to be charged separately).

The terminology can be confusing. To 'assault' someone is usually taken, in ordinary language, to mean 'committed a battery against'. However, in legal terms, an 'assault' means to cause V to apprehend force (for example, shaking a fist at someone's face is an assault), while a 'battery' means to actually apply force to V (for example, punching someone in the face is a battery). Often the two crimes will be committed very close together – drawing your fist back (assault), throwing a punch and connecting with it (battery). Hence the common references to someone committing 'assault and battery'.

Assault

An assault is any act whereby D causes V to (*Fagan v Metropolitan Police Commissioner* [1968]):

- Apprehend

- Immediate

- Unlawful

- Personal violence

Assault was once regarded as attempted battery, but it is not necessary that D intended to do more than cause V to apprehend a battery. Many attempted batteries are assaults, but not necessarily. If D's acts are unobserved by V, because it is dark or D approaches from behind, or V is blind or asleep, then there will be no assault.

Apprehend

It is necessary that V 'apprehends' violence. The word is used in preference to 'fears', because it would severely restrict the law of assault if it had to be proven that V was scared. Aiming a punch at the World Heavyweight Boxing Champion may well make him 'apprehend' violence but he would certainly not 'fear' it.

To 'apprehend' something means to be aware of it, so to apprehend violence simply means that V has to be aware that something violent is about to happen. It does not matter if – in fact – V was not in danger. In *Logdon v DPP*, D showed V a gun in his office desk drawer and said that it was loaded. Although it was, in fact, a fake, this was not obvious from its appearance and V was frightened. D was convicted of assault and the Divisional Court upheld the conviction. But if V had known the gun to be a fake, or that it was real but unloaded, then there would be no assault (see *Lamb* [1967] – Chapter 7). Similarly, there would not be an assault if it was obvious that D had no means of carrying out his threat, for example, by gesticulating at the passengers of a moving train from beside the track.

Immediate

This requirement means that a threat to inflict harm in the future cannot be an assault. However, the courts have tended to take a generous view of immediacy. In *Smith v Superintendent of Woking Police Station* (1983), the Divisional Court decided that D had committed an assault by standing in V's garden, looking at her in her nightclothes through her bedroom window at about 11pm. Kerr LJ said that it was sufficient that D had instilled in V an apprehension of what he might do next. Obviously, as she was inside the house and he was in the garden, he was not in a position to attack her that very second. But nevertheless V had thought that 'whatever he might be going to do next, and sufficiently immediately for the purposes of the offence, was something of a violent nature'.

In *Ireland* (1997), D had made a number of silent phone calls to three women. The House of Lords upheld his convictions of assault occasioning actual bodily harm. There was sufficient evidence that the victims had apprehended immediate violence, because they did not know from where D was making the phone calls; they did not know what D was going to do next, which was sufficient for assault in *Smith*, above.

In *Constanza* (1997), on similar facts to *Ireland*, the Court of Appeal expanded the immediacy test ever-so-slightly. Schiemann LJ held that it was sufficient for the Crown to have proved an apprehension of violence 'at some time *not excluding the immediate future*' (emphasis added). The Court of Appeal did, however, point out that V knew D lived nearby and that 'she thought that something could happen at any time.'

Assault by words alone

It used to be the law that something more than words was required. But in *Ireland* (1997), Lord Steyn said:

> The proposition that a gesture may amount to an assault, but that words can never suffice, is unrealistic and indefensible. A thing said is also a thing done. There is no reason why something said should be incapable of causing an apprehension of immediate personal violence, e.g. a man accosting a woman in a dark alley saying, 'Come with me or I will stab you'.

The words need not necessarily be verbal, as in Lord Steyn's example. In *Constanza*, the Court of Appeal held that words in a written form (i.e. letters) could amount to an assault. Schiemann LJ pointed out that what was important was that V apprehended violence. How that apprehension got there was 'wholly irrelevant'.

Words may negative an assault

Words may negative behaviour that would otherwise be an assault. In *Tuberville v Savage* (1669), D placed one hand on his sword, saying, 'If it were not assize time, I would not take such language from you.' This was held not to be an assault. V knew he was not in danger because the assize judges were in town.

However, in *Light* (1857), where D raised a sword over his wife's head and said 'Were it not for the bloody policeman outside, I would split your head open', this *was* held to be an assault. Someone in her situation would surely have been put in fear – she only had D's word that he was not going to 'split her head open'. If, even fleetingly, it crossed her mind that she was in danger, this was an assault, no matter how convincing D was in stating that she was not in danger. The justification offered for upholding the convictions in *Smith*, *Ireland* and *Constanza* was that the victims did not know what D was going to do next. Presumably Light's wife did not know what D was going to do next either.

Battery

This is the application of unlawful force to the person. Battery does not presuppose an assault. A blow to the back of the head, completely taking V by surprise, is a battery. The merest touching without consent is a battery. In *Collins v Wilcock* (1984), Robert Goff LJ said: 'It has long been established that any touching of another person, however slight, may amount to a battery.'

Of course, every day thousands, if not millions, of people squash onto crowded commuter trains and buses, or squeeze into almost-full lifts. Some physical contact with other people is inevitable. According to Robert Goff LJ, they all commit battery! Except that they do *not*: the answer is that most touchings are not 'unlawful' because implied consent is given to all the touching which is inevitable in the ordinary course of everyday life (see further Chapter 9).

Is there a requirement of hostility?

In *Faulkner v Talbot* (1981), Lord Lane CJ said that a battery 'need not necessarily be hostile, rude or aggressive, as some of the cases seem to indicate.' However, Croom-Johnson LJ in *Wilson v Pringle* (1986), a civil case, stated that a touching had to be 'hostile' in order to be an assault. In *Brown and Others* (1993), the House of Lords approved *Wilson v Pringle*. Lord Jauncey described hostility as 'a necessary ingredient of assault.' Lord Mustill, dissenting, said that 'hostility cannot... be a crucial factor which in itself determines guilt or innocence, although its presence or absence may be relevant when the court has to decide *as a matter of policy* how to react to a new situation' (emphasis added). It is suggested that this latter view is the correct one.

Is there a requirement of directness?

Most batteries are directly applied to V's person, usually by striking that person with a fist or some object, throwing a missile at them, or shooting them. But it is not essential. In *Martin* (1881), D placed an iron bar across the doorway of a theatre, put out the lights and then created general panic and confusion. Various theatregoers were injured. D was convicted of inflicting GBH – but the court accepted that in doing so he had also committed battery. A very recent example of this principle is *Haystead* (2000). D punched a woman who was holding a small child in her arms. As a result of the blows, she dropped the boy on the ground. D was charged with assaulting the boy, and the Divisional Court upheld his conviction of assault. This was proper even though no direct physical contact had occurred between D and the boy.

Actual bodily harm

S.47 of the Offences Against the Person Act 1861 provides that 'Whosoever shall be convicted on indictment of any assault occasioning actual bodily harm shall be liable to imprisonment for not more than five years.'

Actual bodily harm

In *Donovan* (1934), the Court of Criminal Appeal said that 'actual bodily harm' in s.47 bore its ordinary meaning. It included 'any hurt or injury' that interfered with the 'health or comfort' of V. This hurt or injury did not need to be permanent though it had to be 'more than merely transient or trifling.' The definition is deliberately broad. Very slight physical injuries have been held to fall within it, including minor bruises and abrasions. In *Chan-Fook*, the Court of Appeal stated that the injury 'should not be so trivial as to be wholly insignificant.'

'Occasioning'

This is purely a question of causation (see Chapter 1). In *Roberts* (1972), D had tried to remove the coat of his female car passenger and she had jumped out of the motor vehicle to escape. She suffered grazing and concussion for which she was detained in hospital for three days. The jury was directed to convict provided that V's injury was the natural consequence of D's conduct, in the sense that it could have reasonably been foreseen. D's conviction was upheld. In *Notman* (1994), where D ran into V and slightly injured his ankle, D was convicted after the trial judge directed the jury that it was sufficient if his conduct was a 'substantial cause' of V's injury. The Court of Appeal upheld his conviction.

Wounding and grievous bodily harm

Offences Against the Person Act 1861

20. Whosoever shall unlawfully and maliciously wound or inflict any grievous bodily harm upon any other person, either with or without any weapon or instrument, shall be guilty of [an offence triable either way], and being convicted thereof shall be liable to imprisonment for five years.

18. Whosoever shall unlawfully and maliciously by any means whatsoever wound or cause any grievous bodily harm to any person with intent to do some grievous bodily harm to any person or with intent to resist or prevent the lawful apprehension or detainer of any person, shall be guilty of [an offence], and being convicted thereof shall be liable to imprisonment for life.

Caution is advised here. There are many similarities, but some differences, between the two offences. In terms of the *actus reus*, both offences share the common expressions 'wound' and 'grievous bodily harm' but while s.20 uses the verb to 'inflict', s.18 uses the verb to 'cause'. The *mens rea* is very different (see pp. 131 and 135–6).

Wound

To constitute a 'wound', the continuity of the skin must be broken. There are two layers of the skin, an outer layer known as the epidermis or cuticle, and an inner layer called the dermis. It is not enough that the cuticle is broken if the inner layer remains intact. Purely internal bleeding will not suffice for a 'wound'. In *C (a minor) v Eisenhower* (1984), the Divisional Court ruled that internal rupturing of blood vessels in the eye caused by an air-pistol pellet was not a 'wound' because the injury was purely internal.

Grievous bodily harm

The meaning of this expression was considered in Chapter 5, on murder, because it has a common meaning in homicide and non-fatal offences. Essentially, according to Viscount Kilmuir in *DPP v Smith* (1961), 'bodily harm needs no explanation and 'grievous' means no more and no less than 'really serious'. In *Saunders* (1985), where D was convicted despite the judge omitting the word 'really', the Court of Appeal still upheld the conviction.

Inflict and cause

Until 1997 there was much judicial and academic discussion about what differences, if any, there were between the word 'inflict', which appears in s.20, and 'cause', which appears in s.18. The general consensus was that 'cause' was a wider concept. As recently as 1995, the House of Lords had maintained that the words 'inflict' and 'cause' had different meanings (*Mandair*). However, in *Burstow* (1997), the Lords unanimously ruled that the two words should be treated as synonymous. Lord Hope said that 'for all practical purposes there is, in my opinion, no difference between these words... the words 'cause' and 'inflict' may be taken to be interchangeable.'

Mens rea of s.18

4.4.1 Intention

Under s.18, intention is critical to a conviction. Intention has the same meaning as in the law of murder. Where D intends to cause GBH to P, but misses and accidentally causes harm to Q, then he may be convicted under s.18 (this is one application of the 'transferred malice' doctrine, see Chapter 1).

Maliciously

Because s.18 requires 'intent', is the word 'malicious', which appears in s.18, redundant? Remember, according to the leading recklessness case, *Cunningham* (1957), 'maliciousness' means 'intentionally or recklessly'. The answer is: it depends. S.18 really divides up into four crimes, as follows:

- Causing GBH with intent to do some GBH

- Wounding with intent to do some GBH

- Causing GBH with intent to resist arrest

- Wounding with intent to resist arrest

Where the charge is causing GBH with intent to do some GBH, then Diplock LJ in *Mowatt* (1968) was absolutely right when he said, 'in s.18 the word "maliciously" adds nothing'. However, where any of the other crimes are charged, then the word *is* very important. D would *not* be liable under s.18 if, with intent to resist arrest, he *accidentally* injured a policeman – with no foresight of the injuries. To be guilty, D must intend to resist arrest and intend, or be reckless whether, a wound or GBH is caused.

Included offences

S.6(3) of the Criminal Law Act 1967 allows for the conviction of an alternative offence to the one charged 'where the allegations in the indictment expressly or by necessary implication include' that offence. In *Savage* (1992), the Lords ruled that s.47 was included in s.20; and in *Mandair* (1995) the Lords ruled that s.20 was included in s.18. This is very likely to happen where the jury is satisfied that GBH has been caused (or inflicted) but are not convinced beyond reasonable doubt that D intended it. This was the situation in *White* (1995). D, a night-club doorman, had stamped on V's head. He was convicted under s.18 but, before sentence, evidence emerged that he was suffering post-traumatic stress disorder at the time of the assault, and that this might have prevented him forming the intent. The Court of Appeal allowed his appeal but simply substituted a conviction under s.20.

Psychiatric injury

Psychiatric injury as ABH

Psychiatric injury qualifies as 'bodily harm'. In *Chan-Fook* (1994), the Court of Appeal held that 'bodily harm' was capable of including psychiatric injury, although it did *not* include mere emotions such as fear, distress, panic or a hysterical or nervous condition. Hobhouse LJ said:

> The body of the victim includes all parts of his body, including his organs, his nervous system and his brain. Bodily injury therefore may include injury to any parts of his body responsible for his mental and other faculties.

Chan-Fook (1994)

Chan-Fook suspected that V had stolen his fiancée's engagement ring. C-F dragged him upstairs and locked him in a second floor room. V tried to escape but was injured when he fell to the ground. C-F was charged under s.47. It was alleged that even if V had not been physically injured, the trauma he had suffered prior to the escape bid would amount to ABH. However, there was no medical evidence to support this, only V's claim that he felt abused, frightened and humiliated. The trial judge directed the jury that a hysterical or nervous condition was capable of being ABH. C-F was convicted. On appeal, the Court of Appeal quashed the conviction. Although the court held first that ABH was capable of including psychiatric injury, what V had suffered did not qualify.

In *Ireland* (1997), Lord Steyn in the House of Lords approved the decision in *Chan-Fook* (1994), saying that 'the ruling… was based on principled and cogent reasoning and it marked a sound and essential clarification of the law'. He said that, 'one can nowadays quite naturally speak of inflicting psychiatric injury.' D's convictions in that case were upheld, as there was much stronger evidence of psychiatric injury: his victims had suffered palpitations, breathing difficulties, cold sweats, anxiety, inability to sleep, dizziness and stress. In *Constanza* (1997), the Court of Appeal unanimously rejected D's appeal against a s.47 conviction for causing ABH in the form of clinical depression and anxiety.

Psychiatric injury as GBH

Once it had been accepted in *Chan-Fook* that psychiatric injury could amount to 'actual' bodily harm, it logically followed that *serious* psychiatric injury could amount to 'grievous' bodily harm. In *Burstow* (1997), D had mounted a sustained campaign of harrassment against Tracey Sant, with whom he had had a very brief relationship three years earlier. This mainly consisted of silent telephone calls and hate mail, but there was other, more eccentric behaviour. Eventually, she was diagnosed as suffering severe depression. D was convicted of inflicting GBH and the Court of Appeal and the House of Lords dismissed his appeal.

Need for psychiatric evidence

Expert evidence is required before someone can be convicted of causing ABH or GBH where the harm alleged is psychiatric in nature. In *Morris* (1998), where the facts were similar to *Burstow*, the trial judge allowed the case to go to the jury – without any psychiatric evidence. The judge was happy to leave it to the jury to say whether or not V's symptoms – sleeping difficulties, nightmares, cold sweats, nausea, stomach ache and joint pains – amounted to ABH. The Court of Appeal quashed D's conviction – although it did order a retrial.

Transmission of disease

There is no specific legislation to deal with transmission of disease. In *Clarence* (1888), D had sex with his wife despite knowing that he had a venereal disease and yet without telling her. The Court for Crown Cases Reserved decided that he had not assaulted her because of her consent to sex. This forced them to quash his conviction of inflicting GBH – at the time, the courts adopted a much narrower interpretation of 'infliction' than they do now, such that an assault was required as a prerequisite of a successful prosecution for inflicting GBH. Given the decision in *Ireland* (1997) to re-interpret the word to simply mean 'cause', it may be possible to employ this offence, as well as the more serious offence of causing GBH with intent, in cases where D transmits a serious disease.

In 1993, the Law Commission proposed that the intentional or reckless transmission of disease should be a criminal offence as part of their Report on reform of this area. However, in 1998, the Government also published a Report on reform of non-fatal assaults and a draft Bill containing four new offences to replace those in the Offences Against the Person Act and the Criminal Justice Act. One of the proposed new offences is 'intentional serious injury', and the report indicates that intentional transmission of a serious disease comes within that new offence. However, disease transmission is specifically excluded from the other offences. There were two reasons for this:

- 'it would be wrong to criminalise the reckless transmission of normally minor illnesses such as measles or mumps'; and

- 'the law should not seem to discriminate against those who are HIV positive, have AIDS or viral hepatitis or who carry any kind of disease. Nor do we want to discourage people from coming forward for diagnostic tests and treatment... because of an unfounded fear of criminal prosecution.'

The Report concludes that the offence would be used only 'in those rare and grave cases where prosecution would be justified'. An example of what the Government presumably has in mind by 'those rare and grave cases' occurred in Canada in 1998, when a man who had been diagnosed HIV positive had unprotected sex with two women, without telling them of his condition. The Supreme Court of Canada ruled that the consent he had obtained to sex was invalidated by his failure to fully inform them of the risk, making him liable for assault (*Cuerrier* [1998] – see Chapter 9).

The Government's Report and draft Bill will be considered fully at the end of this Chapter.

Stalking

Several of the cases considered above – *Burstow*, *Constanza*, *Ireland*, *Morris* – involved what is commonly known as 'stalking', loosely defined as a sustained campaign of harrassment. At the time when these cases were brought, England had no laws designed to deal effectively with the problem. The Telecommunications Act 1984 and the Malicious Communications Act 1988 contain offences of making indecent, offensive or threatening telephone calls or letters, but they are summary offences with maximum sentences of six months' imprisonment. This compares with five years' imprisonment for inflicting GBH or ABH, the charges in *Burstow* and *Ireland* respectively. It is little wonder, therefore, that the House of Lords was prepared to modify established law on assault (the immediacy requirement; the question whether words alone constituted an assault) in order to uphold the convictions.

In 1996, the Home Office published a consultation paper in which it recognised the scale of the problem – at least 7,000 victims had contacted the National Anti-Stalking and Harrassment (NASH) help-line in less than two years. A year later, specific anti-stalking legislation was brought into force, in the form of the Protection from Harassment Act 1997. There are two offences: harassment (s.1), and causing fear (s.4).

- *Harassment*: it is an offence for a person to 'pursue a course of conduct which amounts to the harassment of another.' The definition section (s.7) provides that 'references to harassing a person include alarming the person or causing the person distress'

- *Causing fear*: A person whose course of conduct causes another to fear, on at least two occasions, that violence will be used against him is guilty of an offence.

S.7 also provides that 'course of conduct' must 'involve conduct on at least two occasions' and that 'conduct' includes speech.

Mens rea of non-fatal offences

Intention *or* recklessness

It is now firmly established that *all* of the non-fatal offences – other than s.18, where proof of intent is essential – may be committed recklessly, as well as intentionally. The word 'maliciously', which appears in s.20 and s.18, means 'intentionally or recklessly' (*Cunningham* [1957]).

In *Venna* (1976), it was argued on appeal that assaults and batteries, including s.47 ABH, could be distinguished from statutory offences requiring 'malice'. It was argued that as s.47 makes no reference to 'malice' or, indeed, any form of *mens rea*, that recklessness was insufficient and only intention would suffice. Four police officers were struggling to arrest D when he lashed out with his legs, kicked one of the officers in the hand and broke a bone. He was convicted after the trial judge directed the jury to convict if they believed he had kicked out 'reckless as to who was there, not caring one iota as to whether he kicked anybody.' Unsurprisingly, the Court of Appeal rejected his appeal. James LJ said: 'In our view the element of *mens rea* in the offence of battery is satisfied by proof that the defendant intentionally or recklessly applied force to the person of another.'

What type of recklessness is required?

The form of recklessness established in *Cunningham* and approved by the Court of Appeal in *Venna* is the subjective form. Following a period of doubt triggered by the decision of the Queen's Bench Divisional Court in *DPP v K (a minor)* (1990), the House of Lords clarified the position in respect of s.20 in *DPP v Parmenter* (1992). Lord Ackner, giving the unanimous decision of the House, said: '*Cunningham* correctly states the law in relation to the word 'maliciously'... in order to establish an offence under s.20 the prosecution must prove either that [D] intended or that he actually foresaw that his act would cause harm.'

What degree of harm must be foreseen?

The next question is, what *degree* of harm need D to have foreseen? This is particularly important where D is accused of either s.47 or s.20. Where those offences are concerned, there is no requirement that D foresee the harm that he in fact causes, whether a broken nose or a bleeding lip. D need not foresee that his acts might cause anything other than a battery. This point was established for s.20 offences in *Mowatt* (1968), and confirmed by the House of Lords in *DPP v Parmenter* (1992), while a similar decision concerning s.47 offences was made by the Court of Appeal in *Roberts* (1972) and approved by the Lords in *Savage* (1992).

D slaps V across the face. He anticipates that V's cheek may be stung. But, D forgot that he was wearing a ring, and V's face is cut deeply. According to the above cases, D faces liability for ABH and/or wounding, each carrying a maximum five years' imprisonment. Is this fair? Should there be a requirement that D foresee the actual injuries caused? Do the above decisions really reflect the courts' insistence that liability for assaults must

---

be decided 'subjectively', using Cunningham recklessness, as opposed to 'objectively'?

Reform

In 1993 the Law Commission published a Report, *Offences Against the Person and General Principles*, which contained a draft Criminal Law Bill. The Law Commission thought that reform in this area was too urgent to wait for the Criminal Code to ever be enacted. In their Report, the Commission made three specific criticisms:

- complicated, obscure and old-fashioned language;

- complicated and technical structure;

- complete unintelligibility to the layman.

Hence the proposed new legislation did away with nineteenth-century terminology including words like 'maliciously' and 'grievous'. However, the Bill was never enacted – but, in 1998, the Labour Government produced its own report, *Violence: Reforming the Offences Against the Person Act 1861*, and a draft Offences Against the Person Bill (the full text of the draft Bill is available from the Home Office website – www.homeoffice.gov.uk/cpd/sou/oapdb.htm). The draft Bill proposes that all the existing offences be scrapped and that four new offences take their place. These are the same as the Law Commission proposed in 1993. The offences are (starting with the least serious):

- Assault

- Intentional or Reckless Injury

- Reckless Serious Injury

- Intentional Serious Injury

'Assault'

Clause 4(1) states that it will be an offence if D:

(a) intentionally or recklessly applies force to or causes an impact on the body of another, or

(b) he intentionally or recklessly causes the other to believe that any such force or impact is imminent.

Clause 4(2) provides that no offence is committed 'if the force or impact, not being intended or likely to cause injury, is in the circumstances such as is generally acceptable in the ordinary conduct of daily life and [D] does not know or believe that it is in fact unacceptable to the other person.'

This seems to restate the law on assault and battery as it currently stands with no significant changes at all. Clause 4(1)(a) is what we now call 'battery', clause 4(1)(b) is what we now call 'assault'. Clause 4(2) states the general rule of implied consent laid down by Robert Goff LJ in *Collins v Wilcock* (1984) – see Chapter 9.

'Injury'

The word 'harm' in the OAPA offences is replaced by 'injury'. Clause 15(1) defines 'injury' as meaning (a) physical or (b) mental injury. Clause 15(2) and (3) define both terms further:

- Physical injury includes pain, unconsciousness and any other impairment of a person's physical condition.

- Mental injury includes any impairment of a person's mental health.

'Serious'

Neither the draft Criminal Law Bill nor the draft Offences Against the Person Bill defines 'serious'. The Home Office Report states that the Government is 'content for the courts to decide what is appropriate in individual cases'. The reform would affect the offences of wounding under s.18 and s.20 in particular. The *actus reus* of those crimes is satisfied on proof of a break in the continuity of the skin – that is, even minor cuts will suffice. But the new offences of intentional and reckless serious injury require 'serious injury' as their *actus reus* – so only those wounds that can be described as 'serious' will lead to liability. Minor cuts are downgraded to the category of intentional or reckless injury.

'Recklessness' and 'Intention'

The Bill's definition of recklessness and intention were considered in the reform sections of Chapters 3 and 6 respectively. The Government makes clear in its Report that the rule established in *Mowatt* (1968) and *Roberts* (1972), and confirmed in *DPP v Parmenter* (1992) and *Savage* (1992), i.e. that it is sufficient if D simply foresees a battery in order to be liable under s.20 or s.47, is to be scrapped. The proposed new offence of reckless serious injury and reckless injury will require proof that D foresaw 'serious injury' and 'injury', respectively.

Figure 5 Reform of Non-fatal offences: summary

Present offences	Proposed new offences	Changes (if any)	Maximum penalty
Wounding, causing GBH with intent, s.18 OAPA	Intentional serious injury	Only wounds that are 'serious' will satisfy the *actus reus*	Life (no change)
Wounding, inflicting GBH, s.20 OAPA	Reckless serious injury	As above. Plus, foresight of risk of 'serious injury' required for *mens rea*	7 years (+2 years)
ABH, s.47 OAPA	Intentional or reckless injury	Foresight of 'injury' required for *mens rea*	5 years (no change)
Assault and Battery, s.39 CJA	Assault	None	6 months (no change)

Summary

- There is a range of offences against the person.

- Assault is an offence under s.39 of the Criminal Justice Act 1988 (CJA). It is defined as intentionally or recklessly causing another person to apprehend immediate unlawful personal violence.

- Battery is also an offence under s.39 CJA. It is defined as the application of unlawful force to another person.

- Assault occasioning actual bodily harm (ABH) is an offence contrary to s.47 of the Offences Against the Person Act 1861 (OAPA).

- Wounding or inflicting grievous bodily harm (GBH) are offences contrary to s.20 OAPA.

- Wounding or causing GBH with intent to do GBH or with intent to resist arrest are offences contrary to s.18 OAPA.

- For an assault, although V must apprehend 'immediate' violence, it is sufficient if V does not know what D is going to do next (*Smith v Superintendent of Woking Police Station, Ireland, Constanza*).

- Assault may be committed by words alone, whether spoken (*Ireland*) or written (*Constanza*). But words may also negative assault (*Tuberville v Savage*).

- ABH has a wide meaning (*Donovan, Chan-Fook*). It includes psychiatric injury (*Chan-Fook, Ireland*).

- Wounding means that the continuity of the skin must be broken (*Moriarty v Brookes*). Purely internal bleeding is not a 'wound' (*C [a minor] v Eisenhower*).

- GBH means really serious harm (*DPP v Smith*) or just serious harm (*Saunders*). It includes serious psychiatric injury (*Burstow*).

- There is no practical distinction between 'inflicting' GBH and 'causing' GBH (*Ireland*).

- The word 'maliciously' in s.20 and s.18 means intentionally or recklessly.

- The subjective *Cunningham* test for recklessness applies to all non-fatal offences (*Savage, DPP v Parmenter*), including those that do not expressly require 'malice' (*Venna*).

- In s.47 and s.20 it is sufficient *mens rea* that D foresees that some harm may be caused by his acts, not necessarily the degree of harm required for the *actus reus*, i.e. ABH, wounding, or GBH (*Mowatt, Roberts, Savage, DPP v Parmenter*).

- The draft Offences Against the Person Bill (1998) would abolish all of the above offences and replace them with four new offences: assault, intentional or reckless injury, reckless serious injury and intentional serious injury. 'Injury' would include physical or mental injury.

9   Consent

Introduction

One thing that should become apparent upon reading this chapter is that the availability of the defence of consent has attracted a good deal of public debate in recent years. This is because consent often involves balancing the freedom of the individual against considerations of public policy as interpreted by the courts.

It is a cornerstone of English law that those charged with a criminal offence have a right to defend themselves. We have already seen that a person charged with murder may seek to raise a special and partial defence to that particular charge, for example provocation or diminished responsibility. There are other so-called general defences such as insanity, automatism, intoxication and mistake which may be pleaded as a defence to most crimes. These are considered in Part 5. The defence of consent will be dealt with here since it is inseparably linked with offences against the person. It is the very essence of all assaults that they are done against V's will. Once the accused raises the defence, the onus of proving lack of consent rests on the Crown (*Donovan* [1934]). Submission (through force, threats or fraud) is *not* the same thing as consent.

It is assumed that you will already have read the preceding chapter, on assaults and aggravated assaults. The same abbreviations will be used, i.e.:
ABH = actual bodily harm
GBH = grievous bodily harm
OAPA = The Offences Against the Person Act 1861. References to s.18,
s.20 and s.47 are all to this Act.

General principles

Consent is (depending on the circumstances) a defence to:

- all non-fatal offences against the person, from assault and battery to causing GBH with intent; and

- all sexual offences including indecent assault and rape. Although rape is not examined in this book, some important consent cases involve the offence.

It may be a defence to constructive manslaughter but is *never* a defence to murder. No one can consent to being killed.

Why is euthanasia illegal?

Consent must be real

The fact that V apparently consents to D's act does not mean that the law will treat that consent as valid. If V is a child, or mentally retarded, this apparent consent may not suffice. The issue is whether V was unable to comprehend the nature of the act. In *Burrell v Harmer* (1967), D was convicted of ABH after tattooing two boys aged 12 and 13 with the result that their arms became inflamed and painful. The court held there was no consent as the boys did not understand the nature of the act. Presumably they understood what a tattoo was, but they would not have understood the level of pain involved.

Consent and mistake

An honestly held (and not necessarily reasonable) belief that V was consenting will be a good defence, as this would deny proof that D carried out an unlawful assault. This is subject to the rules on intoxicated mistakes (see Chapter 17).

Consent obtained by fraud

Fraud does not necessarily negative consent. It only does so in two situations, if it deceives V as to:

* the identity of the person or

* the 'nature and quality' of D's act.

Richardson (1998) involved the first situation. D was a dentist who had been suspended by the General Dental Council. However, she continued to treat patients until she was eventually detected and prosecuted. She was convicted of six counts of ABH, on the basis that her fraud as to her continued entitlement to practise negatived her patients' consent. The Court of Appeal, though describing her treatment as 'reprehensible', allowed the appeal. The patients were consenting to treatment by her. It was irrelevant that they would not have consented had they known the truth.

Clarence (1888) involved the second situation. D had sex with his wife despite knowing that he had a venereal disease and yet without telling her. He was convicted of assaulting her, but his appeal was allowed. His wife had consented to sex with D, so there was no fraud as to the nature and quality of D's act. In *Tabassum* (2000), the Court of Appeal upheld convictions of indecent assault (contrary to s.14 of the Sexual Offences Act 1956) by distinguishing *Clarence*. D had examined the breasts of a number of women after telling them he was medically qualified, when in fact he was not. The Court decided that, as the women were only consenting for medical purposes, they had been deceived as to the 'quality' of D's act and hence there was no consent.

The Court of Appeal's decision in *Tabassum* that the 'nature' and 'quality' of D's act are actually two separate things appears to be new. *Clarence* seemed to treat them as one thing. It is arguable that applying the recent *Tabassum* judgment to the facts of *Clarence* would produce a different result if such a case were to come before the courts again. Selina Clarence was not deceived as to the 'nature' of the act (sex with her husband Charles) but was she deceived as to the 'quality' of it (in the sense that there was a risk of her being infected with a venereal disease)?

The doctrine of 'informed consent'

A very significant judgment has recently been handed down by the Supreme Court of Canada in *Cuerrier* (1998). D was charged with assault after he had unprotected sex with two women, even though he knew that he was HIV positive, without telling them. Although he was originally acquitted, on the basis of consent, the Supreme Court allowed the prosecution's appeal. It was not enough that both women had consented to unprotected sex, it was an assault unless they had specifically consented to have intercourse with a man who was HIV positive.

The Court therefore introduced the doctrine of 'informed consent', long-recognised in medical law, into Canadian criminal law. In *Richardson*, however, the Court of Appeal refused to do the same for English criminal law. Otton LJ said that, although D's failure to communicate the fact of her being suspended to her patients may allow her 'victims' to claim damages, 'we are satisfied that it is not a basis for finding criminal liability.'

Should English law follow the lead of *Cuerrier*?

In medical law, 'informed consent' imposes a duty on doctors to communicate information to a patient about any risks inherent in surgery before consent to the operation can be treated as valid. How would it be defined in criminal law terms?

Consent obtained by duress

A threat to imprison or otherwise harm V if he did not 'consent' would invalidate that consent.

Limitations on consent

There are limits to anyone's right to consent to the infliction of harm upon themselves. In *Attorney-General's Reference (No. 6 of 1980)* (1981), two youths, aged 17 and 18, decided to settle an argument with a bare-knuckles fist fight. One had sustained a bloody nose and a bruised face. Following acquittals, the Court of Appeal held that the defence of consent was not available in this situation. Lord Lane CJ said that 'It is not in the public interest that people should try to cause or should cause each other actual bodily harm for no good reason...'

In *Brown and Others* (1993), the majority's view was that consent was always a good defence to charges of assault and battery, but not to any offence involving ABH, GBH or wounding unless a recognised exception applied. If, therefore, the allegation is that D committed no more than a simple battery, then consent is always a defence. This is an unavoidable conclusion, as Robert Goff LJ made clear in *Collins v Wilcock* (1984):

> Generally speaking, consent is a defence to battery; and most of the physical contacts of ordinary life are not actionable because they are impliedly consented to by all who move in society and so expose themselves to the risk of bodily contact. So nobody can complain of the jostling which is inevitable in, for example, a supermarket, an underground station or a busy street; nor can a person who attends a party complain if his hand is seized in friendship, or even if his back is (within reason) slapped. Although such cases are regarded as examples of implied consent, it is more common nowadays to treat them as falling within a general exception embracing all physical contact which is generally acceptable in the ordinary conduct of daily life.

However, if D is alleged to have gone beyond a battery and committed ABH (or worse), then the situation changes dramatically. No-one impliedly consents to a risk of actual bodily harm just because they are out shopping or at a party. Consent to ABH (or worse) can be given, but only in certain situations. Various courts have suggested lists of activities which carry the risk of serious injury, but where consent would nevertheless provide a good defence to charges of ABH, GBH and wounding. A non-exhaustive list reads as follows:

- contact games and sports including boxing

- surgery

- lawful chastisement

- tattooing

- ear-piercing

Some of these will now be examined in greater detail.

Sport and dangerous pastimes

Boxing

No prosecutions have ever been brought in respect of public boxing matches conducted within the *Queensberry Rules*. The high entertainment value and popularity of the sport is taken to justify V's consent to D trying to punch him very hard about the face and upper body.

However, fights conducted in other circumstances have regularly been held to amount to batteries (*Attorney-General's Reference [No. 6 of 1980]*). This is especially true of bare-knuckle fights staged for 'entertainment' purposes. Any entertainment value they may have is far outweighed by the risk of injury to the fighters. In *Coney* (1882), prosecutions were brought against various spectators at a bare-knuckle prize-fight, for aiding and abetting the unlawful activities. One question for the Court for Crown Cases Reserved was whether the consent of the participants negated the unlawful element of assault. Cave J said that 'a blow struck in sport [wrestling or boxing with gloves] is not an assault' but that 'a blow struck in a prize-fight is clearly an assault'.

Other contact sports

With other contact sports such as football, rugby and ice-hockey, a clear distinction must be drawn between two situations. An off-the-ball incident is, in principle, no different to any other assault. There is no suggestion that players consent, impliedly or otherwise, to the use of force in such situations. In *Billinghurst* (1978), D punched an opposing player, V, in the face in an off-the-ball incident during a rugby union match in South Wales. V's jaw was fractured in two places and D was convicted of inflicting GBH under s.20.

Problems arise where the alleged assault occurs on-the-ball, during play. The players in modern contact sports impliedly consent to D doing what the rules of the particular game permit. Perhaps a breach of the rules ought to establish at least a *prima facie* case; but in any given contact sport game there may be dozens of fouls. Even if only the most serious were prosecuted, the sports would be seriously affected.

The rules themselves only provide a guide as to what has been consented to. In *Moore* (1898) it was said that, 'No rules or practice of any game whatever can make lawful that which is unlawful by the law of the land.' Therefore, where an alleged assault has occurred during play, this should be assessed independently of the rules.

In *Brown and Others*, Lord Mustill referred to a series of Canadian decisions on ice-hockey. All of these cases are of persuasive value on future English decisions involving high-speed, physical contact sports such as rugby, football and ice-hockey itself. In *Cey* (1989), the court provided a helpful list of criteria to determine the scope of implied consent in sport. They include:

- the nature of the game played, whether amateur or professional league and so on;

- the nature of the particular acts(s) and their surrounding circumstances;

- the degree of force employed;

- the degree of risk of injury;

- the state of mind of the accused.

In *Ciccarelli* (1989) the Ontario Court of Appeal considered the significance of the whistle having been blown to stop play before the alleged assault occurred. The whistle had just blown for offside against D when another player, V, who had been skating across to block him, was unable to stop and they collided. D retaliated, using his stick to hit V over the head three times. The officials intervened to separate the pair but D punched out at them too. He was convicted of assault and his appeal dismissed.

> Should the criminal law concern itself with incidents on the field of play? One view is that it should:'the law does not stop at the touchline.'. Another view is that sporting violence should be left exclusively to the various sporting bodies to deal with. What do you think?

Surgery

With 'reasonable surgical interference' there is really no issue of consent as a defence to bodily harm, given that no *harm* is caused or inflicted. But in surgery there is certainly a 'wounding', and the patient must consent to that.

Consent to any recognised surgical procedure is effective; this includes sex-change operations and probably cosmetic surgery.

Tattooing and other forms of branding

Consent is a valid defence in tattooing. In *Wilson* (1997), the Court of Appeal extended this to branding, holding that it was no more hazardous than a tattoo.

> *Wilson* (1997)
> Alan Wilson had branded his initials onto his wife's buttocks using a hot blade. She regarded the branding as 'a desirable personal adornment', and had apparently originally requested that the branding be on her breasts. It was W who persuaded her to have the branding on her buttocks instead. The matter only came to light when her doctor reported the incident to the police. W was convicted of assault occasioning ABH but the Court of Appeal allowed the appeal.

Sexual activity

During sexual intercourse and related activities there is obviously bodily contact; this is not assault as long as it is consented to. This is the case even where the activity is what may politely be termed 'vigorous'. In *Slingsby* (1995), D had penetrated the vagina and rectum of a girl he had met at a nightclub with his hand *with her consent*. However, she suffered internal cuts caused by a ring on D's hand. These injuries were neither intended nor foreseen by D. V was unaware how serious these cuts were and she later died of septicaemia. Was D therefore liable for constructive manslaughter, based on the unlawful act of assault? The answer was no. The judge held that it was clear that all of D's acts on the night in question were all consented to by V and, consequently, there was no assault.

Sado-masochism

The law does not readily tolerate the idea of consent being a defence to injuries inflicted for the sexual gratification of either party. In *Donovan* (1934), D, for his sexual gratification, had beaten a 17-year-old prostitute, with a cane, 'in circumstances of indecency'. When examined by a doctor two days later, she was found to have seven or eight red marks on her buttocks. The doctor concluded she had had a 'fairly severe beating'. D was convicted of common and indecent assault. The Court of Criminal Appeal quashed his conviction, but only because it had not been left to the jury to decide whether D had intended to cause bodily harm.

In the Court of Appeal in *Brown and Others* (1993), Lord Lane CJ said that, 'the satisfying of sado-masochistic libido does not come within the category of good reason nor can the injuries be described as merely transient or trifling.' In the House of Lords, Lord Templeman said that, 'The violence of sado-masochistic encounters involves the indulgence of cruelty by sadists and the degradation of victims. Such violence is injurious to the participants and unpredictably dangerous.'

Brown and Others (1993),
Anthony Brown and the other appellants belonged to a group of sado-masochistic homosexuals who, over a 10-year period willingly and enthusiastically participated in acts of violence against each other for sexual pleasure. Many of these acts took place in rooms designed as torture-chambers. The activities included branding with wire or metal heated by a blow-lamp, use of a cat o'nine tails and genital torture. All the activities were carried out in private with the consent of the passive partner or 'victim'. There were no complaints to the police, no medical attention was ever sought and no permanent injury suffered. The police discovered the activities by accident. All members were charged with various offences, including ABH under s.47 and wounding under s.20. They were convicted and their appeals dismissed by the Court of Appeal and House of Lords (albeit by 3:2).

In *Brown and Others*, the question of consent was approached differently by the Law Lords. The majority clearly viewed what occurred as acts of violence with a sexual motive, as opposed to sexual acts that involved violence. This led them to conclude that what had happened was *prima facie* unlawful. The majority then considered whether the defence applied; they concluded that it did not. Lord Lowry commented that homosexual sado-masochism could not be regarded as a 'manly diversion', nor were they 'conducive to the enhancement of enjoyment of family life or conducive to the welfare of society'. For Lord Jauncey the corruption of young men was a real danger to be considered. Yet no-one was induced or coerced into the activities.

The minority, meanwhile, decided that the activities in question were *prima facie* lawful. Both Law Lords decided that a victim could give valid consent to ABH but not GBH. Lord Mustill identified and analysed the specific policy considerations that might point towards criminal liability, including the risk of infection, in particular AIDS, and decided that this did not justify criminalising all sado-masochistic activity. He observed that as the evidence suggests that consensual buggery was the main cause of transmission, and this was legal, what grounds were there for criminalising what had happened in this case? Lord Slynn thought that the whole area was for Parliament to decide.

Horseplay

The courts have accepted that horseplay is another area in which consensual assaults, even where quite serious injury is caused, may be legally tolerated. Society accepts that community life, such as in the playground, involves risks of deliberate physical contact, but that the criminal law should not get involved. The defence was successfully used in:

- *Jones and Others* (1986) – boys injured having been tossed into the air by schoolmates, and (more controversially),

- *Aitken and Others* (1992) – where serious burns, amounting to grievous bodily harm, were caused to a new RAF officer as part of a bizarre 'initiation ceremony'.

The impact of the Human Rights Act 1998

The coming-into-force of the Human Rights Act 1998 on 2nd October 2000 should not affect this area too greatly. In *Laskey, Jaggard and Brown v UK* (1997), the European Court of Human Rights (ECHR) in Strasbourg upheld the judgment in *Brown and Others*. It had been argued that the criminalisation of private sado-masochistic activities constituted a breach of Article 8(1) of the European Convention on Human Rights, which provides that 'Everyone has the right to respect for his private and family life.' However, like many of the rights protected by the Convention, it is not absolute. Article 8(2) adds that public authorities may interfere with the exercise of this right provided it is necessary in the interests of national security or public safety or the economic well-being of the country, for the prevention of disorder or crime, for the protection of health or morals, or for the protection of the rights and freedoms of others.

In *Laskey*, the ECHR ruled that, once conduct had gone beyond a potential risk with a sufficient degree of seriousness, the involvement of the authorities could not possibly amount to a breach of Article 8(1). In the most recent case in this area, *Emmett* (1999), the Court of Appeal applied the decisions in *Brown and Others* and *Laskey*. D was convicted of two counts of ABH on his girlfriend. The couple enjoyed sado-masochistic sex. One day, during sex, D had placed a plastic bag over her head and tied it tightly around her neck. As a result of lack of oxygen, she nearly lost consciousness, suffered bruising to the neck and ruptured blood vessels in her eyes. A month later, D poured lighter fluid over her left breast and ignited it. As a result of that injury, D persuaded her to go to the doctor, who reported D to the police. The Court of Appeal dismissed his appeals against conviction.

Reform

The Law Commission's draft *Criminal Law Bill* (1993) and their Consultation Paper, *Consent in the Criminal Law* (1995), did not propose any radical changes in the law of consent. The Bill's definition of assault includes a proviso in clause 6 (2) that:

> *No such offence is committed if the force or impact, not being intended or likely to cause injury, is in circumstances such as is generally acceptable in the ordinary conduct of daily life and the defendant does not know or believe that it is in fact unacceptable to the other person.*

This is very similar to the legal situation now. The Consultation Paper states that 'we recommend that the intentional [and reckless] causing of seriously disabling injury to another person should continue to be criminal, even if the injured person consents to such injury or to the risk of such injury.' This also maintains the present legal requirement.

However, the Commission did recommend that the intentional or reckless causing of injury to another person, falling short of the 'seriously disabling' variety, would not be criminal, if the other person had consented to it. This shifts the law slightly, as in *Brown and Others* (1993) the House of Lords had ruled that injury amounting to ABH, or worse, could only be consented to if there was a good reason for it. As the proposed offence of causing injury is designed to replace that of ABH, then the law will be relaxed if the Commission's proposals are ever adopted.

Summary

- Consent is a potentially valid defence to all assaults, including sexual assaults, and rape.

- The alleged victim must be capable of giving a valid consent (*Burrell v Harmer*).

- Where consent is obtained by D's fraud, this will usually not vitiate the consent (*Clarence, Richardson*).

- Persons can consent to all assaults and batteries, in any circumstances.

- But, where the charge is ABH, GBH or wounding (the aggravated assaults), then V's consent is only valid if there was a legally recognised 'good reason' (*Attorney-General's Reference [No. 6 of 1980], Brown and Others*).

- 'Good reasons' include: games and sports, surgery, sexual activity (*Slingsby*), tattooing and branding (*Wilson*), and horseplay (*Jones and Others, Aitken and Others*).

- Sado-masochistic activity is not considered to be a good reason (*Donovan, Brown and Others, Emmett*).

- In sporting contests, consent is no defence if the assault occurred 'off-the-ball' (*Billinghurst*). Otherwise it depends on the level of violence to which the players expressly or impliedly consented.

Questions on Part 3 Offences against the person

NB Many questions on offences against the person are invariably combined with potential defences which may be available to the accused. In some cases they occur alongside other offences. These should be answered only after the chapters on defences (chapters 14–19) have been studied and where examples of further questions appear.

1 Lucy plays for the Barchester Belles hockey team. She has been looking forward to a crucial league game against their main rivals but, as she has been feeling unwell, she takes an illegal drug two hours before bully-off in order to improve her performance. This causes a reaction with other medication she had been taking and makes her dizzy and confused. The referee, Wilf, enters the changing room and asks to inspect the studs in her boots. In her confused state, Lucy thinks he is attacking her and lashes out at him with her hockey stick. Instead, she strikes a fellow team member, Gemma, in the face, causing her mouth to bleed and breaking her glasses.

Analyse the criminal liability, if any, of Lucy.

(OCR 1999)

2 Explain why the courts have sometimes accepted that consent is as a good defence to an offence against the person charge whilst on other occasions it is said to be unavailable? Consider whether the current law satisfactory in this context?

(OCR 2000)

Part 4

Offences against property

10 Theft and making off

Introduction

Theft and other related offences were codified in the Theft Act 1968. Some aspects of the legislation, particularly those dealing with deception offences, proved to be unsatisfactory and a further Theft Act was passed in order to remedy these difficulties in 1978. Even since then, the courts have been frequently asked to interpret the various statutory provisions and their application. Consequently the law in this area is once again, for the student, a challenging mixture of legislation and case law.

S.1(1) of the Theft Act 1968 provides that: 'A person is guilty of theft if he dishonestly appropriates property belonging to another with the intention of permanently depriving the other of it'. Sections 2-6 of the Theft Act 1968 go on to explain what the various component parts of this definition mean – but that is all they do. A common misunderstanding with theft is that there are separate offences contained in these sections – do not make this mistake! There is no offence of 'appropriation', no crime of 'dishonesty' – they are simply elements that go together to make up the crime of theft.

The *actus reus* comprises three elements:

- Appropriation (s.3)

- Property (s.4)

- Belonging to another (s.5)

The *mens rea* comprises two elements:

- Dishonesty (s.2)

- An intention to permanently deprive the owner (s.6)

One of the most common misconceptions in this area of law is that the second element of the *mens rea* belongs in the *actus reus* list, i.e. that for a theft conviction the owner must, in fact, be permanently deprived of their property. This is not the case. There is no requirement that the defendant 'get away' with property before it becomes stolen. The accused simply has to 'appropriate' it with the intention of permanently depriving the owner of it.

This could, for example, lead to a theft conviction if D picks up a chocolate bar in a supermarket and slips it into his pocket – even if he is stopped from leaving the store – because the intention was present at the moment of the appropriation. Of course, as with many elements of the *mens rea*, proving that D had the intent is another matter – this is why many store detectives allow suspected thieves to leave the shop before stopping them. Nevertheless, as a *matter of law*, theft is committed as soon as all the above elements are present.

'Appropriation'

S.3(1) of the Theft Act 1968 states that 'Any assumption by a person of the rights of an owner amounts to an appropriation.' The 1968 Act does not provide any definition of the 'rights of an owner'. However, one fundamental question is whether s.3(1) relates to *all* the rights, or merely *any* of the rights. In *Morris* (1984), counsel argued for the former, but Lord Roskill was unimpressed: 'it is enough for the prosecution if they have proved... the assumption by the defendant of any rights of the owner of the goods in question.' That is not to say that simply touching an item of property amounts to *theft*, of course – it may not be dishonest – but it could be an 'appropriation'.

Relevance of consent or authority

The question of whether D appropriates property when he does do with the authorisation or consent of the owner has troubled the courts for years. In *Lawrence* (1972), the House of Lords decided it was still an 'appropriation'.

Lawrence (1972)

On arrival at Victoria Station in London, an Italian student, Occhi, who spoke little English, showed Alan Lawrence, a taxi-driver waiting outside, a piece of paper on which was written an address in Ladbroke Grove. The address was not far and should have cost 50p. Lawrence, however, said that it was a long journey and would be expensive, at which point Occhi proferred a £1 note. Lawrence said this would not be enough, so Occhi opened his wallet and Lawrence removed a further £1 and a £5 note. Lawrence was convicted of theft, and on appeal the argument that he had not appropriated the money

because he took it with Occhi's consent was rejected by both the
Court of Appeal and a unanimous House of Lords.

After a period of doubt triggered by certain *dicta* of Lord Roskill in *Morris*,
the House of Lords resolved the issue in *Gomez* (1993) by giving their
approval to *Lawrence*. Lord Keith said that 'an act may be an appropriation
notwithstanding that it is done with the consent of the owner.' Where an
honest shopper places goods in a shopping basket, this is not theft, said Lord
Keith, but it is an appropriation. Lord Browne-Wilkinson added that he
regarded 'the word "appropriation" in isolation as being an objective
description of the act done irrespective of the mental state of either the
owner or the accused.'

The *Lawrence/Gomez* definition of 'appropriation' is very wide indeed. So
wide, in fact, that the Court of Appeal seems to be having difficulty in
accepting what the House of Lords very clearly said. In *Gallasso* (1993), for
example, Lloyd LJ said that 'Lord Keith did not mean to say that every
handling is an appropriation. Suppose, for example, the shopper carelessly
knocks an article off the shelf; if he bends down and replaces it on the shelf
nobody would regard it as an act of appropriation.' However, it seems clear
that that is exactly what Lord Keith said and also exactly what he meant to say.

More recently, in *Mazo* (1997), the Court of Appeal stressed that in
Gomez, V's apparent consent had actually been obtained by deception. The
Court in *Mazo* seemed to be suggesting that the *ratio* in *Gomez* be limited to
such cases, that is, where an apparent consent was obtained by deception. The
Court may be reluctant to apply *Gomez* in cases where there is no deception.

Appropriation by keeping or dealing
S.3(1) of the Theft Act 1968 states that 'appropriation' extends to the
situation where D has come by property, innocently or not, though without
stealing it, but later assumes a right to it by 'keeping' or 'dealing with it as
owner'.

'Keeping'
It will be an 'appropriation' by D if he borrows property from V – some item
of DIY equipment, for example – and then refuses to return it, or to simply
hang onto it in the hope that V will forget about it. D is therefore guilty of
theft if he does this with the *mens rea* required.

'Dealing with property as owner'
This would deal with a variation on the situation above where D sells V's
DIY equipment. Having borrowed the equipment in the first place meant

that D was in lawful possession of it, but he would dishonestly appropriate it by selling it, i.e. by 'dealing with' the property as if he owned it.

The exception in favour of bona fide purchasers

Every year hundreds of proprietors of second-hand shops will innocently buy stolen property. Does s.3(1) of the Theft Act 1968 make them thieves if they subsequently discover that the property was stolen, but decide to keep the property or otherwise deal with it, by selling it on to a customer? The answer is no. S.3(2) of the 1968 Act imposes a limitation in favour of persons who purchase property 'in good faith'.

Appropriation as a continuing act

Is 'appropriation' an instantaneous act, or does it continue over time? If the latter is correct, for how long does it continue? At one extreme, appropriation might be said to continue as long as the stolen property remains in D's possession. This would, however, create difficulties for the offence of handling stolen goods. The courts have therefore taken the view that an 'appropriation' continues for so long as the thief can sensibly be regarded as being in the act of stealing.

The leading case is *Atakpu and Abrahams* (1993). D and E had a plan to travel to Frankfurt, Germany, hire a number of expensive cars using false papers, drive them to England and sell them there. The plan worked perfectly and they duly arrived in Dover with two Mercedes and a BMW. However, customs officers were suspicious and they were arrested and charged with conspiracy to steal. On appeal against conviction they argued that no appropriation had taken place in England. The Court of Appeal allowed the appeals. The cars had clearly been stolen in Germany. Once property had been stolen, any further dealing with it did not amount to an 'appropriation' within s.3(1) of the Theft Act. This was so even if the property was stolen abroad. Although, generally speaking, it was for the common sense of the jury to decide how long appropriation continued so that the thief could be sensibly regarded as in the act of stealing, this was not possible in the present case. Ward J said that no jury 'could reasonably arrive at a conclusion that the theft of these motor cars was still continuing days after the appellants had first taken them.'

'Property'

What can be stolen?

S.4(1) of the Theft Act 1968 provides that 'Property includes money and all other property, real or personal, including things in action and other intangible property.'

'Real property'

'Real property' means land. However, s.4(2) goes on to say that 'a person cannot steal land, or things forming part of land and severed from it' except in a limited number of situations. One of these is where D 'appropriates anything forming part of the land by severing it or causing it to be severed.' This could include removing topsoil, or trees and plants, or any structure on the land. Thus in a case in 1972 a man was prosecuted for stealing Cleckheaton Railway Station near Leeds by dismantling and removing it.

S.4(3) provides that wild mushrooms or flowers, fruit or foliage picked from a plant (which in turn includes shrubs or trees) growing wild on any land cannot be stolen – unless D picks them 'for reward or for sale or other commercial purpose.'

Personal property

The vast majority of theft cases involve personal property. In *Kelly and Lindsay* (1998), D, a sculptor, was accused of stealing various body parts from the Royal College of Surgeons where he worked as a laboratory assistant. When arrested he told police that he wanted to 'understand death' and that he had treated all the body parts with respect. He was convicted and on appeal it was argued that parts of bodies were not, in law, capable of being property and therefore could not be stolen. The Court of Appeal dismissed the appeals.

'Things in Action'

A 'thing in action' is property that does not exist in a physical state – it cannot be seen or touched – but can be claimed by legal action. Examples include:

- bank accounts;

- shares;

- intellectual property rights (copyrights, patents, trade marks, design rights, etc.).

What *cannot* be stolen?

Electricity

Electricity cannot be stolen. Instead, s.13 of the Theft Act 1968 provides a separate offence of making dishonest use, wasting or diverting electricity.

Confidential information

Although confidential information has value, and can be sold, it is not 'property'. In *Oxford v Moss* (1979), D, a civil engineering student at

Liverpool University, acquired a draft of his examination paper. He read the contents and then returned it. It was agreed that he had never intended to permanently deprive the University of the paper itself. Instead, he was charged with theft of the information on the paper (the examination questions) on it. The magistrates dismissed the charge and the prosecution's appeal was dismissed.

Wild creatures

Genuinely wild animals are 'property', but cannot be stolen, according to s.4(4) of the Theft Act 1968. The only occasions when a wild animal can be stolen is if it:

* has been tamed; or

* is 'ordinarily kept in captivity', or

* has been reduced into possession and possession of it has not since been lost or abandoned.

Hence, all pets and zoo creatures, as well as something like a tame fox, can be stolen. Pets and zoo animals may be stolen even after they have escaped because they are 'ordinarily kept in captivity'.

Value of the property irrelevant

It is no defence for D to argue that there was no property stolen because the property is practically worthless in commercial terms.

Belonging to another

S.5(1) of the Theft Act 1968 provides that 'Property shall be regarded as belonging to any person having possession or control of it, or having any proprietary right or interest.' In the vast majority of cases D, having no interest in the property, steals from someone who both owns and possesses the property in question. But s.5(1) is wide enough to allow D to steal property which at the relevant time is owned, possessed, or controlled, by different people. So if P lends a book to Q, who shows it to R, and D then grabs it, D has stolen the book from R (who was in possession) and Q (who was in control) and P (who had ownership).

Ownership and 'possession or control'

It is impossible for D to steal property that is wholly owned, possessed and controlled by D himself. This seemingly self-evident proposition has nevertheless been tested in court. In *Powell v McRae* (1977), D, a turnstile operator at Wembley Stadium, dishonestly accepted £2 from a member of the public and admitted him even though he (D) was fully aware that entrance was by ticket only. He was convicted of theft of the £2 from his employers, but his conviction was quashed by the Queen's Bench Divisional Court. By no stretch of language could it be said that the money 'belonged to' his employers. D was simply the recipient of a bribe; he was not a thief.

However, given the possible separation of ownership, possession and control, s.5(1) means that D may, in certain circumstances, steal his own property. In *Turner (No.2)* (1971), D took his car to a garage for repair. He was to pay for the repairs on his return a few days later. When the repairs were practically completed the car was left on the road outside the garage. During the night D surreptitiously took the car using a duplicate key. He was charged with theft of the car. He claimed that, as the car did not 'belong' to anyone other than himself, he could not steal it, but he was held liable. The Court of Appeal upheld the conviction.

'Any proprietary right or interest'

Property may also be stolen from anyone having 'any proprietary right or interest' in it. Once it is established that someone has a proprietary interest, it does not matter that this is precarious or short-lived. It does not matter that someone exists who has a better right to the property than P – one thief may, indeed, steal from another thief.

Joint ownership

Just because D owns property jointly with V, he is still capable of stealing it from him. Thus a partner (in a firm of solicitors, for example) could steal partnership property, even though it is jointly owned by himself.

Property received for a particular purpose

It is clear that in many situations D may be convicted of theft even where he has acquired legal ownership of property, if he was under 'an obligation' to deal with 'that property' in a particular way. In this situation, s.5(3) provides that 'the property or proceeds shall be regarded (as against him) as belonging to the other.'

Suppose D operates a Christmas fund, into which members of a club pay sums during the year, on the understanding that D returns it in a lump sum at Christmas. D, however, misappropriates the money. It is clear that D now owns the money – there is no suggestion that D should return the exact same notes and coins to the members – but s.5(3) would allow D to be treated as a thief. The members of the club retain a proprietary interest in that money.

The obligation must be legal

The obligation referred to must be a legal, as opposed to moral obligation.

The obligation is to deal with 'that property'

In some cases D's conduct will not amount to theft because of the requirement that D deals with 'that property' in a particular way. In *Hall* (1972), D was a partner in a firm of travel agents. He had received money from various customers as deposits for air trips to America. The flights were never arranged and the money, which had been paid into the agency's general trading account, was never returned. D was charged with stealing the customers' money. The Court of Appeal, albeit reluctantly, quashed his convictions. There was no evidence that the customers imposed an obligation on D to deal with the cash in any particular way. The agency simply had an obligation to the customers to provide a holiday in due course. For liability in such a case, it would have to be shown that D was obliged to maintain a fund representing V's deposit and not simply pay the money into a general account.

'Proceeds'

While D may not be under an obligation to deal with particular property, he may be under an obligation to deal with the *proceeds* of the property instead. The case of *Wain* (1995) demonstrates this.

Wain (1995)

Wain had taken part in fundraising for a charity, *The Telethon Trust*, organised by Yorkshire TV, for which he raised £2,833. He paid this into a separate bank account at first. When asked for the cash by Yorkshire TV he made a number of excuses. Eventually the company gave him permission to transfer the money to his own account. Subsequently he withdrew money from the account for his own purposes; a cheque drawn in favour of Yorkshire TV was dishonoured. The Court of Appeal upheld his conviction for theft. McCowan LJ said that D was 'plainly under an obligation to retain, if not the actual notes and coins, at least their proceeds, that is to say the money credited in the bank account which he opened for the trust with the actual property.'

Property acquired by mistake

S.5(4) of the 1968 Act provides that,

> *Where a person gets property by another's mistake, and is under an obligation to make restoration (in whole or in part) of the property or its proceeds or of the value thereof, then to the extent of that obligation the property or proceeds shall be regarded (as against*

> *him) as belonging to the person entitled in restoration, and an*
> *intention not to make restoration shall be regarded accordingly as an*
> *intention to deprive that person of the property or proceeds.*

There has been confusion about the application of s.5(4). It led to an incorrect acquittal in *Attorney-General's Reference (No.1 of 1983) (1985)*. D was an officer with the Metropolitan Police. Her salary was paid into her bank account by direct debit. On one occasion the Met mistakenly overpaid her. She was charged with theft but the judge directed an acquittal. The Court of Appeal, however, held that this case was covered by s.5(4). Although, as a matter of civil law, she became owner of the money as soon as it was paid into her account, she remained under an obligation to restore it to the Met.

The Court of Appeal has held that, as with s.5(3), the obligation must be a legal one. In *Gilks* (1972), Cairns LJ said: 'In a criminal statute, where a person's criminal liability is made dependent on his having an obligation, it would be quite wrong to construe that word so as to cover a moral or social obligation as distinct from a legal one.'

Gilks (1972),
Gilks called into Ladbrokes' betting shop and placed a number of bets. One of these was on a horse called Fighting Scot, which did not get anywhere. Instead the race was won by a horse called Fighting Taffy. However, the relief manager, mistakenly believing that Gilks had backed Fighting Taffy, paid him £106. Gilks kept the cash and was charged with theft. On appeal, he argued that s.5(4) did not apply. Because gambling contracts are not, as a matter of contract law, legally enforceable (fact!) D was under no legal obligation to repay the money. The Court of Appeal agreed: the obligation had to be a legal one.

Ownerless property

A person cannot steal property that is not owned by anyone at the time of the appropriation. This includes property which, although capable of ownership, has never actually been owned by anyone, as well as property that was owned once but has become ownerless.

Lost property and abandoned property

It is insufficient that property is simply lost, it must have been abandoned before it can be said to be ownerless. Abandonment is not lightly inferred:

property is only abandoned when the owner is indifferent as to any future appropriation of the property by others. It is not enough that D has no further use for property. Thus a householder who leaves rubbish outside his house awaiting collection by the refuse authorities has not abandoned it. Property is not abandoned just because the owner has lost it and given up looking for it. The more valuable the property, the less likely it is that the owner has abandoned the hope of ever seeing it again.

'Dishonesty'

The next element that must be proved is that D was dishonest.

Situations covered by s.2(1)

The 1968 Theft Act does not provide a definition of dishonesty. Instead, it provides that in three situations D is not to be regarded as being dishonest if he appropriates the property in the belief that:

- he has in law the right to deprive the other of it, on behalf of himself or of a third person (s.2(1)(a)); or

- he would have the other's consent if the other knew of the appropriation and the circumstances of it (s.2(1)(b)); or

- the person to whom the property belongs cannot be discovered by taking reasonable steps (s.2(1)(c)).

Belief in a 'right to deprive'

If D believes he has a legal right to appropriate V's property, he is not dishonest, no matter how unreasonable that belief. An example is provided by *Holden* (1991). D was charged with theft of scrap tyres from Kwik-Fit, where he had previously been employed. He claimed that other people had taken tyres with the permission of the supervisor. The depot manager, however, gave evidence that taking tyres was a sackable offence. The jury was directed that D was guilty unless he had a reasonable belief that he had a right to take the tyres. The Court of Appeal quashed the conviction: a person was not dishonest if he believed – reasonably or not – that he had a legal right to do what he had done. The question was whether he had – or might have had – an honest belief that he was entitled to take the tyres. The reasonableness (or otherwise) of the belief was no more than evidence as to whether D actually held that belief.

Belief in the 'other's consent'

Suppose D and V share a flat and, one night, D realises that he has no money to spend down the pub. V is away but D finds V's wallet containing money. If D removes £20 from the wallet genuinely thinking that V would not object were he around and knew of the circumstances, then D is not dishonest under s.2(1)(b). The belief may be unreasonable: again, the crux is whether D genuinely believed that V would have consented.

Belief that the owner 'cannot be discovered'

Although s.2(1)(c) does not refer to this situation explicitly, it seems to relate most clearly to the situation where D finds property. If D does find property, and comes to the honest conclusion that the owner cannot be discovered by taking reasonable (as it appears *to him*) steps, then D's appropriation of the property will not be dishonest. The reasonableness (or otherwise) of D's belief is, yet again, no more than evidence as to whether he actually held that belief.

In *Small* (1988), D was convicted of the theft of a car. He claimed that he believed it had been abandoned, because it had been parked in the same place, at an angle on a corner, every day for two weeks, during which time it had not moved at all. On inspection he discovered that the doors were unlocked and the keys were in the ignition. The car appeared to be in a 'forlorn' state: the petrol tank was empty, the battery was flat, as was one tyre; the windscreen wipers did not work. Having filled the tank with petrol he manager to get it started and drove off in it. He did not consider at any time that it was stolen until he observed the police flashing their lights at him, at which point he 'panicked' and ran off. The Court of Appeal quashed the conviction. There was evidence that D might have believed that the car had been abandoned. The question was whether he had – or might have had – an honest belief that the owner could not be traced.

Situations not covered by s.2(1)

Where D's situation does not fall within s.2(1) that does not mean he is dishonest. Rather, he will be subject to the general test of dishonesty. The initial question that arises concerns who should determine honesty. There are three possibilities:

- the defendant (a purely subjective test) – Option 1;

- the magistrates or jury (a purely objective test) – Option 2;

- some combination of the two – Option 3

During the 1970s the Court of Appeal toyed with Options 1 and 2, before plumping for Option 3 in *Ghosh* (1982). Lord Lane CJ said:

In determining whether the prosecution has proved that the defendant was acting dishonestly, a jury must first of all decide whether according to the ordinary standards of reasonable and honest people what was done was dishonest. If it was not dishonest by those standards, that is the end of the matter and the prosecution fails. If it was dishonest by those standards, then the jury must consider whether D himself must have realised that what he was doing was by those standards dishonest.

The problem with having dishonesty decided by the jury is that the determination of dishonesty remains unpredictable. No precedent is ever created by the deliberations of a jury, so each jury must approach the question anew, with no earlier cases to look to for guidance. Questions of fact, determined by a jury, may not be appealed, unlike questions of law. They are therefore not open to consideration and correction by the appeal courts.

In your view, was Robin Hood (who stole from the rich and gave to the poor) dishonest 'according to the ordinary standards of reasonable and honest people'? (see above)

D's willingness to pay not conclusive of honesty

S.2(2) of the Theft Act 1968 provides that 'a person's appropriation of property belonging to another may be dishonest notwithstanding that he is willing to pay for the property.' The effect of s.2(2) is that D may be guilty of theft where he appropriates property and pays for it. Very often the fact that D has paid, or was willing to pay, for property will be strong evidence that he was not dishonest, often on the basis that he genuinely believed V would consent to the appropriation, but it is not conclusive.

'Intention to permanently deprive'

Stealing requires an intention to permanently deprive. It is unnecessary for there to be permanent deprivation *in fact*; theft is committed even if there is no danger of V ever losing his property provided D had the intent that he would. Conversely, the fact that there is permanent deprivation does not make something theft if D did not have the intent. The intent *must* be present at the time of the appropriation.

Circumstantial evidence will be necessary in many cases to determine whether D had the intent or not. In such cases where intent is not obvious it will be for the jury to infer intent from the evidence. For example, if D borrows V's lawnmower and it is found in D's garden, in full view of V or anyone else, the inference that D intended to permanently deprive V of it will not be easy. On the other hand, if V is discovered respraying D's car that he took without permission, the inference will be much easier.

Money

Where D takes money, say from his employer's cash-till, intending to replace an equivalent amount in due course, could it be argued that, as he had intended to repay the money, albeit not the exact notes and/or coins taken, then there was no intention to deprive the owner of the money? In *Velumyl* (1989), the Court of Appeal held that D *does* have such an intent. D, a company manager, took £1,050 from an office safe without authority. He said that a friend owed him money; when this money was repaid he would replace the money in the safe. The Court of Appeal upheld his theft conviction. He had the intention of permanently depriving the company of the money because he had no intention of returning the objects that he had taken. His intention was to return objects of equivalent value, which was not a defence to theft. D had taken something that he was not entitled to take without the consent of the owner and could not force upon the owner a substitution to which the latter had not consented.

Intending to treat property as your own to dispose of regardless of the other's rights

S.6(1) of the Theft Act 1968 provides that 'a person appropriating property belonging to another without meaning the other permanently to lose the thing itself is nevertheless to be regarded as having the intention of permanently depriving the other of it if his intention is to treat the thing as his own to dispose of regardless of the other's rights.'

S.6(1) need only be invoked where D ultimately expects the property to find its way back into the hands of the owner. There are two main situations:

- D takes V's property with the intention of *selling it* back to him. In *Lloyd and Others* (1985), Lord Lane CJ cited an old case in which D took fat from a candlemaker and then offered it for sale to the same man as an example of a situation where s.6(1) would apply today.

- D takes V's property with the intention of *ransoming it*. Thus, in *Lloyd and Others*, Lord Lane CJ gave the following example: if D says, 'I have taken your valuable painting. You can have it back on payment to me of £10,000. If you are not prepared to make that payment, then you are not going to get your painting back.' This would be theft.

Unfortunately confusion has been caused by judges referring to s.6(1) in straightforward theft cases that simply did not require it. The prime example is *Cahill* (1993). D picked up a package of newspapers from outside a newsagent's shop, only to drop it soon after (when he noticed that police officers were watching). He was charged with theft. His story was that he was going to dump the papers on a friend's doorstep for a joke. The trial judge directed the jury in terms of s.6 – but got the wording wrong and forced the Court of Appeal to allow D's appeal. However, it was not necessary for the judge to refer to s.6(1) at all. The question for the jury should simply have been, did D intend that the package be lost to the newsagent forever? If D knew that this would be the effect of depositing the package on the friend's doorstep, that would have been sufficient intent even though D's only purpose was the bizarre practical joke.

In *Cahill*, the judge's reference to s.6(1) allowed D to escape liability on appeal when he was really guilty. The opposite happened in *DPP v Lavender* (1994). D had taken doors from council property undergoing repair and used them to replace damaged doors on his girlfriend's council flat. He was charged with theft but argued he had no intention to permanently deprive. Magistrates dismissed the charge but the Divisional Court disagreed. The question was whether D intended to treat the doors as his own, regardless of the owner's rights; the answer to this was yes.

> Was D a thief? Was he treating the doors as his own? Or was he in fact treating the doors as the Council's? At most, D was 'guilty' of rearranging the Council's property; is this theft?

'Regardless of the other's rights'

What if D takes V's property and is completely indifferent as to whether V ever sees it again? It could be argued that D did not *intend* V to be permanently deprived of his property, hence s.6(1) provides that it is sufficient if D intends to 'treat the thing as his own to dispose of regardless of the other's rights'.

In *Marshall, Coombes and Eren* (1998), D, E and F were caught obtaining London Underground (LU) day tickets from people who had passed through the exit barriers, then selling them on to other people. They were all convicted of theft of the tickets and appealed, on the basis that there was no intention to permanently deprive. The Court of Appeal upheld the convictions. By acquiring and re-selling the tickets the men had demonstrated an intention to treat the tickets as their own to dispose of regardless of LU's rights.

> What 'rights' did the London Underground have over the tickets?

Borrowing or lending

S.6(1) of the Theft Act 1968 goes on to provide that 'a borrowing or lending of (the thing) may amount to (treating the thing as his own to dispose of regardless of the other's rights) if, but only if, the borrowing or lending is for a period and in circumstances making it equivalent to an outright taking or disposal.'

It is clearly not theft if D borrows property intending to return it eventually. However, there may be situations where D merely borrows property from V, fully intending to return the property to D exactly unchanged, but where D could nevertheless be liable for theft. This is where the borrowing is 'for a period or in circumstances making it equivalent to an outright taking or disposal'. An example would be the taking of a battery with the intention of returning it only when its power is exhausted. In *Lloyd and Others* (1985) Lord Lane CJ said:

> The second half of s.6(1)) is intended to make clear that a mere borrowing is never enough to constitute the necessary guilty mind unless the intention is to return the 'thing' in such a changed state that it can truly be said that *all its goodness or virtue* has gone.

Lloyd and Others (1985)
D worked as a projectionist at an Odeon cinema. E and F ran a pirate video operation. Over a period of months D surreptitiously removed a number of films from the cinema and lent them to E and F who quickly copied them onto a master tape from which they produced large numbers of pirate videos. The films were only taken out of the cinema for a few hours at a time. Eventually the three men were caught red-handed in the process of copying *The Missionary*. They were convicted of conspiracy to steal but the Court of Appeal quashed the convictions. Applying the above test to the facts, Lord Lane CJ held that the films had not been stolen. The particular films had 'not themselves been diminished in value at all', there was still virtue in them.

A problem arises if D takes property, and returns it in a changed state where *some* of its goodness or virtue has gone. It is clear that if D takes V's football ticket, intending to return it after the match, then D is guilty of theft although V may well recover the ticket because by then it is simply a piece of paper with no intrinsic value. However, what happens if D takes V's season ticket and returns it after half the season, or even just one game? Does this amount to theft? There do not appear to have been any cases on this issue, but s.6(1) as explained in *Lloyd* would suggest that it is not theft, as the circumstances must make the borrowing 'equivalent to an outright taking or disposal' and it can hardly be said to be outright if a substantial proportion of the value still remains.

Making off without payment

Section 3 of the Theft Act 1978 was introduced in order to cover a loophole situation in the 1968 Act. Where D obtains ownership and possession of property from V, then decides not to pay for it, he is not guilty of theft because by the time he formed the dishonest intention, the property belonged to D. This conduct, commonly referred to as 'bilking', is now provided for as follows. S.3(1) states that 'a person who, knowing that payment on the spot for any goods supplied or services done is required or expected from him, dishonestly makes off without having paid as required or expected and with intent to avoid payment of the amount shall be guilty' of making off without payment.

Actus reus
The *actus reus* elements of the offence are that D:

- Makes off

- Without having paid as required or expected

- For any goods supplied or services done

'Makes off'
'Makes off' is not limited to D leaving by stealth but includes situations where D openly runs off, typically by jumping out of a taxi and running away. To 'make off' means that D must actually leave premises or the point at which payment was expected. For example, if D is caught climbing through a hotel window, he will not have made off (though he may well be guilty of an attempt). In *McDavitt* (1981), D refused to pay his bill for a meal at a restaurant after an argument with the manager. He got up and walked towards a door where he was advised not to leave as the police had been called. At this point he went to the toilet and remained there until the police arrived. He was charged with making off without paying from the restaurant but, at the end of the prosecution case, the judge told the jury to acquit as D had not 'made off'.

Without having paid as required or expected
D's departure must be made without paying. If D hands over forged bank notes he does not 'pay'. On the other hand, where D pays with a cheque

supported by a guarantee card then there is no offence even if he has no funds in his account, because the bank will be obliged to honour the cheque. Similarly, where D pays by credit card, even if he does so without authority because it has been withdrawn or the card is stolen, there is no offence as the card company will honour the debt.

Goods supplied or services done

Goods must be 'supplied' to D, although it is not necessary that the goods be delivered to him. It is sufficient that D is permitted to take them, for example by filling his petrol tank at a self-service filling station, or taking items from a supermarket shelf. Where services are involved, the service must be 'done'. This typically involves letting hotel rooms, supplying meals in restaurants, or valeting D's car. Allowing D to use a facility, such as parking his car in a car park, would be regarded as a service 'done', so that D would commit the offence if he drove away without paying.

> An interesting problem arises if D were charged under s.3 of having sneaked into a cinema to watch a film and then left again without paying. Could this be regarded as a service 'done'?

Excluded goods and services

S.3(3) provides that there is no offence committed 'where the supply of the goods or the doing of the service is contrary to law, or where the service done is such that payment is not legally enforceable'. Examples involving the supply of goods being contrary to law include prohibited drugs, alcohol (where D is under 18), and cigarettes (where D is under 16). Examples of the supply of services being contrary to law would include the situation where D leaves a brothel or an unlicensed casino without paying his debts.

Mens rea

The *mens rea* elements of the offence are:

- Dishonesty

- Knowledge that payment on the spot was required or expected from him

- Intent to avoid payment of the amount

Dishonesty

The *Ghosh* (1982) test applies. See above (pp. 165–166).

Knowledge that payment on the spot was required or expected

D must make off knowing that payment was 'required' or 'expected'. If, for example, D honestly believed that goods were supplied or the service done on credit, and that he would be invoiced later he would not be guilty. Similarly, a foreigner who travels on a bus without paying, because in his country all public transport is free, would not commit the offence because he would not believe that payment was required or expected of him. Two cases involving passengers running away without paying for taxi journeys illustrate what is meant by this element of the offence.

- In *Troughton v Metropolitan Police* (1987), D got into a taxi and asked to be taken to 'Highbury, North London'. He did not give an address. Unable to get an address from D, the exasperated driver drove to the nearest police station, where D got out and ran off. He was convicted but the Divisional Court quashed his conviction.

- In *Aziz* (1993), the taxi had reached the requested destination but D refused to pay a £15 taxi fare. At this the driver set off to drive him back to the point where he had been picked up but, *en route*, decided to drive to a police station. D forced the car to stop and ran off. On appeal, he claimed that the driver's announcement that he was returning meant that his requirement to pay had ceased but the Court of Appeal rejected the argument and upheld the conviction.

The crucial differences in these cases was that in *Troughton v Metropolitan Police*, the journey had never been completed whereas in *Aziz*, it had been completed. The former driver's failure to take D to his destination amounted to a breach of contract, and he was therefore unable to 'require' or 'expect' payment, whereas the fact that the latter driver had then driven off somewhere else was irrelevant, D knew that payment was still required.

Intent to avoid payment of the amount

It was originally believed that the offence was committed where D's intention in making off was merely to avoid payment *at that time*, even though he intended to pay later. However, in *Allen* (1985), the House of Lords held that an intention to avoid payment *permanently* is required.

Allen (1985)
Chris Allen booked a hotel room for ten nights from 15 January 1983. He stayed on thereafter and finally left on 11 February, without paying his bill of £1,286.94, and leaving behind his belongings. He telephoned two days later to say that he was in financial difficulties

and arranged to return to the hotel on 18 February to collect his belongings and to leave his passport as security. He was, however, arrested on his return. At his trial Allen denied that he acted dishonestly and said that he genuinely expected to pay his bill from various business ventures. The Court of Appeal quashed the conviction and the Lords upheld that decision.

Summary

- A person is guilty of theft if he dishonestly appropriates property belonging to another with the intention of permanently depriving the other of it.

- Any assumption of any of the rights of an owner amounts to an appropriation (*Morris*).

- An act may be an appropriation notwithstanding that it is done with the consent of the owner (*Lawrence, Gomez*).

- Appropriation includes keeping property and dealing with it as if you were the owner.

- Appropriation is not instantaneous but may be treated as continuing for so long as the thief can sensibly be regarded as being in the act of stealing (*Atakpu and Abrahams*).

- Property is defined widely (*Kelly and Lindsay*), including personal and intangible property, although real property can only be stolen in certain circumstances.

- Property belongs to any person having possession or control of it, or having any proprietary right or interest in it.

- D cannot steal his own property if he owns, possesses and controls it (*Powell v McRae*) but he can steal property that he owns if it is temporarily in the possession or control of another (*Turner* [No.2]).

- If D received property and was under a legal (*Arnold*) obligation to deal it in a particular way, then either the property itself or the proceeds of it shall be regarded as belonging to another. Because the obligation is to deal with 'that property', D will not be guilty if he was not obliged to deal with it in a particular way (*Hall*) but he may be under an obligation to deal with the proceeds instead (*Wain*).

- Property received by mistake may be treated as belonging to another if D was under a legal (*Gilks*) obligation to make restoration of it (*Attorney-General's Reference* [No.1 of 1983]).

- D must be proved to have been dishonest. The Theft Act 1968 gives three illustrations of when D is not dishonest, all of which depend on D's genuine belief. The Act does *not* define when D is dishonest. This is left to the courts – the test is that laid down in *Ghosh*.

- D must intend to permanently deprive the owner of their property. Taking money from a till is theft even if D intends to replace the cash eventually because the actual notes and coins will be different (*Velumyl*). D has the required intention, even if he intends the owner to get their property back, if D planned to sell, or ransom it back to V.

- Borrowing is not theft, provided D intended to return the property eventually. But D may nevertheless have the required intention if his intention was to return the property in such a changed state that it can truly be said that *all its goodness or virtue* has gone (*Lloyd*).

- Making off without payment is designed to plug a loophole in the definition of theft. D is guilty if he dishonestly makes off, knowing that payment on the spot for any goods supplied or services done is required or expected from him but without having paid as required or expected, and with intent to permanently avoid payment of the amount (*Allen*).

- To 'make off' is to leave the place where payment was required or expected (*McDavitt*)

- 'On the spot' means 'at that time' not 'at that particular place' (*Troughton v Metropolitan Police, Aziz*).

11 Robbery

Introduction

S.8 of the Theft Act 1968 provides that 'a person is guilty of robbery if he steals, and immediately before or at the time of doing so, and in order to do so, he uses force on any person or puts or seeks to put any person in fear of being then and there subjected to force.'

The *actus reus* of robbery

'Steals'

Robbery is an aggravated form of theft; it is therefore necessary to prove theft. If D has not committed theft he cannot be convicted of robbery even though he uses force to deprive V of the property. This may occur if D honestly believes that he has a right to the property and is, therefore, not dishonest (*Robinson* [1977]). In such cases D could, of course, be charged with the appropriate offence against the person. In *Robinson*, D had approached a man who owed his wife money, brandishing a knife. After a struggle, D grabbed a £5 note. When he was charged with robbery, the judge directed the jury that it was necessary for D to have honestly believed that he was entitled to get his money in that particular way. The jury convicted but the Court of Appeal quashed the conviction.

Robbery is complete when D has appropriated the property. There is no requirement that D succeed in 'getting away' with the property (*Corcoran v Anderton* [1980]).

Corcoran v Anderton (1980)
Chris Corcoran and a friend, P, agreed to steal a handbag from a woman, Mrs Hall, whom they had seen walking along the street in Manchester. P hit her in the back and tugged at her bag to release it, while Corcoran participated. Mrs Hall released the bag and it fell to the ground but in doing she also fell to the ground. She also screamed and at this the pair ran off empty handed. Mrs Hall recovered her bag. Corcoran was subsequently convicted of robbery. He appealed but the

> Queen's Bench Division upheld the conviction. An appropriation did not require either defendant to have sole control of the handbag.

'Force'

In *Dawson and James* (1976), D nudged a man so that he lost his balance, at which point E, who was in position jury behind V, was able to take his wallet. The Court of Appeal held that 'force' was an ordinary word and was therefore to be determined by the jury. This approach was confirmed in *Clouden* (1987), below.

'On any person'

Prior to the 1968 Act, robbery required that force be used to overpower V or to make him give up his property. This is no longer the case and robbery may be committed, for example, by wrenching a shopping bag from V's grasp, as in *Clouden*. The Court of Appeal held that, in applying force to the bag, D was taken to apply force to the woman as well. In most cases, the person on whom the force is used or against whom it is threatened will be the same person against whom theft is committed. However, the Act does not limit robbery to this situation. Thus, if D threatens P and takes jewellery belonging to Q, P's wife, then this will also be robbery.

Threat of force

S.8 of the Theft Act 1968 defines robbery as including the situation where D 'puts... any person in fear of being then and there subjected to force'. Thus, a threat of future force will not suffice for robbery (although it may constitute blackmail, contrary to s.21 of the 1968 Act).

However, it is not necessary that V be aware of the threat; or, if he is aware, that he is in fact fearful. The Act simply requires that D '*seeks* to put' him in fear of force. Thus, if V is blind and does not see D waving a knife at him while he takes his wallet, this is nevertheless robbery.

'Immediately before or at the time of' stealing

Given that theft is complete as soon as property is appropriated, a problem may arise where D uses force to effect his escape with stolen property in his possession. That is, the use of force is arguably not 'immediately before or at the time of' the theft and, therefore, there is no robbery.

To tackle this problem, the courts are prepared to treat appropriation as a continuing act. In *Hale* (1978), D and E forced their way into a house owned by Mrs Carrett after she answered the door to them. D put his hand over her mouth to stop her from screaming, while E went upstairs where he found a jewellery box. Before leaving the house, they tied her up. D was charged with, and convicted of, robbery. On appeal, he argued that, as theft was complete as soon as E laid hands on the box, any force used when tying Mrs Carrett up was irrelevant, but this had not been made clear to the jury. That is, he had not used force 'at the time of' the stealing, but afterwards. The Court of Appeal dismissed the appeal. Eveleigh LJ said:

> To say that the conduct is over and done with as soon as he laid hands on the property... is contrary to common-sense and to the natural meaning of words... the act of appropriation does not suddenly cease. It is a continuous act and it is a matter for the jury to decide whether or not the act of appropriation has finished... As a matter of common sense [D] was in the course of committing theft; he was stealing.

In *Lockley* (1995), D, caught shoplifting, had used force on a store security man who was trying to stop him to make good his escape. It was argued on appeal against his robbery conviction that the decision of the House of Lords in *Gomez* (1993), considered in Chapter 10 above, had impliedly overruled *Hale*. However, the Court of Appeal confirmed the continuing application of the *Hale* principle: it is for the jury to decide whether the appropriation was still continuing while D was endeavouring to escape and, hence, whether the use of force was 'at the time of' the theft. Of course a line must be drawn somewhere, but the matter is one for the jury to decide.

'In order to' steal

The force, or the threat of force, must be used 'in order to' steal. Thus, if D punches V in a fight, knocking him unconscious, and then removes his watch, this would not be robbery, as the force was not used 'in order to' steal.

The *mens rea* of robbery

Obviously D must steal, so this requires the *mens rea* of theft. See Chapter 10.

Summary

- To be guilty of robbery a person must 'steal', thus they must commit theft. If there is no theft, for whatever reason, there is no robbery (*Robinson* [1977]).

- As in simple theft, there is no requirement that D escape with the property (*Corcoran v Anderton* (1980). It is sufficient if D appropriates property, belonging to another, dishonestly with the intention of permanently depriving the other of it.

- The use of force is not actually essential for robbery. Robbery may also be committed if D puts or seeks to put any person in fear of being then and there subjected to force.

- However, if the allegation is that 'force' was used, this is an ordinary word that can simply be left to the jury (*Dawson and James* [1976]).

- Force must be used 'immediately before or at the time of' stealing – but the appropriation element of theft is a continuing act and it should be left to the jury to decide when it has stopped (*Hale* [1978], *Lockley* [1995]).

- Force must be used 'on any person' – but force can be used on property, e.g. a bag snatch is robbery (*Clouden* [1987]).

- D must use force, or put or seek to put any person in fear of being then and there subjected to force, 'in order to' steal. Simply using force, and then later stealing something from the same person, does not amount to robbery.

12 Burglary

Introduction

Burglary replaced the old offence of breaking and entering. Section 9 of the Theft Act 1968 creates two separate offences of burglary. In many, if not most, cases D will commit both offences – but they are separate.

Theft Act 1968
9 (1) A person is guilty of burglary if –

(a) he enters any building or part of a building as a trespasser and with intent to commit any such offence as is mentioned in subsection (2) below; or
(b) having entered any building or part of a building as a trespasser he steals or attempts to steal anything in the building or that part of it or inflicts or attempts to inflict on any person therein any grievous bodily harm.

(2) The offences referred to in subsection (1)(a) above are offences of stealing anything in the building or part of a building in question, of inflicting on any person therein any grievous bodily harm or raping any person therein and of doing unlawful damage to the building or anything therein.

(4) References in subsections (1) and (2) above to a building… shall also apply to an inhabited vehicle or vessel, and shall apply to any such vehicle or vessel at times when the person having a habitation in it is not there as well as at times when he is.

Actus reus of burglary

The *actus reus* elements – which are common to both burglary offences – are that D must have:

- Entered

- A building or part of a building

- As a trespasser

Furthermore, depending on exactly what it is that D is alleged to have done, the word 'therein' requires some explanation.

'Entry'

The 1968 Act does not explain what is meant by 'entry'. In *Collins* (1973), the Court of Appeal offered some guidance. The facts of the case are unusual to say the least. D did not deny climbing a ladder, wearing only his socks, and entering the bedroom of an 18-year-old girl in the middle of the night and having sex with her. However, he claimed that, whilst balanced on the windowsill, the girl had sat up and then knelt on the bed before putting her arms around his neck and pulled him into the bed. Apparently, the girl – who had been drinking – had assumed that D was her boyfriend paying her an 'ardent nocturnal visit'! It was only after they had started to have sex that she discovered that D was not her boyfriend, slapped his face and demanded that he leave. When he was charged with burglary (entry with intent to rape), contrary to s.9(1)(a), he denied having entered the building as a trespasser, on the basis that he was still outside the building when the girl pulled him into the bedroom.

Although he was convicted the Court of Appeal quashed the conviction. Edmund-Davies LJ said that the jury had to be 'entirely satisfied' that D had to make an 'effective and substantial' entry into the building before a conviction was possible. The Court made it very clear that D did not have to have his entire body inside the building before he had entered it.

The 'substantial and effective entry' test was modified in *Brown* (1985). D was observed with the top half of his body inside a shop window rummaging around, and was convicted of burglary (entry with intent to steal), contrary to s.9(1)(a). The Court of Appeal held that all that was required was that D had made an 'effective' entry, and that this was a question of fact for the jury.

This approach suggests that what is an effective entry in some circumstances may not be in others. While D's entry is effective for stealing goods if he can reach into a shop window, it will rarely, if ever, be effective for inflicting grievous bodily harm and still less for rape. It is difficult to think of a situation where anything less than D having his whole body inside a building would amount to an effective entry where his intent is to commit rape.

More recent developments suggest that the requirement that entry be 'effective' has also been removed. In *Ryan* (1996), D was discovered stuck in the downstairs window of an elderly man's house in the middle of the night.

His head and right arm were inside the house but the rest of his body was in the garden. He was completely trapped and the fire brigade had to be called to release him. The Court of Appeal upheld his conviction of burglary (entry with intent to steal), contrary to s.9(1)(a). The Court dismissed his argument that his actions were incapable of amounting to entry because he could not have stolen anything. The question had correctly been left to the jury.

Do you agree that Ryan had made an 'entry' into the old man's house?

'Any building or part of a building'

The maximum sentence that may be imposed depends on the type of building entered. The maximum penalty for conviction on indictment is 14 years if the building in question is a 'dwelling'. For other buildings, the maximum is ten years.

'Building'

The word is not defined in the 1968 Act but it must be a fairly permanent structure. A temporary, prefabricated structure would probably be a 'building'; a tent is not. It is not clear when a structure under construction becomes a 'building'. If D wanders onto a building site and enters a partly finished house with no roof or fittings and causes criminal damage, has he entered a 'building'? Similarly, does there come a point when a dilapidated and/or partly demolished house ceases to be a 'building'? At present there is no answer to these questions.

'Inhabited' vehicles, such as caravans, or vessels, like houseboats, are buildings. There is no requirement that the occupier has to be in at the time when D enters. But would a caravan be 'inhabited', and therefore a building, if it was left empty for months, as many holiday caravans are during the winter? The answer may be that a caravan or houseboat is only a building if it is *actively* occupied. Meanwhile, vehicles such as mobile libraries, blood transfusion centres and army recruitment offices are not buildings as they are not 'inhabited'.

'Part of a building'

It is sufficient that D enters 'part of a building' as a trespasser. D may have permission to enter parts of a building but not others; he may commit burglary if he enters those other parts. A guest in a hotel has permission to enter his own room and communal rooms (the foyer, bar, restaurant, for example), but not other guests' rooms or parts of the hotel used exclusively by staff. If D were to enter another guest's room or the manager's office intending to steal this could be burglary.

'Part of a building' does not necessarily mean a separate room; any separate section of a room will suffice. In *Walkington* (1979), D entered Debenhams department store in Oxford Street, London one evening. It was 20 minutes before closing time and the store was quiet. On the first floor was a three-sided counter, with a till, the drawer of which was partially open. D entered the counter area, opened the drawer and, after looking inside and finding it empty, slammed it shut and left the store whereupon he was arrested. He was convicted of burglary (entry with intent to steal) contrary to s.9(1)(a) and the Court of Appeal upheld the conviction. Whether the counter area was a 'part' of a building was a question of fact for the jury.

'As a trespasser'

Whether D is charged under s.9(1)(a) or (b), it is essential that D entered a building, or part of a building, as a trespasser. If D, having lawfully entered a shop, remains behind after closing by hiding somewhere, then moves throughout the display area he will not be a trespasser unless he leaves that 'part' of the shop and enters another 'part'.

Trespass is a civil concept, a tort. It basically means being on someone else's property without their permission or without some legal right to be there. While the tort of trespass may be committed negligently, the crime of burglary requires *mens rea*, and this means that D must enter the building, or part of the building, either:

- intending to trespass; or

- being reckless whether or not he is trespassing.

In *Collins* (1973), Edmund Davies LJ said (emphasis added):

> There cannot be a conviction for entering premises 'as a trespasser'... unless the person entering does so *knowing* that he is a trespasser and nevertheless deliberately enters, or, at the very least, *is reckless* as to whether or not he is entering the premises of another without the other party's consent.

The form of recklessness in burglary is subjective. In *Collins*, D's conviction was quashed after the trial judge directed the jury that civil trespass was sufficient; the question of D's *mens rea* had not therefore been left to the jury. Further, D's entry must be voluntary. Thus there would be no trespass if D stumbled into a building, or was dragged into a building against his will.

Permission to enter

The person who is in possession of a building, or part of it, is the per
may give permission to others to enter. The person in possess
authorise others to give permission to enter. A husband who owns th.. ...
home expressly, or more usually impliedly, authorises his wife and children
to invite people into the house. Those people do not enter as trespassers,
even if the husband does not know about the entry.

The person in possession may, equally, forbid the entry of certain
persons, for example his daughter's boyfriend. If the boyfriend nevertheless
enters, and either knows or thinks that the father has refused him permission
to be there, he enters as a trespasser. If he were then to remove some item
of property he would commit burglary.

Exceeding consent

A question arises about the limit of consent to enter a building. A father
might well consent to his 15-year-old daughter's boyfriend coming round to
see her – but almost certainly does not consent to them having sex in her
bedroom. Would this make the boyfriend a trespasser? Suppose D, who is
grown up and left home, still has consent to enter his father's house. One
night he enters the house and steals a television set. Is consent impliedly
limited in some way, so that D is a trespasser and hence a burglar?

In *Jones and Smith* (1976), where this exact situation occurred (although
Chris Smith, along with his friend John Jones, actually stole two televisions
from Alfred Smith's house), the Court of Appeal answered this question:
'Yes'. James LJ said that in such cases the prosecution had to prove that D
'entered with the knowledge that entry was being effected against the
consent or in excess of the consent that had been given'.

This suggests that, where D is given permission to enter for one purpose
(say to look after a flat while the owner is away on holiday), but enters for
another (say to have wild parties), then D will enter as a trespasser. There is
no requirement that the latter entry be for an unlawful purpose. Of course,
if D merely enters a flat in order to have wild parties this will not necessarily
make him a burglar! Similarly, if D has permission to enter one part of a
building, but then enters another, he will be trespassing. A TV repairman
may be invited into the living room but, if he then enters the kitchen to
search for money, he would enter that room as a trespasser.

The courts have never had to tackle the issue of where the limit of
permission to enter shops is drawn. However, it would seem that D, a
shoplifter, may commit burglary if he enters a shop intending to steal from
the very outset. The shopkeeper's permission to enter is impliedly limited to
the purpose of inspecting and/or purchasing goods. A conviction under
s.9(1)(a) would be unlikely, given the problem of proof, unless D were to
confess or was found to have gone equipped for shoplifting. A conviction

under s.9(1)(b) would seem more feasible once D has actually appropriated goods.

'Therein'

Both offences of burglary under s.9(1)(a) and (b) refer to entering a building, etc., and either intending to commit various offences or actually committing them 'therein'. This word is ambiguous. Does it mean that the property to be stolen, destroyed or damaged, or the person to be raped or harmed, has to be inside the building already? Or is it sufficient that they arrive there at the same time as D, or even later? If the latter interpretation is correct it would mean that if D and E both entered a building together as trespassers intending to steal, and D then stole E's jacket, D would be guilty of burglary (under s.9(1)(a) and (b)). However, as the purpose of the offence is the protection of persons or property in buildings, the former, more restrictive interpretation, appears more correct.

The *mens rea* of burglary

The *mens rea* required depends on whether D is charged with the s.9(1)(a) or (b) offence.

Section 9(1)(a): intent to commit another offence

Under s.9(1)(a) it must be proved that D, when entering a building or part of a building, had the intention to commit one of the offences referred to in s.9(2):

- theft

- criminal damage (strictly the 1968 Act refers to 'unlawful damage' but this presumably means the offence of criminal damage, which was only introduced by the Criminal Damage Act 1971.)

- GBH; or

- rape.

A conditional intent will suffice. In *Attorney-General's References (Nos. 1 and 2 of 1979)* (1979), there were two cases. D1 was caught inside a house. D2 was caught fiddling with a set of French windows. Both claimed that they planned to steal whatever they could find 'lying around' (D's actual words in the second case). D1 was charged with burglary and D2 with attempted burglary; in each case the trial judge directed an acquittal. However, the Court of Appeal held that the trial judges had got the law wrong. It was no defence to burglary for D to claim that he had not intended to steal any specific objects. An intention to steal whatever there was worth stealing is, nevertheless, an intention to steal.

Presumably, applying this argument, D also commits burglary if he enters a building with intent to rape or inflict GBH on anyone he finds sitting around inside. As far as guilt is concerned it would not matter that no-one was, in fact, inside; it is D's intent that defines the offence.

If D enters a building as a trespasser with intent to kill, is he a burglar?
If D enters a building as a trespasser with intent to commit robbery, is he a burglar?

Section 9(1)(b)

Under s.9(1)(b), the actual offences of theft, the infliction of GBH, or an attempt to commit either, must be proven. D must have the requisite *mens rea* states for these. Suppose D enters a house, as a trespasser, intending to commit criminal damage. Once inside he gets distracted by a magazine and starts reading it. Subsequently, he absent-mindedly places the magazine into his bag and leaves. Whilst he is certainly guilty under s.9(1)(a), has he committed burglary contrary to s.9(1)(b)?

Summary

- There are two offences of burglary.

- In either case, D must have entered a building or part of a building as a trespasser.

- Under s.9(1)(a), D must have entered with the intent to commit theft, rape, criminal damage of grievous bodily harm. A conditional intent will suffice *(Attorney-General's References (Nos. 1 and 2 of 1979) (1979))*.

- Under s.9(1)(b), D must have entered and then gone on to steal, inflict grievous bodily harm, attempted to steal or attempted to inflict grievous bodily harm.

- 'Entry' does not require that D get the whole of his body inside *(Collins* [1973]; *Brown* [1985])*.

- 'Entry' is an issue simply left to the jury to decide (*Ryan* [1996]).

- It does not appear that the entry has to be either 'substantial' or effective' (*Ryan*).

- A 'part' of a building does not have to be a separate room. Whether D has entered a 'part' of a building is a jury question (*Walkington* [1979]).

- 'Trespass' means to enter a building or part of a building without the consent of the person in possession.

- D must trespass either knowingly or recklessly (*Collins* [1973]).

- D may have consent to enter but still be a trespasser if he exceeds that consent (*Jones and Smith*).

13 Criminal damage

Introduction

The 'offence' of criminal damage was introduced in 1971 to replace the old offence of malicious damage. However, some of the pre-1971 cases are still relevant, on issues such as 'damage'. There are really four main criminal damage offences: criminal damage, aggravated criminal damage, arson and aggravated arson.

- *simple criminal damage* occurs if D intentionally or recklessly destroys or damages property belonging to another.

- *aggravated criminal damage* occurs if D intentionally or recklessly destroys or damages his own or someone else's property, intending or being reckless whether life would thereby be endangered.

- *arson* occurs if D intentionally or recklessly destroys or damages property, by fire.

- *aggravated arson* occurs if D intentionally or recklessly destroys or damages property, by fire, intending or being reckless whether life would thereby be endangered.

Criminal damage

> *Criminal Damage Act 1971*
> *1 (1) A person who without lawful excuse destroys or damages any property belonging to another intending to destroy or damage any such property or being reckless as to whether any such property would be destroyed or damaged shall be guilty of an offence.*

'Destroys or damages'

This is a question of fact and degree. It includes physical harm, whether permanent or temporary, and the permanent or temporary impairment or usefulness of property. It may occur in many ways. One test would seem to be whether the owner of property is put to expense in cleaning or repairing the property. Thus, in *Hardman v Chief Constable of Avon and Somerset* (1986), drawing or painting on the pavement even with water-soluble chalks or paints was 'damage' because the local authority was put to expense in cleaning the pavement. But spitting on a policeman's coat does not constitute damage where the spittle can be removed with a damp cloth (*A* [1978]). However, if the policeman's coat had required dry-cleaning then spitting would have been damage.

The nature of the property may also be relevant. In *Morphitis v Salmon* (1990) the Divisional Court held that a scratch to a scaffolding bar could not constitute damage as it involved no impairment of its value or usefulness. But a scratch to the bonnet of a car would be damage as the owner would expect to have this repaired.

Alteration, tampering, etc.

Property can be damaged where it is simply tampered with, or parts are removed from it, especially if the property is machinery so that it no longer works. Where D has removed parts from a machine he should be charged with damaging the machine, not the parts, unless they have also been damaged.

Damage to computer programs

Does the Criminal Damage Act 1971 apply to damage done to computer programs? Fortunately, such difficulties have been avoided by the passage of the Computer Misuse Act 1990, s.3(6) which provides that 'For the purposes of the Criminal Damage Act 1971 a modification of the contents of a computer shall not be regarded as damaging any computer or computer storage medium unless its effect on that computer or computer storage medium impairs its physical condition.' Instead, a new offence of 'unauthorised modification of computer material' has been created by s.3(1) of the 1990 Act.

'Property'

Criminal Damage Act 1971

10 (1) In this Act 'property' means property of a tangible nature, whether real or personal, including money and-

(a) including wild creatures which have been tamed or are ordinarily kept in captivity, and any other wild creatures or their carcasses if, but only if, they have been reduced into possession which has not been lost or abandoned or are in the course of being reduced into possession; but
(b) not including mushrooms growing wild on any land or flowers, fruit or foliage of a plant growing wild on any land.

This is similar to the definition of property in s.4 of the Theft Act 1968, with some differences. First, land cannot be stolen, though it can, and often is (especially arson to buildings) damaged. Second, wild plants and flowers cannot be damaged but they can, in certain circumstances, be stolen. Thirdly, property in the 1971 Act is confined to tangible property.

'Belonging to another'

S.10(2) of the 1971 Act provides that property belongs to another if that person has:

- custody or control of it, or

- has any proprietary right or interest in it, or

- has a charge on it.

It is possible for D to commit criminal damage of property which he actually owns if V has a proprietary interest in it. Suppose D hires his car to V but tampers with the engine, this may be criminal damage as V has a proprietary interest in the car.

'Intention'

Under s.1(1) it must be proved both that D intended to damage property belonging to another. If he honestly intended to damage his own property, but mistakenly damaged V's, then that is insufficient. In *Smith* (1974), D, the tenant in a flat, damaged certain fixtures that he had installed when removing wiring for his stereo equipment. He believed that the fixtures belonged to him, when in law they became the property of the landlord. His conviction was quashed because he did not intend to 'damage property belonging to another'.

'Recklessness'

See Chapter 3.

Aggravated criminal damage

Criminal Damage Act 1971

1 (2) A person who without lawful excuse destroys or damages any property, whether belonging to himself or another –

(a) intending to destroy or damage any property or being reckless as to whether any property would be destroyed or damaged; and
(b) intending by the destruction or damage to endanger the life of

another or being reckless as to whether the life of another would be thereby endangered;

shall be guilty of an offence.

Professor Sir John Smith has criticised the inclusion of the aggravated offence because it introduces an *offence against the person* into the Criminal Damage Act 1971, a statute that is designed to deal with offences against property. The decision in *Merrick* (1995) illustrates this point. In that case, D was convicted of aggravated criminal damage when, in removing old electrical equipment, he left live wires exposed for about six minutes. The Court of Appeal held that this created a risk of endangering life, and D had been reckless with respect to that risk. Yet, if D had left live wires exposed when installing new equipment, there would be no offence, because there would have been no damage! Yet the dangerous situation is exactly the same. Surely, both situations should be illegal (i.e. an offence of creation of danger to life, for example), or neither.

Actus reus
This is largely the same as for criminal damage, although the property may belong to D himself. If D, frustrated that his car will not start, starts shooting at it with a rifle, oblivious as to whether anyone might get hit by flying glass or metal, he might be liable under s.1(2).

No requirement that life be endangered in fact
The fact that lives were not, in fact, endangered is irrelevant if it was D's intention to endanger life or, more likely, that he was reckless whether life would be endangered. In *Sangha* (1988), D, who had been drinking all day, set fire to a mattress and two chairs in his neighbour's flat in Southall. The flat, which was gutted, was unoccupied at the time. Moreover, the block itself was of a particular design, such that the occupants of neighbouring flats were not, in fact, endangered. When charged under s.1(2), D argued that this meant he was not reckless as to whether life would be endangered. However, the Court of Appeal upheld his conviction. Tucker J said that the fact that there were 'special features' which prevented a risk of death from materialising was 'irrelevant'. Tucker J said:

> The test to be applied is this: is it proved that an ordinary prudent bystander would have perceived an obvious risk that property would be damaged and that life would thereby be endangered? The ordinary prudent bystander is not deemed to be invested with expert knowledge relating to the construction of the property, nor to have the benefit of hindsight. The time at which the perception is relevant is the time when the fire started.

Mens rea

The Crown must prove that D's state of mind was one of the following:

- *intent* to damage property, and *intent* by that damage to endanger the life of another; or

- *intent* to damage property, and *recklessness* as to whether life would thereby be endangered; or

- *recklessness* as to whether property would be damaged, and *recklessness* as to whether life would thereby be endangered.

D must intend that, or be reckless whether, life would be endangered by the damage that he causes, not by the means employed to cause the damage. This point was established in *Steer* (1988). D had fired a rifle through V's bungalow window. His conviction of aggravated criminal damage was quashed – it had not been proven that he had been reckless whether lives would be endangered by the damage, i.e. by shards of broken glass flying around, as opposed to being endangered by the act which caused the damage, namely the bullets.

Steer was distinguished in two Court of Appeal cases heard in 1995, *Webster*, *Asquith and Seamans* and *Warwick*. In the former case the three defendants pushed a heavy stone from the parapet of a railway bridge onto the roof of a passenger train, showering the passengers with debris; in the latter case D had thrown bricks at a police car from a stolen car, smashing the rear window and showering the officers with broken glass. In both cases the court decided that the defendants had been reckless whether lives would be endangered by the damage they had caused and upheld their convictions.

> D drops a brick from a motorway fly-over onto the windscreen of a car travelling at 70mph in the middle lane. The brick hits the passenger side of the windscreen and shatters it; the brick lands on the passenger seat. The driver, who was alone in the car, swerves in shock but manages to avoid hitting other cars and eventually regains control, moves over onto the hard shoulder and stops. If D is charged with aggravated criminal damage, would you convict him?

'Without lawful excuse'

There are two 'lawful excuses' contained in s.5(2) of the 1971 Act.

- Belief in consent (s.5(2)(a))

- Belief that other property was in immediate need of protection (s.5(2)(b))

S.5(3) states that 'it is immaterial whether a belief is justified or not, provided it is honestly held'. It need not be a reasonable belief – though the more unreasonable the belief, the more likely that D will simply not be believed. However, if D's belief was the result of extreme intoxication, it will nevertheless provide him with a good excuse under s.5(2). Indeed, in *Jaggard v Dickinson* (1980), the court accepted a defence under s.5(2)(a) based on a drunken belief that would in all probability never have been accepted had D been sober at the time. Once D has adduced evidence of lawful excuse, the onus is on the prosecution to disprove it.

Belief in consent: s.5(2)(a)

Under s.5(2)(a), D has a lawful excuse if, at the time of the alleged criminal damage he believed that the person(s) 'whom he believed to be entitled to consent to the destruction of or damage' – not necessarily the owner – either:

- had so consented, or

- would have done so if he or they had known of the destruction or damage and its circumstances.

If D honestly believes that the owner of property (or some other person entitled to give consent) has consented to his damaging property, then no offence of criminal damage is committed. In *Denton* (1982), D, a cotton mill worker, thought that his employer had asked him to set fire to the mill and the machinery in order to make a fraudulent insurance claim. One evening D entered the mill and set fire to the machinery, and caused £40,000 damage. The Court of Appeal quashed his conviction, applying s.5(2)(a).

The 'person entitled to consent' must be a human being or corporate body. In *Blake v DPP* (1993), D, a vicar, had been convicted of criminal damage. Using a marker-pen he wrote a Biblical quotation on a concrete pillar at the Houses of Parliament, as part of a protest against the use of military force in Kuwait and Iraq. In his defence he claimed to be carrying out the instructions of God, and so had a lawful excuse under s.5(2)(a). This meant that God was the person entitled to consent to the damage of property. This defence was rejected and D's conviction was confirmed.

Belief that other property was in immediate need of protection: s.5(2)(b)

D is not guilty of criminal damage if he destroyed or damaged property 'in order to protect property belonging to himself or another', provided he believed that:

- the other property was 'in immediate need of protection' and

- the means of protection adopted were 'reasonable having regard to all the circumstances'

In order to protect property

It is for the court to determine whether, as a matter of law, D's purpose was to protect property. If D has some ulterior motive other than protecting his or another's property then this defence will not be available. In *Hunt* (1978), D, who assisted his wife in her post as deputy warden of a block of old people's flats, set alight to some bedding in order, he claimed, to draw attention to the state of a defective fire alarm. The judge withdrew the defence; this was upheld in the Court of Appeal. The act was not done to protect property.

The case of *Hill* (1988) provides a good illustration of the application of s.5(2)(b). The Court of Appeal held that the correct approach was to decide whether it could be said, as a matter of law, on the facts believed by D, that the damage or destruction had been done in order to protect property or a right or interest in property.

Hill (1988)

Valerie Hill was a member of CND (the Campaign for Nuclear Disarmament). She claimed that, by cutting the fence surrounding the US naval base at Brawdy, a strategic military target, she was protecting her nearby home from blast-damage or radiation fall-out in the event of a Russian nuclear missile strike on the base. If enough people cut the fence and irritated the Americans enough they might move the base somewhere else. However, she was convicted and the Court of Appeal dismissed her appeal, holding that her purpose was not to protect her property but to get the US navy out.

In *Blake v DPP* (1993), above, D also claimed he was damaging government property in order to protect the property of others (i.e. civilians in Kuwait and Iraq). This was also rejected. B's damage was not capable of protecting property in those countries.

In April 2000, a criminal damage case was brought against Lord Melchett, a director of Greenpeace, and several members of that organisation, accusing them of damaging genetically modified (GM) crops in a Norfolk field. They did not deny the damage but relied upon s.5(2)(b), claiming that the damage was done in order to protect non-GM crops in neighbouring fields from contamination with airborne GM pollen. The judge at Norwich Crown Court allowed the defence to go to the jury, but the jury was unable to agree on a verdict and a retrial was ordered. At the retrial, the new jury acquitted.

The adoption of an objective test for this question is odd: how can a purpose be anything other than subjective? The position should be that if D honestly believed he was protecting his or another's property, s.5(2)(b) should apply (subject to the two questions below). The fact that, objectively, his chosen methods are incapable of achieving D's purpose is, really, irrelevant.

D must believe he is acting in order to protect 'property'. If D is acting in order to protect human life, for example, he is not covered by the Act. In *Baker and Wilkins* (1997), B and W were charged with causing criminal damage to the door of a house, in which they believed B's daughter was being held, in order to rescue her. On appeal against conviction they argued s.5(2)(b), unsuccessfully.

Belief that property was in immediate need of protection
It is up to D to provide evidence that he held this belief, and for the prosecution to disprove that he held it. While D's beliefs may be (objectively) wholly unreasonable, this is not fatal to the defence; but the more unreasonable D's beliefs appear, the less likely it is that the court will believe D.

D must adduce evidence that they believed the other property was in *immediate* need of protection. In *Hill* (1988), above, D was forced to admit that she did not expect a nuclear bomb 'to fall today, or tomorrow', which clearly counted against her.

Belief that the means adopted were reasonable having regard to all the circumstances
In *Hill* (1988), the Court of Appeal held that the test is whether, on the facts as D believed them to be, the measures taken could be said, objectively, to amount to something reasonably done to protect D's property or some right or interest of his in property. That is, it is not for D to say that he thought the means adopted were reasonable but whether the court thinks that they were.

No application to the aggravated offence
The provisions of s.5(2) do not apply to aggravated criminal damage. Thus, the fact that D believes that he has consent, or believes other property is in immediate need of protection, is irrelevant if D damages or destroys property intending to or being reckless whether life be endangered.

Arson and aggravated arson

Criminal Damage Act 1971

1 (3) An offence committed under this section by destroying or damaging property by fire shall be charged as arson.

Actus reus

For arson there must be some damage or destruction 'by fire'. The damage need not be severe. It would be sufficient that wood was charred, or that some material was singed. However, it would seem that blackening property by smoke would be insufficient, as there is no damage or destruction 'by fire'.

Mens rea

To be liable for arson, D must intend to destroy or damage property, or be reckless whether property is destroyed or damaged, by fire. Similarly, to be liable for aggravated arson, D must intend to endanger life, or be reckless whether life be endangered, by fire.

Summary

- There are four main criminal damage offences: criminal damage, aggravated criminal damage, arson and aggravated arson. There are also related offences of threatening criminal damage and possessing anything with intent to commit criminal damage.

- Damage is defined very widely – property is damaged if the owner of property is put to expense in cleaning or repairing it (*Roe v Kingerlee*).

- With the aggravated offence, D must intend or be reckless whether life be endangered by the damage itself, not by the means of causing the damage (*Steer, Webster, Asquith and Seamans, Warwick*).

- There is no requirement that anyone's life be endangered in fact (*Sangha*).

- Two defences of lawful excuse are available – but only if D is charged with criminal damage, not aggravated criminal damage.

- D may have a defence to criminal damage if he honestly believed that he had consent to damage or destroy property (*Denton*).

- D may have a defence to criminal damage if he did it in order to protect other property provided he honestly believed that the other property was in immediate need of protection, and that the means adopted to do so were reasonable.

- Whether D acted in order to protect other property is a question of law (*Hunt, Hill*).

Questions on Part 4 Offences against property

1 Fingers was a professional thief. He went into a branch of the National Building Bank and waited for a customer to make a large cash withdrawal. Brenda came into the bank and drew out £400. Fingers watched her put the money into her purse which she then placed into her bag. While she was distracted by someone dropping some coins on the floor Fingers took the purse from her bag. Brenda realised what was happening , and shouted out. Fingers dropped the purse and went to run out of the bank. Kevin, a customer, tried to block his way but Fingers pushed him aside causing him to fall and bruise his arm.

   Once outside, Fingers immediately hailed a taxi and asked the driver to take him to the railway station. When they arrived at the station Fingers asked if he could pay by cheque and the taxi driver reluctantly agreed. Fingers 'paid' with a stolen cheque.

   Discuss Fingers' criminal liability.

   (OCR 1998)

2 Discuss whether the law relating to dishonesty and appropriation in theft is now in a satisfactory state.

   (OCR 1995)

3. Hugh and Keith, who are both aged 18, are cocaine addicts sharing a squat. They frequently steal goods which they sell to finance their habit. Hugh knows that his father, Colin, has put a mountain bike in the shed at the top of his garden saying that he doesn't use it any more. One night, Hugh sneaks round to his father's house and takes the bike with a view to selling it. Keith drinks half a bottle of whisky and, while Hugh is out, searches through Hugh's jacket intending to take any money he might find. He doesn't find any so he drinks the rest of the bottle of whisky and walks down to the local supermarket. There he places several items inside his coat unaware that Aziza, a store detective, is watching him. As soon as he passes the cash till without paying for any of the items Aziza stops him. Keith pushes Aziza aside causing her to fall and bruise her arm. Keith then runs out of the store.

   Advise Hugh and Keith of their criminal liability.

   (OCR 2000)

Part 5

Defences

General introduction

This Part of the book deals in detail with those defences that are often termed general defences. We have already seen that there are special and partial defences that may be raised on a murder charge and that the defence of consent has specific relevance to offences against the person. In addition, s.2 of the Theft Act provides the so-called 'partial dishonesty defences' which may allow a jury to conclude that a defendant on a charge of theft has not acted in a dishonest manner when appropriating property belonging to another.

Lest this should appear confusing the following chart may assist in clarifying when particular defences may be raised in the context of various offences.

Figure 6 Table showing the relationship between offences/defences

Defence / Offence	Duress	Diminished responsibility	Provocation	Automatism	Insanity	Intox	Self defence
Murder	no defence	guilty of voluntary manslaughter	guilty of voluntary manslaughter	acquittal	special verdict hospital	guilty of involuntary manslaughter	acquittal
Involuntary manslaughter	acquittal	no	no	acquittal	special verdict discretion	no defence	acquittal
s.18	acquittal	no	no	acquittal	special verdict discretion	guilty of s.20	acquittal
s.20, s.47 and battery	acquittal	no	no	acquittal	special verdict discretion	no defence	acquittal

14 Intoxication

Introduction

Beginning on a Sunday morning and continuing until Monday night, Robert Majewski went on a 36-hour drugs and drink marathon. Over that time he consumed a combination of barbiturates, amphetamines (speed), and alcohol. On the Monday evening he got involved in a pub brawl and assaulted a customer, the manager and several police officers sent to deal with him. He was eventually arrested and charged with three offences of assault occasioning actual bodily harm and three offences of assaulting a police officer in the execution of his duty. His defence was that he was suffering from the effects of the alcohol and drugs at the time. He claimed that he was intoxicated, that this prevented him from foreseeing the consequences of his actions, that he was not, therefore, reckless in the *Cunningham* sense, and hence not guilty.

Would you allow him a defence?

Although Robert Majewski's intake of intoxicants was fairly extreme, hundreds if not thousands of people get involved in drink and/or drug related violence every week. Everyone knows that alcohol and other intoxicants affect our ability to think clearly and coolly, to react appropriately in certain situations. Alcohol is described as a 'depressant'. This does not mean that it makes you depressed! But it does 'depress' your inhibitions and other, more sophisticated, brain functions. If alcohol and/or drugs were to be allowed as a defence to crimes such as assault, rape and criminal damage (on the basis that it prevented D from foreseeing the consequences of his or her actions) then a very dangerous message would be sent out: basically, the more intoxicated you get, the stronger your potential defence! Unsurprisingly, therefore, the law does not allow intoxication as a general defence.

In *DPP v Majewski* (1977), D was convicted of all charges after the trial judge directed the jury that they should ignore the effect of drink and drugs. Effectively they were told to look at what he did and convict him if satisfied that he would have had the necessary *mens rea* had he been completely sober. The Court of Appeal and House of Lords upheld his convictions.

Legal principle *vs* public policy

Intoxication is not a true defence, like duress: it is no excuse for D to say that they would not have acted as they did but for their intoxication. Instead, it is a means of putting doubt into the minds of the jury as to whether D formed the necessary *mens rea*. Alcohol and many other drugs – barbiturates, amphetamines (speed and 'E'), hallucinogens (LSD), tranquilisers – all have an influence on a person's perception, judgement and self-control, and their ability to foresee the consequences of their actions. In extreme cases, D may be so drunk that they are rendered an automaton.

Generally, if enough members of the jury form a reasonable doubt as to D's *mens rea* then they are required to acquit. This creates a dilemma for the law. Application of legal principle would mean that the more intoxicated D became, the better their chances of acquittal. Policy demands the opposite. The law has tried to achieve a compromise, but perhaps inevitably it is policy that has prevailed.

D's intoxication must be extreme in order to prevent them from foreseeing *any* of the consequences of their actions. Lord Simon in *DPP v Majewski*, however, was not convinced that matters should be left entirely to the jury. He thought that, without special rules for intoxicated defendants, the public would be 'legally unprotected from unprovoked violence where such violence was the consequence of drink or drugs having obliterated the capacity of the perpetrator to know what he was doing or what were its consequences.'

Of course the criminal law should seek to protect the public from violence. But surely the number of cases where D might escape conviction – if the matter were simply left to the jury – would be very few. The approach of the leading courts in New Zealand (*Kamipeli* [1975]) and Australia (*O'Connor* [1980]) has been to leave the question of D's intoxication to the jury in all cases. The result has not been a proliferation of acquittals.

As well as protecting the public, the law must also protect the rights of the individual, including D. However, this issue did not unduly trouble Lord Elwyn-Jones LC in *DPP v Majewski*. His attitude was that those who caused harm while intoxicated should not be allowed to go unpunished. He said: 'If a man of his own volition takes a substance which causes him to cast off the restraints of reason and conscience, no harm is done by holding him answerable criminally for any harm he may do while in that condition.'

The evidential burden

D is required to adduce evidence of intoxication before the matter becomes a live issue. The question of whether D's intoxication is sufficient is a question of law for the judge. In *Groark* (1999), D had, apparently, consumed 10 pints of beer before striking V in the face with a 'knuckleduster'. He was charged with wounding with intent to do GBH under s.18 OAPA. At trial he gave evidence that he had known what he was doing but that he had acted in self-defence. The judge, therefore, did not direct the jury as to intoxication and D was convicted of the s.18 offence. The Court of Appeal dismissed his appeal: because D had not raised the defence, then there was no obligation on the judge to do so. The same conclusion was reached in *McKnight* (2000).

> Compare the approach of the Court of Appeal in *Groark* (1999) with that of the same court in *Rossiter* (1994), which was considered in Chapter 6. Both cases involved defendants pleading self-defence (as a tactical move, hoping for an acquittal) but having that defence rejected and appealing against their convictions. Rossiter's appeal was successful because the judge should have directed the jury on provocation; Groark's appeal was dismissed. But why? If there is an obligation on the judge to direct the jury on provocation, why not intoxication?

Voluntary intoxication

The present law is comparatively lenient. Until the mid-nineteenth century, voluntary intoxication was not regarded as any form of defence at all. But as time passed the courts began to relax the strict approach. In *DPP v Beard* (1920), Lord Birkenhead considered the situation where D pleaded intoxication to deny malice aforethought, the *mens rea* for murder. He concluded that, if D was rendered incapable of forming the intent to kill or cause GBH, then he would not be guilty of murder, but would be guilty of manslaughter. He emphasised that intoxication was merely a means of demonstrating that D lacked, on a particular charge, the mental element necessary:

> Where a specific intent is an essential element in the offence, evidence of a state of drunkenness rendering the accused incapable of forming such an intent should be taken into consideration in order to determine whether he had in fact formed the intent necessary to constitute the particular crime.

This principle has remained largely unchanged since, though it is now firmly accepted that D need not be incapable of forming intent; it is sufficient if he does not in fact do so. Conversely, D may be very drunk indeed and yet still form the *mens rea* required. According to *Sheehan* (1975), where D raises intoxication in an attempt to show lack of *mens rea*, the jury should be directed as follows:

> The mere fact that the defendant's mind was affected by drink so that he acted in a way in which he would not have done had he been sober does not assist him at all, provided that the necessary intention was there. A drunken intent is nevertheless an intent.

This was essentially the outcome in *Groark*, above. Indeed, the cases where any defendant has successfully avoided conviction on account of intoxication are very rare.

Basic and specific intent

In *Beard* Lord Birkenhead used the expression 'specific intent'. By this he meant that where a particular crime required a particular intent to be proven, then the case was not made out until that proof was achieved. At no point did Lord Birkenhead refer to anything called 'basic intent'. Nevertheless, his analysis was developed into a legal doctrine, according to which crimes divide into two categories. In *Bratty* (1963), Lord Denning said:

> If the drunken man is so drunk that he does not know what he is doing, he has a defence to any charge, such as murder or wounding with intent, in which a specific intent is essential, but he is still liable to be convicted of manslaughter or unlawful wounding for which no specific intent is necessary, see *Beard's* case.

In *DPP v Majewski* (1977), Lord Elwyn-Jones LC said that 'self-induced intoxication, however gross and even if it has produced a condition akin to... automatism, cannot excuse crimes of basic intent such as... assault.' One objection to the denial of the intoxication defence in basic intent crimes is based on s.8 of the Criminal Justice Act 1967. This statutory provision requires juries, when deciding whether D was reckless, to consider all the evidence before deciding whether D foresaw the results of his actions. However, in *DPP v Majewski*, Lord Elwyn-Jones LC dismissed this argument. He said that when s.8 refers to 'all the evidence' it only means 'all the relevant evidence'. Because intoxication was irrelevant as far as basic intent crimes are concerned, then evidence of intoxication was also irrelevant.

> Do you agree with Lord Elwyn-Jones on this point?

Distinguishing basic and specific intent offences

DPP v Majewski, then, confirms the distinction between crimes of specific and basic intent. However, it does not tell us which offences belong in which category. One explanation that was rejected in *Majewski* is the 'fallback' argument. This would limit specific intent crimes to those where D, were he to be acquitted because of intoxication, would only convict himself of some lesser offence of basic intent. Many specific intent offences do have this fallback; to use the examples given by Lord Denning in *Bratty*, murder has the fallback of manslaughter, wounding with intent has the fallback of unlawful wounding. However, some specific intent crimes, like theft, do not have a fallback crime. Instead, the approach that has prevailed is that:

- specific intent crimes can only be committed intentionally;

- basic intent crimes may be committed recklessly.

In *Caldwell* (1982), Lord Diplock stated that: 'self-induced intoxication is no defence to a crime in which recklessness is enough to constitute the necessary *mens rea*.' The courts have now assigned most crimes to one category or another, as follows.

Crimes of specific intent

- Murder

- Wounding with intent (s.18 OAPA)

- Causing grievous bodily harm with intent (s.18 OAPA)

- Theft

- Robbery

- Burglary

- Attempts

Crimes of basic intent

- Manslaughter (involuntary)

- Rape

- Wounding (s.20 OAPA)

- Inflicting grievous bodily harm (s.20 OAPA)

- Assault occasioning actual bodily harm (s.47 OAPA)

- Assault and battery

- Criminal damage

There are some passages in *DPP v Majewski* that suggest that D will be automatically guilty, merely because he committed the *actus reus* of a basic intent offence whilst drunk. That is, his intoxication substitutes for the *mens rea* of the offence, his intoxication is conclusive proof that he was reckless. For example, Lord Elwyn-Jones LC said that when D reduced himself to an intoxicated condition this

> supplies the evidence of *mens rea*, of guilty mind certainly sufficient for crimes of basic intent. It is a reckless course of conduct and recklessness is enough to constitute the necessary *mens rea* in assault cases... The drunkenness is itself an intrinsic, an integral part of the crime.

The other judges either agreed or made speeches to the same effect. However, in more recent cases, the courts have softened their approach. Although intoxication is still viewed as no defence to basic intent offences, simply committing the *actus reus* whilst intoxicated no longer invites an automatic conviction (*Richardson and Irwin* [1999]).

Richardson and Irwin (1999)
D, E and V were all students at Surrey University. One night, after drinking about five pints of lager each, they returned to D's accommodation and began indulging in 'horseplay' – something the group did regularly – during the course of which V was lifted over the edge of a balcony and dropped about 10 feet, suffering injury. D and

E were charged with inflicting GBH. The prosecution case was that they had foreseen a risk that dropping V from the balcony might cause him harm but, nevertheless, took that risk. Their defence was that V had consented to the horseplay and/or that his fall was an accident. The jury was directed to consider each man's foresight of the consequences on the basis of what a reasonable, sober man would have foreseen. D and E were convicted but the Court of Appeal quashed the convictions. The question was *not* what the reasonable, sober man would have foreseen, but what these particular men *would have foreseen had they not been drinking*. Clarke LJ, showing commendable insight into modern student psychology, said that, 'the defendants were not hypothetical reasonable men, but University students.'

Thus, the rule in 'basic intent' crimes appears to be that the jury should be directed to assume that D was sober, and assess what he would have foreseen in that condition. They should not consider what the reasonable man would have foreseen. Of course this is still a hypothetical question, but it is better (from the defence point of view) than the suggestions in *DPP v Majewski* that simply being drunk is automatically reckless.

Involuntary intoxication

The *Majewski* rules only apply where D was *voluntarily* intoxicated. The rules are relaxed when D becomes intoxicated without his knowledge or against his wishes. D is not entitled to be automatically acquitted but is entitled to have the evidence of intoxication considered, even where the offence is one of basic intent. If the intoxication negatives *mens rea* he is entitled to an acquittal but, if not, he remains liable, even though he would not have acted as he did had he remained sober.

In *Kingston* (1995), the House of Lords confirmed this proposition after the Court of Appeal had cast doubt upon it. The Court of Appeal had allowed D's appeal against a conviction of indecent assault contrary to s.14 of the Sexual Offences Act 1956 (a basic intent offence) on the basis that it was not his fault that he had become drunk. Academic reaction to this approach was mixed (to put it mildly). In the end the House of Lords reversed the decision of the Court of Appeal and restored the conviction.

Kingston (1995)
Barry Kingston, 48, was known to have paedophiliac and homo-

sexual tendencies. Kevin Penn, who had been hired by former business associates of Kingston's, blackmailed him. P had lured a 15-year-old boy to his flat and drugged him. While the boy was asleep, P invited K to abuse him. This he did, and P photographed and tape-recorded him doing it. K claimed that he could remember nothing about the night's events, and it appeared that P may have drugged his coffee. K was convicted of indecent assault, following a direction that the jury could convict if sure that, despite the effect of any drugs, he had still formed the *mens rea* of indecent assault. The Court of Appeal quashed the conviction but, following the Crown's appeal, the House of Lords restored the conviction.

There are four main situations where D's intoxication will be treated as involuntary, namely where the intoxicating substance was:

- taken under medical prescription, or

- commonly known to have a 'soporific or sedative' effect, or

- taken by D without his knowledge;

- taken under duress.

Where any one of these is the case then D will be entitled to have his evidence of intoxication considered, even where the crime is one of 'basic intent'.

Drugs taken under medical prescription

In *Bailey* (1983), the Court of Appeal held that there was a distinction between intoxication arising from alcohol and 'certain sorts of drugs to excess', on one hand, and intoxication arising from the unexpected side-effects of therapeutic substances, on the other. Griffiths LJ said: 'The question in each case will be whether the prosecution have proved the necessary element of recklessness.' If D knew that in taking some medicine was 'likely to make him aggressive, unpredictable or uncontrolled' then it would be open to a jury to find him reckless and hence guilty.

Bailey (1983)

John Bailey, a diabetic, had struck his ex-girlfriend's new boyfriend

over the head with an iron bar causing a 10-inch cut. He was charged
with wounding (a basic intent offence). He said that he had taken
insulin but failed to take food afterwards, which triggered a loss of
consciousness and that he therefore had no *mens rea*. The trial judge
directed the jury that, as his condition was self-inflicted, it was no
defence, and they convicted. On appeal, the Court of Appeal held that
the judge's direction was wrong. Provided it was not due to alcohol
or drugs, intoxication *could* provide a defence to a crime of basic
intent. The question was whether Bailey's conduct, in the light of his
knowledge of the likely results of taking insulin but not eating
afterwards, had been sufficiently reckless to establish the *mens rea*
necessary for the offence.

'Soporific or sedative' drugs

The next situation involves drugs that do not have an inhibition-lowering
(e.g. alcohol) or mind-expanding (e.g. LSD) effect but instead have a
'soporific or sedative' effect. An example would be intoxication caused by
tranquilisers. In such cases, the jury should again be directed to consider
whether the taking of the drug was reckless. In *Hardie* (1985), D was
depressed because his girlfriend had told him to move out of their flat.
Before leaving, he took some of her Valium tablets. He returned to the flat
that night and set fire to a wardrobe in the bedroom. He was charged with
arson, but said that he did not know what he was doing because of the
Valium. The jury was directed to ignore the effects of the tablets and they
convicted. However, the Court of Appeal quashed the conviction. Parker LJ
said:

> Valium is... wholly different in kind from drugs which are liable to
> cause unpredictability or aggressiveness... if the effect of a drug is
> merely soporific or sedative the taking of it, even in some excessive
> quantity, cannot in the ordinary way raise a conclusive presumption
> against the admission of proof of intoxication... such as would be the
> case with alcoholic intoxication or incapacity or automatism resulting
> from the self-administration of dangerous drugs.

The use of 'conclusive' in *Hardie* is to the same effect as 'without more' in
Bailey. There *may* be situations where D realises that morphine or Valium,
instead of soothing him or calming him down, might induce 'aggressive,
unpredictable conduct'. If the jury thinks that such is the case and that D
went on to take that risk, he could be said to be reckless.

Lack of knowledge

Intoxication is involuntary when, for example, D's soft drink has been drugged or 'laced' without his knowledge, as in *Kingston* itself. It is imperative that D did not know that he was taking an intoxicating substance. It is no defence for D to claim that he did not know exactly what effect an intoxicating substance would have on him. Otherwise, people experimenting with drugs would be able to claim a defence. In *Allen* (1988), D was given some home-made wine, which he did not realise had a particularly high alcohol content. As a result he became extremely drunk and in that state carried out a serious sexual assault. He was convicted of buggery and indecent assault and the Court of Appeal upheld the convictions. There was no evidence that Allen's drinking was anything other than voluntary.

However, D may be able to rely upon a defence of involuntary intoxication when his drink is spiked with an entirely different type of intoxicant. In *Eatch* (1980), D had smoked a small amount of cannabis and then drunk a can of beer to which another, stronger drug had been added without his knowledge. The judge directed the jury that it was up to them to decide whether D's condition was 'due solely to voluntary intoxication'.

Intoxication under duress

Although the question has not been judicially considered in England, there is American authority for the proposition that 'intoxication under duress' should be regarded as involuntary.

'Dutch courage'

In *Attorney-General for Northern Ireland v Gallagher* (1963), D decided to kill his wife, bought a knife and a bottle of whisky, drank much of the whisky in order to provide himself with 'Dutch courage', then killed her with the knife. He was convicted of murder, the jury deciding that he had formed the specific intent for murder at the time of the stabbing, despite being drunk, and this was upheld by the House of Lords. Lord Denning, however, went on to consider, obviously *obiter*, what the outcome would have been if the jury had decided that D was too drunk to form the specific intent when he stabbed his wife. He concluded that D would not be entitled to a defence:

> If a man, whilst sane and sober, forms an intention to kill and makes preparation for it knowing it is a wrong thing to do, and then gets himself drunk so as to give himself Dutch courage to do the killing, and whilst drunk carries out his intention, he cannot rely on this self-induced drunkenness as a defence to murder, not even as reducing it to manslaughter.

Intoxication and other defences

Insanity

Where intoxication produces insanity as defined in the M'Naghten Rules (see Chapter 15) then those latter rules apply. In *Davis* (1881), where D claimed that a history of alcohol abuse had caused the disease called *delirium tremens*, and based his defence on insanity, Stephen J directed the jury that, 'Drunkenness is one thing and disease to which drunkenness leads are different things.' This was approved by the House of Lords in both *DPP v Beard* and *Gallagher*. Some American states allow an insanity defence where intoxication has produced temporary insanity.

Automatism

An act done in a state of (non-insane) automatism (see Chapter 16) will negative criminal liability *except* where the state is self-induced, this is most obviously the case where it is due to intoxication. In such cases the normal *DPP v Majewski* approach applies. *Lipman* (1970) is the clearest example of this. Robert Lipman and his girlfriend, Claudie Delbarre, had taken the hallucinogenic drug LSD before falling asleep in her flat. During the night Lipman went on a 'trip', where he thought he was at the centre of the Earth under attack from snakes. When he awoke, Claudie was dead. She had been strangled and had 8 inches of sheet stuffed into her mouth. Lipman was convicted of manslaughter, even though at the time of the killing he was an automaton, and the Court of Appeal confirmed the conviction. In *Sullivan* (1984), Lord Diplock stated that the defence of automatism did not apply when 'self-induced by consuming drink or drugs'.

Developments in Canada: the rule in Daviault

There has been a very interesting development in Canada in this area. Until recently the law in Canada was essentially exactly the same as in England, with crimes divided into specific intent and basic intent categories. However, in *Daviault* (1995) the Supreme Court of Canada held that a defence of intoxication could be available for a person charged with a basic intent offence, if the intoxication was so extreme as to have produced a state of automatism. The burden of proof is on D to prove this automatism, on the balance of probabilities. The sort of extreme drunkenness required, for the new rule to apply, would obviously be very rare. Expert evidence would be required to confirm that D was probably in an automatic state. Having established this new rule, the Court quashed D's conviction of sexual assault (equivalent to the basic intent crime of indecent assault in English law) and ordered a retrial. The trial judge had naturally ruled out evidence that D was intoxicated, although this was fairly extreme: he had consumed a bottle of brandy and several bottles of beer.

> Do you prefer the approach of English courts (Lipman, Sullivan), or the Canadian courts (Daviault), to self-induced automatism?

Diminished responsibility

The impact of intoxicants on the defence of diminished responsibility was considered in Chapter 6.

Mistake

The issue of intoxicated mistakes will be dealt with in Chapter 17.

Reform

The Law Commission's Criminal Code Bill (1989) confirmed the *Majewski* rule for voluntary intoxication. Clause 22(1) provides that, when D is charged with a basic intent offence, i.e. one which 'requires a fault element of recklessness', and pleads voluntary intoxication, he is not automatically guilty but that he 'shall be treated... as having been aware of any risk of which he would have been aware had he been sober'. Clause 22(5) defines 'intoxicant' as 'alcohol or other thing which, when taken into the body, may impair awareness or control' and 'voluntary intoxication' as 'the intoxication of a person by an intoxicant which he takes, otherwise than properly for a medicinal purpose, knowing that it is or may be an intoxicant.' Clause 22(6) deals more fully with intoxication caused by medicines. It states that 'An intoxicant, although taken for a medicinal purpose, is not properly so taken if:

(a) (i) it is not taken on medical advice; or (ii) it is taken on medical advice but the taker fails then or thereafter to comply with any condition forming part of the advice; and

(b) the taker is aware that the taking, or the failure, as the case may be, may result in his doing an act capable of constituting an offence of the kind in question.

A new offence of dangerous intoxication

It has been suggested on more than one occasion that Parliament should reform the law on intoxication by abolishing the *DPP v Majewski* rule and allowing intoxication to be used as a defence to all crimes. This would bring England into line with other common law countries like Australia and New Zealand. However, rather than stop there, it has further been suggested that a new offence, perhaps called 'dangerous intoxication', should be created.

One of the leading proponents of this reform, the Butler Committee, proposed that in the 'occasional' situation when intoxication negatived *mens rea* for a basic intent offence, then the jury should be directed to acquit of that offence but then convict D of 'dangerous intoxication', if they found that D, while voluntarily intoxicated, had done an act (or made an omission) that would have amounted to a 'dangerous offence' if it were done or made with the requisite state of mind for that offence. This new offence would never be charged in the first instance, but would only come into play when intoxication had been successfully raised as a defence to a basic intent crime.

A leading law reform body in Canada (where the law is essentially the same as in England) recommended something very similar in 1982 when they proposed that 'anyone committing what would, but for his intoxication, constitute an offence' should be convicted instead of 'criminal intoxication'. This would be subject to an affirmative defence (that is, the burden of proof is on the defence) to prove that his intoxication was due to 'fraud, duress, physical compulsion or reasonable mistake.'

More recently, the Law Commission also recommended the abolition of the *DPP v Majewski* rule and its replacement with a new offence, in a 1993 consultation document. By 1995, however, they had dramatically retreated from this after receiving very hostile criticism of their proposals and much support for the retention of the present rule. Completely contradicting their recommendations two years previously, when they had criticised the *Majewski* rule for being arbitrary and unfair, they concluded that the present law approach operated 'fairly, on the whole, and without undue difficulty'. In a very watered-down reform, they reverted back to the Draft Code by concluding that it was both 'desirable and necessary' to set out the relevant principles clearly in codified form.

A new verdict

The Butler Committee's recommendation did not have the full backing of its members. A very distinguished minority, Professors John Smith and Glanville Williams, suggested an 'improved version' of the majority's proposal: the creation of an alternative *verdict*. Under their proposal, evidence of voluntary intoxication was to be taken into account for any offence, for the purpose of determining whether D had formed an intention, 'specific or otherwise' and, in the absence of it, he would be acquitted. However, if the jury was satisfied that all the other elements of the offence other than the mental element were proved, and that D would have been aware of the risk had he not been intoxicated, they were to find him 'not guilty of the offence charged but guilty of doing the act (or making the omission) while in a state of voluntary intoxication.'

Summary

- With the defence of intoxication, two crucial distinctions must be made: between voluntary and involuntary intoxication, and between crimes of specific intent and basic intent.

- Involuntary intoxication is a defence to crimes of specific intent and basic intent (*Kingston*).

- Voluntary intoxication is a defence to a crime of specific intent (*Beard, Lipman*) but is never a defence to a crime of basic intent (*DPP v Majewski*).

- Voluntary intoxication means the consumption of alcohol and other drugs generally known to make people aggressive, unpredictable or uncontrolled.

- Involuntary intoxication occurs if D consumes an intoxicating substance under medical advice (*Bailey*), consumes an intoxicant commonly known to be 'soporific or sedative' (*Hardie*), does not know he is consuming an intoxicant, perhaps because their soft drink has been spiked (*Kingston*), or if they are forced into consuming it.

- When D pleads intoxication, whether voluntary or involuntary, they may still be convicted if, despite their intoxicated state, they formed the *mens rea* required (*Sheehan* – voluntary, *Kingston* – involuntary).

- Specific intent crimes are those that can only be committed intentionally – e.g. murder, theft, wounding with intent, causing grievous bodily harm with intent.

- Basic intent crimes are that that may be committed recklessly – e.g. manslaughter, wounding, inflicting grievous bodily harm, assault and battery, criminal damage.

- If D plans a specific intent crime but then intoxicates himself so as to give themselves the 'dutch courage' to commit it, they are still guilty of that specific intent crime (*Attorney-General for Northern Ireland v Gallagher*).

- Intoxication producing insanity is insanity (*Davis*) but intoxication producing automatism is still intoxication (*Lipman*).

Figure 7 Intoxication flowchart

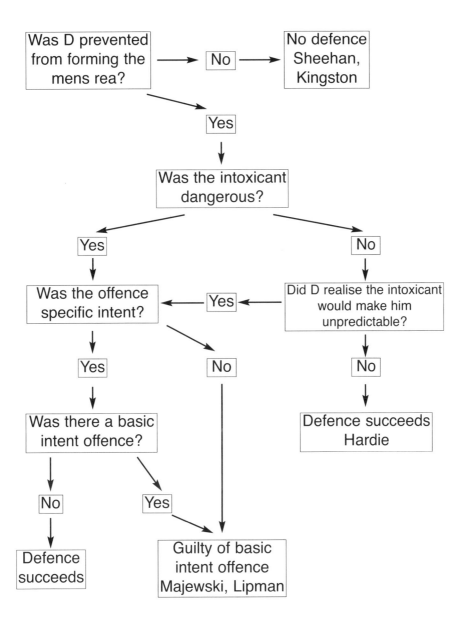

15 Insanity

Introduction

Despite everything that is written about the insanity defence, it is rarely used. Its importance had been much reduced, particularly in murder cases, by the abolition of the death penalty, and the introduction of the diminished responsibility defence.

The M'Naghten rules

The law of insanity in England is contained in the M'Naghten Rules, the result of the deliberations of the judges of the House of Lords in 1843. Media and public outcry at the acquittal of one Daniel M'Naghten led to the creation of the Rules as an attempt to clarify the defence. The joint opinion of 14 Law Lords is not binding as a matter of strict precedent. Nevertheless, the Rules have been treated as authoritative of the law ever since. The 'general part' of the Rules is as follows:

> *The jurors ought to be told in all cases that every man is presumed to be sane, and to possess a sufficient degree of reason to be responsible for his crimes, until the contrary be proved to their satisfaction; and that to establish a defence on the ground of insanity it must be clearly proved that, at the time of the committing of the act, the party accused was labouring under such a defect of reason, from disease of the mind, as not to know the nature and quality of the act he was doing, or, if he did know it, that he did not know he was doing what was wrong.*

M'Naghten (1843)
Daniel M'Naghten was charged with the murder of Sir Robert Peel's secretary, one Edward Drummond. M'Naghten was described as 'an extreme paranoiac entangled in an elaborate system of delusions', which led him to believe he was being persecuted by the 'Tories', who were to blame for various personal and financial misfortunes. He had intended to murder Sir Robert himself. Medical witnesses

testified that he was insane. The jury accepted his plea and found him not guilty on the grounds of insanity, though he was committed to Broadmoor (where he remained until his death 20 years later).

The Divisional Court has recently held that the defence is only available where *mens rea* is an element of the offence. In *DPP v H* (1997), D was charged with driving with excess alcohol – a strict liability offence. There was evidence that he was suffering 'manic depressive psychosis'. The magistrates acquitted him on insanity grounds. The prosecution appealed to the Divisional Court – where it was held that the magistrates should have convicted.

'Defect of reason'

The phrase 'defect of reason' implies that D's powers of reasoning must be impaired, as opposed to a failure by D to use those powers. In *Clarke* (1972), Ackner J said that the Rules apply only to 'persons who by reason of a 'disease of the mind' are deprived of the power of reasoning. They do not apply and never have applied to those who retain the power of reasoning but who in moments of confusion or absent-mindedness fail to use their powers to the full.'

Clarke (1972),
May Clarke went into a supermarket. She selected three items, including a jar of mincemeat, and put them into her own bag. She left the store without paying for them and was charged with theft. She claimed to have lacked the *mens rea* of theft (the intention to permanently deprive) on the basis of absent-mindedness caused by diabetes and depression. She had no recollection of putting the items into her bag. She did not even want the mincement as neither her nor her husband ate it. The trial judge ruled that this amounted to a plea of insanity, at which point she pleaded guilty. On appeal, her conviction was quashed: she had not been deprived of her powers of reasoning but had simply failed to use them.

'Disease of the mind'

'Disease of the mind' is a legal, not a medical, term. In *Kemp* (1957), D made an entirely motiveless and irrational attack on his wife with a hammer. He was charged with inflicting grievous bodily harm. He was suffering from arteriosclerosis, or hardening of the arteries, causing a congestion of blood on the brain. This produced a temporary loss of consciousness, during which time D attacked. He admitted that he was suffering a 'defect of reason', but argued that this did not arise from a 'disease of the mind'. He argued that arteriosclerosis was a physical, as opposed to mental, disease. A physical disease which caused the brain cells to deteriorate would be a disease of the mind but, until that happened, his condition was a temporary interference with the working of the brain, comparable with concussion. Therefore the true defence was automatism entitling him to an acquittal. Devlin J, rejecting this argument, held that:

> The law is not concerned with the brain but with the mind, in the sense that 'mind' is ordinarily used, the mental faculties of reason, memory and understanding. If one read for 'disease of the mind' 'disease of the brain', it would follow that in many cases pleas of insanity would not be established because it could not be proved that the brain had been affected in any way, either by degeneration of the cells or in any other way. In my judgment the condition of the brain is irrelevant and so is the question whether the condition is curable or incurable, transitory or permanent.

Sane and insane automatism
The law draws a distinction between two causes of automatism:

- Automatism caused by a 'disease of the mind' (insane automatism). Here the M'Naghten Rules apply, and the verdict should be one of not guilty by reason of insanity.

- Automatism *not* caused by a 'disease of the mind' (sane automatism). Here the verdict is an acquittal – unless D's condition was self-inflicted, e.g. by drink or drugs, as in *Lipman* (1970).

The question of whether D's condition is sane or insane automatism is one of law for the judge (*Bratty* [1963]). Judges base their decision on medical evidence. However, because disease of the mind is a legal concept, judges will also take account of policy. There have been two distinct approaches:

- The continuing danger theory, which says that any condition likely to present a recurring danger to the public should be treated as insanity;

- The external cause theory, which says that conditions stemming from the psychological or emotional makeup of the accused, rather than from some external factor, should lead to a finding of insanity.

The two theories are clearly closely linked and overlap to a considerable degree: an internal cause is more likely to recur than an external one. The continuing danger theory was the test used by English courts until 1973. Although the external cause theory was introduced into English law from New Zealand as a qualification to that test, it has since developed into a test in its own right. This has had unhappy consequences, particularly for sleepwalkers.

The continuing danger theory

The leading authority is the House of Lords case of *Bratty* (1963). D had killed an 18-year-old girl by removing one of her stockings and strangling her with it. When arrested he did not deny doing it but said that 'something terrible came over me... I had some terrible feeling and then a sort of blackness'. He claimed that it happened during an epileptic seizure. The trial judge ruled that this amounted to an insanity plea; the House of Lords upheld this. Lord Denning said:

> It seems to me that any mental disorder which has manifested itself
> in violence and is prone to recur is a 'disease of the mind'.

Lord Denning approved *Kemp* (1957) but disapproved of the earlier case of *Charlson* (1955). There, D had hit his 10-year-old son on the head with a hammer and thrown him into a river. D was charged with various offences including inflicting grievous bodily harm. Medical evidence suggested that he was suffering from a cerebral tumour that left him liable to motiveless outbursts of impulsive violence over which he would have no control. The jury acquitted after the judge directed them to consider only automatism. Under Lord Denning's direction, above, D would have been found not guilty by reason of insanity.

The converse of Lord Denning's test should not be taken to represent the law, i.e. even where there is no danger of recurrence a condition may still amount to a disease of the mind. In *Burgess* (1991), Lord Lane CJ said that 'a danger of recurrence that may be an added reason for categorising the condition as a disease of the mind' but it was not a prerequisite. Thus: the greater the likelihood of recurrence, the more likely a condition will be treated as a disease of the mind; but presence or otherwise of recurrence is not conclusive.

The first automatism case to reach the House of Lords after *Bratty* was *Sullivan* (1984). Lord Diplock, like Lord Denning before him, suggested a test based upon the likelihood of recurrence. He said that it was irrelevant whether the source of D's defect of reason was 'organic, as in epilepsy, or functional, or whether the impairment itself is permanent or is transient and intermittent, provided that it subsisted at the time of the commission of the act.'

> *Sullivan* (1984)
> Patrick Sullivan had suffered from epilepsy since childhood. He had been known to have fits and to show aggressiveness to anyone coming to his aid. One day he was sitting in a neighbour's flat with a friend of his, Mr Payne, aged 80. The next thing he remembered was standing by a window; Mr Payne was on the floor, injured. Sullivan was charged with assault. The judge ruled that his plea of automatism, based upon an epileptic seizure, amounted to a 'disease of the mind'. To avoid hospitalisation, Sullivan pleaded guilty. This was accepted and the Court of Appeal and House of Lords rejected his appeals against conviction.

The external factor theory

In 1973, the Court of Appeal adopted the external factor theory, first used by the New Zealand Court of Appeal in *Cottle* (1958). This theory was not designed to replace the recurring danger theory but to complement it. Simply put, if a disorder is internal to D, then there is a greater chance of recurrence. In *Quick* (1973), Lawton LJ said:

> A malfunctioning of the mind of transitory effect caused by the application to the body of some external factor such as violence, drugs, including anaesthetics, alcohol and hypnotic influences cannot fairly be said to be due to disease.

In *Sullivan*, Lord Diplock also gave his support to the external factor theory. He agreed that sane automatism might be available 'in cases where temporary impairment results from some external physical factor such as a blow on the head causing concussion or the administration of an anaesthetic for therapeutic purposes'. In *Hennessy* (1989), Lord Lane CJ confirmed both the external cause and recurrent danger theories. D claimed to be having marital problems that left him suffering stress, anxiety and depression. These, he argued, were external causes. Lord Lane CJ rejected the argument. He said that 'stress, anxiety and depression ... constitute a state of mind which is prone to recur. They lack the feature of novelty or accident, which is the basis of the distinction drawn by Lord Diplock in *Sullivan*.' The external cause theory has also been approved by the Supreme Court of Canada (*Rabey* [1980]).

Applying the law

In *Quick*, Lawton LJ said that 'it seems to us that the law should not give the words defect of reason from disease of the mind a meaning which would be regarded with incredulity outside a court'. How has this *dictum* been applied in practice?

Epilepsy

Epilepsy is a functional disease of the brain, characterised by seizures. It affects several hundred thousand people in the UK. Yet, in both *Bratty* and *Sullivan*, the House of Lords held that epileptics were legally insane.

Diabetes

Diabetes is a disorder of the pancreas, which results in erratic quantities of the insulin hormone being produced. Injections of insulin are needed to control the body's blood-sugar level. If the blood-sugar level gets too high or too low, a seizure may result. There are two types of diabetic seizure, which may eventually lead to a loss of consciousness. Prior to the onset of coma, however, the sufferer may become uncontrollably aggressive and violent. The two seizure types are:

- *Hypoglycaemia* (low blood-sugar), caused by taking too much insulin or by taking insulin and failing to eat afterwards;

- *Hyperglycaemia* (high blood-sugar), caused by failing to take any or enough insulin.

In the cases of *Quick* (1973) and *Hennessy* (1989), each defendant was a diabetic.

> *Quick* (1973)
> William Quick, a nurse at a mental hospital, had taken his insulin one morning but had eaten little afterwards. That afternoon he attacked a patient, causing him two black eyes, a fractured nose, a split lip and bruising. Another nurse found Quick sitting aside the patient, glassy-eyed and apparently unable to talk. He pleaded not guilty to assault; he had suffered a hypoglycaemic episode and could not remember what he had done. The judge ruled that this was a plea of insanity. Quick pleaded guilty and appealed. The Court of Appeal quashed his conviction. The cause of his automatic state was not his diabetes, but his insulin; as this was an external factor, automatism should have been left to the jury.

This creates a highly anomalous situation. One diabetic, who falls into a hypoglycaemic state is setting up automatism and should be acquitted (Quick); another diabetic, who falls into a hyperglycaemic state, must be treated as pleading insanity (*Hennessy*). If only to achieve consistency, any form of diabetic seizure should be regarded as a disease of the mind. It is a mental disorder that is prone to recur. The strange distinction has occurred because of the emphasis placed upon the external factor theory in *Quick*. It is not the theory itself which is wrong, but the application of it. What really caused Quick's automatic state? The insulin was *a* cause – but the *underlying* cause was his diabetes. In 1973, when *Quick* was decided, those found insane faced indefinite hospitalisation. Perhaps Lawton LJ was reluctant to say that an epileptic was insane and send him to Broadmoor. But in 1991, compulsory hospitalisation was abolished (for all cases except murder). It is time to recognise that *Quick* was wrongly decided.

Somnambulism

Somnambulism or sleepwalking is a sleep disorder, very common in children but also found in about 2 per cent of adults. For a long time acts committed whilst asleep were treated as raising sane automatism. However, the position has changed, as a result of the courts' emphasis, since *Quick* and *Sullivan*, on the external cause theory. In *Burgess* (1991), Lord Lane CJ said that sleepwalking was 'an abnormality or disorder, albeit transitory, due to an internal factor'.

video recorder – which he had unplugged – and then grasping her by the throat. She suffered cuts to her head. To a charge of unlawful wounding, Burgess pleaded automatism on the basis that he had been sleepwalking. The trial judge ruled he was pleading insanity and the jury returned the special verdict. The Court of Appeal dismissed his appeal.

The Supreme Court of Canada, in *Parks* (1992), took a very different view. D had got up in the middle of the night, dressed, got into his car and then drove 15 miles to the home of his in-laws where he stabbed and killed his mother-in-law and severely injured his father-in-law. Throughout this whole sequence of events he was, apparently, sleepwalking. He was charged with murder and attempted murder. At his trial, the judge left automatism to the jury, who acquitted on all charges. The Supreme Court upheld these acquittals. The leading judge held that, 'Accepting the medical evidence, the respondent's mind and its functioning must have been impaired at the relevant time but sleepwalking did not impair it. The cause was the natural condition, sleep.'

Another judge pointed out that the external cause theory was 'meant to be used only as an analytical tool, and not as an all-encompassing methodology'. Sleepwalking was not suited to analysis under the external cause theory. 'The particular amalgam of stress, excessive exercise, sleep deprivation and sudden noises in the night that causes an incident of somnambulism is, for the sleeping person, analogous to the effect of concussion upon a waking person, which is generally accepted as an external cause of non-insane automatism.'

Hence, leading courts in England and Canada have found totally different solutions to the same problem! That is not to say that one case must be right and the other wrong: there are distinguishing features. In *Parks*, there was evidence that D was under considerable pressure and stress at work, which may have triggered his sleep-walking. The implication is that, when those stresses were removed, he would not repeat his actions, i.e. there was less evidence that he might repeat his behaviour.

Dissociation

Dissociative states are medically classified as 'hysterical neuroses'. The most prominent feature is a 'narrowing' of the field of consciousness, commonly accompanied or followed by amnesia. There may be dramatic, but temporary, personality changes. A 'fugue' – wandering state – is also possible. The body remains capable of carrying out complex, purposive actions. The condition is brought on by psychological reasons, such as overwhelming emotion. The leading cases on this problem come from overseas: Canada and Australia.

In *Rabey* (1977), D had developed an attraction towards a girl. When he discovered that she regarded him as 'nothing', he hit her over the head with a rock and began to choke her. He was charged with causing bodily harm, and pleaded automatism, based on dissociation. He argued that the dissociative state was a psychological blow, akin to being physically struck on the head, and hence not a disease of the mind. The trial judge ordered an acquittal but the Ontario Court of Appeal allowed the prosecution appeal. The judge said that the 'ordinary stresses and disappointments of life which are the common lot of mankind do not constitute an external cause... the dissociative state must be considered as having its source primarily in [D's] psychological or emotional make-up'.

Note here that Lord Denning's test in *Bratty* is satisfied: where D has such a fragile personality that everyday situations are liable to make him violent, then the likelihood of recurrence is high. In *Burgess* (1991), considered above, the Crown psychologist suggested that D had not been sleepwalking at all, but had fallen into a dissociative state caused by emotional trauma (he was in love with the unfortunate Miss Curtis). The Court of Appeal, like the Canadian court in *Rabey*, thought that even if this was so, the defence was still insanity: the disappointment or frustration caused by unrequited love was not to be equated with something like concussion.

In *Rabey*, the judge referred to the 'ordinary stresses... of life'. The position, presumably, is different when there is an *extraordinary* stress. The shock of seeing a loved one murdered, for example, could cause a dissociative state in anyone. Consequently, where an event is deemed, objectively, to be extraordinary, then this qualifies it as an external cause entitling D to an acquittal. This seems to be the explanation of the decisions in *T* (1990) and *Falconer* (1990), considered in Chapter 16. In *Falconer*, the High Court of Australia distinguished mental states which 'may be experienced by normal persons', from those which are 'never experienced by or encountered in normal persons'. The former implies sane automatism, the latter insanity. Rather than concentrating exclusively on whether the cause was internal or external, the Court suggested a radical, new distinction, between the reaction of:

- a sound mind to external stimuli including stress (sane automatism), and

- an unsound mind to its own delusions or to external stimuli (insane automatism)

'Disease of the mind': a summary

On the whole, the courts in England have restricted the automatism defence. The defendant who pleads automatism based on epilepsy, diabetes or even sleepwalking faces being labelled as insane. This is perhaps justifiable where D has committed acts of violence. Yet not all the cases have involved violence, for example *Hennessy* (though it must be conceded that Hennessy was a danger to the public, driving in his condition).

Arguably, the label of insanity should not extend beyond those who, although they do not realise what they are doing, carry out acts of a violent or dangerous nature. This would cover offenders like Bratty and Burgess, who were acting in a purposive manner. On the other hand, Sullivan, who happened to strike someone while thrashing around during an epileptic fit, was not so acting. Sullivan seems to enjoy the 'feature of novelty or accident' which characterises automatism. The courts have not made such a distinction, but it would provide justice without jeopardising the policy of social protection.

Until recently, the insanity verdict meant indefinite hospitalisation and left defendants like Quick, Sullivan and Hennessy pleading guilty to offences when all the evidence pointed to a total lack of *mens rea*. With the Criminal Procedure (Insanity and Unfitness to Plead) Act 1991 relaxing the restrictions available to the judge as to disposal following the special verdict, the insanity defence becomes a more realistic prospect. Nevertheless there remains the stigma of being labelled insane. A new verdict is long overdue. Clause 35 of the Law Commission's Criminal Code Bill (1989) contains such a verdict – 'mental disorder'.

'Nature and quality of the act'

For this limb of the defence to work, D's lack of knowledge must be fundamental. An example often used is when D cuts a woman's throat under the idea that he is cutting a loaf of bread – such a person clearly does not know the 'nature and quality' of his act. In another well-known example, if D chops off a sleeping man's head because it would be great fun to see him looking for it when he wakes up, then he is not guilty of murder by reason of insanity; he does not understand the consequences of his act.

In these situations D lacks *mens rea* but, because this is due to a 'disease of the mind', he is not entitled to an acquittal but the special verdict instead. If, on the other hand, D kills a man whom he believes, because of some paranoid delusion, to be stalking him, then he is still responsible for his act because his delusion has not prevented him from understanding that he is committing murder.

'Wrong'

If D claims he did not realise that what he was doing was 'wrong', what exactly does that mean? 'Wrong' is an ambiguous concept. It could mean:

- Legally wrong (Option 1); or

- Morally wrong (Option 2); or

- Both legally and morally wrong (Option 3); or

- Either legally or morally wrong (Option 4)

In M'Naghten the Lords seemed to support Option 1, when they said that D was sane 'if he knew... that he was acting contrary to law; by which expression we... mean the law of the land.' However, they foresaw a problem with that: if a jury was to be directed 'solely and exclusively' with reference to 'the law of the land', this might confuse a jury into thinking that ignorance of the law was a defence, when it is not. So, the Lords concluded that 'If the accused was conscious that the act was one which he ought not to do, and if that act was at the same time contrary to the law of the land, he is punishable.' This seemed to indicate Option 3. Then, in *Codere* (1916), the Court of Criminal Appeal stated that D would be denied the defence if he knew his act was wrong 'according to the ordinary standard adopted by reasonable men'. This indicated that Option 2 was correct. This confusing and contradictory mess was finally resolved by the Court of Criminal Appeal in *Windle* (1952), when they supported Option 1. Lord Goddard CJ said that 'there is no doubt that... "wrong" means contrary to the law.'

Windle (1952)

Windle was unhappily married to a woman, some 18 years his senior, who was always speaking of committing suicide and who, according to medical evidence at the trial, was certifiably insane. Eventually he killed his wife by giving her 100 aspirins. On giving himself up to the police, Windle said, 'I suppose they will hang me for this?' Despite medical evidence that he was suffering from a form of communicated insanity known as *folie à deux*, both sides agreed that this statement showed he was aware of acting unlawfully. The defence was withdrawn from the jury, Windle was convicted of murder. The Court of Criminal Appeal upheld the conviction.

> If the facts of Windle occurred now, what defence (other than insanity) would you advise him to plead?

The position therefore is: Option 1. If D did not realise his act was illegal then he is entitled to the special verdict. If D knew his act was illegal, then he is guilty. This is the case even if D is suffering from delusions which cause him to believe that his act was morally right.

> Suppose D believes his mother is possessed and being tortured by demons. He has enough of a grasp on reality to realise that killing her is the crime of murder, but is nevertheless convinced that to do so would be 'right', in the moral sense of the word. He tries to kill her but fails to do so. If charged with attempted murder (where there is no diminished responsibility defence) should he be guilty or have the defence of insanity?

In Australia and Canada, meanwhile, the highest courts have refused to follow *Windle* and decided that morality, and not legality, is the concept behind the use of 'wrong'; that is, Option 2 (*Stapleton* [1952] – High Court of Australia; *Chaulk* [1991] – Supreme Court of Canada). Finally, in Northern Ireland, the defence of insanity is available if the defendant is prevented from appreciating that what he is doing is either morally wrong or illegal: that is, Option 4.

> What should 'wrong' mean – legally, morally, either or both?

The presumption of sanity

If D wishes to raise the insanity defence he must do more than simply introduce evidence to that effect and invite the prosecution to rebut it. Instead the defence are required to prove that D was insane, albeit on a balance of probabilities. This proposition stems from M'Naghten itself. It was confirmed in the celebrated case of *Woolmington v DPP* (1935), where Viscount Sankey said

> Throughout the web of the English Criminal Law one golden thread is always to be seen, that it is the duty of the prosecution to prove the prisoner's guilt subject to... the defence of insanity.

However, just because the courts have adopted a presumption of sanity does not explain *why* the legal burden of proving D's insanity lies on D. A presumption of sanity need mean no more than that D bears a burden of introducing evidence of insanity, sufficient to raise a reasonable doubt. This is the position with other defences, such as provocation and duress. But remember that in diminished responsibility the burden of proof is also on D.

'Irresistible impulses'

Until the early twentieth century, a plea of 'irresistible impulse', that D was physically unable to control his actions, was a good defence. However, in *Kopsch* (1925), the law was changed. Lord Hewart CJ described the irresistible impulse argument as a 'fantastic theory' which, if it were to become part of the law, 'would be merely subversive'. The reluctance of the courts to recognise a defence of irresistible impulse is based on two grounds:

- The difficulty of distinguishing between an impulse caused by a disease of the mind, and one motivated by greed, jealousy or revenge;

- The view that the harder an impulse is to resist, the greater is the need for a deterrent.

In 1953, the Royal Commission on Capital Punishment suggested adding a third limb to the M'Naghten Rules, that D should be considered insane if at the time of his act he 'was incapable of preventing himself from committing it.' Although this was not taken up, the Commission report led to the introduction of the diminished responsibility defence; this, in turn, has allowed the irresistible impulse defence into murder (*Byrne* [1960]).

In the United States, irresistible impulse defences are accepted. The American Law Institute's Model Penal Code (not unlike the Law Commission's Criminal Code Bill (1989), except that this has been converted into legislation in many states) includes a defence of insanity. This is available if, as a result of mental disease or defect, D lacks 'substantial capacity' either to appreciate the criminality/wrongfulness of his conduct or to 'conform his conduct to the requirements of law.' This version of the defence was widely adopted at one time but, in the immediate aftermath of the attempted assassination of President Reagan by John Hinckley in 1982, the American Congress passed the Insanity Defense Reform Act 1984. This removed the irresistible impulse defence in cases where D was charged with federal crimes.

The special verdict

If D is found to have been insane then the jury should return a verdict of 'not guilty by reason of insanity' (s.1, Criminal Procedure (Insanity) Act 1964), otherwise referred to as the *special verdict*. Until quite recently this verdict obliged the judge to order D to be detained indefinitely in a mental hospital. In many cases the dual prospect of being labelled 'insane' and indefinite detention in a special hospital such as Broadmoor discouraged defendants from putting their mental health in issue. In some cases it led to guilty pleas to offences of which defendants were probably innocent, and relying on the judge's discretion as to sentence (*Quick, Sullivan, Hennessy*). The prevailing attitude prior to 1991 was that the special verdict was the 'psychiatric equivalent of a life sentence' (Dell, *Wanted: An Insanity Defence that can be Used* [1983]). This was, clearly, an extremely unsatisfactory state of affairs that required reform.

The 1991 reforms

The position has been modified by the Criminal Procedure (Insanity and Unfitness to Plead) Act 1991. The Act made a number of changes but, most significantly, s.3 substituted a new s.5 into the Criminal Procedure (Insanity) Act 1964. Under the new section, the judge is allowed much greater discretion with regard to disposal on a special verdict being returned. A judge now has a range of options – except in murder cases (see below). The courts' options are:

- A Hospital Order, with or without restrictions

- A Guardianship Order

- A Supervision and Treatment Order

- Absolute Discharge

The latter option is particularly useful where the offence is trivial and/or the offender does not require treatment. The new range of disposals should make the special verdict more attractive. Nevertheless, the 1991 Act does not tackle the definition of insanity, and so the stigma of being labelled 'insane' remains. Ironically, that reform may be further away than ever now that mandatory commitment has been removed.

The special verdict and murder

For those defendants charged with murder the position is unchanged; D found not guilty of murder by reason of insanity must be hospitalised indefinitely. Of course, the vast majority of defendants charged with murder plead diminished responsibility instead. One advantage of doing so is that if D is hospitalised, following conviction for manslaughter, he is entitled to be discharged by a Mental Health Review Tribunal once it is satisfied that he is no longer mentally disordered. But, if D is hospitalised following a special verdict, then his release is entirely at the discretion of the Home Secretary. On the other hand, the trial judge may impose a term of imprisonment following a manslaughter conviction, and potentially this could be a life sentence.

Procedure

Often D does not specifically raise the defence of insanity, but places the state of his mind in issue by raising another defence such as automatism. The question whether such a defence, or a denial of *mens rea*, really amounts to the defence of insanity is a question of law to be decided by the judge on the basis of medical evidence. Whether D, or his medical witnesses, would call it insanity or not is irrelevant.

Importance of medical evidence

If the judge decides the evidence *does* support the defence, then he should leave it to the jury to determine whether D was insane. S.1 of the 1991 Act provides that a jury shall not return a special verdict except on the written or oral evidence of two or more registered medical practitioners, at least one of whom being approved as having special expertise in the field of medical disorder.

The jury must act upon the evidence before them. If this points towards D being insane, but they nevertheless convict, then such a conviction may be overturned on the ground that no reasonable jury could have reached such a verdict. But, if there is evidence to the contrary, then a jury verdict will not be quashed simply because there was medical evidence supporting the defence.

Reform

Writing about the M'Naghten Rules, the academic Morris commented in 1953:

> As a rigid, precise definition of a defence to a criminal charge they are woolly, semantically confused, psychologically immature nonsense [but] as a means whereby juries work rough justice in a difficult peripheral area of law and morality they are reasonably satisfactory.

Various criticisms that can be made about the M'Naghten Rules include:

- The word 'insanity' is itself inappropriate in many cases and stigmatising in all of them. The Butler Committee and, more recently, the Law Commission's Criminal Code Bill (1989), at least recommend a change to 'mental disorder' – defined broadly so as to include mental illness, arrested or incomplete development of mind, and psychopathic disorders. This change has also been effected in Canada.

- The defence is based on a legal definition of insanity, not a medical one. 'Disease of the mind' is a meaningless concept to any psychiatrist.

- The over-reliance on the external factor test produces bizarre abnormalities (*Quick* and *Hennnessy*). It means that diabetics (sometimes), epileptics and sleepwalkers are legally, but not medically, insane.

- The emphasis on legality in deciding whether D knew his acts were 'wrong' is inappropriate and too narrow.

- There is no irresistible impulse defence.

Summary

- Insanity is subject to the M'Naghten Rules from 1843.

- Everyone is presumed to be sane. With insanity, D must prove all the elements of the defence, on the balance of probabilities.

- The result of a successful defence is the 'special verdict'. Apart from murder cases, which means indefinite hospitalisation, the judge can impose a variety of orders.

- D must be suffering a 'defect of reason'. This means being deprived of the power of reason, not simply failing to use it (*Clarke*).

- The 'defect of reason' must be the result of a 'disease of the mind'. This is a legal, not a medical, term. Whether D has such a disease is a question of law for the judge (*Bratty*).

- In determining whether D had a 'disease of the mind' judges use two tests: whether or not the disease is prone to recur (*Bratty*) and whether it was caused by an internal or external factor (*Quick, Sullivan*).

- Thus, epileptics (*Sullivan*) and sleepwalkers (*Burgess*) are insane. Diabetics who fail to take insulin are also insane (*Hennessy*). But diabetics who take too much insulin are not (*Quick*). People who suffer a dissociative state caused by emotional trauma are probably insane (*Rabey, Burgess*) – unless the trauma was extraordinary (*T, Falconer*).

- If D is suffering a disease of the mind, he must be prevented from knowing the 'nature and quality' of his act or that it was 'wrong'.

- 'Wrong' means legally, as opposed to morally, wrong (*Windle*).

- There is no irresistible impulse defence.

16 Automatism

Introduction

In *Bratty v Attorney-General for Northern Ireland* (1963), Lord Denning said that: 'The requirement that (the act of the accused) should be a voluntary act is essential ... in every criminal case. No act is punishable if it is done involuntarily.' The classic example of this is when A grabs B's hand, in which B happens to be holding a knife, and plunges the knife into C. Although B 'stabbed' C, he is excused liability. Not only does B have no *mens rea*, he also has the defence of automatism. Voluntariness is an essential element of the *actus reus*.

What is 'automatism'?

'Automatism' is a phrase that was brought into the law from the medical world. There it has a very limited meaning, describing the state of unconsciousness suffered by certain epileptics. In law it seems to have two meanings. In *Bratty*, Lord Denning said:

> Automatism... means an act which is done by the muscles without any control by the mind such as a spasm, a reflex action or a convulsion; or an act done by a person who is not conscious of what he is doing such as an act done whilst suffering from concussion or whilst sleepwalking.

Mental capacity is presumed. Hence, if D wishes to plead automatism, it is necessary for him to place evidence in support of his plea before the court. In *Hill v Baxter* (1958), Devlin J explained the reasoning behind this rule. He pointed out how 'unreasonable' it would be if in every single criminal case the Crown had to prove that D was 'not sleepwalking or not in a trance or black-out'. He concluded that 'such matters ought not to be considered at all until the defence has provided at least *prima facie* evidence' that his acts were involuntary. The evidence of D himself will rarely be sufficient, unless it is supported by medical or other evidence, because otherwise there is a possibility of the jury being deceived by spurious or fraudulent claims. It is insufficient for D to simply say 'I had a black-out' because that was 'one of the first refuges of a guilty conscience and a popular excuse', according to Lord Denning in *Bratty* (1963). Although the evidence will usually be medical it is not essential. If D's condition 'is said to be due to concussion, there should be evidence of a severe blow shortly beforehand' – Lord Denning once again.

Examples of automatism

Over the years, the courts have given a number of examples of possible causes of automatism:

- severe blows to the head,

- hypnotism,

- the administration of anaesthetic,

- being attacked by a swarm of bees (the famous *hypothetical* example given in *Hill v Baxter*).

In some cases the courts have been prepared to rule that a 'dissociative state' caused by some extraordinary event may be classed as automatism. In *T* (1990), Miss T pleaded automatism to charges of robbery and assault occasioning actual bodily harm. She had been raped three days earlier. A psychiatrist diagnosed that she was suffering post-traumatic stress disorder, and at the time of the alleged offences had entered a dissociative state. The judge allowed automatism to be left to the jury: 'such an incident could have an appalling effect on any young woman, however well-balanced normally.'

This also represents the law in Australia. In *Falconer* (1991), D shot her husband at point-blank range with a shotgun, killing him instantly. She was charged with murder. In court she testified that he had sexually assaulted her, hit her across the face and taunted her; she had also just been informed that he was facing charges of incest involving their two daughters. D claimed that she could remember nothing until he was found dead. She was convicted of murder but, on appeal, a majority of the High Court of Australia held that automatism was available.

However, in *Burgess* (1991) it was held that a dissociative state, if caused by the *ordinary* stresses of life, such as unrequited love, will be classed as insanity. This was also the decision of the Supreme Court of Canada in *Rabey* (1977). *Parks* (1991), another Canadian case, decided that somnambulism was an example of automatism, but that conflicts with the decision of the Court of Appeal in *Burgess*, where it was held that sleepwalking was an example of insanity. All of these cases were discussed fully in Chapter 15.

Extent of involuntariness required

How unconscious does D have to be before he can be said to be an automaton? There are many possible levels of consciousness. When dealing with something as abstract as 'consciousness', it is more a matter of degree. There is no clear dividing line at which point D becomes an automaton. It seems that the extent of involuntariness required to be established depends on the offence charged. There are two categories.

Crimes of strict liability

D must show that he was exercising no control over his bodily movements whatsoever. If, despite some lack of control, he was still able to appreciate what he was doing and operate his body to a degree, then the defence is not made out. The position has been demonstrated in a series of driving cases. In *Hill v Baxter* (1958), D claimed to have become unconscious as a result of being overcome by a sudden illness, the Queen's Bench Divisional Court found that the facts showed that D was 'driving', in the sense of controlling the car and directing its movements, and rejected D's plea of automatism. In *Watmore v Jenkins* (1962), the Divisional Court said that only 'a complete destruction of voluntary control... could constitute in law automatism'. There had to be some evidence to raise a reasonable doubt that D's bodily movements were 'wholly uncontrolled and uninitiated by any function of conscious will'. In *Isitt* (1978), Lawton LJ said:

> It may well be that, because of panic or stress or alcohol, the appellant's mind was shut to the moral inhibitions which control the lives of most of us. But the fact that his moral inhibitions were not working properly... does not mean that the mind was not working at all.

These decisions may be explained on the ground that the automatism must be of such a degree that D cannot be said to have performed the *actus reus* voluntarily. But it seems harsh. D who, though not completely unconscious, retains the merest grasp on his senses, faces conviction. Clause 33 of the Law Commission's Criminal Code Bill (1989) proposes that a lack of control to the extent that D is no longer in *effective* control of his bodily movements should suffice for the defence. Such a reform is to be welcomed. There is little to be said for a rule of law which criminalises behaviour which D was incapable of preventing.

Crimes of *mens rea*

In this category the degree of automatism is, or should be, much reduced. D should have a good defence provided he was prevented from forming *mens rea*. There is a dearth of English case law on this point. In *T*, above, the crimes with which Miss T had been charged both required *mens rea*. The prosecution had claimed that her opening of a pen-knife blade had required a 'controlled and positive action', that this was a case of partial loss of control only and that, following *Issit*, automatism was therefore not available. However, the trial judge distinguished *Issit* and held that T was 'acting as though in a dream' and the defence was available after all.

The *mens rea* required for robbery is intent and dishonesty; for assault it is intent or, at least, subjective *Cunningham* recklessness. However, where D is charged with a crime requiring objective *Caldwell* recklessness, then a partial loss of control will not suffice. This was the decision of the Court of Appeal in *Attorney-General's Reference (No. 2 of 1992)* (1993). D had crashed his lorry into a stationary vehicle, killing two people. Charged with causing death by reckless driving, he pleaded that he was suffering from the condition 'driving without awareness', a trance-like state brought on by the lack of visual stimuli on long journeys on motorways. The Court decided that, because this condition induced only partial loss of control, i.e. the driver was largely unaware of what he is doing but unawareness was not total, then the defence of automatism was not available.

Self-induced automatism

Where the automatism was due to D's consumption of alcohol and/or drugs, then the rules of intoxication apply (*Lipman* [1970]). This principle could apply whenever automatism is self-inflicted. A driver who suffers an epileptic fit whilst driving may still be held liable for a motoring offence should he cause an accident, depending on the degree and frequency of epileptic attacks he has suffered in the past. Likewise, the driver who feels drowsy but continues to drive, then falls asleep (*Kay v Butterworth* [1945]).

Reflex actions

A 'reflex action' was one of the examples given by Lord Denning in *Bratty* of an involuntary act. That case did not involve reflex actions; so Lord Denning's view is *obiter*. In *Ryan* (1967), a defence of reflex action was advanced, but the High Court of Australia was unsympathetic. Windeyer J said that there were only two legally recognised categories of involuntary 'act':

- those which were involuntary because 'by no exercise of the will could [D] refrain from doing it', such as convulsions or an epileptic seizure; and

- those which were involuntary 'because he knew not what he was doing', such as the sleepwalker or a person rendered unconscious for some other reason.

However, reflex actions did not bear true analogy to either category. It is not surprising that the Court was unsympathetic: D had shot a petrol station attendant, V, at point blank range with a shotgun after V had moved while D was trying to tie him up. He claimed that when V struggled this led to D pulling the trigger involuntarily. The Court, quite rightly, upheld his conviction. So the case – which is persuasive authority at the most anyway – is not authority for the proposition that reflex actions are never a good defence.

Reform

The Law Commission's Criminal Code Bill (1989) provides an interesting definition of 'automatism', one which, if it were ever to be adopted, would change the present law. Clause 33(1) states that 'a person is not guilty of an offence if':

> *(a) he acts in a state of automatism, that is, his act (i) is a reflex, spasm or convulsion; or (ii) occurs while he is in a condition (whether of sleep, unconsciousness, impaired consciousness or otherwise) depriving him of effective control of his act; and*
>
> *(b) the act or condition is the result neither of anything done of omitted with the fault required for the offence nor of voluntary intoxication.*

The inclusion of 'sleep' as one of the causes of automatism involves a reversal of the Court of Appeal decision in *Burgess* that a sleepwalker is legally 'insane' and a tacit approval of the Supreme Court of Canada's decision in *Parks*.

Clause 33(2) states that 'a person is not guilty of an offence by virtue of an omission to act if':

> *(a) he is physically incapable of acting in the way required; and*
>
> *(b) his being so incapable is the result neither of anything done or omitted with the fault required for the offence nor of voluntary intoxication.*

Summary

- Automatism is a defence if D's act was involuntary (*Bratty v Attorney-General for Northern Ireland*).

- It includes: spasms, reflex actions or convulsions or situations where D was unconscious through, for example, concussion or hypnotism (*Bratty*). In *Ryan* a 'reflex action' defence was, however, denied.

- Automatism may include dissociative states – but only those caused by an extraordinary event (*T, Falconer*). Dissociative states caused by ordinary events are classed as insanity (*Parnekar, Rabey, Burgess*).

- Crimes of strict liability require a total destruction of voluntary control (*Hill v Baxter, Watmore v Jenkins, Isitt*). Similarly, crimes using objective recklessness *(Attorney-General's Reference [No.2 of 1992])*.

- For crimes requiring *mens rea*, automatism that prevents proof of *mens rea* should suffice for a good defence.

- Self-induced automatism, e.g. through drink and/or drugs, is classed as intoxication (*Lipman*).

- Automatism caused by a 'disease of the mind' is classed as insanity – see Chapter 15.

Figure 8 Relationship between intoxication, insanity and automatism

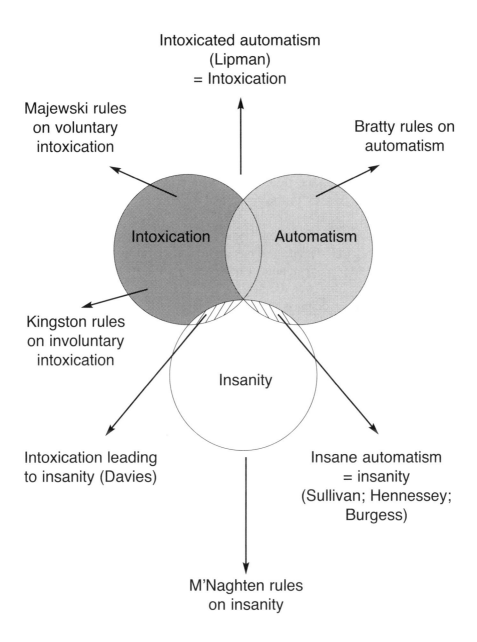

Intoxicated automatism
(Lipman)
= Intoxication

Majewski rules
on voluntary
intoxication

Bratty rules on
automatism

Intoxication

Automatism

Kingston rules
on involuntary
intoxication

Insanity

Intoxication leading
to insanity (Davies)

Insane automatism
= insanity
(Sullivan; Hennessey;
Burgess)

M'Naghten rules
on insanity

17 Mistake

Introduction

It is a basic principle of English criminal law that D is entitled to be judged against the facts as he honestly supposed them to exist. This is the position even if he is mistaken as to the facts, and even if the mistake was quite unreasonable.

At first glance, this may seem unduly favourable towards an accused. You may think that all the accused has to do is to swear in court that 'I was mistaken at the time your honour. I believed that the victim was going to attack me so I hit him over the head with a glass ashtray'. However, the crucial element in a defence of mistake claim is that the accused must convince a bench of magistrates or a jury of the honesty of his belief. The reality is that the more far-fetched the claim that the accused is making, the less likely it is that a jury will believe that it could have been honestly held at the time of the offence.

General principles

The leading cases are *Morgan and Others* (1976), *Kimber* (1983) and *Williams* (1987). In *Morgan and Others* and *Kimber* the question was whether D was guilty of rape and indecent assault, respectively, if he honestly thought (wrongly as it happens) that the victim was consenting. The House of Lords in *Morgan* held that a genuine, mistaken belief in consent was a good defence, because it denied the *mens rea* in rape (which is either knowledge or recklessness that V is not consenting to intercourse). Crucially, the Court stressed that mistake is a good defence even if D's belief is unreasonable, provided that it was honestly held. However, the more unreasonable a belief, the more likely it is that a jury will decide that D was lying and did not really have that belief at all.

Morgan and Others (1976)
Morgan, a senior officer in the RAF, invited three junior officers to his house to have sex with his wife. The other officers were at first incredulous but were persuaded when Morgan told them about his

wife's sexual behaviour and provided them with condoms. They also claimed that Morgan said to expect some resistance, but not to take this seriously as it was simply pretence on his wife's part to stimulate her own excitement. In due course the officers had sex with Morgan's wife, despite her struggling and screaming for her son to call the police. The officers were convicted of rape and Morgan of aiding and abetting rape, after a jury direction that their belief in consent had to be based on reasonable grounds. The Court of Appeal and the House of Lords actually rejected their appeals (applying the proviso – this means the court thought that a reasonable jury, properly instructed, would also have convicted), on the basis that the whole story was 'a pack of lies'. But Lords Cross, Hailsham and Fraser nevertheless held that the trial judge had misdirected the jury by telling them that the defendants' belief had to be reasonable.

In *Kimber* the Court of Appeal confirmed that the principles established in *Morgan* were not limited to rape but were of general application to all offences. In *Williams* the Court of Appeal decided that honest mistakes could also be used to support a defence, such as self-defence, as well as deny proof of *mens rea*. Lord Lane CJ attempted to sum up the role of mistake in criminal law generally, as follows:

> The reasonableness or unreasonableness of [D]'s belief is material to the question of whether the belief was held by [D] at all. If the belief was in fact held, its unreasonableness, so far as guilt or innocence is concerned, is neither here nor there. It is irrelevant.

Williams (1987)
Gladstone Williams was charged with assaulting a man called Mason. His defence was that he was preventing M from assaulting and torturing a young man. Williams claimed that he was returning from work on a bus when he saw M repeatedly punching the youth who was struggling and calling for help. Williams was so concerned at this that he got off the bus and approached M to ask him what on earth he was doing. M replied that he was arresting the youth for mugging an old lady (which was true) and that he was a police officer (which was not true). Williams asked to see M's warrant card, which was of course not forthcoming, at which point a struggle broke out between them. As a result of this altercation M sustained injuries to his face, loosened teeth and bleeding gums. Williams did not deny punching

> M but claimed that he did so in order to save the youth from further
> beatings and torture. The jury was directed that Williams only had a
> defence if he believed *on reasonable grounds* that M was acting
> unlawfully. The Court of Appeal quashed his conviction.

In *Scarlett* (1993), Beldam LJ pointed out that in *Williams* the Court of
Appeal had decided that D was entitled to be acquitted if he had been
genuinely mistaken about the need to use *any* force. He decided that the
same approach should be adopted in cases where D was mistaken as to the
degree of force necessary.

> *Scarlett* (1993)
> D, a pub landlord in Halifax, was charged with manslaughter
> following his forceful ejection of a drunk from his pub. The drunk, L,
> described as a 'large, heavily built man', had arrived in the pub
> shortly after closing time. D refused to serve him and told him to
> leave. L refused to leave and tried to punch D, who dodged the blow,
> grabbed L from behind and bundled him towards the door. What
> happened next was disputed. The prosecution case was that D shoved
> L down some stairs using excessive force. What was undisputed was
> that L banged his head on the pavement, suffering fatal injuries. The
> jury was directed to convict if they thought that the degree of force D
> used was excessive (because that would make the shove an assault,
> an unlawful act for the purposes of constructive manslaughter). The
> Court of Appeal quashed the conviction. Leaving the decision to the
> jury to decide on a purely objective basis was incorrect.

Beldam LJ went on to say that a jury ought not to convict 'unless they are
satisfied that the degree of force used was plainly more than was called for
by the circumstances as they believed them to be.' That much is entirely
consistent with the approach in *Williams* and is perfectly unremarkable.
Regrettably, Beldam LJ added that 'provided he believed the circumstances
called for the degree of force used, he is not to be convicted even if his
belief was unreasonable.' In *Owino* (1996), D had been convicted of assault
after repeatedly punching his wife in the face. He claimed that she had 'gone
for him' and he had simply used force in order to restrain her. The jury
thought that, whatever his wife had done, D had used excessive force and
convicted. D appealed, arguing that Beldam LJ had lain down a purely
subjective test. However, the Court of Appeal managed to 'explain' what

Beldam LJ meant to say, even if he did not actually say it. The law is simply that, when the jury is assessing whether the amount of force used was reasonable, they should put themselves in the situation that D supposed (rightly or wrongly, reasonably or unreasonably) to exist.

Intoxicated mistakes

An important exception to the general rule (above) is where D's mistake was caused by voluntary intoxication. A drunken mistake is likely to be honest – but unreasonable. To allow D to rely upon intoxicated mistakes as a defence would create an alarming loophole in the law. Thus, D should not be entitled to rely upon a mistaken belief in the need to use force in self-defence if charged with assault, or a mistaken belief in a woman's consent if charged with rape, if D was intoxicated at the time.

Indeed, this is the position. Take the following case as an example. In *Fotheringham* (1988), D, a middle-aged man, had been out drinking with his wife. When they returned home, D went to bed. Finding a woman already in the bed he assumed that it was his wife and proceeded to have sex with her. In fact, it was the couple's teenage babysitter, who had felt tired and gone to sleep in their bed. No doubt D's drunken condition hindered his ability to tell the difference between his middle-aged wife and a teenaged girl. He was charged with rape, contrary to s.1 of the Sexual Offences Act 1956. However, the law at the time meant that it was legally impossible for a man to rape his wife because it was assumed that she always consented (this ancient legal rule was only reversed by the House of Lords in *R* [1992]). Hence, D pleaded not guilty, because he honestly believed that the woman with whom he had sex was, in fact, his wife. But he was convicted and the Court of Appeal upheld the conviction. Intoxicated mistake was no defence to a basic intent crime such as rape, whether the issue was mistaken belief as to consent or, as in this case, mistaken belief as to identity.

So, where the offence is one of 'basic intent' – which includes assault and battery, wounding, actual and grievous bodily harm, indecent assault and rape – D cannot use evidence of intoxication to support a plea that he made a genuine mistake. The policy of protecting the public that was stressed in the leading intoxication case, *DPP v Majewski* (1977), makes this position inevitable.

However, by the same token, D should still be able to rely upon an intoxicated mistake if charged with a specific intent offence. However, the Court of Appeal has not always accepted the logic of this argument. In *O'Grady* (1987), D and his friend V had been drinking heavily when they fell asleep in the former's flat. D claimed that he awoke as V began hitting him, picked up an ashtray and hit V with it, then went back to sleep. In the morning, V was dead. D was convicted of manslaughter. The Court of Appeal upheld the conviction, distinguishing *Williams* and on the ground that it was not directly concerned with intoxicated mistakes.

So much is unremarkable. But then, Lord Lane CJ went on to say, *obiter*, that, for public policy reasons, intoxicated mistakes should not be available even as a defence to specific intent crimes such as murder. Lord Lane was particularly concerned that, because the mistaken use of force in self-defence is a good defence in the case of the sober defendant, dangerous harm-doing could go unpunished were this to be applied to the intoxicated one. He said:

> There are two competing interests. On the one hand the defendant who has only acted according to what he believed to be necessary to protect himself, and on the other hand that of the public and the victim in particular who… has been injured or perhaps killed because of the defendant's drunken mistake. Reason recoils from the conclusion that in such circumstances a defendant is entitled to leave the court without a stain on his character.

However, while 'reason' would, of course, 'recoil' from allowing someone like O'Grady to 'leave the court without a stain on his character', it is not necessary to deny someone like him a defence to murder. While a *sober* defendant would be entitled to an acquittal, having used fatal force in self-defence, even if wrong about the need to use force, the *intoxicated* one would not. Look again at the case of *Lipman* (1970), considered in Chapter 14. Even if not guilty of murder, D's intoxication would supply the *mens rea* for the basic intent offence of manslaughter. In *O'Grady*, D could have easily been convicted of constructive manslaughter on the basis that he had assaulted his friend, that this act was dangerous and it caused death.

Suppose D, staggering home from the pub one night, thinks that a large man walking towards him wearing a fur coat is a bear about to attack him. D picks up a brick and delivers a fatal blow to the man's head. If charged with murder, and D pleads self-defence, how should the jury be directed regarding D's intoxication? (Bear in mind the rules in DPP v Majewski [1977], which state that intoxication is a defence to a specific intent offence.)

The Criminal Law Revision Committee and the Law Commission have both recommended that intoxication should be considered as relevant evidence in murder cases. That is, the law as stated in *O'Grady* should be rejected.

Summary

- Where D is charged with an offence but denies *mens rea*, an honestly held, but mistaken, belief that prevents the Crown from proving *mens rea* will be a good defence (*DPP v Morgan, Kimber*). Typically this belief will relate to whether the victim of rape has consented to sexual intercourse (*Morgan*).

- Where D is charged with an offence and pleads self-defence, then an honestly held, but mistaken, belief in the need to use force will be a good defence (*Williams, Beckford*).

- When a jury is assessing whether D used reasonable force in self-defence, then D is entitled to be judged on the circumstances as he genuinely, but mistakenly, believed them to be (*Scarlett, Owino*).

- In all cases, the crucial point is that D's mistake must be honest but need not necessarily be reasonable. However, the more unreasonable the belief, the more likely it is that the jury will decide that D was lying.

- Intoxication cannot be used to support a claim of mistake, certainly in cases of basic intent (*Fotheringham*) and, according to *O'Grady*, not even in cases if specific intent.

18 Duress

Introduction

Imagine that you are standing in a queue at your bank. Suddenly, armed robbers burst into the store, waving guns around and shouting at everyone to get down on the floor and shut up. One of them then comes over to you – it's obviously not your lucky day – and tells you to help them fill their bags with cash. There is a gun pointed at your head. What do you do? Of course, if you don't pass out, you do exactly what you're told. Five minutes later the robbers have gone and it's all over. Or is it? What if the police decide to charge *you* with participating in the robbery? After all, without your help, the robbers might not have succeeded. Well, relax: there is a defence ready and waiting – duress.

With duress, D claims that, although he committed the *actus reus* of the offence, with *mens rea*, he did so because he had no effective choice, being faced with threats of serious injury or death. Duress is a 'concession to human frailty'.

Sources of the duress

Duress comes in two types:

- Duress by threats

- Duress of circumstances (sometimes referred to as necessity)

The principles applying are identical in either case.

Duress by threats

Here, D is threatened by another person to commit a criminal offence. For example, D is ordered at gunpoint to drive armed robbers away from the scene of a robbery. Duress by threats is only available if D commits a criminal offence of a type that was nominated by the person making the threat. In *Cole* (1994), moneylenders had pressured D for money. They had threatened D, his girlfriend and child, and hit him with a baseball bat. Eventually, D robbed two building societies. To a charge of robbery he pleaded duress but the judge held the defence was not available. The duressors had not said, 'Go and rob a building society or else.'

Duress of circumstances

Here, the threat does not come from a person but the circumstances in which D finds himself. Duress of circumstances has really only received official recognition from the appellate courts in the last fifteen years. Coincidentally, the first cases all involved driving offences.

The very first case, *Willer* (1986), involved a charge of reckless driving. D had been driving around town with two friends. As they drove down a narrow alley, their car was suddenly surrounded by a gang of youths who issued death threats. D realised that the only opportunity to escape was to drive onto the pavement. This he did, quite slowly, about 10mph. Having made his escape, he drove to the police station. He was subsequently charged with reckless driving. The trial judge ruled that he had no defence, but the Court of Appeal allowed his appeal. It should have been left to the jury to consider whether or not D was 'wholly driven by force of circumstance' into doing what he did. Subsequent cases following *Willer* included:

- *Conway* (1988), another reckless driving case. D claimed that his extremely hazardous driving was prompted by a (mistaken) belief that two men were trying to assassinate his passenger.

- *Martin* (1989), a case of driving while disqualified. D's wife had become hysterical and had threatened to kill herself if D did not drive her son, who was late, to work. D agreed to this even though he was disqualified.

It was not until *Pommell* (1995) – involving possession of an illegal firearm – that the defence was confirmed to be of general application.

The seriousness of the threat

The threats must be of death or serious personal injury (*Hudson and Taylor* (1971). A threat to damage or destroy property is insufficient. Threats to expose sexual immorality are certainly insufficient (*Valderrama-Vega* [1985]). In *Baker and Wilkins* (1997), the Court of Appeal refused to extend the scope of the defence to cases where D feared serious psychological injury.

Although there must be such a threat, it need not be the sole reason why D committed the offence with which he is charged. In *Valderrama-Vega*, D claimed that he had imported cocaine because of death threats made by a mafia-type organisation. But he also needed the money because he was heavily in debt to his bank. His conviction was quashed: the jury had been directed that he only had a defence if the death threats were the sole reason for acting.

Threats against whom?

As well as threats to D himself, threats to other people will also support the defence. This will often, but need not necessarily, involve members of D's family. The cases reveal the defence being available where threats were made to D's wife, girlfriend, mother – even his friends – as in *Willer* and *Conway*.

> Suppose armed robbers accost D while he is sitting in his car and they demand that he drive them away – or they will shoot randomly into a group of schoolchildren at a nearby bus stop. If D is subsequently charged with aiding and abetting armed robbery, should he have a defence? What would you do in that situation?

Imminence of the threat

The threat must have been operative on D, or other parties, at the moment he committed the offence. The Court of Appeal has recently confirmed that, for the defence to be available, the threat to D must be 'imminent' – but it does not have to be 'immediate'. In *Abdul-Hussain and Others* (1999), the defendants were all Shiite Muslims from Iraq who had fled to Sudan to escape punishment and execution. As they feared deportation back to Iraq they boarded a plane bound for Jordan and hijacked it, using plastic knives and imitation grenades made from mustard bottles. The plane eventually reached the UK where the hostages were released and the hijackers surrendered. They were charged with hijacking. The trial judge decided that the perceived danger had to be so 'close and immediate' as to give rise to a 'virtually spontaneous reaction'; hence, as the danger was not 'immediate', the defence was denied. The Court of Appeal disagreed and quashed the convictions. Duress of circumstances should have been put to the jury. The trial judge had interpreted the law too strictly.

Escape opportunities and police protection

D will be expected to take advantage of any opportunity he has to escape. If he fails to take it, the defence may fail. In *Gill* (1963), D claimed that he and his wife had been threatened with violence if he did not steal a lorry. The Court of Criminal Appeal expressed doubts whether the defence was open as there was a period of time in which he could have raised the alarm and wrecked the whole enterprise.

D will also be expected to seek police protection as soon as possible. In *Pommell* (1995), D was found in bed one morning with a loaded gun in his hand. He claimed to have persuaded another man, E, to hand over the gun, as E appeared determined to use it and D wanted to prevent that happening. This had been in the early hours of the morning; D had intended to hand the gun into the police the next day. However, D was convicted of possessing a prohibited weapon after the judge refused to allow the defence of duress on the basis of the time delay. The Court of Appeal allowed the appeal and ordered a retrial, where the defence would be available. In some cases a delay, especially an unexplained one, would deny the defence but, in this case, the delay of a few hours was not excessive and in any case D had offered an explanation for the delay (it was the middle of the night).

In *Hudson and Taylor* (1971), the Court of Appeal took a very pragmatic approach to the realities of many duress causes. The Court recognised that, in some cases, the police would be unable to provide effective protection against later reprisals.

Hudson and Taylor (1971)

Linda Hudson, 17, and Elaine Taylor, 19, were the principal prosecution witnesses at the trial of a man called Jimmy Wright, who had been charged with wounding another man in a Salford pub. Both girls were present in the pub and gave statements to the police. However, at the trial, the girls refused to identify Wright as the assailant, and he was acquitted. In due course, the girls were charged with and convicted of perjury (lying in court under oath). Hudson claimed that a man called Farrell, who had a reputation for violence, had threatened her that if she 'told on Wright in court' she would be cut up. Hudson passed this threat on to Taylor. They were frightened by this and resolved not to identify Wright. This resolve was strengthened when they arrived in court and saw Farrell in the public gallery. The trial judge withdrew the defence of duress from the jury because the threat of harm could not be immediately put into effect when they were testifying in the safety of the courtroom. Their convictions were quashed.

Voluntary exposure to risk of compulsion

D will be denied the defence if he voluntarily places himself in such a situation that he risks being threatened with violence to commit crime. This may be because he joins a criminal organisation. In *Fitzpatrick* (1977), D pleaded duress to a catalogue of offences including murder even though he was a voluntary member of the IRA. The trial judge rejected the defence. The Northern Ireland Court of Appeal dismissed the appeal. Lowry LCJ said:

> It would be only too easy for every member of an unlawful conspiracy and for every member of a gang except the leader to obtain an immunity denied to ordinary citizens. Indeed, the better organised the conspiracy and the more brutal its internal discipline, the surer would be the defence of duress for its members. It can hardly be supposed that the common law tolerates such an absurdity.

In *Sharp* (1987), Lord Lane CJ identified the features that deny the defence in this situation:

- D must 'voluntarily' join a criminal organisation or gang;

- He must have 'knowledge of its nature';

- He must know that other organisation or gang members 'might bring pressure on him to commit an offence'; and

- He must have been 'an active member when he was put under such pressure'.

Sharp (1987)

David Sharp, along with two men, A and H, had attempted an armed robbery of a sub-post office in Wraysbury, which resulted in the death of the sub-postmaster. Sharp claimed that he was only the 'bagman', he was not armed and only took part in the robbery because he had been threatened with having his head blown off by H if he did not co-operate. The judge withdrew the defence, and Sharp was convicted of manslaughter, robbery and attempted robbery. The Court of Appeal upheld the convictions.

In *Ali* (1995), this principle was extended to include not just those who join criminal organisations or gangs, but also those who voluntarily associate themselves with persons of a violent disposition. This case, like the more recent cases of *Baker and Ward* (1999) and *Heath* (2000), involved drug users or dealers who had become heavily indebted to their suppliers and were subsequently forced to commit crimes (typically robbery) in order to pay their debts or face violence or even death.

One of the conditions in *Sharp* is that D must have 'knowledge of the nature' of the organisation or gang before he joins it. Consequently, if D joins a criminal enterprise not known to have a propensity to violence, the defence may be available to him. In *Shepherd* (1987), D was a member of a gang of organised, non-violent shoplifters. They would enter a shop and one of them would distract the shopkeeper while the rest made off with as much booty as they could, usually boxes of cigarettes. No violence against the shopkeepers was involved. D was charged with theft and pleaded duress on the basis that he had tried to leave the gang but one of the others had threatened him and his family with violence unless he continued to participate. The trial judge withdrew the defence from the jury but, on appeal, his conviction was quashed. The question should have been put to the jury of whether D knew of a propensity to violence when he joined the gang.

The test for duress

The defence is not available just because D reacted to a threat; the threat must be one that the ordinary man would not have resisted. In *Graham* (1982), D was a practising homosexual living in a 'bizarre *menage-a-trois*' with his wife, Betty, and another homosexual, King. The latter was jealous of Betty and wanted to kill her. One day he wrapped a percolator flex around her neck and told D to hold the other end of the flex. D did so but only, he claimed, because he was afraid of King. Both men were convicted of murder; D appealed. The Court of Appeal upheld his conviction. Lord Lane CJ laid down the definitive test. It contains a subjective and objective element:

> The correct approach on the facts of this case would have been as follows: (1) Was the defendant, or may he have been, impelled to act as he did because, as a result of what he reasonably believed King had said or done, he had good cause to fear that if he did not so act King would kill him or... cause him serious physical injury? (2) If so, have the prosecution made the jury sure that a sober person of reasonable firmness, sharing the characteristics of the defendant, would not have responded to whatever he reasonably believed King said or did by taking part in the killing? The fact that a defendant's will to resist has been eroded by the voluntary consumption of drink or drugs or both is not relevant to this test.

In *Howe and Bannister* (1987), the House of Lords approved the *Graham* test. The test is carefully framed in such a way to ensure the burden of proof remains on the prosecution at all times (although D must raise evidence of duress). If the jury feel D *may* have been threatened, and that the reasonable man *might* have responded to it, then they *must* acquit D. Both *Graham* and *Howe* were duress by threats cases. In *Conway* (1988), the Court of Appeal applied the same test to the defence of duress of circumstances.

The first question

The first question is whether D was, or might have been, impelled to act as he did because, as a result of his reasonable belief, he had good cause to fear that if he did not so act, he would die or suffer serious physical injury. This test concentrates on D's belief.

> *Cairns* (1999)
> V, who was inebriated, stepped out in front of D's car, forcing him to stop. V climbed onto the bonnet and spreadeagled himself on it, with his face pressed up against the windscreen. In an attempt to get away, D drove off with V on the bonnet. A group of V's friends ran after the car, shouting and gesticulating (they claimed later that they just wanted to stop V, not do any harm to D). D had to brake in order to drive over a speed bump, V fell off in front of the car, and was run over, suffering serious injury. D was convicted of inflicting grievous bodily harm, after the trial judge ruled that the defence of duress of circumstances was only available when 'actually necessary to avoid the evil in question'. The Court of Appeal quashed the conviction: the judge should have directed the jury on the defence.

In duress cases, the issue is whether D acted as he did because he *reasonably believed* that if he did not do so he would suffer death or serious injury – that is, it was not necessary that the threat, the 'evil in question', was, in fact, real. In *Cairns*, D may have reasonably believed that V's friends were determined to attack him, so the defence should have been left to the jury.

However, the test does not just concentrate on D's subjective view of the threat or circumstances (as the case may be):

- D's belief must have been 'reasonable'. If D *unreasonably* believed that he was being threatened and committed an offence, the defence is unavailable.

- D's belief must have given him 'good cause' to fear death/serious injury. The defence will, therefore, fail if, viewed objectively (i.e. in the opinion of the jury), death or serious injury was unlikely.

Arguably the test is too strict. There is a good case for saying that the first question should be *purely* subjective; that is, D should be judged on the basis of what he *actually* believed, and what he *actually* feared. It would appear lack of faith in the jury to detect the bogus defence lies at the root of the objective 'glosses' on the first question. But juries are not daft: the more unlikely the grounds for fear, the less likely D is to be believed. The requirement that D's belief be reasonable was challenged, *obiter*, by the Queen's Bench Divisional Court in *DPP v Rogers* (1998) but, for the time being at least, it remains an essential part of the law of duress.

The second question

The second question is whether a 'sober person of reasonable firmness' – but sharing D's characteristics – would have responded to whatever it was that D reasonably believed would happen to him, by committing a criminal offence. Put another way, the defence is unavailable if the ordinary person, sharing D's characteristics, would have resisted the threats.

The relevant characteristics will include age, sex, and certain other permanent physical and mental attributes which would affect the ability of D to resist pressure and threats. In *Bowen* (1996), the Court of Appeal said that the following characteristics were obviously relevant:

- age: a young person may not be so robust as a mature one;

- pregnancy: where there was an added fear for the unborn child;

- serious physical disability: as that might inhibit self-protection;

- recognised mental illness or psychiatric condition: such as post-traumatic stress disorder leading to learnt helplessness. Psychiatric evidence might be admissible to show that D was suffering from such condition, provided persons generally suffering them might be more susceptible to pressure and threats. It was *not* admissible simply to show that in a doctor's opinion D, not suffering from such illness or condition, was especially timid, suggestible or vulnerable to pressure and threats.

- Finally, sex *might* be relevant, although the Court of Appeal thought that many women might consider they had as much moral courage to resist pressure as men.

Where D wished to submit that they had some characteristic from the list, that had to be made plain to the judge. In most cases it was probably only the age and sex of D which was relevant. If so, the judge should, as he had done in this case, confine the characteristics to those.

> *Bowen* (1996)
> Bowen was convicted of obtaining property by deception. He claimed to have been acting under duress. Two men had accosted him in a pub and told him that he and his family would be petrol-bombed if he did not obtain goods for them. The judge had left duress to the jury but did not mention Bowen's low intelligence (his IQ was only 68). The Court of Appeal dismissed the appeal. A low IQ, falling short of mental impairment or mental defectiveness, could not be said to be a characteristic that made those who had it less courageous and less able to withstand threats and pressure.

The decision of the Court of Appeal in *Bowen* to allow evidence of post-traumatic stress disorder leading to learnt helplessness as a characteristic is interesting, and not particularly easy to reconcile with the earlier decision in *Horne* (1994). There, D was charged with fraud and pleaded duress. He sought to support it with psychological evidence that he was unusually pliable and vulnerable to pressure. The judge refused to consider the evidence, D was convicted, and the Court of Appeal dismissed his appeal.

> Suppose you were on the jury in a case where duress was pleaded following threats of violence. How would you react to the question, 'Would the sober person of reasonable firmness but suffering from learnt helplessness have yielded to the threat?'

Self-induced characteristics

In *Bowen*, the Court of Appeal also clearly distinguished *Morhall* (1996), the leading provocation case, by holding that characteristics due to self-imposed abuse, such as alcohol, drugs or glue-sniffing, could not be relevant. This is consistent with the earlier case of *Flatt* (1996). D was addicted to cocaine and owed his supplier £1,500. The dealer had apparently told him to look after some drugs and, that if he did not, D's mother, grandmother and girlfriend would be shot. Some 17 hours later, the drugs were found in D's flat by the police. He pleaded duress but was convicted of possession of drugs with intent to supply. On appeal, he argued that the judge should have told the jury that, in assessing the response of the reasonable person to the threats, they should have considered his drug addiction. The Court of Appeal held, dismissing the appeal, that self-induced addiction was *not* a characteristic.

The rationale for this exclusion is not absolutely clear. There are two possible explanations. Either self-induced conditions are excluded, generally, as a matter of policy; or D's condition did not affect his ability to resist threats. Clearly the former is a much broader principle. If this is the correct explanation, then there appears to be a conflict of authority between *Flatt* and *Morhall*, considered in Chapter 6, where the House of Lords held that an addiction to glue-sniffing was admissible as a characteristic.

Limits to the defence

As the cases considered above demonstrate, duress may be pleaded as a defence to a wide range of offences. Indeed, it seems that duress may be accepted as a defence to any crime *except* murder and attempted murder.

Murder

Duress is no defence to murder. In *Dudley and Stephens* (1884), D and S had been shipwrecked in the South Atlantic Ocean in a boat with another man and a cabinboy. After several days without food or water, they decided to kill and eat the boy, who was the weakest of the four. Four days later they were rescued. They pleaded what would now be called duress of circumstances but this was rejected and they were sentenced to death. In the event, Queen Victoria intervened and exercised the 'royal prerogative' to spare their lives.

The proposition that duress is no defence to murder was confirmed in *Howe and Bannister* (1987). At one point in time, duress was a defence for accessories to murder (*Lynch* [1975]). This distinction was difficult to justify: if D plans a murder, makes a bomb but, rather than plant it himself, persuades E to plant it for him, why should he have a defence while E does not? Hence, in *Howe and Bannister*, the Lords overruled *Lynch*.

In *Howe and Bannister*, the House of Lords gave a variety of reasons for withholding the defence from murderers, none of which are totally convincing:

- *Reason*: The ordinary man of reasonable fortitude, if asked to take an innocent life, might be expected to sacrifice his own. Lord Hailsham said that he could not 'regard a law as either "just" or "humane" which withdraws the protection of the criminal law from the innocent victim, and casts the cloak of protection on the cowards and the poltroon in the name of a concession to human frailty'. *Response*: why should the law require heroism? Indeed it doesn't – Lord Lane CJ's test in *Graham* (approved in *Howe*) sets the standard as the 'sober person of reasonable firmness'. If the reasonable man would have killed in the same circumstances, why should D be punished – with a life sentence for murder – when he only did what anyone else would have done?

- *Reason*: One who takes the life of an innocent cannot claim he is choosing the lesser of two evils (*per* Lord Hailsham). *Response*: This may be true if D himself is threatened; but what if D is told to kill V and that if he does not a bomb will explode in the middle of a crowded shopping centre? Surely that is the lesser of two evils. The situation where D's family are held hostage and threatened with death if D does not kill a third party is far from uncommon.

- *Reason*: The Law Commission had recommended in 1977 that duress be a defence to murder. That recommendation was unimplemented; that suggested Parliament was happy with the law as it was. *Response*: Parliament might equally be taken to have approved *Lynch* (1975), which allowed duress for accessories to murder and was not overruled until *Howe*.

- *Reason*: Hard cases could be dealt with by not prosecuting, or by action of the Parole Board or exercise of the royal prerogative of mercy in ordering D's early release. *Response*: D still faces being branded as, in law, a 'murderer', and a morally innocent man should not have to rely on an administrative decision for his freedom. In *Lynch*, Lord Wilberforce said: 'A law which required innocent victims of terrorist threats to be tried and convicted as murderers, is an unjust law.'

- *Reason*: To recognise the defence would involve overruling *Dudley and Stephens* (1884). According to Lord Griffiths, that decision was based on 'the special sanctity that the law attaches to human life and which denies to a man the right to take an innocent life even at the price of his own or another's life'. *Response*: the *ratio* of *Dudley and Stephens* is not absolutely clear. It could be, and usually is, taken to mean that duress is no defence to murder – but, instead, it could be taken to mean that, on the facts of the case, duress was not available.

- *Reason*: Lord Griffiths thought the defence should not be available because it was 'so easy to raise and may be difficult for the prosecution to disprove'. *Response*: this would apply to most defences! It also ignores the fact that in *Howe*, like *Lynch*, the jury had rejected the defence and convicted. Indeed, Lord Hailsham said that 'juries have been commendably robust' in rejecting the defence in other cases.

- *Reason*: Lord Bridge thought that it was for Parliament to decide the limits of the defence. *Response*: why? Duress is a common law defence, so the judges should decide its scope. In *Lynch*, Lord Wilberforce said that, 'The House... would not discharge its judicial duty if it failed to define the law's attitude to this particular defence in particular circumstances.'

Howe and Bannister (1987)

Michael Howe, 19, and John Bannister, 20, together with two other men, Bailey, 19, and Murray, 35, participated in the torture, assault, and then strangling of two young male victims at a remote spot on the moors near Buxton in Derbyshire. On the first occasion, H and B had kicked and punched V1, while Bailey had strangled him to death. On the second occasion, however, they jointly strangled V2. On a third occasion V3 escaped on a motorbike. At their trial on two counts of murder and one of conspiracy to murder, they pleaded duress, arguing that they feared for their lives if they did not do as M directed. M was not only much older than the others but had appeared in court several times before and had convictions for violence. They were convicted of all charges, and their appeals failed in the Court of Appeal and House of Lords.

Should duress in murder cases operate as a partial defence, like provocation, and reduce D's liability to manslaughter? If this reform were to come about, should the House of Lords carry it out or is it a job for Parliament?

Attempted murder

In *Gotts* (1991) D was a 16-year-old who had been threatened with death by his father unless he tracked his mother down to a refuge (where she had gone with her two other children to escape the father's violence) and killed her. D stabbed his mother intending to kill her but, although seriously injured, she survived. The trial judge withdrew the defence and D was convicted. The Court of Appeal and House of Lords (by 3:2) upheld his conviction. Lord Jauncey said that he could 'see no justification in logic, morality or law in affording to an attempted murderer the defence which is withheld from a murderer'. If anything the opposite was true, because attempted murder requires an intent to kill, whereas murder requires an intent to kill or an intent to cause grievous bodily harm; Lord Jauncey said that the 'intent required of an attempted murderer is more evil than that required of a murderer'.

Should duress be a defence to a person charged with causing grievous bodily harm with intent, contrary to s.18 OAPA? (Bear in mind that a person can be guilty of murder if they killed having intended to do no more than cause really serious injury.)

Reform

In *Abdul-Hussain and Others* (1999), Rose LJ observed that, as the defence of duress of circumstances had developed on a case-by-case basis, its scope is imprecise and there is a need for Parliament to provide legislation to establish precision. This is in fact the fourth time in five years that a Court of Appeal judge has made such a request. However, there is no sign of Parliament responding to these pleas.

Summary

- Duress comes in two types: duress by threats and duress of circumstances (sometimes referred to as necessity). The principles applying are identical in either case (*Howe and Bannister*).

- The threats must be of death or serious personal injury (*Hudson and Taylor*).

- As well as threats to D himself, threats to family members or even other people will also support the defence (*Conway*).

- The threat must have been operative on D, or other parties, at the moment D committed the offence (*Hurley and Murray*). The threat to D must be 'imminent' – but it does not have to be 'immediate' (*Abdul-Hussain and Others*).

- D will be expected to take advantage of any opportunity to escape. If he fails to take it, the defence may fail (*Gill*) unless D can proffer some explanation for it (*Pommell*).

- D will be denied the defence if he voluntarily places himself in such a situation that he risks being threatened with violence to commit crime. This may be because he joins a criminal organisation (*Fitzpatrick*) or gang (*Sharp*), or even if he associates with people known to be violent criminals like drug dealers (*Ali, Baker and Ward, Heath*). But the position is different if the organisation was not known to be violent (*Shepherd*).

- The twofold test for duress is whether D's reasonable belief gave him good cause to fear death or serious injury (subjective test) and whether the 'sober person of reasonable firmness', sharing D's characteristics, would have done as D did (objective test) (*Graham, Howe and Bannister*).

- D's belief is crucial. There is no requirement that the threat be real (*Cairns*).

- Relevant characteristics include age, physical disability and recognised mental illness (*Bowen*). Certain characteristics are never relevant, e.g. pliability, low IQ (*Hegarty, Horne, Bowen*).

- Duress is no defence to murder (*Dudley and Stephens*, *Howe and Bannister*).

- Duress is no defence to attempted murder (*Gotts*).

19 Self-defence and the prevention of crime

Introduction

While it is accepted that a person may generally defend himself and his property from attack, the courts and Parliament have always been mindful of minimising the risk of encouraging over-zealous retaliation in such a situation. There is always the danger that the defender may take on the rôle of attacker. Public policy also dictates that revenge attacks or vigilante-type behaviour must be discouraged at all costs. For this reason, the use of any force in self-defence must always pass the test of *reasonableness*. In essence, this is a question of fact for the jury, taking into account all the relevant factors in the case.

Force causing damage to property, injury or even death to other persons may be justified if the force was reasonably used in the defence of certain public or private interests. If D is charged with unlawful malicious wounding and pleads self-defence, he is arguing that the wounding was justified and, thus, lawful. The use of lawful force is not an offence; an element of the *actus reus* is missing. There are three situations where force can be used:

- Self-defence. This is regulated purely by the common law.

- Prevention of crime. This is covered by s.3(1) of the Criminal Law Act 1967, which provides that a 'person may use such force as is reasonable in the circumstances in the prevention of crime, or in effecting or assisting in the lawful arrest of offenders or suspected offenders or of persons unlawfully at large.'

- Defence of property. This is partially but not exclusively covered by s.5(2) of the Criminal Damage Act 1971 (see Chapter 13).

This chapter will concentrate on self-defence and the prevention of crime defence. There is the potential for overlap between the two defences. Suppose a married couple are walking home one night when they are confronted by a mugger. If the man uses force to fight and overpower the mugger he is using self-defence is respect of himself as well as using force in order to prevent crime (robbery). For convenience, the rest of this chapter will simply refer to self-defence unless specific reference to the prevention of crime defence is required. Where this happens the defence will be called 'the s.3 defence'.

Where there is evidence of self-defence this must be left to the jury. However, there must be evidence before the court on which a reasonable jury might think it was reasonably possible that D was acting in self-defence. The judge is not required to direct a jury on what appears to him to be a fanciful or speculative matter.

Scope of the defence

Self-defence is usually raised to charges of offences against the person, but is not confined to them. In *Symonds* (1998), a case of 'pedestrian rage', D was convicted of careless driving after the trial judge omitted to direct the jury on the possibility that he had driven his car in self-defence to escape an irate pedestrian. The Court of Appeal acknowledged that there was some difficulty (though more of theory than substance) with deploying self-defence to offences other than those where force is involved but nevertheless held that the judge should have directed the jury on the defence. The Court's hesitancy about allowing self-defence was justified: on the facts, the more appropriate defence was surely duress of circumstances (see Chapter 18).

Limits on the defence

When D pleads self-defence, the onus is placed on the prosecution to disprove it. The prosecution must prove that:

- the use of *any* force was unnecessary or, if some force was justifiable, that;

- the actual degree of force used was unreasonable.

The necessity of force

The use of *any* force is not justified if it is not necessary. The test is whether it was necessary *in the circumstances as they appeared to D*. The danger that D apprehends must be sufficiently specific or imminent to justify his actions, and of a nature which could not reasonably be met by more pacific means.

Threats and pre-emptive strikes

It is not necessary for there to be an attack in progress. It is sufficient if D apprehends an attack. In *Beckford* (1988), Lord Griffiths said, 'A man about to be attacked does not have to wait for his assailant to strike the first blow or fire the first shot; circumstances may justify a pre-emptive strike.'

It follows that it will be permissible for D to issue threats of force, even threats of death, if that might prevent an attack upon himself or prevent a crime from taking place. In *Cousins* (1982), D believed that a contract had been taken out on his life. He armed himself with his nephew's double-barrelled shotgun and paid a visit to the father of the person he thought was behind the contract. D told the father that when he saw his son, 'I'm going to kill him. I'm going to blow his brains out.' D was charged with making threats to kill and relied upon the s.3 defence. The trial judge directed the jury that the defence was unavailable because D's life was not in immediate jeopardy. He was convicted but the Court of Appeal quashed the conviction. Milmo J said: 'It can amount to a lawful excuse for a threat to kill if the threat is made in the prevention of crime or for self-defence, provided it is reasonable in the circumstances to make such a threat.'

Preparing for an attack

Where D apprehends an attack upon himself, may he make preparations to defend himself, even where that involves breaches of the law? In *Attorney-General's Reference (No. 2 of 1983)* (1984), D's shop had been attacked and damaged by rioters. Fearing further attacks he made petrol bombs. He was charged with possessing an explosive substance contrary to the Explosive Substances Act 1883. He pleaded self-defence and the jury acquitted. The Court of Appeal accepted that this was correct.

Thus, acts preparatory to justifiable acts of self-defence may be justified. Otherwise D, caught up in a police shootout, who picks up a gun lying on the ground and uses it to shoot one of the criminals, would have a defence to murder – but not to being in possession of a firearm without a certificate contrary to the Firearms Act 1968!

Is there a duty to retreat?

The leading case in this area concerns a violent incident at a house party in West London. In *Bird* (1985), D was convicted of wounding after the trial judge directed the jury that D must have demonstrated by her actions that she did not want to fight. The Court of Appeal, allowing the appeal, made it clear that this direction 'placed too great an obligation' on D. In particular, it was going too far to say that it was 'necessary' for her to demonstrate a reluctance to fight.

Bird (1985)
Debbie Bird was celebrating her seventeenth birthday at a house in Harrow when a former boyfriend of hers, M, turned up with a new

girlfriend. Bird and M began arguing and, eventually, she poured a glass of Pernod over him. M slapped her and Bird lunged at him with her hand, which still contained the glass. The glass broke in his face and gouged his eye out. Exactly why Bird lunged at him was disputed, but the defence claimed that M was holding her against a wall and had threatened to hit her if she did not shut up, and she had struck out and in the 'agony of the moment', not realising that she was holding the glass. The Court of Appeal quashed her conviction of wounding.

The reasonableness of force

The general principle is that only such force may be used as is reasonable in the circumstances. This is a question for the jury. However, although the question of what is reasonable force is to be judged by the jury, it is critical that they put themselves in the circumstances which D supposed (whether reasonably or not) to exist. The jury should be reminded not to disregard the state of mind of D altogether. This recognises that the force will commonly be used in a moment of crisis. In the Privy Council case of *Palmer* (1971), Lord Morris said that

> a person defending himself cannot weigh to a nicety the exact measure of his... defensive action. If a jury thought that in a moment of unexpected anguish a person attacked had only done what he honestly and instinctively thought was necessary that would be most potent evidence that only reasonable defensive action had been taken.

The Court of Appeal has affirmed this passage. In *Whyte* (1987), Lord Lane CJ said that 'in most cases... the jury should be reminded that [D]'s state of mind, that is his view of the danger threatening him at the time of the incident, is material. The test of reasonableness is not... a purely objective test.' Ironically, the *Whyte* case itself was not one of those cases! D had called on V, his downstairs neighbour, with a lock-knife already locked open and ready to use in his back pocket. D claimed that V swung a punch at him at which point he produced the knife to use in self-defence. Lord Lane CJ said that, even if the jury believed D's version of events, which Lord Lane CJ thought highly unlikely, D had clearly used excessive force. It was 'perfectly plain that on any view the use of an already prepared knife... could not possibly be reasonable under any circumstances, whether the direction in *Palmer* was given or not.'

Should excessive force causing death reduce murder to manslaughter?

Currently, if the jury conclude that D used more force than was reasonable in self-defence and death results, then he is guilty of murder. That is, excessive self-defence is no defence at all. In *Palmer* (1971), Lord Morris said: 'If the prosecution have shown that what was done was not done in self-defence then that issue is eliminated from the case.... The defence of self-defence either succeeds so as to result in an acquittal or it is disproved in which case as a defence it is rejected.'

However, it has been argued that excessive force should, like provocation and diminished responsibility, reduce murder to manslaughter. In *Attorney-General's Reference (No. 1 of 1975)* (1977), Viscount Dilhorne said: 'It may be that a strong case can be made for an alteration of the law to enable a verdict of manslaughter to be returned where the use of some force was justifiable [but excessive force was used] but that is a matter for legislation and not for judicial decision.'

The most recent case is *Clegg* (1995). D's murder conviction was upheld by the Northern Ireland Court of Appeal on the basis that he had used a 'grossly excessive and disproportionate' use of force. On further appeal, the House of Lords found that, as the danger had passed when D fired the fatal shot, there was no necessity to use force at all, excessive or otherwise. Nevertheless, Lord Lloyd rejected the proposition that excessive force used in self-defence and/or the prevention of crime and/or in arrest, should reduce liability from murder to manslaughter.

Clegg (1995)

Lee Clegg, a soldier of the Parachute Regiment, was on duty at a checkpoint in Belfast one night. A car approached Clegg's section at speed with its headlights full on. Somebody shouted to stop the car. Clegg fired three shots through the windscreen as the car approached, and a fourth at the car as it passed. This last shot hit a female passenger, Karen Reilly, in the back, and killed her. Forensic evidence showed that, when the last shot was fired, the car would already have been ten yards away. On trial for murder, Clegg pleaded self-defence. He was convicted after the trial judge found that this last shot could not have been fired in self-defence because, once the car had passed, Clegg was no longer in any danger. His conviction was upheld.

Australian courts used to recognise a defence of excessive self-defence reducing murder to manslaughter, but in *Zekevic* (1987), the High Court of

Australia reversed this decision. The Criminal Law Revision Committee and the Law Commission (Criminal Code Bill [1989], clause 59) and the Select Committee of the House of Lords on Murder and Life Imprisonment (1989) have all recommended that the use of excessive force in self-defence should reduce what would otherwise be murder to manslaughter.

Following *Clegg*, the then Home Secretary, Michael Howard, announced a review of the position. The subsequent report (*Report of the Inter-Departmental Review of the Law on the Use of Lethal Force in Self-Defence or the Prevention of Crime* [1996]) expressed the view that a verdict of manslaughter where excessive force had been used 'might assist in a comparatively small number of cases', but did not consider that the availability of such an option 'would enable the court or jury to achieve a result which would necessarily always be seen as just.' The report concluded that a change in this area alone would be difficult 'without taking a more fundamental look at the scope and operation of the law on, and the penalty for, murder.'

In May 2000, a jury at Norwich Crown Court returned a verdict of guilty of murder in the case of *Tony Martin*, a Norfolk farmer. Martin shot and killed a 15-year-old whom he thought was about to burgle his property, known as Bleak House Farm. The jury rejected a plea that Martin was simply using force to defend his property from burglars. The reaction to this case included calls from the Leader of the Conservative Party, William Hague, that changes to the law relating to self-defence and force used in the prevention of crime were urgently needed.

Summary

- Force may be used to protect oneself or to prevent a crime from being committed.

- There must be evidence of self-defence. If there is evidence, then the issue must be left to the jury (*DPP v Bailey*). The burden of proof is on the prosecution to show either that it was not necessary to use any force at all, or that the amount of force in fact used was unreasonable.

- Self-defence will normally be pleaded to as a defence to assaults and murder. However, it is not restricted to these crimes (*Symonds*).

- D does not have to wait to be attacked, he may make a pre-emptive strike (*Beckford*).

- He may also issue warnings and threats against perceived attackers (*Cousins*).

- There is no requirement of spontaneity. D may arm himself in preparation for a perceived attack on himself and not be guilty of firearms of explosives offences (*Attorney-General's Reference [No. 2 of 1983]*).

- There is no obligation on D to demonstrate an unwillingness to fight (*Bird*).

- Whether force used was reasonable is a question for the jury. However, they must assess that question by putting themselves in the position that D believed to exist (*Palmer, Whyte*).

- Excessive force in self-defence that causes death does not reduce liability for murder to manslaughter (*Palmer, Clegg*).

Questions on Part 5 Defences

1 Critically evaluate the principles governing the law on intoxication.

(OCR 1998)

2 Compare and contrast the defences of diminished responsibility and insanity.

(OCR 1999)

3 Lucy plays for the Barchester Belles hockey team. She has been looking forward to a crucial league game against their main rivals but, as she has been feeling unwell, she takes an illegal drug two hours before bully-off in order to improve her performance. This causes a reaction with other medication she had been taking and makes her dizzy and confused. The referee, Wilf, enters the changing room and asked to inspect the studs in her boots. In her confused state, Lucy thinks he is attacking her and lashes out at him with her hockey stick. Instead, she strikes a fellow team member, Gemma, in the face, causing her mouth to bleed and breaking her glasses.

Analyse the criminal liability, if any, of Lucy.

(OCR 1998)

4 Identify the circumstances in which a mistake will relieve a defendant of criminal liability? How satisfactory is the present law in this area?

(OCR 1999)

5 The defences of duress, necessity and duress of circumstances all recognise that a person ought not always to be regarded as criminally liable if he or she feels compelled to act against their will. Critically evaluate how and why the courts have limited the availability of these defences.

(OCR 1998)

Part 6

General principles 2

20 Participation

Introduction

Many crimes are committed by defendants working alone. But a great number are committed with the help or assistance of possibly just one, or possibly a large number, of other people. These people could be locksmiths, getaway drivers, lookouts… the range of situations where other people – known as 'accomplices' or 'accessories' or, sometimes, 'secondary offenders' (the terms are more or less interchangeable) – may participate in a criminal offence is infinitely variable. A slightly different situation occurs where two or more defendants work as a team; this is known as a 'joint enterprise', although many of the legal principles are the same in both situations. How has the law responded to the difficulties posed by the many and varied roles played by accomplices?

Principals and secondary parties

The person who directly and immediately causes the *actus reus* of the offence is the 'perpetrator' or 'principal', while those who assist or contribute to the *actus reus* are 'secondary parties', or 'accessories'. The law for indictable offences (including murder, manslaughter, rape, etc.) is set out in s.8 of the Accessories and Abettors Act 1861, as amended. This provides that 'Whosoever shall aid, abet, counsel or procure the commission of any... is liable to be tried, indicted and punished as a principal offender'. S.44 of Magistrates' Court Act 1980 provides the same for summary offences (including assault and battery).

The significance of this provision lies in the discretion given to a judge to sentence the accomplice according to the degree of blame for which he or she deserves to be punished. For example, villains who make a living from organised crime are notoriously difficult to convict. They may provide the money and brains behind criminal operations but rarely expose themselves to the risk of being caught. Often, a so-called 'Mr Big' will use a combination of cunning and intimidation to ensure that it is a 'fall-guy' who takes the blame should any planned crime go wrong. However, when the opportunity does actually arise to convict such a villain it is essential that a judge has the power to sentence them accordingly for their part in counselling the offences. It is for this reason that such an accessory may receive a sentence which is greater than that given to the actual principal offender.

Innocent agency

Where the perpetrator of the *actus reus* of a crime is an 'innocent agent', someone without *mens rea*, or not guilty because of a defence such as infancy or insanity, then the person most closely connected with the agent is the principal. So if D, an adult, employs his 8-year-old son to break in to houses and steal, the child is an innocent agent, and the father liable as principal.

There may be more than one principal

Just because two or more parties are involved, it does not mean one has to be the principal and the other their accessory. They may be both principals, provided each has *mens rea* and together they carry out the *actus reus*. Suppose two friends agree to burgle a house together, or two brothers agree to gang up on their abusive father and beat him up (as in *Pearson* [1992] – see Chapter 6). This is known as a 'joint enterprise', and will be dealt with later on.

What if the principal lacks *mens rea*, or has a defence?

The accessory may nevertheless be liable here: the presence of the *actus reus* is crucial. In the following cases, the accessory was held liable even though the principal offender was not liable. In *Bourne* (1952), B forced his wife on two occasions to commit buggery with the family dog. His conviction of aiding and abetting the offence was upheld, even though she could not be convicted, had she been tried, because of his duress. The *actus reus* of buggery had been committed.

In *Cogan and Leak* (1976), L terrorised his wife to have sex with C. C's conviction for rape was quashed, because of a misdirection, but L's rape conviction was upheld. The Court of Appeal thought it irrelevant that C may not have had the *mens rea* for rape and L's conviction was upheld on the basis that he simply procured the *actus reus* of rape. Lawton LJ said that, 'the act of sexual intercourse without the wife's consent was the *actus reus*; it had been procured by [L] who had the appropriate *mens rea*, namely his intention that [C] should have sexual intercourse with her without her consent'. Hence, L's conviction was upheld on the basis that he simply procured the *actus reus* of rape.

Neither of these cases affect the decision in *Thornton v Mitchell* (1940). If there is no *actus reus* at all then D cannot be liable for participating in whatever it was that E was doing. A bus driver, H, was reversing his bus relying on the signals of his conductor, Thornton. Two pedestrians behind the bus were run over. H was cleared of driving a motor vehicle without due care and attention – as he *had* driven the bus with due care and attention – but Thornton was nevertheless convicted of aiding and abetting the offence. The Divisional Court quashed this conviction: there was simply no *actus reus* to aid or abet.

Actus reus of secondary parties

Generally

An accessory will be charged with aiding, abetting, counselling or procuring the particular offence, and is liable if it can be proved that he participated in any one or more of the four ways. The Court of Appeal has held that the words should simply bear their ordinary meaning. In *Attorney-General's Reference (No.1 of 1975)* (1975), Lord Widgery CJ said:

> We approach s.8 of the 1861 Act on the basis that the words should be given their ordinary meaning, if possible. We approach the section on the basis also that if four ordinary words are employed here – aid, abet, counsel or procure – the probability is that there is a difference between each of those four words and the other three, because, if there were no such difference, then Parliament would be wasting time in using four words where two or three would do.

There is considerable overlap between them and it is quite possible for D to participate in several different ways.

Does there have to be a 'meeting of minds'?

Yes and no. For D to abet or counsel another person, it seems that there must be some common understanding between them. For aiding and procuring, D may participate without the other even knowing what D is doing, or even against the other's wishes – especially where procuring is concerned. In *Attorney-General's Reference (No.1 of 1975)* (1975), D surreptitiously added alcohol to E's drink for a joke. When E drove home he was arrested and charged with drink–driving. D was charged with procuring the offence. D's addition of alcohol to E's drink was the direct cause of the offence, and would, the Court of Appeal thought, amount to procuring. Lord Widgery CJ said:

> It may... be difficult to think of a case of aiding, abetting or counselling when the parties have not met and have not discussed in some respects the terms of the offence which they have in mind. But we do not see why a similar principle should apply to procuring... To procure means to produce by endeavour. You procure a thing by

setting out to see that it happens and taking the appropriate steps to produce that happening.

What about a causal connection?

Again, yes and no. It is essential in procuring. In *Attorney-General's Reference (No.1 of 1975)* (1975), the Court of Appeal held that 'you cannot procure an offence unless there is a causal link between what you do and the commission of the offence'. However, for aiding, abetting and counselling there is no requirement of a *strong* causal connection. In *Calhaem* (1985), the leading counselling case, Parker LJ said that there was 'no implication in the word itself that there should be any causal connection between the counselling and the offence'. The only 'connection' required was that 'the actual offence must have been committed and committed by the person counselled' and did not happen accidentally.

Calhaem (1985)

Kathleen Calhaem was so infatuated with Shirley Rendell's boyfriend that she hired a hitman, a private detective called Zajac, to carry out her murder. Zajac apparently changed his mind about the killing but nevertheless went to Rendell's house armed with a hammer, knife and a loaded shotgun wrapped in a parcel intending to make it look like he had at least tried to do the killing. However, once at the house, something made him go 'berserk' and he hit Rendell several times with the hammer and then stabbed her in the neck. He pleaded guilty to murder and Calhaem was convicted of counselling. On appeal, she argued that the causal connection between her instigation of the crime and the killing was broken when Zajac decided to kill Rendell of his own accord. However, the conviction was upheld.

Aiding and abetting

These are often taken together. The threshold of involvement is very low. The Court of Appeal in *Giannetto* (1996) stated that 'any involvement from mere encouragement upwards would suffice' for conviction of abetting. The Court commented that if E was to say to D 'I am going to kill your wife', then if D patted him on the back, nodded, or said 'Oh goody' then that would make D liable for abetting 'because he is encouraging the murder.'

Mere presence at the scene of the crime

It is possible for D's mere presence at the scene of a crime to amount to aiding and abetting. In *Coney and Others* (1882), an illegal, bare knuckle fight was held in a makeshift ring by the road between Ascot and

Maidenhead. A large crowd gathered to watch. Many of the crowd were seen to be actively encouraging the fighters. The three defendants, who were in the crowd but were simply watching, were convicted of abetting assault – but the conviction was quashed on appeal. The jury had been directed that persons watching an illegal fight were guilty by virtue of their mere presence. Hawkins J laid down the following propositions:

- Encouragement may be intentional (e.g. by expressions, gestures or actions intended to signify approval) or unintentional (e.g. by misinterpreted words, or gestures, or by silence). However, only intentional encouragement amounts to aiding and abetting.

- Generally speaking, it is not criminal to stand by, to be a mere passive spectator of a crime; some active steps by word or action are required. However, there is an exception if a person was 'voluntarily and purposely present' at the scene of a crime and offered no opposition or did not even express dissent. This might, under some circumstances, 'afford cogent evidence' upon which conviction for aiding and abetting would be justified.

From this, and other cases, the following requirements can be identified before liability can be imposed on spectators for mere presence at the scene of a crime:

- D must have intended to encourage the principal; and

- D's presence must have actually encouraged the principal.

In *Coney and Others*, the convictions were quashed because the first requirement was missing. A similar result occurred in *Clarkson and Others* (1971). An 18-year-old girl, Elke von Groen, had been subjected to a brutal gang-rape at a British Army barracks in West Germany. Although Clarkson and others were present in the room, there was no evidence that they had done anything – such as hold the girl down, or even shout encouragement – other than just watch. Their convictions of rape were quashed. Megaw LJ stated that it was not enough 'that the presence of the accused person has, in fact, given encouragement. It must be proved that he intended to give encouragement; that he *wilfully* encouraged.'

Meanwhile, in *Allan* (1965), the second requirement was missing. D was present – but totally passive – at an affray. Apparently, he had a secret intention to join in to help his 'side' if need be. The Court of Appeal quashed his conviction for abetting the others. Although he *was* present, it seems clear the affray would have taken place anyway – so there was no encouragement *in fact*. This decision must be correct: upholding the trial court's decision would have been tantamount to convicting Allan for his thoughts alone.

An example of a successful conviction, i.e. where both elements were established, occurred in *Wilcox v Jeffrey* (1951). An American saxophonist, Coleman Hawkins, appeared at a concert in London, despite a legal prohibition on him being employed in the UK. Herbert Wilcox, the proprietor of a magazine, *Jazz Illustrated*, had attended the concert and then written a 'most laudatory' review in his magazine. The King's Bench Division upheld his conviction for aiding and abetting Hawkins' illegal employment. Wilcox's presence in the audience was intended to encourage, and did in fact encourage.

Figure 9 The elements needed for a conviction of aiding and abetting

Case	Encouragement in fact?	Intention to encourage	Guilty of aiding and abetting
Coney & Others	Yes	No	No
Clarkson & Others	Yes	No	No
Allan	Yes	No	No
Wilcox v Jeffrey	Yes	Yes	Yes

Aiding and abetting by omission

If D has knowledge of the actions of E, plus the duty or right to control them, but deliberately chooses not to, then he may be guilty of aiding or abetting by omission. In *Tuck v Robson* (1970), Lord Parker CJ asked the rhetorical question, whether 'inaction, passive tolerance, can amount to assistance so as to make the accused guilty of aiding and abetting' – and answered it in the affirmative. D, a pub landlord, with the authority to remove persons from the pub, tolerated after-hours drinking. He was convicted of aiding and abetting breaches of the Licensing Act.

'Counselling'

In *Calhaem* (1985), Parker LJ said that, 'we should give to the word "counsel" its ordinary meaning, which is... "advise", "solicit", or something of that sort...'.

Figure 10 Actus reus of secondary parties: a summary

Form of Participation	Meaning/examples	At or before?	Meeting of minds?	Causal Connection?
Aiding	Help or assistance. Examples: supplying information or equipment; acting as lookout or driver	EITHER	NO	NO
Abetting	Encouragement. Examples: verbal support; gesturing; nodding approval	AT	YES	NO
Counselling	Encouragement; making proposals; offering suggestions, instigating an offence. Example: hiring a hitman	BEFORE	YES	NO
Procuring	To 'produce by endeavour'. Example: spiking a motorist's soft drink with alcohol	BEFORE	NO	YES

'Procuring'

Traditionally it was thought that 'to procure means to produce by endeavour' *(Attorney-General's Reference (No.1 of 1975)* (1975), *per* Lord Widgery CJ). However, in *Millward* (1994), D, a farmer, instructed an employee to drive a tractor on public roads. The tractor was poorly maintained and a trailer became detached, hit a car and killed a passenger. D was convicted of procuring the offence of causing death by reckless driving. Yet D certainly did not 'endeavour' to produce the passenger's death. All that seems to be required now is a causal connection between D's act and the principal's commission of the offence.

Mens rea of secondary parties

The accessory must:

- Have *intended* to assist, encourage, etc., the commission of the offence; and

- Have *knowledge* of the circumstances which constituted the offence.

Intention

D must have intended to participate in the commission of the offence. Any motives or desires that D may have had are, of course, irrelevant. It is therefore no defence that D is utterly indifferent as to whether the principal commits the offence or not. In *National Coal Board v Gamble* (1959), a colliery weighbridge operator, H, allowed a lorry driver to leave the colliery and drive onto a public road even though it was overweight. The Coal Board was found guilty (vicariously, that is, by assuming responsibility for the actions of its employee) of aiding and abetting the offence of driving an overloaded lorry on the public roads. It was no defence that H was indifferent to the commission of the offence.

This gives accessorial liability a very wide scope. The problem was discussed in *Gillick v West Norfolk and Wisbech* AHA (1986), a civil case. G was seeking a declaration that it would be unlawful for a GP to give contraceptive advice to a girl under 16, because this would amount to aiding and abetting the girl's boyfriend to have unlawful sexual intercourse. The House of Lords thought that the GP would not be acting illegally, provided what they did was 'necessary' for the girl's physical, mental and emotional health. Lord Scarman said that the '*bona fide* exercise by a doctor of his clinical judgment must be a complete negation of the guilty mind which is an essential ingredient of the criminal offence of aiding, abetting the commission of unlawful sexual intercourse.'

> Does this decision mean that motive is relevant in criminal law?
>
> What difference is there between a gun salesman, only interested in cash, and a GP, only interested in the best interests of a 15-year-old girl?

Of course, *Gillick* is a civil case and anything said therein is not binding on courts dealing with criminal cases. However, Lord Scarman's statement received the approval of Lord Hutton in the criminal case of *English* (1997) – see pp. 281–2 below.

Knowledge of the circumstances

D must have knowledge of the circumstances that constitute the offence. In *Johnson v Youden and Others* (1950), Lord Goddard CJ said:

> Before a person can be convicted of aiding and abetting the commission of an offence he must at least know the essential matters which constitute that offence. He need not actually know that an offence has been committed, because he may not know that the facts constitute an offence and ignorance of the law is no defence.

The 'essential matters' will be the circumstances and consequences of the *actus reus*. If D is not aware of these he cannot be liable. In *Ferguson v Weaving* (1951), D was the landlady of a large pub. One night, customers were found drinking after time; an offence under s.4 of the Licensing Act 1921. Crucially, there was no evidence that D actually knew that her customers were drinking after hours. A charge of counselling and procuring the customers' offences was dismissed and the King's Bench Divisional Court confirmed that decision.

Extent of knowledge required: the contemplation principle

> Suppose D supplies E with a screwdriver – what else (if anything) should D need to know before he can be held liable as an accessory to burglary if the screwdriver is subsequently used in order to break into a house?
>
> Suppose D and E are on a joint enterprise to commit burglary. D knows that E is armed with a screwdriver. If they are disturbed and E uses the screwdriver to kill the householder, with intent, does this make D guilty of murder?

Secondary parties

If D is accused of aiding, abetting, etc., then there must be proof that he was aware that a crime of a particular type may be committed. D does not need to know the *exact* details but he must be aware of more than that some illegality is planned. In *Bainbridge* (1960), D had purchased some oxygen-cutting equipment for E, which E used six weeks later in breaking into the Midland Bank at Stoke Newington, north London. The equipment was left behind and it was subsequently traced back to D. He was convicted of aiding and abetting burglary and the Court of Criminal Appeal dismissed his appeal. Lord Parker CJ laid down the following propositions:

- D need not have knowledge of 'the precise crime' or 'the particular crime';

- However, D must know 'the type of crime that was in fact committed';

- But is not enough that D merely knows that 'some illegal venture is intended'.

Applying these principles, it was sufficient that D knew the equipment was going to be used for stealing money from a bank. It was not necessary that he knew in advance that it was going to be the Midland Bank, or the date on which the raid was to take place. But it would not suffice for a conviction if he simply knew that the equipment was going to be used to dispose of stolen property.

In *DPP for Northern Ireland v Maxwell* (1978), D was a member of the UVF, a Protestant terrorist organisation. One night he guided other members of the UVF to a Catholic pub, where one of them threw a bomb. He was convicted of doing an act with intent to cause an explosion and possession of a bomb. He appealed on the basis that he was unaware of the precise nature of the attack but the House of Lords upheld his conviction. The Lords took the opportunity to confirm – and extend – the *Bainbridge* principle. Both Lord Fraser and Lord Scarman said that D was guilty if he knew that any one of a 'range' of crimes might be committed. This extends *Bainbridge*, which only referred to crimes of certain 'type'. Lord Scarman said (emphasis added):

> A man will not be convicted of aiding and abetting any offence his principal may commit, but only one which is within his contemplation. He may have in contemplation only one offence, *or several*; *and the several which he contemplates he may see as alternatives*. An accessory who leaves it to his principal to choose is liable, provided always the choice is made from *the range of offences* from which the accessory contemplates the choice will be made.

Joint enterprise

The slight difference here is that D and E are already committed to carrying out one crime, typically robbery or burglary. The question is whether D can be held liable for other crimes, typically murder or manslaughter, that are in fact committed, usually because things do not go according to plan. What is required is proof that that D participated in the joint enterprise with foresight of those other crimes. D is liable for *all* crimes committed by E as a result of carrying out the joint enterprise, *provided* that they were contemplated, in advance, by D. In *English* (1997), Lord Hutton said:

> Where two parties embark on a joint enterprise to commit a crime and one party foresees that, in the course of the enterprise, the other party may commit, with the requisite *mens rea*, an act constituting another crime, the former is liable for that crime if committed by the latter in the course of the enterprise.

The requirements for liability are as follows:

* D must have foresight that E may commit another crime;

* D must foresee that E will have the requisite *mens rea* at the time of committing it;

* The crime foreseen must be committed in the course of the enterprise.

In *English* (1997), Philip English and a man called Weddle agreed to attack a police officer with wooden posts. However, in the course of the attack, W produced a knife with which he killed the officer. English said that he did not know that W was armed with the knife. The judge nevertheless directed the jury to convict English of murder if they believed that he knew that W might cause really serious injury with the wooden post. The House of Lords quashed English's conviction.

Ultimately, it is a question of what was within the scope of the joint enterprise. In *Anderson and Morris* (1966), Lord Parker CJ said that if one member of a joint enterprise 'departed completely' from what had been agreed, 'suddenly formed an intent to kill' and acted upon it, then to hold the other members liable even for manslaughter was 'something which would revolt the conscience of people today'. This was approved in *English*. The unforeseen use of the knife took the killing outside the scope of the joint venture altogether, which meant that English could not be found guilty of either murder or manslaughter.

Justification of the contemplation principle

In *English* (1997) it was argued that the different standards of liability for imposition of murder liability on the members of the joint enterprise, where one of the members kills, was anomalous. The law is as follows:

- The perpetrator (the person who actually does the killing) must be proven to have malice aforethought;

- The other members of a joint enterprise need only foresee that the principal might commit murder.

Lord Steyn took a forthright view. He said that 'the answer to this supposed anomaly... is to be found in practical and policy considerations'. He specifically referred to 'the utility of the accessory principle' and how it would be 'gravely undermined' if the law required proof of intention on the part of all members of the enterprise. The reasons for this stance are twofold.

1 The *difficulty in establishing proof of intention*. Lord Steyn thought that it would 'almost invariably be impossible for a jury to say that the secondary party wanted death to be caused or that he regarded it as virtually certain.'

2 The *desirability of controlling gangs*. Lord Steyn said that the criminal law had to deal 'justly but effectively with those who join with others in criminal enterprises'. He stated that 'joint criminal enterprises only too readily escalate into the commission of greater offences. In order to deal with this important social problem the accessory principle... cannot be... relaxed.'

Withdrawal

An accessory, or a member of a joint enterprise, may withdraw, and escape liability for the full offence. The principles appear to be identical in either case. However, a crucial distinction must be drawn between, on the one hand, pre-planned criminal activity, and, on the other, spontaneous criminal behaviour.

Pre-planned criminal activity

In this situation, the fundamental principle is that mere repentance without action is not enough. Specifically, D will need to satisfy two conditions:

- He must communicate his withdrawal to E;

- He must (depending on how advanced the crime is) take active steps to prevent it.

Communication

In *Becerra and Cooper* (1975), a joint enterprise case, Roskill LJ said that there must be 'timely communication' by the person wishing to terminate their involvement in the enterprise. Roskill LJ said that:

> What is 'timely communication' must be determined by the facts of each case but where practicable and reasonable it ought to be such communication, verbal or otherwise, that will serve unequivocal notice upon the other party to the common unlawful cause that if he proceeds upon it he does so without the further aid and assistance of those who withdraw.

Becerra and Cooper (1975)
Becerra, Cooper were in the middle of the burglary of an old woman in Swansea when they were disturbed by a neighbour, a Mr Lewis. B shouted, 'Come on, let's go', climbed out of the window and ran off. There was a struggle and C, who had the knife, stabbed Lewis four times, once in the heart. C then escaped through the window. B and C were convicted of murder. B appealed, *inter alia*, on the ground that by the time C stabbed Lewis he had withdrawn from the common enterprise. The Court of Appeal upheld the convictions. Roskill LJ was clearly unimpressed with B's argument: he said that something 'vastly different and vastly more effective' was required for withdrawal than shouting 'Let's go'.

Thus in *Whitefield* (1984), where D had tipped off a burglar that his neighbours' flat was unoccupied, but subsequently informed the man of his wanting no more to do with it, his withdrawal was effective. However, in *Rook* (1993), where D had been heavily involved in the planning stage of a contract killing, his failure to tell anyone of his decision to withdraw meant that his disappearance before the killing took place was insufficient.

Spontaneous criminal activity

In *Mitchell and King* (1999), the Court of Appeal held that communication of withdrawal from a joint enterprise was only a necessary condition for cases of *pre-planned* criminal activity, as in *Rook*, above. This was not the case where the criminal behaviour was *spontaneous*, as in this case, where an argument quickly developed into a fight outside a fast-food takeaway. In such cases, it was possible to withdraw merely by walking away.

Victims as accessories

The mere fact D is also a victim does not prevent him from accessorial liability. Suppose D, a masochist, allows E, a sadist, to wound him for sexual gratification, then D should be liable for aiding and abetting E's unlawful assault.

Occasionally a statute may protect a particular class or type of person, for example a child, so that they may not be convicted. In *Tyrell* (1894), D, a 14 year-old girl, was convicted of aiding and abetting her father to have incest *with her*, contrary to s.5 of the Criminal Law Amendment Act 1885. Her conviction was quashed. The Court of Criminal Appeal thought it impossible that an Act designed to protect young girls could have been intended to punish them instead.

Reform

In 1993, the Law Commission published a Report, *Assisting and Encouraging Crime*. It involves a radical reform of the existing law. As well as abolishing all of the familiar – but arguably too old-fashioned – words in the Accessories and Abettors Act 1861, the Report recommends the abolition of the rule that an accessory 'is liable to be tried, indicted and punished as a principal offender.' Instead, accessories become liable for an independent offence of 'assisting crime'. The proposals may be summarised thus:

- Aiding, abetting, counselling and procuring all abolished;

- New offence of 'assisting crime' created;

- *Actus reus*: D commits this if he 'does any act', which 'includes giving the principal advice' as to how to commit the offence or to 'avoid detention or apprehension before or during the commission of the offence';

- *Mens rea*: D must 'know or believe' that the principal will commit a criminal offence with the *mens rea* required for that offence; D must also 'know or believe' that his act assists or will assist the principal in committing it.

This proposed reform is now eight years old, but is nowhere near implementation.

Summary

- An accomplice is anyone who aids, abets, counsels or procures the principal offender to commit a criminal offence. The words bear their ordinary meaning (*Attorney-General's Reference [No.1 of 1975]*).

- A joint enterprise occurs where two defendants embark on a criminal venture together (*Pearson*).

- Accessories are liable to be 'tried, indicted and punished' as a principal offender.

- Accessories may be liable even if the principal offender is not guilty for some reason – provided the principal performed the required *actus reus* (*Bourne, Cogan and Leak*).

- Mere presence at the scene of a crime does not, generally speaking, amount to aiding and abetting (*Coney and Others*). There must be encouragement in fact and an intention to encourage (*Wilcox v Jeffrey*). If only one or other of these is present there is no liability (*Clarkson and Others, Allan*).

- The accessory must have intended to aid, abet, etc., the commission of the offence (*National Coal Board v Gamble*) and have knowledge of the circumstances which constitute the offence (*Johnson v Youden and Others*).

- D does not need to know the *exact* details of the offence but he must be aware of more than that some illegality is planned (*Bainbridge, DPP for Northern Ireland v Maxwell*).

- In joint enterprise cases, D is liable for all crimes committed by their co-defendant committed within the scope of the joint enterprise (*English, Anderson and Morris*). This includes all offences that D contemplated that the other might commit. However, D must foresee that the other would have the required *mens rea*, as well as the *actus reus*. D's awareness of the other being armed – and, if so, with what weapon – may be a crucial factor in establishing what crimes D contemplated.

- An accessory, or a member of a joint enterprise, may withdraw, and escape liability for the full offence.

- If the criminal offence was pre-planned, then they must, at the least, communicate their unequivocal withdrawal (*Becerra and Cooper, Rook*).

- If the criminal offence was spontaneous, then simply walking away might suffice (*Mitchell and King*).

- Victims cannot be guilty of offences under statutes designed for their own protection (*Tyrell*).

21 Attempts

Introduction

If D poisons his mother's drink, fully intending to kill her so that he can inherit under her will, but she drops dead from a heart attack by some freak coincidence before drinking it, should D escape liability because he failed to kill her? If D bursts into a post office with a sawn-off shotgun, terrifies the staff and customers, but leaves empty-handed because one of the staff reacted quickly enough to press the alarm, should he escape liability because he failed to steal anything? Of course both defendants are not liable for murder or robbery respectively, as they did not complete the crime. But they would almost certainly be guilty of an attempt. Indeed, the first illustration is taken from the facts of *White* (1910), where D tried to kill his own mother with potassium cyanide, only for her to die of natural causes. However, D was found guilty of attempted murder.

The law relating to attempts perfectly illustrates that element of criminal liability which addresses the significance of *mens rea* or the guilty mind. Clearly, in the above examples the accused is intent upon committing an offence but fails in the attempt. It would be ludicrous to regard their actions as innocent. They deserve to be sentenced for their actions just as much as they would have been punished had their attempted crime been successful. After all, they intended to commit a criminal offence. However, a person cannot be convicted for harbouring evil thoughts by themselves. Feeling like killing the examiner for not setting a question on your favourite topic is, perhaps fortunately, not in itself a crime. Students should note, however, that each of the inchoate offences does in fact consist of its own *actus reus* which the prosecution must prove has occurred in order to gain a conviction. In incitement the accused must be proved to have *proposed, suggested or encouraged another* to commit an offence. In conspiracy there must be *an agreement* between two or more people to commit a crime. In an attempt it must be shown that the accused has done an act which is *more than* merely preparatory to the intended offence.

Attempt, incitement and conspiracy are examples of what are collectively termed inchoate offences. Incitement and conspiracy will be examined in the next chapter. The term inchoate refers to the situation where a person has done something which can be regarded as a preparatory criminal act with the intention that a substantive offence should be carried out.

Apart from the moral justification of punishing a person who intends to commit criminal activity there is a practical reason for the existence of these crimes. After all, it is the duty of the police to prevent crime as well as to detect it. It would do little for the protection of the public were the police always required to wait until a substantive offence had actually been committed before being able to carry out an arrest. If an informant reveals that a gang is planning a robbery, for example, it makes sense for the police to pre-empt the danger to the public that could accompany such a venture. Provided there is good evidence that an agreement to commit the robbery has been entered into the police may arrest and charge those concerned with the offence of conspiracy.

The *actus reus* of attempts

S.1(1) of the Criminal Attempts Act 1981 provides that 'If, with intent to commit an offence to which this section applies, a person does an act which is more that merely preparatory to the commission of the offence, he is guilty of attempting to commit the offence.' Although the judge must decide whether there is evidence on which a jury could find that there has been such an act, the test of whether D's acts have gone beyond the merely preparatory stage is essentially a question of fact for the jury (s.4(3) Criminal Attempts Act 1981). If the judge decides there is no such evidence, he or she must direct them to acquit; otherwise the question must be left to the jury, even if the judge feels the only possible answer is guilty.

'More than merely preparatory'

When is D guilty of an attempt? When he has gone beyond the 'merely preparatory' stage. But when is that? Consider the following scenario: Ken discovers that his girlfriend is seeing another man (F). Ken decides to do something about it. He decides to kill this love rival. But at which point does he become liable for attempted murder?

- He buys a shotgun.

- He shortens the barrel.

- He loads it.

- He leaves his house, wearing overalls and a crash helmet with the visor down, carrying a bag containing the loaded gun.

- He approaches F's car as F drops his daughter off at school.

- He opens the car door and gets in.

- He says he wants to 'sort things out'.

- He takes the shotgun from the bag.

- He points it at F, and says, 'You are not going to like this'.

At this point F was able to grab the end of the gun, throw it out of the window and escape. These are the facts of *Jones* (1990), who was convicted of attempted murder; the Court of Appeal upholding his conviction. Taylor LJ said that obtaining the gun, shortening the barrel, loading the gun, and disguising himself were clearly preparatory acts but – once Jones had got into the car and pointed the loaded gun – then there was sufficient evidence of an attempt to leave to the jury.

The common law offence of attempt was abolished by the Criminal Attempts Act 1981. The 1981 Act is a codifying Act. This means that the 'natural meaning' of the statutory words must be considered first but, if any provision is 'of doubtful import', then previous cases may be referred to. They are not binding, but are persuasive. At common law, there were a variety of tests used by the courts in determining whether D had done an act which could be described as 'an attempt' to commit an offence.

The 'proximity' test

The Law Commission thought that the most suitable of these tests was the 'proximity' test. In *Eagleton* (1855), it was said that 'acts remotely leading towards the commission of the offence are not to be considered as attempts to commit it, but acts immediately connected with it are.' This test was applied in *Robinson* (1915). D, a jeweller, insured his stock against theft. He then concealed it around his shop, then tied himself up and called for help. He told the police that he had been attacked and his safe robbed. However, his scheme was discovered. Although D confessed, his conviction for attempting to obtain £1,200 from his insurers by false pretences was quashed. He still had to approach the insurers for a claim form, fill it in, submit it, etc. His acts were not 'immediately connected' with the substantive offence.

However, the Law Commission's support for this test was surprising. First, the expression 'immediately connected' could be interpreted very narrowly, as Robinson shows. Second, the proximity test looked *backwards* from the commission of the full offence, to see if D's acts were close to that. The 'more than merely preparatory' looks *forward* from the point of preparatory acts to see whether D's acts have gone beyond that stage.

The 'Rubicon' test

Obviously the Law Commission's views on what test the courts should use was not binding, and in an early case after the enactment of the new legislation, *Widdowson* (1986), the Court of Appeal adopted a different common law test, the 'Rubicon' test as proposed by Lord Diplock in *Stonehouse* (1978). He stated that there was only an attempt where D had 'crossed the Rubicon and burnt his boats': that is, gone beyond the 'point of no return'. In *Widdowson*, D wished to obtain a van on hire purchase but, realising that his application would be rejected, filled in the form under a false identity. The Court of Appeal quashed his conviction of attempting to obtain services by deception. The acts he had done were too remote from the substantive offence. Too many acts remained unperformed; in particular he had not actually submitted the form to the hire purchase company. He had not 'burned his boats'.

The 'series of acts' test

However, in *Boyle and Boyle* (1986), the Court of Appeal referred to another pre-1981 Act test: the 'series of acts' test, put forward by the academic Stephen, according to whom 'an attempt to commit a crime is an act done with intent to commit that crime, and forming part of a series of acts which would constitute its actual commission if it were not interrupted'. In *Boyle and Boyle*, the defendants were convicted of attempted burglary, having been found by a policeman standing near a door, the lock and one hinge of which were broken. The Court of Appeal upheld this conviction.

Progress!

This divergence of approaches even after the 1981 Act was clearly unsatisfactory. However, progress was made in *Gullefer* (1990). D had placed an £18 bet on a greyhound race at Romford Stadium. Seeing that his dog was losing, he climbed onto the track in front of the dogs, waving his arms and attempting to distract them, in an effort to get the stewards to declare 'no race', in which case he would get his stake back. His conviction of attempted theft was quashed; his act was merely preparatory. He still had to go to the bookmakers and demand his money back. Lord Lane CJ recognised that the problem with Stephen's test was that it did not specify *when* the 'series of acts' begins. Further, acts which were obviously merely preparatory could be described as part of a series. Instead, he said:

> The words of the Act seek to steer a midway course. [A crime] begins when the merely preparatory acts have come to an end and [D] embarks upon the crime proper. When that is will depend of course upon the facts in any particular case.

In *Jones* (1990), above, Taylor LJ agreed with Lord Lane CJ, adding that the correct approach was to 'look first at the natural meaning of the statutory words, not to turn back to earlier case law and seek to fit some previous test to the words of the section.' In the light of the more expansive approach signalled by *Gullefer* and *Jones*, the decision in *Campbell* (1991) is surprisingly narrow. D was arrested by police when, armed with an imitation gun, he approached to within a yard of a Post Office door. His conviction for attempted robbery was quashed: the Court of Appeal thought there was no evidence on which a jury could 'properly and safely' have concluded that his acts were more than merely preparatory. It seems the police should have waited until D had entered the Post Office, or even approached the counter.

However, further progress was made in *Geddes* (1996), when the Court of Appeal offered another formulation for identifying the threshold. A member of school staff discovered D lurking in the boys' toilet. He ran off, leaving behind a rucksack, in which was found various items including string, sealing tape and a knife. He was charged with attempted false imprisonment of a person unknown. The judge ruled that there was evidence of an attempt and the jury convicted. On appeal, the conviction was quashed. There was serious doubt about whether he had gone beyond the mere preparation stage. He had not even tried to make contact with any pupils. The Court of Appeal postulated the following questions:

- Had the accused moved from planning or preparation to execution or implementation?

- Had the accused done an act showing that he was actually trying to commit the full offence or had he got only as far as getting ready, or putting himself in a position, or equipping himself, to do so?

In *Tosti* (1997), the Court of Appeal followed the *Geddes* approach. D and his co-accused, White, had provided themselves with oxy-acetylene equipment, drove to a barn which they planned to burgle, concealed the equipment in a hedge, approached the door and examined the padlock. They then became aware that they were being watched and ran off. The Court of Appeal upheld their convictions of attempted burglary. The conviction seems right: the men were clearly 'actually trying to commit the full offence' of burglary by examining a padlock.

More than merely preparatory: conclusion

When D might be said to be 'embarked on the crime proper' (*Gullefer* [1990]) or when he was 'actually trying to commit the full offence' (*Geddes* [1996]), he has committed an act that is 'more than merely preparatory' and is guilty of an attempt.

The *mens rea* of attempt

Intention

The essence of attempt is D's intention. The acts which may amount to the *actus reus* will very often be objectively neutral; it is the *mens rea* which converts them into an attempt. In *Whybrow* (1951), the Court of Appeal held that although on a charge of murder, an intention to cause GBH would suffice, where attempted murder was alleged, nothing less than an intent to kill would do; 'the intent becomes the principal ingredient of the crime'.

In *Mohan* (1975), the Court of Appeal defined 'intent' as 'a decision to bring about, insofar as it lies within [D]'s power, the commission of the offence which it is alleged [D] attempted to commit, no matter whether [D] desired that consequence of his act or not'. 'Intent' clearly includes D's purpose. If D is *trying* to do something, then it does not matter whether he views his chances of success are remote, or even just possible. In *Walker and Hayles* (1990), the Court of Appeal applied the *Nedrick* (1986) direction (see Chapter 5) on oblique intent in the common law to 'intent' in s.1 of the 1981 Act.

Conditional intent

Attempted theft and burglary cases have caused difficulties when it comes to framing the indictment. The problem is that most burglars, pickpockets, etc. are opportunists who do not have something particular in mind. Two cases from the 1970s illustrated the problem:

- *Easom* (1971) – D, who had been observed rummaging in a handbag in a cinema but did not take anything from it, was charged with the theft of a handbag, purse, notebook, tissues, cosmetics and pen. He was convicted but the Court of Appeal quashed his conviction following a misdirection. The Court declined to substitute a conviction of attempted theft of those articles.

- *Husseyn* (1977) – D and another man had been observed loitering near the back of a van. As police approached they ran off. D was convicted of attempting to steal a quantity of sub-aqua equipment that was in the van. The Court of Appeal quashed the conviction.

Eventually, in *Attorney-General's Reference (Nos. 1 and 2 of 1979)* (1979), the Court of Appeal got around the problem. The difficulties in *Easom* and *Husseyn* were all caused because D in each case had been charged with the attempted theft of some specific thing(s). Instead, if D is charged with an attempt to steal 'some or all of the contents' of the holdall, handbag, box, pocket, etc., the problem disappears.

The relevance of recklessness
Consequences

Recklessness has a role to play in attempts. In *Attorney-General's Reference (No.3 of 1992)* (1994), the Court of Appeal held that D could have been convicted of attempting to commit arson, being reckless as to whether life would be endangered, contrary to s.1(3) of the Criminal Damage Act 1971. D had thrown a petrol bomb towards a car containing four men but it missed and smashed harmlessly into a wall. The trial judge ruled that there was no case to answer as he concluded that it had to be shown that D both intended to damage property *and* to endanger life. The Court of Appeal held this was wrong. It was enough that D intended to damage property by fire, recklessness as to whether life would be endangered was sufficient.

Circumstances

If D is charged with attempted rape, does it have to be proved that he:

- intended to have sex, being reckless as to whether V consents, or

- intended to have non-consensual intercourse?

The Law Commission, in their report preceding the 1981 Act, took the view that intention as to every element was required; that is, knowledge as to circumstances was required. However, this had not been the position before the Act, and the Court of Appeal did not change it afterwards. In *Khan* (1990), D, along with three others, was convicted of the attempted rape of a 16-year-old girl at a house in Uxbridge. All four of the men had tried to have sex with her, unsuccessfully. Their convictions were upheld despite the trial judge's direction that, on a charge of attempted rape, it was only necessary for the Crown to prove that they had intended to have sex, knowing that the girl was not consenting, or not caring whether she consented or not.

Excluded offences

S.1(4) of the Criminal Attempts Act 1981 excludes attempts to commit the following:

- conspiracy; and

- aiding, abetting, counselling or procuring the commission of an offence (except where this amounts to a substantive offence, e.g. complicity in another's suicide, procuring others to commit homosexual acts).

S.1(1) also implicitly excludes other attempts. There must be 'an act', so it is impossible to attempt to commit a crime which can only be committed by omission (e.g. D cannot attempt to fail to provide a breath test). Where a crime cannot be committed intentionally (such as involuntary manslaughter), it is impossible to attempt it. Furthermore, because diminished responsibility and provocation are no defence to attempted murder, there is therefore no offence of 'attempted manslaughter' (though the Law Commission suggested creating it, see below).

Successful attempts

Is failure essential to a conviction for attempt? The answer, perhaps surprisingly, is no. D may be convicted of an attempt, notwithstanding that he is also shown to be guilty of the completed offence. In *Webley v Buxton* (1977), police officers observed D sitting astride a motorbike outside a pub at about 1a.m. He was seen using his feet to push it 8 feet across a pavement towards the road. When the officers got out of their vehicle, he jumped off the bike and ran off. D was convicted of attempting to take the bike, an offence under s.12 Theft Act 1968. The Divisional Court held that, although D had committed the full offence – that is, taking the bike, because the slightest movement of it would suffice – he could nevertheless be convicted of the attempt. This seems right: the greater includes the less. Once D goes beyond preparation, he is guilty of attempt. It should not disappear simply because the attempt happens to succeed. Of course, D could not be convicted of *both* the full offence *and* the attempt.

Impossibility

If a crime is impossible to commit, obviously no-one can be convicted of committing it. However, it does not automatically follow that no-one can be convicted of attempting it. The question is whether the crime in question was possible. (This is different from the situation where D attempts to commit what is not in fact a crime, even if he thinks it is. Here there is no offence. Thus, in *Taaffe* [1983], which was considered in Chapter 1, D would not have been guilty of 'attempting to import currency' either – there is simply no such offence.)

There may be an offence where D fails to commit the substantive crime, because he makes a mistake or is ignorant as to certain facts. The crime may be:

- *physically impossible* (e.g. D attempts to pick V's pocket, which, unknown to D, is in fact empty; or D attempts to murder V who, unknown to him, died that morning); or

- *legally impossible* (D attempts to handle goods, believing them to be stolen, when they are not in fact not stolen)

There are also situations where the crime is physically and legally possible, but in the actual circumstances, because of the inadequate methods D plans to use, or does use, it is impossible to commit the substantive offence (e.g. D attempts to break into a three-inch thick titanium steel safe using a screwdriver). That the crime was 'impossible' because D used inadequate methods is certainly no defence (in *White* [1910], above, had D given his mother sugared water instead, he would not have avoided liability).

But, at common law, there was no liability if the crime attempted was physically or legally impossible. S.1(2) of the Criminal Attempts Act 1981 was intended to abolish that loophole. The subsection provides that 'A person may be guilty of attempting to commit an offence to which this section applies even though the facts are such that the commission of the offence is impossible.' Despite the statutory provision, in *Anderton v Ryan* (1985), the House of Lords decided that the 1981 Act had not been intended to affect the situation of physical impossibility.

> *Anderton v Ryan* (1985)
> D bought a video recorder for £110 from a person whom she declined to name. Later she said to police officers who were investigating a burglary at her home, 'I may as well be honest, it was a stolen one.' When asked why she had bought it if she knew it to be stolen, she said: 'Well everyone's at it. I didn't think I'd get discovered.' She was convicted of attempting to handle a stolen video recorder worth £500. But her conviction was quashed because the video recorder was not in fact stolen.

Lord Roskill said that 'a defendant who is possessed of [an] erroneous belief and who after doing innocent acts which are more than merely preparatory to fulfilling his intention for some reason subsequently fails to achieve that which he intends is not liable to be convicted of an attempt to commit a crime.'

In *Shivpuri* (1987), this decision was overruled less than a year later. Lord Bridge (who, much to his obvious embarrassment, sat in both cases) said:

> The concept of 'objective innocence' is incapable of sensible application in relation to the law of criminal attempts. The reason for this is that any attempt to commit an offence which involves 'an act which is more then merely preparatory to the commission of the offence' but which for any reason fails, so that in the event no offence

is committed, must *ex hypothesi*, from the point of view of the criminal law be 'objectively innocent'. What turns what would otherwise... be an innocent act into a crime is the intent of the actor to commit an offence.

Shivpuri (1987)

Pyare Shivpuri, on a visit to India, was approached by a man who offered to pay him £1,000 if, on his return to England, he would receive a suitcase, which a courier would deliver to him containing drugs. S would then receive instructions as to how he was to distribute the drugs. The suitcase was duly delivered to him. S then received instructions to go to Southall station to deliver some of the drugs. However, he was arrested outside the station. A package containing a powdered substance was found in his bag. At his flat, he produced the suitcase and more packages of the same powdered substance. S, believing the powder to be either heroin or cannabis, fully confessed to receiving and distributing illegally imported drugs. Subsequently, the powder was scientifically analysed and found to be snuff or some similar harmless vegetable matter. S was convicted of attempting to be knowingly concerned in dealing in prohibited drugs, and the Court of Appeal and Lords dismissed his appeal.

It has been argued that in this sort of case, D is being punished solely for his criminal intention. However, for an attempt, there must be a 'more then merely preparatory act'. Furthermore, defendants like Shivpuri who intend to smuggle drugs are dangerous; prosecution and conviction is in the public interest. In many cases, the 'objectively innocent' nature of the acts means that the attempt will not come to light. But, in those cases where it does, D should not escape punishment.

Reform

Should there be a crime of attempted manslaughter? No such offence presently exists but the Law Commission has recommended that it should. This would occur if D pleaded diminished responsibility, provocation or excessive force in self-defence to a charge of attempted murder. Under the current law, none of these pleas would amount to any defence at all, but under the draft Criminal Law Bill (1989), they would result in a conviction for attempted manslaughter.

Summary

- D is guilty of attempting an offence if he does an act which is more than merely preparatory to the commission of that offence, under the Criminal Attempts Act 1981.

- The Act replaced the common law crime of attempt. The Act does not give any definition of when the 'more than merely preparatory' stage is reached – it is left entirely to the courts. However, the Law Commission recommended the old 'proximity' test established in *Eagleton*, *Robinson*, be used.

- Cases decided just after the Act used the 'Rubicon' test established in *Stonehouse* instead (*Widdowson*). Then courts began to use another old test, the 'series of acts' test (*Boyle and Boyle*).

- Now the courts have eschewed the old tests and developed new ones, based on the words of the Act itself (*Gullefer*, *Jones*). One test is whether D has 'embarked on the crime proper' (*Gullefer*). Another is whether D was 'actually trying to commit the full offence' (*Geddes*, *Tosti*).

- Intent is 'the principal ingredient' of attempt (*Whybrow*).

- A conditional intent will suffice (*Attorney-General's Reference [Nos. 1 and 2 of 1979]*).

- Recklessness has a role in attempt (*Attorney-General's Reference [No.3 of 1992]*, *Khan*).

- Legal or physical impossibility is no defence (*Shivpuri*).

22 Conspiracy and incitement

A Conspiracy

Introduction

S.1(1) of the Criminal Law Act 1977, as amended, provides that,

if a person agrees with any other person or persons that a course of conduct shall be pursued which, if the agreement is carried out in accordance with their intentions… will necessarily amount to or involve the commission of any offence or offences by one or more of the parties to the agreement, he is guilty of conspiracy.

The *actus reus* of conspiracy

'Agreement'

The offence is complete as soon as there is an agreement. The agreement continues until the substantive offence is performed, abandoned or frustrated (*DPP v Doot* [1973]). Thus further parties may join a subsisting conspiracy at any time until then.

'The parties'

It is essential is that there is a common purpose or design, and that each alleged conspirator has communicated with at least one, but not necessarily all, of the others.

Excluded parties: s.2(2) Criminal Law Act 1977

S.2(2) specifically provides there is no conspiracy if D agrees with:

(a) his spouse – applied in;

(b) a person under age of criminal responsibility; or

(c) the intended victim.

The *mens rea* of statutory conspiracy

The parties must:

- *agree that a course of conduct shall be pursued* which,

- if the agreement is carried out *in accordance with their intentions* will necessarily amount to or involve the commission of any offence or offences by one or more of the parties to the agreement.

Agreement on a 'course of conduct'

This is not limited to the physical acts, but includes the consequences of those acts too. It is necessary to establish exactly what consequences were agreed upon. If D and E agree that E will kneecap V, this is a conspiracy to wound or cause GBH – it does not metamorphose into a conspiracy to murder if D actually does the kneecapping and V happens to die.

'In accordance with their intentions...'

Does this mean that, if D and E agree to commit a crime but D, secretly, has no intention of seeing it through, there will be no conspiracy? In *Anderson* (1986), the House of Lords decided that the answer to this question was no. D had been convicted of conspiracy to effect the escape of a prisoner from Lewes prison. D stood to receive £20,000 for his part in the escape, which was to purchase and supply equipment, transport and accommodation. D's appeal – that he had no intention of seeing the plan put into effect – was rejected. Lord Bridge said that the *mens rea* of conspiracy was 'established if, and only if, it is shown that the accused, when he entered into the agreement, intended to play some part in the agreed course of conduct in furtherance of the criminal purpose.'

Lord Bridge was concerned to see that a 'perfectly respectable citizen' who went along with a conspiracy 'with the purpose of frustrating and exposing the objective of the other parties' should not be liable, and thought he was doing so. In fact, he may have achieved quite the opposite.

Suppose that D is a criminal mastermind. According to Lord Bridge, he is not guilty of conspiracy if he never intended to 'play some part'. On the other hand, an undercover policeman could well be guilty of conspiracy if he intended to play an active role in order to remain undetected and/or to gather evidence. This led the Court of Appeal to undertake a damage-limitation exercise in *Siracusa* (1989). O'Connor LJ said that 'the intention to participate in the furtherance of the criminal purpose is also established by his failure to stop the unlawful activity.' This deals with the problem of the mastermind, although it still requires that he fails to prevent someone else to do something.

As for the undercover policeman, he appears liable for conspiracy precisely because he does intend to 'play some part.' In *Yip Chiu-Cheung* (1994), the Privy Council used this positively in order to uphold a conviction. D had conspired with E, an undercover US drug enforcement officer, to smuggle heroin from Hong Kong to Australia. The judge directed the jury that, if they found that E intended to export the heroin from Hong Kong, he was in law a co-conspirator and, hence, they could convict D of conspiring with him. They convicted and the Privy Council upheld D's conviction: the mere fact that E would not have been prosecuted were he to export the drugs did not mean he did not intend to do it. D and E had conspired to commit the offence.

'If the agreement is carried out…'

In *Jackson* (1985), D and E agreed with V that they would shoot him in the leg if V, who was then on trial, was convicted of burglary, in order to encourage the court to sentence him more leniently! They were convicted of conspiracy to pervert the course of justice. The Court of Appeal upheld their convictions, dismissing their argument that there was no conspiracy because V may have been acquitted.

> If D and E agree to rob a bank if it is quiet when they get there, have they agreed on a course of conduct which will 'necessarily' amount to the commission of an offence?

Impossibility

At common law, impossibility was a defence (except where it was down to D's choice of method being inadequate). However, the Criminal Law Act 1977 abolished that defence. Hence, D and E could be convicted of a conspiracy to murder a particular politician on the basis of an agreement even if – unknown to them – the politician in question had died in his sleep the previous night.

Jurisdiction

An agreement in England to commit an offence abroad is only triable here if the substantive offence would be too. This would include conspiracies to commit murder abroad. What about the reverse position: if D and E agree in France to commit murder (or indeed any offence) in England? In *DPP v Doot* (1973), the House of Lords thought such a conspiracy could be prosecuted here if the agreement was subsequently performed, wholly or in part, in England. Five American citizens had conspired in either Belgium or

Morocco to smuggle cannabis from Morocco to the United States *via* England. They were caught by customs officers and charged with conspiracy to import cannabis. The House of Lords upheld their convictions. Lord Salmon said: 'It is obvious that a conspiracy to carry out a bank robbery in London is equally a threat to the Queen's peace whether it is hatched, say, in Birmingham or in Brussels.'

Summary

- Conspiracy is governed by the Criminal Law Act 1977.

- It requires an agreement between at least two parties.

- Certain parties are excluded: spouses, young children and the intended victim.

- The parties must agree on a course of conduct that will necessarily amount to the commission of an offence by one of them. It is probably not necessary that the conspirators know that what they are planning is illegal (*Siracusa*).

- There may still be a conspiracy even if one party has no intention of seeing it through – provided he intended 'to play some part' (*Anderson*). But playing a part has been taken to include failing to stop the conspiracy (*Siracusa*).

- It is no defence for D to conspire with an undercover policeman – there was still an agreement to commit an offence (*Yip Chiu-Cheung*).

- There is a conspiracy even if the agreement was conditional on some future event or circumstance (*Jackson*).

- Impossibility is no defence.

- A conspiracy made abroad can be tried in England if the agreement was subsequently performed, wholly or in part, in England (*DPP v Doot*).

B Incitement

Introduction

At common law it was an indictable offence to incite someone to commit any offence. Now incitement to commit a summary offence is triable summarily, incitement to commit an indictable offence is triable on indictment. In the former case, the maximum penalty is the same as for the substantive offence; but in the latter the penalty is totally at the discretion of the court – regardless of the penalty for the substantive offence.

Parliament has also created statutory offences of incitement, such as incitement to murder (s.4, Offences Against the Person Act 1861). There is now an offence of incitement to commit certain sexual acts outside the United Kingdom, contrary to the Sexual Offences (Conspiracy and Incitement) Act 1996.

The *actus reus* of incitement

Incitement could take various forms:

- suggestions,

- proposals,

- requests,

- persuasion,

- goading.

In *Marlow* (1997), D wrote a book on the cultivation and production of cannabis. Some 500 copies were sold and several customers followed the instructions. He was charged with incitement to commit an offence under the Misuse of Drugs Act 1971. The trial judge directed the jury, using the phrases 'may encourage or persuade'. This, it was argued, set the test too low, but the Court of Appeal dismissed the appeal; describing the use of the word 'encourages' as representing 'as well as any modern word can the concept involved'.

In Gianetto (1996), a counselling case, the Court of Appeal suggested that, for D to respond to being told by someone that they were going to kill his wife by saying 'Oh goody!', would make him liable for murder. Would it make him liable for incitement?

Incitement may be to an individual, or to the whole world. In *Invicta Plastics Ltd v Clare* (1976), the company was convicted of inciting the readers of *What Car* magazine to commit the offence of using unlicensed apparatus under the Wireless Telegraphy Act 1949 by advertising a device, 'Radatec', which they claimed could give drivers advance warning of the police using radar speed-traps. There was little chance of the licensing authorities granting drivers licences to use the devices.

The act incited must constitute an *actus reus*

If D persuades E to do an act, he is only liable for incitement if that act would constitute the *actus reus* of an offence. In *Whitehouse* (1977), D was convicted of inciting his 15-year-old daughter to commit incest with him. Had intercourse taken place, he would have been guilty of incest; the girl, however, would have committed no offence (because of the rule that prevents people from being convicted of crimes designed to protect them). D's conviction was quashed.

The *mens rea* of incitement

D must intend that the offence incited be committed. He must also know of (or be wilfully blind as to) all the circumstances which make the act an offence.

Impossibility

Incitement is still governed by the common law. Hence, impossibility is a defence except where it relates to the adequacy of the methods to be used. If D incites E to break into a titanium safe using a screwdriver which, unknown to them, will never work, D should be guilty.

In *Fitzmaurice* (1983), D's father asked him to find someone to rob a woman taking wages to a bank in Bow, East London. D, believing the robbery was to take place, approached E, who he knew was short of money, and encouraged him to take part in the proposed robbery. In fact the proposed robbery was a complete fiction, invented by the father to enable him to collect reward money from the police! D was convicted of inciting E to commit robbery and appealed, arguing that as the woman did not exist it would be impossible to rob her. However, the Court of Appeal dismissed his appeal. Although the court held that, in most cases, impossibility was a good defence to a charge of incitement, the offence incited by D was possible: he had incited E to rob a woman on her way to a bank, and it would have been possible for E to go ahead and rob such a woman.

Reform

In 1993, the Law Commission produced a Report, *Assisting and Encouraging Crime*. The Commission proposed a new offence to replace that of incitement, called simply 'encouraging crime'. This would be committed by anyone who 'solicits, commands or encourages another' to commit a crime, intending that the crime should be committed and knowing or believing that the other person would have the *mens rea* for the offence at the time. The 'solicitation, command or encouragement' would have to be 'brought to the attention' of the other, but it would be irrelevant to D if the other failed to react to the solicitation, command or encouragement.

Although this reform was welcomed in some quarters, it has not been adopted – yet – by the Government; nor is there any indication that it will be in the near future.

Summary

- Incitement consists of encouragement of another to commit a criminal offence. It extends to threats or pressure (*Race Relations Board v Applin*).

- Incitement may be to an individual, or to the world (*Invicta Plastics Ltd v Clare*).

- D is only liable for incitement if the act incited would constitute the *actus reus* of an offence (*Whitehouse*).

- D must intend that the offence incited be committed.

- D must also know of (or be wilfully blind as to) all the circumstances which make the act an offence.

- Impossibility is a defence except where it relates to the adequacy of the methods to be used (*Fitzmaurice*).

Questions on Part 6 General Principles 2

Participation

1 Del and Rodney agree to steal jewellery from Lady Windermere's country house. Del buys a gun from Max, who knows of Del's reputation as a violent criminal. When Rodney finds out that Del is going to be carrying a gun he decides to withdraw from their plan. When he tells Del this, Del threatens to inform Rodney's wife of an affair Rodney is having with another woman unless Rodney agrees to go ahead. Rodney reluctantly gives in to these threats on condition that Del agrees not to use the gun except to frighten anyone they might encounter.

On the night in question Rodney sees that Del has a revolver apparently loaded with bullets. 'They are only blanks!', Del assures him.

Rodney isn't sure whether to believe him or not. They break in and carry out their plan but, as they are leaving, are suddenly confronted by Soames, Lady Windermere's valet. Del pulls out the gun and deliberately shoots Soames dead.

Discuss the liability, if any, of Del, Rodney and Max for the death of Soames.

(OCR 1998)

2 'We approach s.8 of the 1861 [Accessories and Abettors] Act on the basis that the words should be given their ordinary meaning, if possible. We approach the section on the basis also that, if four words are employed here, "aid, abet, counsel or procure", the probability is that there is a difference between each of those four words and the other three, because, if there were no such difference, then Parliament would be wasting its time in using four words where two or three would do.'
– per Lord Widgery CJ in *Attorney-General's Reference* (No 1 of 1975)

Critically consider how the courts have interpreted the words 'aid, abet, counsel or procure'.

(OCR 1999)

Inchoate offences (incitement, conspiracy, attempt)

3 In order to secure a conviction for an attempted crime the accused must be proved to have done an act which is 'more than merely preparatory' to the intended offence.
How satisfactory has this definition proved to be?

(OCR 1998)

4 'All inchoate offences should be abolished on the theory that society is not harmed until the crime is completed.'
Critically evaluate the strengths and weaknesses of the above proposition using examples drawn from any of the inchoate offences of incitement, conspiracy and attempt.

(OCR 2000)

Part 7

General questions on criminal law

23   Additional questions

Essay and problem questions have so far been included at the end of each Part of the book, and relate predominantly to the subject matter of the preceding Part. All these questions have been taken from OCR papers, reflecting their approach to assessment and setting questions on criminal law. The following chapter provides a range of questions on criminal law which range more broadly across the subject matter covered in this book as a whole, reflecting the approach taken by AQA. Any student will benefit, however, from tackling either type of question, and in testing and improving their understanding of different aspects of criminal law.

Before beginning each of the questions which follow, read through them carefully, noting the area of criminal law involved in each part, and then also note the mark allocation. This will help you to plan your time, as this should be roughly in proportion to the mark allocation. The total time allowed for the AQA questions is 1 hour 30 minutes.

Question 1

Amy, who was 16 years old, took her four-year-old brother, Ben, to the park. Whilst Ben was playing on the slide, Amy went off into the trees with some friends and smoked some cannabis. When she returned, Ben was complaining that he was cold and wanted to go home. Amy dragged him to the swings and, even though he was crying and trying to get off the swing, pushed him vigorously. Ben fell awkwardly from the swing and cut his face as he slid along the ground. It was later discovered that Ben's sight was impaired.

Claire, Amy and Ben's mother, was devastated when she discovered what Amy had done and she began to behave very oddly. She stopped looking after herself properly, lost her temper easily and wandered the streets at all hours of the day and night in a dishevelled state. Whilst walking through the town on one night, she encountered a neighbour, Derek, who made comments about her appearance and suggested that Amy and Ben needed a proper mother. About five minutes later, she saw Derek again. He was waiting to cross a busy road and she ran up behind him and pushed him. Derek stumbled into the road and was killed by a passing car.

(a) Considering any defence(s) which she may raise, discuss Amy's criminal liability arising out of her treatment of Ben and for the injuries which he suffered. (25 marks)

(b) Considering any defence(s) which she may raise, discuss Claire's criminal liability for the murder of Derek. (25 marks)

(c) Discuss whether the defences to murder dealt with by the Homicide Act 1957 are in need of some clarification or reform. (25 marks)

AQA 2001/2002

Question 2

Harry and Ian had already had a few drinks in a bar when Harry slipped a tablet of 'powerblast' (a drug which increased feelings of strength and aggression) into Ian's drink whilst he was not looking. Shortly afterwards, John and Karl entered the bar. Ian and John knew each other and some good-natured banter developed, which ended with Ian challenging John to an arm-wrestling contest to which John readily agreed. During the contest, Ian suddenly exerted a great deal of strength, twisting John's arm very awkwardly and severely damaging tendons in John's wrist.

Two days later, Ian's wife, Laura, returned home to find that the message, 'Ian you are scum you will die' had been sprayed on the front door. Subsequently, telephone calls were made at various times during the night, in which no one spoke but screaming could be heard, as if a person was in terrible pain. Laura became anxious and depressed, and imagined she was about to be attacked whenever she was out in the street. On one such occasion, she lashed out with her bag at Martin, a perfectly innocent pedestrian who happened to be walking past her. Martin suffered a heart attack and died. It was later established that Karl was responsible for the message and telephone calls.

(a) Considering any defence(s) that he may raise, discuss Ian's criminal liability for the injury to John. (25 marks)

(b) Considering any defence(s) which Laura may raise, discuss her criminal liability for the death of Martin, and discuss the criminal liability of Karl arising out of his actions. (25 marks)

(c) How satisfactory is the law on intoxicated defendants? (25 marks)

AQA 2001/2002

Question 3

Stella and her friend Tina went for a meal in a restaurant. At the end of the meal, they paid separately and Stella realised that drinks she had ordered and consumed had not been included on her bill. When the cashier asked her to check the bill, Stella said that it was fine. As they left, a waiter said to Tina, 'Do not forget this, madam', and put something into her shopping bag which she assumed was some advertising for the restaurant. Later in the day, Tina discovered that the waiter had actually put a purse containing £60 into her bag, presumably thinking that she had left it behind. Tina subsequently spent the £60.

They went to a department store where Stella used her sister's store card to buy a pair of shoes and Tina saw some underwear that she really wanted to buy but felt that she could not afford. She took it to the changing room with the idea of trying to put it on and leave the store whilst still wearing it. However, Vera, the changing room attendant, became suspicious and Tina pushed her over before throwing the underwear down and running out of the store.

(a) Discuss Stella's criminal liability arising out of the incidents described above. (25 marks)

(b) Discuss Tina's criminal liability arising out of the incidents described above. (25 marks)

(c) To what extent should the claim that the defendant has made an honest, but not necessarily reasonable, mistake be a good defence in criminal law? (25 marks)

AQA 2001/2002

Question 4

David had been involved in drug dealing with Edward and now owed him a lot of money, which he could not repay. Edward, who had a reputation for violence, said to David, 'Get that money for me by next week or your children will not be safe. Steal it, rob someone, just get it.' David went into a branch of his local building society intending that, if he thought it was safe to do so, he would threaten one of the cashiers into handing over money. However, just before he was about to threaten the cashier, he noticed a closed circuit television camera pointing at him and he immediately left without saying anything. In his hurry to get out, he knocked down Frances, an 80-year-old woman who was in the queue behind him. Frances broke her hip when she hit the floor.

Later, when David was visiting his friend Gina, she went to collect her children from school, leaving David alone in the house. He went into her bedroom, forced open a locked drawer and took some jewellery. Seeing Gina returning, he climbed out of the kitchen window, putting his weight on a gas pipe as he did so. The pipe broke and gas escaped. Gina did not detect any smell of gas whilst she was in the house but an explosion occurred shortly after she went out again with her children.

(a) Considering any defence which he may raise, discuss David's criminal liability arising out of the incidents at the building society. (25 marks)

(b) Discuss David's criminal liability arising out of the incidents at the house of his friend, Gina. (25 marks)

(c) Discuss whether Caldwell (objective) recklessness is an appropriate state of mind on which to base criminal liability. (25 marks)

AQA 2001/2002

Question 5

Alice and Ben have been married for ten years, during five of which Ben has been addicted to heroin. In consequence, Alice has had to endure unpredictable behaviour from Ben, including verbal and physical abuse to herself and their children, unexplained absences, lack of money and loss of her possessions to Ben for the purchase of drugs. During the last two years, Alice has increasingly resorted to drink and her own behaviour has become unpredictable. In particular, she has become anxious, depressed and short-tempered, and has engaged in casual prostitution to supplement their income. In turn, this behaviour has led to further abuse from Ben and to two fights between them in which Alice suffered quite serious injuries.

Two days ago, Alice returned from seeing a 'client' and immediately drank half a bottle of whisky in front of Ben, whom she accused of being no use to her in any way at all. Ben punched her, called her a drunken whore and said that he would 'finish the job properly' after he had injected a dose of heroin. He then went upstairs whilst Alice pushed the television set off its stand, broke a mirror and poured whisky over the furniture as well as drinking more of it. She then went into the kitchen and made and drank a cup of coffee.

About ten minutes after the incident with Ben, she armed herself with a knife and went upstairs. There, she found Ben unconscious and surmised that he had taken an excessively large or pure dose of heroin. She went back downstairs and paced around in an agitated manner, throwing pictures and other objects around the room from time to time until about an hour had gone by. She then telephoned for an ambulance. However, when the ambulance arrived, the medical emergency team failed to revive Ben and a doctor pronounced him dead.

(a) Explain the elements of the offence of murder and, ignoring Alice's anxiety and depression and Ben's behaviour towards her, apply them to determine whether Alice could be guilty of murdering Ben. (10 marks)

(b) Considering, especially, Alice's anxiety and depression and Ben's behaviour towards her, explain the elements of any defence(s) which Alice may raise to seek to reduce the crime to manslaughter and apply them to determine whether she would be successful in doing so. (10 marks)

(c) Explain the elements of unlawful act manslaughter and gross negligence manslaughter and consider whether, if a murder charge were to fail, Alice could be guilty of either. (10 marks)

(d) Alice might have difficulty in being able to pay for legal advice and representation. Explain what statutory provision is made to assist accused persons in her position. (10 marks)

(e) In answering parts (a) – (c) above, you have discussed rules of law concerning the offences of murder and manslaughter and related defences. Select either the offences or the defences and consider what criticisms may be made of the rules and what improvements might be suggested. (10 marks)

AEB 1997

Question 6
After drinking all day in public houses, Andy and his friends went to the fair.

Encouraged by his friends, Andy tried his luck at a coconut shy, where he persistently failed to knock any of the coconuts out of their stands with the hard wooden balls with which he was provided. Everyone, including the owner of the shy, was laughing at his attempts and he became convinced that the coconuts were fixed in the stands. When the owner of the shy suggested that Andy should let 'a man' try, Andy turned and threw a ball at him with all his might. The ball completely missed the owner of the shy, struck a post supporting the stand and was deflected onto a small dog belonging to Betty. The dog was killed instantly and Betty was so shocked by this the she suffered a heart attack shortly afterwards and died.

Meanwhile, Colin, who had just come out of hospital where he had been receiving treatment for paranoid delusion, had gone to the fair on his own. His attention was attracted by the commotion at the coconut stall, and the noise, together with the music and flashing lights from other fairground attractions, caused him to experience strange sensations. He ran to the 'waltzer', knocked the operator out of the way, shut off the power and then turned it on again. At that point, Dave was collecting money from customers in the waltzer cars. Colin's actions caused the machinery to give a sudden jerk which threw Dave off the back of one car and resulted in his being struck by another. He died from a broken skull. Colin's subsequent explanation seemed to indicate that he believed himself to be experiencing the events in a film he had seen a few months before, in which the main character (Colin) had been instructed to kill a spy (Dave).

(a) Taking account of any possible defences which Andy might raise, discuss his liability for the murder of Betty. (15 marks)

(b) Taking account of any possible defences which Colin might raise, consider whether he might be guilty of murder or manslaughter in connection with Dave's death. (15 marks)

(c) In examining (a) and (b) above, you have considered various offences and defences. Discuss who bears the burden of proof in those offences and defences, and what standard of proof is required. (5 marks)

(d) Being careful to give your reasons, explain what changes you would propose to the current law on unlawful homicide. (15 marks)

AEB 1999

Question 7

Gerry and Henry were both aged 15 and were obsessed with playing dangerous games. Their latest game was to suspend a rope from the branch of a tree and for one of them to use it to swing out high above a shallow river. Meanwhile, the other would shake the branch in an attempt to dislodge him. Instead of just shaking the branch when Gerry was swinging from the rope, Henry also climbed part way along it. As the branch started to break, Gerry desperately tried to swing back and wrap his legs around Henry to stop himself falling. However, he only succeeded in catching Henry's face with the metal tip of his shoe and Henry suffered a long, deep cut to this cheek. Meanwhile, Gerry fell and dislocated his knee.

Until then, Gerry's mother, Ellen, and Henry's mother, Frances, had always been good friends but as soon as Ellen heard what had happened, she telephoned Frances and said, 'From now on, you and your family will not be safe.' Frances was so shocked by this that she became hysterical and had to receive medical treatment. When Frances's husband, Ian, went round to see Ellen to complain about her behaviour, Ellen mistakenly thought that he was about to punch her and she slammed the door on his hand, partly severing two of this fingers.

(a) Taking into account any defences which each may be able to plead, discuss the liability of Gerry and Henry in connection with the injuries suffered by each. (15 marks)

(b) Taking into account any defence(s) which she may be able to plead, discuss Ellen's liability arising out of the telephone call to Frances and the injury to Ian. (15 marks)

(c) Explain what factors would be considered by the Crown Prosecution Service in determining whether, and for which offence(s), Ellen might be prosecuted. Consider how she could obtain legal advice and representation if she had little money. (10 marks)

(d) If Ellen, Gerry and Henry were to be convicted of any offence(s), discuss what aims might be pursued in sentencing them and suggest what sentence(s) might be appropriate. (10 marks)

AEB 1999

Question 8

Before Adam and his friend Ben went to a party, Adam suggested that they have a drink. Unknown to Ben, Adam put an hallucinogenic drug into the drink, which he then poured out for both of them. Shortly after their arrival at the party, Ben began to behave strangely and insisted that he was going to fly from the balcony of the sixth-floor flat in which the party was being held. Adam merely giggled and watched him go out onto the balcony. Ben fell towards the road below but his fall was partly broken by a sloping roof. However, Clare, who was walking to the party with her boyfriend, Daniel, was so startled by Ben's fall towards her that she stepped back into the road and was struck and killed by a passing car.

Shortly afterwards, Adam came down and found Clare dead and Ben seriously injured. Adam and Daniel began to argue and then fight when Adam kept giggling and making flying gestures. Adam was punching Daniel when Elaine, another partygoer, tried to break up the fight just as Daniel responded by thrusting a knife at Adam. The knife pierced Elaine's heart, killing her instantly.

(a) Discuss the criminal liability of Adam and Ben for the manslaughter of Clare. (15 marks)

(b) Discuss Daniel's criminal liability for Elaine's death. (15 marks)

(c) Any trials for homicide would be before a jury. Explain and evaluate the role of the jury in criminal trials. (10 marks)

(d) Discuss the extent to which the rules of law you have explained and applied in answering parts (a) and (b) above reveal evidence of the importance of establishing fault in criminal liability. (10 marks)

AEB 1998

Part 8

Studying criminal law

24 Criminal law in context

Introduction

Criminal law does not exist in isolation and any student of criminal law soon realises that it is but one of many branches of law that govern the complex relationships that exist in a modern society. That very complexity is, these days, forcing most practising lawyers to specialise in one or two branches of law. Many specialise in criminal law. The era of the small firm of family solicitors, made up of one or two partners, dealing with every type of legal problem is rapidly disappearing.

Even so, for many the mention of the words 'the law' does still immediately conjure up selective images of the police, criminals, jury trials and judges sentencing villains to terms of imprisonment. The truth is that law touches almost every aspect of our daily lives in one way or another. It imposes duties upon parents to make sure that their children are properly maintained and educated; it imposes duties upon employers to make sure that their employees enjoy a safe working environment; it imposes duties upon motorists to tax and insure their vehicles. All of these potentially carry criminal sanctions should the duties be broken.

'The law', however, casts its net far wider than this. There are laws governing the making of wills, the buying and selling of houses, the formation of contracts, marriage and divorce, the relationships between neighbours, the rights of citizens of the European Union, the licensing of goods and services, etc. The list is virtually endless and reflects the complicated social, economic and political nature of a democracy in the twenty-first century. Any study of criminal law is bound to recognise this wider context since criminal offences cover almost every aspect of social conduct.

Having studied the earlier chapters in this book, the reader will be aware of some of the major offences, the main defences and the general principles underlying criminal liability. However, it would be a mistake to assume that you are now a complete expert in criminal law. There exist many related issues that it is not possible to address in a work of this length as well as numerous offences that have not even been mentioned. Nevertheless, it is hoped that attention will have been drawn to some of the factors which contribute to the continuing development of criminal law and which have shaped the evolution of these general principles and offences as they exist today. Let us now consider some of these factors.

Morality

It is traditionally accepted that there must normally be some moral foundation or justification for branding an individual as 'criminal'. 'Morality' is an elusive concept. It is often regarded as a matter for the individual conscience. In many ways this represents the acknowledgement of the ideal concept of freedom of individual thought. Criminal law, however, must pay attention to the needs of society as a whole, which may sometimes conflict with the right of the individual to behave exclusively according to his or her own moral code.

Consider the following scenario:

Helen chooses to drive into a city centre to work rather than to take public transport, although doing so would alleviate problems of congestion and pollution. One of her reasons for using her car is so she can give a lift in secret to her lover George. Helen has told her husband Barry that she takes the car so that she can listen to her favourite music on the way to work. During their journey to work, a bulb has failed and they are now driving a vehicle with a defective brake light.

In this scenario, some would regard an individual's decision to drive to work as being anti-social whereas others would defend the right of a car owner to drive to work as a basic freedom. Others may focus on other aspects of Helen's conduct. She is apparently intent on committing adultery and, at the very least, being deceitful to her husband about it. You could imagine many arguments and points of view about the morality of these features of her behaviour. Can we properly rush to a moral judgement about this aspect of her activities without knowing about the full circumstances surrounding Helen's married life? Is it our business anyway?

On the other hand, ironically, Helen is technically committing a criminal offence by driving a car with a defective brake light. Few would regard the failure of a light bulb as an event deserving moral blame, let alone one that can be said to justify the imposition of criminal liability. Sometimes the interests of an individual and the rest of society are potentially in conflict with one another, just as the elements of law and morality in the two situations might appear difficult to fully reconcile. These two conflicting interests are balanced in our society by the mechanisms of the State. The

Crown Prosecution Service, representing the State in the name of the Crown, brings criminal prosecutions.

Law and morality are often represented as two overlapping spheres of influence. On certain issues the way an individual behaves is acknowledged as being entirely up to their own individual conscience. On other issues the criminal law actually imposes liability where there appears to be doubtful moral justification for doing so.

Figure 11 The relationship between law and morality

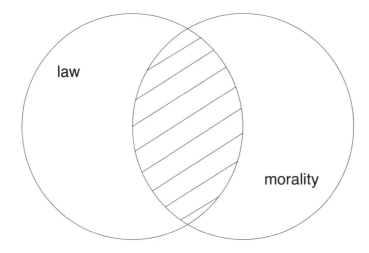

There is, however, a very large area where the two concepts of law and morality appear to happily coincide. A good example is the crime of murder. Few would argue that a murderer does not deserve to be punished for intentionally taking the life of another.

There can be little doubt that a system of criminal law which lacked any basis in morality would have little credibility and would soon lose its authority. For this reason alone Parliament and the judiciary must pay some heed to the influence of moral values.

Many offences involve issues of morality. In theft one of the key rôles for the jury is to assess whether the conduct of an accused is dishonest. A discussion of this issue can be found in the Court of Appeal decision in *Ghosh* (1982) – see pp. 165–166.

I What moral and legal arguments surround the topic of euthanasia?
2 Should we implement a 'Good Samaritan' law to encourage people to give assistance to victims of an emergency situation? (Chapter 2)
3 Was the fourteen-year-old defendant in Elliott v C morally to blame for

setting fire to the garden shed? (Chapter 3)

4 What moral blame attaches to someone who attempts the impossible but fails? (Chapter 21)

5 Do you agree that criminal law should confine itself to the minimum rules necessary for the protection of society from harm, or should it intervene to promote higher standards of social behaviour generally?

Policy issues

It is important to remember that the tension at the centre of many issues in criminal law is the critical balance to be achieved between the interests and freedom of the individual and the wider interest of society at large to enjoy protection from the harmful acts or omissions of the individual. Inevitably the development of criminal law is affected by a variety of policy issues. These range from social and political to economic and philosophical. Examples of the influence of policy can be seen in aspects of legislation and the common law alike.

However, the implementation of policy is a complex process. Any government is duty bound by convention at least to consult interested parties when proposing major change in the criminal law. Parliamentary procedures must be observed. There may be influential reports and consultation papers to consider such as those produced by the Law Commission or following a judicial or public enquiry. Full and proper consultation fulfils a valuable function in a democracy by, at the very least, giving the illusion that the views of interested groups are being taken into account and, at its best, informing an open debate prior to proposing new law. Governments are also influenced by events and political factors. In recent years the Protection from Harassment Act 1997 provides a good example of this (see Chapter 8) as do a number of changes that have occurred in sentencing policy in the field of criminal justice.

Equally, there are many examples of the way that the appeal courts have acknowledged the importance of policy issues when considering landmark judgements. The Privy Council in *Gammon* (1985) listed a whole number of policy factors that would assist judges when justifying the imposition of strict liability (see Chapter 4). The House of Lords in *Brown and others* (1993) weighed up the arguments surrounding the freedom of the individual to consent to being the victim of an assault (see Chapter 9). It is worth reading these judgements to appreciate the way in which the judiciary has adopted views about the function of the public interest in determining criminal liability. It has often been questioned whether it is the rôle of the judges to act in this manner. After all, they are not democratically elected and hold office by way of appointment and cannot easily be removed from office. Students should always be prepared to debate the arguments that surround 'public policy', as interpreted by the judges, and recognise that decisions involving such issues are frequently open to challenge.

Criminal justice

Criminal law, like all branches of law, must also be susceptible to rational and logical analysis. Should Parliament or the courts create or develop rules which appear to be capricious then the law would rapidly fall into disrepute. For this reason the lawyer must be able to analyse the basis of liability in crime according to proven logical principles. Much of this is to do with the need to avoid any miscarriage of justice by following a due process of law. Many rules exist to protect the individual against a wrongful conviction, and the appeals system is designed to ensure that any mistakes in the administration of justice may be corrected.

Just as importantly the student must always remember that sentencing theory and practice exists to complement the law. A finding of guilt means that the sentencing powers of the appropriate court are invoked. You will recall from studying the machinery of justice in the English legal system that, for the vast majority of offences, magistrates or judges exercise their discretion in choosing the suitable sentence. There are few mandatory sentences that automatically apply. The mandatory life sentence for murder is an obvious exception and partly explains why English law has sought to maintain a clear distinction between the definitions of the offences of murder and manslaughter. Of course, the rôle of the sentencer in nearly all other situations is to choose the appropriate sentence after taking into consideration his or her powers and the circumstances of the case. It should not be forgotten that policy in sentencing has been altered over the years as a result of legislation, particularly the Criminal Justice Act 1991. In addition, judges in the Crown Court must also pay attention to Court of Appeal 'guideline' judgements in this capacity. In recent years these have tended to recognise the needs of the individual victim of a crime as well as the wider interests of society at large.

The relationship between criminal liability and the choice of the appropriate sentence is a significant one. For example, it helps to explain the partial defences of diminished responsibility and provocation which allow a judge to exercise discretion following a murder charge. Here, the accused has put forward a successful mitigation and has been convicted of voluntary manslaughter in circumstances which may vary enormously. The use of discretion in sentencing enables a notion of justice in its natural sense to be incorporated into a technically proper finding of guilt.

Finally, it should be remembered that, in some circumstances, sentences cannot be justified in terms of fairness or natural justice. Strict liability cases have provided examples of technical convictions occurring where it is not easy to attribute blame or fault. (See for example, *Storkwain* in Chapter 4). We have seen that it may be difficult to say that a defendant in such cases is truly 'blameworthy' or at fault. The only real justification for imposing a sentence (usually a fine) is therefore one based upon the protection of society.

Conclusion

The modules of study for the AS level in law are in part designed to prepare students for the in-depth study of a particular branch of substantive law such as criminal law. Hopefully, it is not difficult to recognise the relevance of legislation and the common law as central features of the evolution of the principles and rules that comprise criminal law. As has been emphasised above, it is equally important to recognise and understand the wider context within which you are studying these rules and principles of liability in crime. Curriculum 2000 places a new emphasis on this relationship with the specification as a whole, and seeks to build the specific knowledge acquired in the A2 module upon the foundation that you gained during your AS-level studies.

All boards include marks for analytical content in marking essay questions. This is nothing new and has been happening for years. What is different, however, is that the new A2 specifications (for the full A-level award) must include a clear element of synoptic assessment relating criminal law to the wider context of the English legal system. (See Chapter 25).

25 Sources of law

Introduction

All A-level law students are required to develop a knowledge and understanding of sources of law as part of the study of the general principles underlying English law as a whole. English law does not grow on trees, neither was it handed to Moses on top of a mountain. It is derived from Acts of Parliament (statute law) and from the decisions of judges in decided cases (common law). Students of this book will have already read, in each chapter, countless references to case decisions and to Acts of Parliament. When reading about a particular branch of law, such as criminal law the significance of these major sources of law becomes apparent. These are the *primary sources* of law. Writers and lawyers, including judges, must take them as the starting point for what the law actually is. Most of the things that you have read in this book are merely the informed interpretations that the authors of this book have placed upon these primary sources. Consequently, most of the views put forward in this book are merely a *secondary source* of reference.

Textbooks as secondary sources

One of the advantages of textbooks as secondary sources is that they provide a summary version of the very complex and detailed wording that typifies many case law judgments and Acts of Parliament. However, any such summaries or interpretations do carry with them the risk that these may not be completely accurate, and they will certainly not be comprehensive. Accuracy is so vital in law that it is essential that law students are encouraged to read at least some samples of primary sources in order to begin to develop an understanding of their importance. One reason for this is that the original source often contains the purest logical statement of the appropriate law.

It follows that the study of primary sources is important. This is not necessarily an easy task since most A-level students probably do not have easy access to them. The increasing availability of the internet, however, is allowing free access to important judgments in the House of Lords and Court of Appeal as well as to Acts of Parliament which have been passed since 1996. For an example you should consult the Parliament website www.parliament.uk/. A list of useful legal websites is contained in an Appendix at the end of this book.

Primary sources

Case law

If you have already studied the general principles underlying the working of the English legal system, you will be aware of the significance of reported cases and how a system of precedent incorporates them into what is known as the common law. Whole areas of criminal law are still based upon these common law case decisions. The offence of murder is an obvious example. The definition originates in a seventeenth-century statement of the then Lord Chief Justice, Coke. However, this common law definition has been relatively recently developed by the House of Lords decision in *Woollin* (1998).

As stated earlier, however, the courts are constantly being required to interpret existing statutory provisions and the student must be aware of this. Therefore, case law is also important when interpreting and evolving the meaning and application of legislation. This is particularly true of criminal law. For example, the House of Lords ruled in *Burstow* (1997) that serious psychiatric injury caused by silent phone calls can amount to grievous bodily harm for the purposes of s.18 of the Offences Against the Person Act 1861.

Statute law

Statute law in the form of legislation is increasingly important in all branches of law and criminal law is no exception. Many new criminal offences have been created in recent years. However, successive governments appear to have been rather reluctant to implement changes in the more serious offences. This is odd since there have been many proposals for the reform and even codification of the criminal law over the past twenty years. There has been a Draft Criminal Code Bill in existence since 1985 but it has never been implemented. At the time of writing there is little indication that the Offences Against the Person Bill (1998) will become law in the immediate future.

Most of these proposals for the reform of the criminal law are the work of the Law Commission, a permanent body whose rationale is to research, consult and make recommendations to Parliament on reforming the existing law. One area that is ripe for Parliamentary reform is the law relating to involuntary manslaughter which has been subject to much criticism in its present form. The Law Commission has proposed detailed changes recently in its Report No. 237 (1996), *Legislating the Criminal Code – Involuntary*

Manslaughter, which are very good examples of the role of the Law Commission as it exists to reform and improve the existing law. What is far less predictable is whether any government has the time and the will to introduce these proposals into its legislative programme and present them to Parliament for its consideration. Very often desirable, long-term reform is postponed indefinitely in the interests of short-term, political expediency. Publications from the Law Commission can be viewed online at their website www.lawcom.gov.uk/, and downloaded if necessary.

Synoptic assessment based on sources

Following various recommendations by Sir Ron Dearing and QCA (the Qualification and Curriculum Authority), A-level teaching and learning is now in modular form, with assessment by the examination of six units. The final unit is designed to incorporate elements of so-called 'synoptic assessment'. Students need not be unduly anxious about what this means. Essentially, it involves students being invited to demonstrate a knowledge and understanding of a subject that has been acquired over the full period of study. Rather than being assessed in the final unit, purely upon what they have learned in the sixth and final module, a student studying criminal law will be expected, quite properly, to demonstrate their awareness of the way in which criminal law exists within the broader context: not in isolation, but rather as a product of the machinery of justice in England as operated by the courts and personnel of the legal profession.

The synoptic assessment in the OCR specification comprises a study of published materials of relevance to a specific topic. If you are taking this specification these published materials will indeed be your own 'source materials', the evidence provided for you to study and upon which a large part of your synoptic assessment will be based. Using these materials as a basis, you will be expected to answer questions about the particular subject or topic with which they deal, for example, involuntary manslaughter or non-fatal offences against the person. In addition, you will be expected to demonstrate your broader understanding of these issues by applying other knowledge you have acquired over your entire period of study.

It is therefore vital that you familiarise yourself thoroughly with the relevant published source material and that you consider the surrounding issues which you could fairly expect to see examined on the question paper. You will be provided with a copy of the source material in the examination but you will not be allowed to take your previously issued version (which you will probably have annotated) into the exam room with you.

The current pre-released material for OCR, which has a 'shelf life' of two years, follows. We will examine some of the issues which could provide a useful source of enquiry, comment, analysis and criticism. In future years

327

it is very likely that students may expect to see source materials based upon themes in criminal law such as the development of case law reasoning or the interpretation of criminal law statutes.

A further important point to note is that the final question on the Synoptic Special Study Paper is a problem question designed not merely to assess the candidate's knowledge and understanding of a topic but to see whether they can apply that knowledge to a hypothetical scenario.

OCR special study source materials (with commentary)

1 Extract from Farrar, J H (1974) *Law Reform and the Law Commission*, Sweet & Maxwell, pp. 28–9

Section 3 of the Law Commissions Act 1965 defined the duties and powers of the Law Commissions. First it was their basic duty to take and keep the law under review with a view to its systematic development and reform, including in particular codification, the elimination of anomalies, the repeal of obsolete enactments, consolidation and generally the simplification and modernisation of the law. It is to be noted that although the act contemplated codification it did not in fact require it. To execute their basic duty they were authorised to consider proposals for reform, to submit to the appropriate Minister (i.e. for England and Wales, the Lord Chancellor) programmes of law reform, and then, when approval had been given, to undertake the examination of particular items in the programme and to formulate proposals for reform by means of draft Bills or otherwise.

Where the programme covered a branch of law which seemed likely to be controversial in a political sense or to have a broad social trend it was unlikely that the detailed review would be entrusted to the Commissioners themselves. In cases like that it was thought by the Government that it would be more appropriate that the matter should be referred in accordance with the usual practice to a royal commission or a departmental committee.

The Commissioners were further authorised to prepare (at the request of the Minister), comprehensive programmes of consolidation and statute law revision and to undertake the preparation of draft Bills, to give advice and information to government departments and other bodies at the instance of the government, together with proposals for reform of any branch of law and lastly, the Commissioners were authorised and instructed to obtain such information on other legal systems as appeared to them likely to facilitate the performance of any of their functions.

The Act set out certain procedures with regard to Law Commission business. Section 3(2) provided that the Minister should lay before Parliament any programmes prepared by the Law Commission and approved by him and any proposals for reform formulated by the Commission pursuant to the programmes. Each Commission should make an annual report to the Minister of their proceedings and the Minister should lay the report before Parliament with such comments (if any) as he thought fit (s3[3]).

The general effect of these provisions was described by Sir Leslie Scarman in his Manitoba Law School Foundation Annual Lecture in 1967. By the Act, he said, the law of England and Scotland shifted its emphasis from reliance on judicial law making to reliance on legislation to reform the law. It meant that Parliament has accepted 'a greater, continuing responsibility for the reform of the law than in our history it has ever accepted before.' However, 'Parliament in matters of law reform, is an extremely amateur and indolent body. It requires advice, it requires spurring on and to be stimulated into action.' The Act was, therefore, an attempt to provide Parliament with the advice which it needs in order to reach a skilled decision and to provoke it to action.

2 Extracts from 'The Law Commission Report on Involuntary Manslaughter: (1) The Restoration of a Serious Crime', by Heather Keating (Senior Lecturer in Law, University of Sussex) *Criminal Law Review*, August 1996 (published by Sweet & Maxwell)

As long ago as 1980, the Criminal Law Revision Committee emphasised that 'so serious an offence as manslaughter should not be a lottery'. Liability for involuntary manslaughter, it is argued, may arise from an unlucky combination of events. Moreover, the difficulties created by the breadth of the offence are universally acknowledged. Whilst the fact of causing death remains constant, the degree of 'unintentional' fault may range from that which is almost murderous to that which is almost accidental. Serious doubts exist as to whether the present law can act either as an effective mechanism for censuring conduct or as guide for sentencers. In terms of 'applicability, certainty, clarity, intellectual coherence and general acceptability' the present law has little to recommend it.

It is not the purpose of this article to dissect these deficiencies in any detail. The case for reform is overwhelming. This is true even after the House of Lords decision of *Adomako* (1993) which revives the concept of gross negligence manslaughter. Whilst some commentators have welcomed the removal of 'much unnecessary complication and injustice', others have been less sanguine about the development. Moreover, problems remain with the test adopted by Lord MacKay in this case. First, it is circular: the jury must be directed to convict the defendant of a crime if they think his conduct 'criminal'. In effect, this leaves a question of law to the jury, and, because juries do not have to give reasons for their decisions, it is impossible to tell what criteria will be applied in an individual case. Secondly, the mixture of the civil concepts of 'negligence' and 'duty of care' with that of criminal liability is an unhappy one, giving rise to the fear that liability for manslaughter by omission has been at one and the same time both broadened and restricted. More fundamentally, of course, the decision in *Adomako* left untouched the law relating to constructive manslaughter. The Law Commission summarises the defects of this law thus:

> [W]e consider that it is wrong in principle for the law to hold a person responsible for causing a result that he did not intend or foresee, and which would not even have been *foreseeable* by a reasonable person observing his conduct. Unlawful act manslaughter is therefore, we believe, unprincipled because it requires only that a foreseeable risk of causing *some* harm should have been inherent in the accused's conduct, whereas he is actually convicted of causing death, and also to some extent punished for doing so.

Commentary

The above passage is taken from an article published in the *Criminal Law Review*, a monthly publication which discusses and reviews issues and developments in criminal law. The extract forms a useful starting point since it sets out to review the proposals of the Law Commission for the reform of the law on involuntary manslaughter. If you are not clear about the broad classifications of this topic you should remind yourself by looking again at Chapter 7. The extract should almost immediately indicate to you that the present law on involuntary manslaughter is unsatisfactory.

Q What was the role of the Criminal Law Revision Committee in 1980 and why do you think it implied that the offence of manslaughter is sometimes 'a lottery'? Notice too that the Law Commission's proposals of 1996 were largely a response to developments which had occurred and forced themselves to the forefront for consideration. In particular there was the 1994 House of Lords decision in *Adomako*, the first time that the House of Lords had considered involuntary manslaughter in over ten years Secondly, there had been widespread public dissatisfaction with the failure to bring a series of prosecutions in corporate manslaughter. 'These followed a number of disasters where many victims had been killed in circumstances in which it appeared that companies and their policies had been seriously at fault and yet escaped conviction. Examples were the loss of 187 lives when the Herald of Free Enterprise capsized of Zeebrugge, the King's Cross fire in which 31 people died, the Piper Alpha oil platform disaster in which there were 167 fatalities and the Clapham rail crash, in which 35 people died. Since the report was published there has of course been the Ladbroke Grove train disaster outside Paddington in October 1999, where many more lives were lost.

Q. What is the role and composition of the Law Commission. Do you think that the Law Commission can help to reform -to such outside factors. If so why?

...*Abolition of constructive manslaughter*

In its review of offences against the person the Criminal Law Revision Committee recommended that reckless killing should be the only form of involuntary manslaughter. In proposing that unlawful act manslaughter and gross negligence manslaughter be abolished it was firmly of the view that the 'offenders' fault falls too far short of the unlucky result' in such instances. The Law Commission agrees that these two forms of manslaughter should go. One might have thought that few would lament the passing of unlawful act manslaughter. However, the proposal in the Consultation Paper to abolish it met with a mixed response. Some commentators argued that those who embark upon a course of criminal conduct 'involving, albeit slight, violence should take the consequences if the results turn out to be more catastrophic than they expected'. But the doctrine of constructive crime does not fit within the principles espoused by the Law Commission and is a legacy from harsher times. The Law Commission is, therefore, right to state:

> We consider that the criminal law should properly be concerned with questions of moral culpability, and we do not think that an accused who is culpable for causing *some harm* is sufficiently blameworthy to be held liable for the unforeseeable consequences of death.

... the abolition of unlawful act manslaughter is, therefore, sound in principle, but it would not mean that many defendants would, in practice, escape liability. Many such defendants would be liable for reckless killing. If not, liability may be based upon the second form of manslaughter, for unlike the Criminal Law Revision Committee, the Law Commission has recommended a further species of manslaughter: killing by gross carelessness.

Commentary
The concept of constructive manslaughter, the idea that a person should be made liable for a death resulting from another unlawful act, is harshly criticised in the above passage. The Law Commission favours its abolition.
Q. What are the arguments for and against the abolition of constructive manslaughter?
(See also the extracts from Church, Lowe and Lamb below)

...The Law Commission's proposals: reckless killing

It is not, perhaps, surprising that the first recommendation of the Report is that there should be an offence of subjectively recklessly causing death:

> We are quite certain that a person should ... be held criminally responsible for causing *death* in circumstances where she unreasonably and knowingly runs a risk of causing death (or serious injury). Indeed – and we are sure that many people would agree with us – we consider this type of conscious risk-taking to be the most reprehensible form of unintentional homicide, on the very borders of murder...

...The new offence is defined as:

> Reckless killing, which would be committed if
> (1) a person by his or her conduct causes the death of another;
> (2) he or she is aware that his or her conduct will cause death or serious injury; and
> (3) it is unreasonable for him or her to take that risk, having regard to the circumstances as he or she believes them to be....

... In addition, the Law Commission argues that there is 'a very thin line between behaviour that risks serious injury and behaviour that risks death, because it is frequently a matter of chance, depending on such factors as the availability of medical treatment, whether serious injury leads to death.' To this small extent, at least, the Law Commission is prepared to allow defendants to run the gauntlet of luck. Such an approach is certainly more justifiable than the existing law because the 'moral distance' between the harm done and that foreseen is lessened. Someone who foresees *some* harm resulting from their actions should not be held responsible for the consequence of death.... .

We consider that the criminal law should properly be concerned with questions of moral culpability, and we do not think that an accused who is culpable for causing *some harm* is sufficiently blameworthy to be held liable for the unforeseeable consequence of death.

Commentary

The above passage addresses the concept of reckless manslaughter. It is perhaps easier to see sound reasons for imposing liability on this basis since it is easier to agree a moral justification for saying that a person who is consciously willing to take a risk of causing death or serious injury deserves to answer to the consequences of their actions should death result. Notice, too, that the Law Commission distinguishes between the causing of serious harm and some harm but does not distinguish between the risk of death and the risk of serious injury.

Q. How does the Law Commission justify this distinction?

Unfortunately the term 'reckless' was complicated in its application to criminal liability by the introduction of so-called 'Caldwell recklessness' in the 1980s (See Chapter 3).

Q. Distinguish between the two types of recklessness that exist in criminal law as a possible basis for liability and try to justify each type.

At one time the House of Lords approved the introduction of 'Caldwell recklessness' into manslaughter by its decision in Seymour in 1983. The House of Lords overruled its own decision in Seymour in the more recent case of Adomako in 1994.

Q. Why and how was the House of Lords prepared to do this?

Q. In Caldwell, you will find references to 'advertent risk-taking' and 'inadvertent risk-taking'. Try to explain in your own words what these two phrases mean.

Killing by gross carelessness

… Having been persuaded that inadvertence may be culpable, the Law Commission had to determine the boundaries for a law which would hold a defendant liable for a death she neither intended nor foresaw. Two criteria are insisted upon. First, the harm has to be foreseeable:

If the accused is an ordinary person, she cannot be blamed for failing to take notice of a risk if it would not have been apparent to *an average person in her position*, because the criminal law cannot require an *exceptional* standard of perception or awareness from her. If the accused held herself out as an expert of some kind, however, a higher standard can be expected of her; if she is a doctor, for example, she will be at fault if she fails to advert to a risk that would have been obvious to the average doctor in her position.

As with the offence of reckless killing, the Law Commission restricts the risk of harm to that of death *or* serious injury.

The second criterion is that the accused must have been capable of perceiving the risk:

> We consider that there is a clear distinction, in terms of moral fault, between a person who knowingly takes a risk and one who carelessly fails to advert to it, and that the worse case of advertent risk-taking is more culpable than the worst case of inadvertent risk-taking.
>
> Since the fault of the accused lies in her failure to consider a risk, she cannot be punished for this failure if the risk in question would never have been apparent to her, no matter how hard she thought about the potential consequences of her conduct. If this criterion is not insisted upon, the accused will, in essence, be punished for being less intelligent, mature or capable than the average person.

Hart has persuasively argued for an assessment of capacity to be included in the definition of negligence. Explicitly doing so in the reform proposals should lay the ghost of *Elliot v. C* finally to rest. The offence which is proposed, based upon these two criteria, is that of killing by gross carelessness. It is modelled, to some extent at least, on the test of 'dangerousness' in the offence of causing death by dangerous driving. The Report comments that this test is one with which lawyers, the courts and the public are familiar and, moreover, seems to have worked well.

It recommends that the new offence would be committed if:

> (1) a person by his or her conduct causes the death of another;
> (2) a risk that his or her conduct will cause death or serious injury would be obvious to a reasonable person in his or her position;
> (3) he or she is capable of appreciating that risk at the material time; and
> (4) *either* (a) his or her conduct falls far below what can reasonably be expected of him or her in the circumstances, or (b) he or she intends by his or her conduct to cause some injury, or is aware of, and unreasonably takes, the risk that it may do so, *and* the conduct causing (or intended to cause) the injury constitutes an offence.

Commentary
The decision in Adomako it is widely felt to be unsatisfactory and that gross negligence is an inappropriate phrase to apply in criminal liability since 'negligence' seems to be borrowed from the concept of negligence in civil

law. The Law Commission favours the use of the term 'Killing by gross carelessness'. Is this really any different? Clearly, yes. For a start the 'circular test' to be asked by the jury in Adomako would be abolished.

Q What is this so-called 'circular test'?

Secondly, the Law Commission bases its definition of killing by gross carelessness on a risk of death or serious injury that would be 'obvious to the reasonable person'.

On the other hand, the Law Commission is careful to propose a definition which apparently 'lays to rest the ghost of Elliott'.

Q What do you think this means and how does the Law Commission's definition achieve the 'laying' of this 'ghost'?

3 Extract from the judgment of Edmund Davies J in *R v Church* [1965] 2 All ER 72

It appears to this court, however, that the passage of years has achieved a transformation in this branch of the law and, even in relation to manslaughter, a degree of *mens rea* has become recognised as essential. To define it is a difficult task, and in *Andrews v DPP* (1937) AC 576 Lord Atkin spoke of 'the element of "unlawfulness" which is the elusive factor'. Stressing that we are here leaving entirely out of account those ingredients of homicide which might justify a verdict of manslaughter on the grounds of (a) criminal negligence or (b) provocation or (c) diminished responsibility, the conclusion of this court is that an unlawful act causing the death of another cannot, simply because it is an unlawful act, render a manslaughter verdict inevitable. For such a verdict inexorably to follow, the unlawful act must be such as all sober and reasonable people would inevitably recognise must subject the other person to, at least, the risk of some harm resulting therefrom, albeit not serious harm. See, for example, *R v Franklin* (1883), *R v Senior* (1899).

Commentary

Q Select the phrase from the above judgement which is used by Lord Edmund Davies to justify what he terms 'the element of mens rea' in unlawful act manslaughter. Do you agree that this really represents the necessary ingredient of mental guilt in manslaughter?

Q Suppose an unarmed burglar is disturbed at night by the occupier of a house. In his rush to escape, the burglar collides in the dark with the occupier and sends him tumbling down the stairs to his death. Is he liable for the death? Should he be liable for the death?

4 Extract from the judgment of Phillimore LJ in *R v Lowe* [1973] 1 QB 702

We think that there is a clear distinction between an act of omission and an act of commission likely to cause harm. Whatever may be the position with regard to the latter it does not follow that the same is true of the former. In other words, if I strike a child in a manner likely to cause harm it is right that, if the child dies, I may be charged with manslaughter. If, however, I omit to do something with the result that it suffers injury to health which results in its death, we think that a charge of manslaughter should not be an inevitable consequence, even if the omission is deliberate.

Commentary

The above extract concerns a case of constructive manslaughter by omission. It appears that there can be no liability on this basis since there is literally no unlawful 'act', merely an omission to act.

Q. On what basis would you ever charge a person who 'omits to do something with the result that (a child) suffers injury'... if the omission is deliberate'?

(see Chapter 2)

---

5 Extract from the judgment of Sachs LJ in R v Lamb [1967] 2 QB 981

[Prosecution counsel] had at all times put forward the correct view that for the act to be unlawful it must constitute what is called 'a technical assault'. In this court moreover he rightly conceded that there was no evidence to go to the jury of any assault of any kind. Nor did he feel able to submit that the acts of the defendant were on any other ground unlawful in the criminal sense of that word. Indeed no such submission could in law be made: if, for instance, the pulling of the trigger had had no effect because the striking mechanism or the ammunition had been defective no offence would have been committed by the defendant.

Another way of putting it is that *mens rea*, being now an essential ingredient in manslaughter...that could not in the present case be established in relation to the first ground except by proving that element of intent without which there can be no assault.

Commentary

Imagine that you were on the jury in this case. Would you be happy to acquit Terry Lamb having heard his evidence alone? (see pp 105–6 for details of

---

this case in the text). In one sense justice was done on a legal technicality. There was no assault therefore no unlawful act.

Q. Do you think that Lamb was aware of the risk of firing the bullet from the revolver?

Q. Do you think he may have considered the risk but wrongly concluded that there was none?

6 Extract from the judgment of Lord Mackay LC in R v Adomako [1995] 1 AC 171

...in my opinion the ordinary principles of the law of negligence apply to ascertain whether or not the defendant has been in breach of a duty of care towards the victim who has died. If such a breach of duty is established the next question is whether that breach of duty has caused the death of the victim. If so, the jury must go on to consider whether that breach of duty should be characterised as gross negligence and therefore as a crime. This will depend on the seriousness of the breach of duty committed by the defendant in all the circumstances in which the defendant was placed when it occurred. The jury will have to consider whether the extent to which the defendant's conduct departed from the proper standard of care incumbent upon him, involving as it must have done a risk of death to the patient, was such that it should be judged criminal.

It is true that to a certain extent this involves an element of circularity, but in this branch of the law I do not believe that is fatal to its being a correct test of how far conduct must depart from accepted standards to be characterised as criminal. This is necessarily a question of degree and an attempt to specify that degree more closely is I think likely to achieve only a spurious precision. The essence of the matter which is supremely a jury question is whether, having regard to the risk of death involved, the conduct of the defendant was so bad in all the circumstances as to amount in their judgment to a criminal act or omission....

... I consider it perfectly appropriate that the word 'reckless' should be used in cases of involuntary manslaughter, but as Lord Atkin put it, 'in the ordinary connotation of that word'. Examples in which this was done, to my mind with complete accuracy, are *R v Stone* (1977) QB 354 and *R v West London Coroner, ex parte Gray* (1988) QB 467.

Commentary

Lord Mackay's judgment shows that he is clearly aware of the difficulties associated with the current law on gross negligence manslaughter. For example, he admits that the test is somewhat 'circular' because it invites the jury to decide whether or not the crime of manslaughter has been committed on the facts of the case. The jury must decide whether or not the duty of care is owed in the first place. This in itself is uncertain. To whom is the duty of care owed? Should it be confined to 'special duty' situations such as doctor and patient, road user to road user and parent and child. Alternatively, does it extend to the 'neighbour test' laid down in the leading civil case of *Donoghue v Stevenson* – we all owe a duty of care towards anyone whom we can reasonably foresee is likely to be affected by our acts or omissions.

The jury also has to decide from the evidence whether the duty has in fact been breached. They then must decide whether the degree of negligence is so 'gross' as to amount to manslaughter. In practice, no doubt they will receive a good deal of advice and guidance from the presiding judge but this still does not solve the problem that in the end it is, according to Lord Mackay, 'supremely a jury question'. Perhaps it will lie more in the hands of the Crown Prosecution Service who will have to decide when to prosecute gross negligent conduct that results in death.

Q. On further reflection do you think that the Law Commission's definition of 'killing by gross carelessness' is preferable to Lord Mackay's in Adomako?

---

7 Extract from William Wilson, *Criminal Law* (Longman, 1998)

A more precise and meaningful fault element was identified by Watkins LJ in *R v West London Coroner, ex. parte Gray* (1987) 2 All ER 129, at 136, which likewise passed over *Lawrence* recklessness, this time in favour of a more cogent indifference-based test.

> To act recklessly means that there was an obvious and serious risk to the health and welfare of [the deceased] to which [the accused], having regard to his duty, was indifferent or that, recognising that risk to be present, he deliberately chose to run the risk by doing nothing about it. It should be emphasised, however, that a failure to appreciate that there was a risk would not by itself be sufficient to amount to recklessness.

This statement suggests that a satisfactory direction to the jury would require them to consider whether the failure to attend to appreciate the risk was due to inexperience, forgetfulness, stress or incompetence however gross, or was due to the defendant not caring enough to act in accordance with standards of safety and care which would minimise any risk. Only in the latter case would they be entitled to find recklessness.

One desirable feature in Lord Mackay's circular, if 'jury friendly', test of gross negligence is the explicit reference to 'the risk of death'. Before *Adomako* it was by no means certain that the defendant's conduct must be such as to create the risk of death. In *Stone and Dobinson* it was said to be enough that the accused's conduct provoked the risk injury to 'health and welfare'. More recently Lord Taylor CJ spoke of the risk of injury to health. Both seem to set the standard too low, quite apart from the unacceptable vagueness characterising 'welfare' in *Stone*. Most authorities provide, however, that the risk must be of death or grievous bodily harm. This coheres with a notion of homicide separated only by the type of decision made by the accused. Thus intention characterises murder and culpable risk-taking, and manslaughter. However, given that manslaughter does not require proof of deliberate risk-taking, it is submitted that fairness to the accused requires the risk to be of death, or at least serious injury.

Commentary

Wilson's extract both criticises and commends different aspects of the decision in Adomako.

Q. Where do you think that the extract from West London Coroner (ex parte Gray) corresponds more with the Law Commission's proposal of 'killing by gross carelessness'?

Q. Which aspect of Lord Mackay's judgment in Adomako does Wilson approve of and why?

Questions based on Criminal Law special study (OCR Specimen Paper)

Time allowed: 1 hour 30 minutes

You are reminded of the importance of including relevant materials from all areas of your course, where appropriate including the English Legal System.
Answer ALL Questions

1   The Law Commission recommends changes to the criminal law in its 1996 Report, Legislating The Code – Involuntary Manslaughter. Critically consider the rôle of the Law Commission in assisting Parliament to change the law.

[20 marks]

2   Discuss why Lord Mackay's definition of gross negligence manslaughter in the House of Lords' decision in R v Adomako (1994) has been criticised as unsatisfactory.

[20 marks]

3   Examine how decided cases have developed the offence of unlawful act/ constructive manslaughter.

[30 marks]

4   David and Imran, both aged 22, are in David's house while David's parents are away on holiday. David tells Imran that his father has got a revolver in a drawer in his bedroom. They agree that it would be fun to get it and pretend to be gangsters by pointing the gun at each other and making exaggerated threats. David knows his father has also got some 'dummy' bullets and some live bullets in a box next to the gun. He tells Imran they are only dummy bullets. They put six of these bullets into the chamber. They then take turns pointing the gun at each other and pulling the trigger. Unfortunately one of the bullets is real and when David squeezes the trigger for the third time he shoots Imran dead with a real bullet.

When questioned David admits that he didn't really know the difference between the dummy bullets and the real ones but he hoped they were all dummy bullets.

David has now been charged with manslaughter. Discuss his liability:
(a) under the existing law, and
(b) under the Law Commission's proposals for the reform of involuntary manslaughter.

[30 marks]

Suggested answer guidelines are found on pp 393–5.

26 Key skills

Introduction

Whether students are used to thinking about them or not, certain key skills have always underpinned learning and build upon the basic skills that have already been acquired in the early years of education. They are certainly nothing to be afraid of. On the contrary, key skills provide an opportunity for the first time for students to acquire recognition for these skills. Key skills are in fact the means through which learning takes place and which, in a rapidly changing world, must be updated throughout life. What is new is that a key skills qualification, valued by employers and higher education institutions, is now available at Levels 2, 3 and (probably 4). This chapter is intended to provide some general advice and guidance to students and teachers and also points out some specific suggestions about how evidence for the key skills qualification can be produced on the A-level Law specification. (specification, remember, is the new term for syllabus – see the Introduction to this book).

Key skills to be assessed

The 'Main' key skills at Level 3

- C3 Communication

- N3 Application of number

- IT3 Information technology

The 'Wider' key skills at Level 3

- WO3 Working with others

- LP3 Improving own learning and performance

- PS3 Problem solving

At present the wider key skills do not form part of the qualification for the purposes of assessment but they are nevertheless seen as integral to post-16 education and training, and the Government has made it clear that these wider skills must be developed and promoted. Consequently, all new specifications have 'signposted' these wider skills.

In order to enable as many students as possible to achieve a key skills qualification, developing and assessing these skills is designed to be a straightforward task. Examples of the 'keys to attainment' may be essays, oral presentations or information displays using technology or graphical interpretation.

To achieve the new qualification, students must pass internal (e.g. portfolio and coursework) and external (set assignments, tests) components of assessment. Extra information, support and guidance concerning assessment is available on two websites:

- www.qca.org.uk/keyskills/newunits/htm, and

- www.dfee.gov.uk/qualify/key.htm, where case studies and exemplars of students' work to specified standards is available.

Although key skills underpin all learning, they are not actually embedded in each specification. Rather, key skills should be the subject of a separate qualification with opportunities for producing relevant evidence 'signposted' within each specification. In this way, it is hoped that undue artificiality and repetition in key skills assessments will be avoided or minimised. The rest of this chapter deals with the variety of opportunities that exist for students and teachers for the compilation of such evidence within the Law specifications concerning criminal law.

Opportunities for evidencing key skills

Communication (C3)

C3.1a: Contribute to a group discussion about a complex topic

- what is the moral significance of assessing a person's guilty mind? (Chapter 1)

- how have the courts developed an approach to the coincidence of *actus reus* and *mens rea* and what is the significance of these terms? (Chapter 1)

- when and why is it possible to justify imposing criminal liability upon a person who simply fails to act? (Chapter 2)

- why is there a need for two tests to assess 'recklessness'? (Chapters 3, 7, 8 and 13)

- how can strict liability offences be justified? (Chapter 4)

- why is there a need to distinguish between different forms of homicide? (Chapter 5)

- how should the offence of involuntary manslaughter be reformed? (Chapter 7)

- is the law on assaults satisfactory? (Chapter 8)

- what might be the impact of the Human Rights Act 1998? (Chapter 9)

- is the law relating to dishonesty and appropriation in a satisfactory state? (Chapter 10)

- how can the decision in *Elliott v C* be justified? (Chapters 3 and 13)

- how does the law address the problems of conduct whilst intoxicated? (Chapter 14)

- should the law on insanity be reformed? (Chapter 15)

- justify the limitations on the availability of duress as a defence? (Chapter 18)

- is the law relating to participation in crime fair? (Chapter 20)

- why is there a need for inchoate offences? (Chapters 21 and 22)

C3.1b: Make a presentation about a complex subject using at least one image to illustrate complex points

- describe the principles of causation using a flow chart to illustrate this. (Chapter 2)

- illustrate the distinctions between subjective and objective recklessness by means of a diagram. (Chapter 3)

- by means of a flow chart illustrate the historical development of the law on foresight of consequences as a means of assessing the concept of intention. (Chapter 5)

- produce a diagrammatic analysis of the offence of homicide. (Chapters 5, 6 and 7)

- demonstrate the operation of the defence of intoxication using a chart. (Chapter 14)

- compare and contrast the defences of insanity and automatism by means of a flow chart or diagram. (Chapters 15 and 16)

- illustrate the availability of the various general defences. (Chapters 14–19)

- produce a chart showing how liability for participation in crime may be analysed. (Chapter 20)

- using a diagram, illustrate the classification of inchoate offences. (Chapters 21 and 22)

C3.2: Read and synthesize information from two extended documents that deal with a complex subject. One of these documents should include at least one image.

- access to an extended document should not be a problem – a case report or legal article ought to be readily available to most students either in hard copy or via the internet (a list of useful legal websites appears in an Appendix at the end of this book). Interesting and relevant cases among many would be *Woollin* (Chapter 5), *Brown* (Chapter 9) or *Pommell* (Chapter 18).

- in addition, there are many examples of Law Commission reports (e.g. 237 on Corporate Manslaughter), draft bills and recent legislation available on the internet. The *Times*, *Independent* and *Guardian* newspapers all carry dedicated law reports and features.

- other sources are legal journals such as the *New Law Journal*, published weekly, and the *Criminal Law Review*, published monthly. Access to these may be more limited but many colleges and some libraries take these publications. Graphs, tables or illustrations are often contained in these publications.

C3.3: Write two different types of documents about complex subjects. One piece of writing should be an extended document and include at least one image.

- there are ample opportunities to produce this element of evidence. Extended essays on almost any criminal law topic should satisfy the first criterion, e.g. on the concept of dishonesty in theft.

- draft an advice on legal liability based on a scenario arising from homicide using a scattergram to illustrate the various issues involved.

Information technology (IT3)

IT 3.1: Plan and use different sources to search for and select information required for two different purposes

- a number of opportunities exist. Students can research the internet (in some cases in-house intranet systems) and commercially available CD ROMs for Acts of Parliament, law reports, legal databases, Home Office Reports, etc. (See Appendix at the end of the book).

IT 3.2: Explore, develop and exchange information and derive new information to meet two different purposes

- design a mini-project involving the creation of a database of cases and statutes in criminal law using one field to contain a key word to identify the main topic of the case or related statute. You could work as a team on this so that a large number of cases can be entered. This could be used for:

- fellow students to access a set of cases on a topic by entering a query

- the production of a law magazine

- e-mailing a list of cases on a particular topic in response to requests by other students.

IT 3.3: Present information from different sources for two different purposes and audiences. Your work must include at least one example of images and one example of numbers.

- create a report and presentation for members of staff, describing how you compiled your database. Illustrate how the system works and how it is possible to incorporate some of the results into a law magazine. Show a table of cases requested and construct a chart to show how many times they were requested.

- create a series of supplementary related references and/or questions arising from the issues addressed by the cases.

- create a presentation to explain the current criticisms surrounding involuntary manslaughter, using graphical representations of the various issues.

- extend into synoptic topics by presenting a review of the various proposals for reform of involuntary manslaughter put forward by the Law Commission.

Working with others (WO3)

The evidence for this area of skill needs to be produced in at least two substantial activities that each includes tasks for WO3.1, WO3.2 and WO3.3 respectively. You need to show that you can work in a group and in one-to-one situations. The aspects of activity for which you are required to supply evidence are:

WO3.1: Plan a group activity, agreeing objectives, responsibilities and working arrangements.

WO3.2: Work towards achieving the agreed objectives, seeking to establish and maintain co-operative working relationships in meeting individual responsibilities.

WO3.3: Review the activity with others against the agreed objectives and agree ways of enhancing collaborative work.

Suggested activities

This is an opportunity to combine one or more aspects of the machinery of justice and criminal procedure so as to incorporate them synoptically into the specification. Aspects of procedure and sentencing are particularly appropriate for this purpose.

1 Organise a moot, debate or rôle play based on a given scenario (e.g. a problem question from the examples given at the end of chapters in the book). The stages could be:

- meet as a group and agree upon the chosen scenario.

- create an action plan to:

  - organise the breakdown of tasks.

  - agree pairings or groupings to undertake the various tasks to include the following:
    research of different aspects of the legal problem;
    obtain case/statute details and references and research them;
    prepare a report and presentation;
    plan meetings or appoint a chair responsible for co-ordinating the work;
    agree deadlines and methods of communication, e.g. e-mail;
    monitor progress and working relationships;
    review progress and goals;
    review and change action plans where necessary.

- Hold the moot/debate inviting others to attend or preside.

- Arrange a post-moot discussion group to review and provide feedback on the exercise and make conclusions and recommendations for improvement.

2 Make a presentation as a small group, to the class as a whole, on a given topic of general interest from the specification. For example, whether the defence of duress should be extended from its current limitations or whether the current law on consent to assaults amounts to an undue restriction on individual freedom.

- meet as a group and organise the distribution of tasks.

- create OHPs or a 'Powerpoint' presentation.

- agree on the allocation of tasks and responsibilities for research, oral presentation, etc.

- agree on deadlines and methods of co-ordination and communication.

- invite others to attend the presentation.

- arrange a post-presentation discussion group to review and provide feedback on the exercise and make conclusions and recommendations for improvement or produce a questionnaire to elicit staff and student perceptions of the exercise.

Improving own learning and performance (LP3)

An increasingly important aspect of improvement is that students are involved in planning, managing and reviewing their own learning. To provide evidence of improvement you need to examples of study-based learning, two examples of activity-based learning and one example of using learning from at least two different contexts to meet the demands of a new situation. For this assessment it is important that you arrange to meet a tutor who will support you in providing the necessary evidence. An action plan could be drawn up to include the following steps:

LP3.1: Agree targets and plan how these will be met using support from tutors.

LP3.2: Use your plan, seeking and using feedback and support from relevant sources to help meet your targets using different ways of learning to meet new demands.

LP3.3: Review your progress in meeting targets, establishing evidence of achievements and agree action for improving performance using support from appropriate people.

Suggested activity

You can monitor your progress in several ways, but each should include appropriate feedback, recording of achievement and setting of targets:

- through essay writing and solving hypothetical situations as homework assignments.

- through timed essays.

- through set tests.

- through oral and practical contribution to group activities.

- by attending court and writing an appropriate report.

- by attending student law conferences.

- by improving literacy and ICT skills.

Problem solving (PS3)

For this skill you need to undertake an activity which involves identifying, solving and validating the proposed solution to a complex problem. You can easily find a problem scenario from criminal law – most of the problem questions at the end of the Parts, and in the Additional Questions Chapter, would be suitable. Identifying, analysing and suggesting a solution to legal problems is a central feature of this specification. However, you cannot properly implement the solution since the scenarios presented are hypothetical in nature, not real cases which will be taken to court. Accordingly your evidence here will be limited to PS3.1 and PS3.2.

PS3.1: Recognise, explore and analyse the problem and agree how to show success in solving it.

PS3.2: Plan and compare at least two options that could be used for solving the problem and justify the option chosen.

Suggested activity

Choose a complex problem question and research it in detail – for example, question 2 at the end of Chapter 7. Compile your answer to the problem, and review the work done. Consider any practical alternative solutions. In such an instance, it may again be possible to incorporate a synoptic element by considering the various sentencing alternatives that might be appropriate in such a scenario.

Conclusion

Remember that the total portfolio of evidence you produce for your key skills qualification will not normally be drawn exclusively from the study of law. Indeed, a study of A-level law will provide very limited opportunity to display evidence of N3: Application of Number, other than in a highly artificial context. It is therefore important that you develop a strategy with your tutors which will enable you to gather appropriate evidence from all your AS and A2 studies. It should be clear that law provides many opportunities to compile the necessary evidence for the key skills addressed above.

Legal resources on the internet

General awareness sites
Excellent starting points for free and subscription services
www.venables.co.uk
www.the-lawyer.co.uk
www.lawzone.co.uk
www.bailii.org

Legislation
Acts of Parliament www.hmso.gov.uk/acts
Statutory Instruments www.hmso.gov.uk/stat
Parliamentary Bills, etc www.parliament.the-stationery-office.co.uk
The Law Commission www.lawcom.gov.uk
More Government information www.coi.gov.uk, www.criminal-justice-system.gov.uk

Case law
House of Lords decisions www.parliament.the-stationery-office.co.uk
The Court Service www.courtservice.gov.uk
Criminal Cases Review Commission www.ccrc.gov.uk
Casetrack www.casetrack.com
The Lord Chancellor's Department www.open.gov.uk/lcd
The Times www.the-times.co.uk
General www.lawreports.co.uk

Professional bodies
www.lawsociety.org.uk
www.barcouncil.org.uk
www.ilex.org.uk

Academic websites
www.cardiff.ac.uk
www.law.warwick.ac.uk
www.newcastle.co.uk

European law sites
www.europa.eu.int
www.europa.eu.int/celex
www.europa.eu.int/eur-lex/en/index.html
www.europarl.eu.int/dors/oeil/en
www.curia.eu.int
www.eurotext.ulst.ac.uk

Magazines/journals, etc
www.lawgazette.co.uk
www.butterworths.co.uk
www.smlawpub.co.uk

Answers guide

A. END OF PART QUESTIONS

Part 1 General Principles 1 (p. 64)

Question 1

- Define the concept of causation as a determinant of whether or not an accused can be said to have committed the *actus reus* of a particular crime, giving examples of situations where causation may be an issue, e.g. typically homicide;

- Refer to the 'but for' test or *sine qua non,* e.g. in *White,* and explain the essential principle that causation is a question of both fact and law (*Pagett*).

- Identify and illustrate what the phrase 'chain of causation' means, recognising the potential presence of a *novus actus interveniens;*

- Review the possibility of there being a number of contributory factors to the eventual commission of the *actus reus* and refer to:

  - the victim's own conduct (*Pitts, Curley, Roberts*).

  - the foreseeability of the events in the chain (*Pagett, Williams*) etc.

  - the A's conduct does not need to be the sole and exclusive cause of the prohibited consequence, e.g. *Jordan, Smith, Cheshire.*

- Evaluate the legal analysis and principles which determine responsibility, e.g. taking one's victim as one finds him/her (*Blaue*).

- Consider to what extent policy has shaped judicial attitudes to the development of the law in relation to supporting the police and the medical services in the performance of their duties e.g. (*Jordan, Smith, Cheshire*) etc.

- Evaluate the merits of placing the entire blame upon the originator of a chain of events.

- Comment on the value of employing principles of causation to avoid problems apparently posed by the apparent lack of coincidence of *actus reus* and *mens rea* in some cases (*Thabo Meli, Church, Fagan, Le Brun*).

Question 2

- Recognise that the vast majority of true crimes involve prohibited conduct, e.g. an act in unlawful killing, an appropriation in theft, etc., but identify that some offences may be brought about by omission e.g. gross negligence manslaughter.

- Describe 'duty' situations that may arise from statute, public office, common law, close relationship, voluntary assumption of care, *Gibbins v Proctor, Dytham, Pittwood, Stone v Dobinson, Miller.*

- Examine the uncertainty over defining when a 'caring duty' ought to be imposed.

- Discuss the imposing of standards of 'good practice' on the holders of public office.

- Refer to the issues arising in the *Bland* case and consider defining the extent of these duties.

- Comment upon legal and moral codes of behaviour in this context.

- Suggest whether the criminal law strikes an appropriate balance in this regard or whether it may be desirable to adopt a more prescriptive approach as in the Netherlands and France.

- Analyse the principles concerning coincidence and prior fault discussed in *Miller, Fagan*, etc.

Question 3

- Explain that there are two concepts of recklessness, one subjective and one objective, and distinguish between the relevant principles, giving definitions of *Cunningham* and *Caldwell.*

- Identify and discuss the harshness of *Elliott* and subjective characteristics.

- Refer to some of the relevant offences to which *Cunningham*-and *Caldwell*-type subjective/objective recklessness have been applied, including perhaps a very brief account of their historical relationship by reference to their statutory context within the Offences Against the Person Act 1861 and the Criminal Damage Act 1971 respectively;

- Cite other relevant cases such as *Stephenson, Satnam and Kewal, Savage and Parmenter.*

- Realise and explain the difficulties of the lacuna in *Shimmen, Reid and Merrick.*

- Recognise the significance of *Adomako* in this context.

- Views of the Law Commission and provisions of the draft Offences Against the Person Bill.

- Argue the moral distinction between an advertent and inadvertent risk taker.

- Explain the significance of policy behind Lord Diplock's decision in *Caldwell* setting 'acceptable' standards of conduct relating to intoxication and the *Majewski* rules.

- Consider the difficulties of punishment theory: how do you deter conduct, i.e. risk taking, of which the actor is unaware in *Caldwell*? Distinguish *Cunningham* where the punishment of deliberate or advertent risk taking is appropriate.

Question 4

- Define the concept of strict liability referring to the lack of requirement of *mens rea*.

- Emphasise the common law presumption of *mens rea*, e.g. in *Sweet v Parsley*.

- Identify the statutory nature of strict liability offences and realise the significance of statutory interpretation in this context.

- Recognise the summary nature of strict liability offences (road traffic, licensing, food safety, pollution, etc) and relevant cases, e.g. *Sherras v De Rutzen, Alphacell, Smedleys v Breed, James and Son v Smee*, etc.

- Refer to the distinction between 'absolute' and 'strict' liability.

- Give examples of 'no negligence'/'due diligence' defences.

- Refer to some of the social benefits claimed or injustices caused such as the regulatory nature or administrative convenience or the possible injustice of imposition of liability without fault in 'spiking' of drinks or 'planting' of drugs (*Warner, Gammon, Storkwain, Lim Chin Aik*, etc.).

- Criticise the potential unfairness of such offences by a consideration of some of the potential injustices arising from a willingness to dispense with proof of a 'guilty mind'– too much inconsistent use of discretion used by prosecuting agencies (more Parliamentary guidance as to fault element preferable?)/conviction of the morally innocent is never justifiable. Public respect for the criminal law is potentially undermined by dubious prosecutions/room for the development of criminal responsibility based on negligence?

- Comment on of some of the following 'benefits':
  protection of society from harmful acts; the 'quasi-criminal' nature of strict liability offences creates little stigma; regulatory nature, promotes high

standards of care in socially important activities; practical effectiveness, i.e. too many polluted rivers, too many drunk drivers as it is; administrative convenience, difficulty of establishing *mens rea* in many such cases removed.

Part 2 Homicide (pp. 120-1)

Question 1

- Define murder and explain the phrase 'malice aforethought' as interpreted by the courts, i.e. intention to kill or do serious harm (*Moloney*); distinguish motive and intention (*Steane*).

- Consider Lord Mustill's idea of 'indiscriminate malice' in *A-G Ref No. 3 of 1994* (1997).

- Consider the doctrine of transferred malice (*Latimer*) and apply the doctrine of transferred malice to Patrick as an unforeseen victim and conclude that Rupert may nevertheless remain liable for his death.

- Identify that Rupert is a *sine qua non* of Patrick's death in terms of causation (*Pagett*).

- Analyse whether Rupert's mental state may lead to a conviction for murder or manslaughter by the application of *Moloney; Woollin* and the *Nedrick* direction on oblique intention and perhaps other hypothetical examples.

- Observe that whether Rupert has oblique intention is a question for the jury on consideration of all the evidence, and infer that an accused intends the natural consequences of his actions (s.8 Criminal Justice Act 1967).

- Perhaps consider unlawful act manslaughter.

- Perhaps consider and dismiss the defence of duress.

Question 2

- Define the offence of murder (*Moloney,* etc), and refer to the concept of specific intent.

- Assess whether Sandra acted with an intention to kill or do serious harm.

- State sections 3 and 2 of the Homicide Act 1957, provocation and diminished responsibility.

- Explain the significance of special and partial defences on a charge of murder.

- Explain provocation and demonstrate knowledge and understanding of relevant cases, e.g. *Duffy, Camplin, Thornton, Morhall, Humphreys, Dryden, Smith* etc.

- Define diminished responsibility (s.2), (*Byrne*), and describe its relationship with provocation through the development of 'Battered Woman Syndrome' (*Ahluwalia, Thornton, Luc, Parker, Smith*, etc.)

- Analyse whether Sandra was provoked into suffering from a sudden and temporary loss of self-control (*Duffy*), and whether the previous systematic regime of violence towards her is relevant as cumulative provocation (*Ahluwalia, Thornton*).

- Consider whether the reasonable person would have lost control in the circumstances.

- Examine which characteristics may be applied to Sandra?

- Consider whether 'BWSome' is capable of amounting to a 'characteristic'? (*Camplin, Morhall, Humphreys, Dryden, Parker, Smith, Ahluwalia, Thornton*).

- Analyse the alternative scenario: has Sandra now lost the availability of the defence of provocation due to the 'cooling-off' period (*Duffy, Ibrams* and *Gregory, Thornton*)?

- Consider whether there is evidence of 'abnormality of mind' sufficient to sustain a defence of diminished responsibility?

- Perhaps consider and dismiss self-defence.

Question 3

- Identify the concept of intention in criminal law as an aspect of *mens rea and appreciate* the relevance of intention to crimes of specific intent.

- Recognise the development of intention through the common law (*DPP v Smith, Mohan, Hyam, Moloney, Woollin*, etc), and distinguish motive (*Steane*).

- Refer to different aspects of intention – direct/oblique.

- Appreciate the fact that foresight of intention is not the same as intention but may be used in conjunction with s.8 Criminal Justice Act 1967 – evidence from which intention may be inferred by the jury.

- Consider the difficulties inherent in distinguishing between degrees of probability.

- Evaluate the need to distinguish between, e.g. murder and manslaughter, by reference to the gravity of the offence in terms of blameworthy states of mind.

- Discuss whether juries should be able to make such moral judgements on morally reprehensible facts in murder trials as in *Moloney, Hancock (Woollin)*.

- Comment on the Law Commission's proposals

Question 4

- Recognise the potential issue of constructive/unlawful act manslaughter in relation to both Sarah and Mary; there is no basis for a murder charge.

- Recognise the potential causation issues when related to medical negligence (*Pagett, Smith, Jordan, Cheshire*).

- Define constructive manslaughter by reference to *Church, Newbury and Jones*, etc.

- Identify the unlawful act – criminal damage or possibly assault upon Angela?

- Analyse the 'dangerousness' of the unlawful act and the harm suffered by Mary (*Dawson, Goodfellow*) whether the act need be directed at the victim? (*Dalby/Goodfellow*).

- Does Dennis take Mary as he finds her? (*Blaue, Dawson, Watson*)

- Can a *Caldwell* reckless *mens rea* be transferred to an unforeseen victim (*Latimer* and transferred malice), or is it simply a matter of causation?

- Sarah: analysis of the facts, arguments as to whether the hospital negligence relieves Dennis of liability; probably does but either conclusion may be justified.

Question 5

- Identify the current forms of involuntary manslaughter.

- Define constructive/unlawful act manslaughter and gross negligence manslaughter.

- Unlawful act variety: must be criminal; must be dangerous (*Church*); need not be 'aimed' at the victim (*Goodfellow*); relevant *mens rea* that of the unlawful act (*Newbury and Jones*).

- Gross negligence variety: more than mere compensation as between the parties *Andrews;* may arise from a voluntary assumption of a duty of care (*Stone and Dobinson*); the significance of *Adomako,* and criticise the uncertainty surrounding the categories of involuntary manslaughter despite, or, indeed because of, the House of Lords decision in *Adomako.*

- Criticise the so-called 'circular-test' of liability enunciated by Lord Mackay in *Adomako.*

- Appreciate the criticism and potential unfairness surrounding constructive manslaughter where an accused could be found liable for a death which may never have been foreseen.

- Comment upon the Law Commission proposals on involuntary manslaughter including corporate manslaughter.

Part 3 Offences against the person (p. 151)

Question 1

Refer to/consider the following offences/aspects:

- the injury – it seems the bleeding mouth must be at least actual bodily harm, s.47 OAPA. Whether it amounts to a wound and the possibility of sections 18 and 20 is also something which ought to be considered (*Eisenhower*). A cut on the inside of the cheek has been held to satisfy the definition of a 'wound' (*Waltham*). Appropriate definitions of the relevant offences should be provided.

- Does she possess the necessary *mens rea*? s.18 requires proof of intention.

- *damage to Gemma's glasses* – appropriate definition s.1 Criminal Damage Act.

- *attempted assault on Wilf* – definition of an attempt/assault/battery.

- *mens rea and mistaken use of force in self-defence* – *Gladstone Williams* where the accused mistakenly uses force in self-defence. She is entitled to put forward the defence on the basis that she honestly believed he was entitled to use force, whether or not that belief would be considered honest. If force is unreasonable in the imagined circumstances, however, the defence may be lost (*Hughes*).

- *intoxication and self-defence* – according to *O'Grady* and *O'Connor,* where the mistaken belief has arisen out of voluntary intoxication, whether the accused is to be judged according to the facts as they actually were, or is the defence unavailable?

- *automatism* – some definition might be reasonably expected on the basis of *Bratty*. Self-induced automatism only provides a defence to crimes of specific intent and would be no defence to a s.47/s.20 charge. Does it even amount to automatism? (*A-G's Ref [No.2 of 1992]*).

- *transferred malice* – a recognition of the problem of the unforeseen victim and the way the law deals with it by reference, for example, to *Latimer*.

Question 2

- Note that consent to minor assaults in the course of everyday life is generally implied; indicate with appropriate citation that a true consent may excuse what would otherwise be an assault, e.g. surgery, injections, tattooing, body piercing for cosmetic purposes, physical contact sports.

- Recognise the limitations imposed upon the availability of consent (e.g. not available to a charge of homicide; euthanasia is not recognised in the UK; aiding and abetting a suicide is an offence).

- Refer to policy decisions restricting the availability of consent as a defence, e.g. not to prize-fighting with bare fists (*Coney*), nor to agreeing to settle differences by means of a fight or duel (*A-G's Reference No.6 of 1980*), nor to sado-masochistic activities deemed to be against the public interest (*Brown*).

- An assault may be prosecuted should a participant exceed what is allowable within the rules of that sport or game; deliberate harm is the essence of boxing but unacceptable in a variety of ball sports such as football, rugby or hockey.

- Comment upon the social utility of surgical treatment as a justification for the defence, whether or not the patient is conscious and capable of giving consent.

- Evaluate the reasons for the decisions given in *Brown Slingsby* and *Wilson*.

- Comment upon when and why it is appropriate for the law to interfere with individual freedom of choice on the grounds of public interest and consider whether the judiciary are in the better position to proceed on a case-by-case basis rather than Parliament attempting to lay down general principles in this regard.

- Discuss whether euthanasia should be made lawful?

Part 4 Offences against property (p. 196)

Question 1

Students should outline the law relating to the following issues:

- Theft in connection with the bag snatch (*Corcoran v Anderton* and s.1 Theft Act 1968); the question of the abandoning of the purse makes no difference – why?

- Burglary s.9(1)(a) entry as a trespasser in excess of permission *Jones and Smith,* and/or

- Burglary s.9(1)(b) is this technically committed if he had no pre-formed intent?

- *Robbery* s.8 definition and interpretation of the use of force 'in order to steal' (*Hale*). Although theft may be a continuing offence had the theft ended when he dropped the purse?

- *Assault* probably actual bodily harm contrary to s.47 Offences against Property Act 1861; refer to, e.g., *Miller, Savage* and *Spratt*.

- *Obtaining services by deception* s.1 Theft Act 1978, brief definition.

- *Evasion of liability* s. 2 (1)(b) Theft Act 1978, brief definition and, perhaps, *Gilmartin*.

- *Making off without payment* s.3 Theft Act 1978, question of consent by accepting a cheque (*Hammond*)? Potential liability here is less clear as he has clearly had the consent of the taxi driver to leave. By analogy with *Gomez* in connection with the problem in theft it seems that Fingers has made off without payment despite the apparent consent of the taxi driver.

Question 2

- Define theft and further define dishonesty and appropriation by reference to sections 1–3 Theft Act 1968.

- Explain the partial dishonesty provisions in s.2(1) (a),(b) and (c) by use of cases such as *McIvor* and *Robinson* and hypothetical examples regarding the honest finder.

- Refer to the test for dishonesty in all other cases citing *Feeley* and *Ghosh* and note that a person is not to be regarded as honest merely by demonstrating a 'willingness to pay'.

- Give the s.3 definition 'any assumption of the rights of an owner' and explain that rights amount to a 'bundle of rights' and not merely physical possession.

- Comment upon the fact that theft requires any appropriation to be coupled with a dishonest intention in order to establish liability.

- Comment that in all cases dishonesty is a mixed question of law and morality for the magistrates or a jury (*Feeley* and the two-tier *Ghosh* test), identifying the objective and subjective tests to be applied and giving hypothetical examples such as the 'Robin Hood' scenario or foreign visitor on a bus.

- Recognise the potential for juries in particular to apply differing standards of dishonesty to the same set of facts.

- Analyse the problems posed by *Lawrence* and *Morris* regarding an owner's apparent consent to appropriation where the accused nevertheless has a secret dishonest intention, and identify the connection between dishonesty and appropriation as later demonstrated in *Gallasso* and *Atakpu*.

- Consider whether the decision in *Gomez* satisfactorily reconciled the problems of *Lawrence* and *Morris*.

Question 3

- Identify and define theft and its elements (sections 1–6 Theft Act 1968).

- Identify and define burglary and its elements (s.9 (i) (a) and (b) Theft Act 1968).

- Identify and define attempt and attempting the impossible (Criminal Attempts Act/*Shivpuri*).

- Identify and define robbery and its elements (s.8 Theft Act 1968).

- Identify and define assault and battery at common law and s.47 Offences against Property Act 1861.

- Identify and define intoxication as a defence and refer to the *Majewski* principles.

- Consider Hugh's liability and identify some or all of the following offences:

  - does he commit burglary when he enters the shed belonging to his father?

  - consider 9 (i) (b) if he only formed the intention to steal after entry.

  - is the shed a building?

  - has he entered his father's premises as a trespasser (*Jones* and *Smith*)?

  - was the bike abandoned? The courts are reluctant to infer this.

  - did he intend to permanently deprive? Was he dishonest? (*Ghosh*, etc.)

- Consider Keith's liability and identify some or all of the following offences:

  - can a conditional intent to steal from the jacket amount to theft?

  - is it an attempted theft notwithstanding the impossibility element?

  - is he guilty of theft when he places items inside his coat? (*Morris, Gomez, McPherson*)

  - whether s.9 (i) (a) or (b) depends upon his state of mind when entering.

  - assault relevant to a possible robbery charge. Was the force used in order to steal?

  - likely to be a s.47 Offences against Property Act charge since there is bruising, recklessness in the subjective sense will suffice (*Savage, Parmenter*).

- consider intoxication as a defence. Did the intoxication prevent the formation of the necessary *mens rea*? If so, it would be a defence to the theft-related offences but not to the assault or criminal damage offences which are crimes of basic intent.

Part 5 Defences (p. 268)

Question 1

- Identify that intoxication is only ever relevant as a defence if it actually prevents the formation of the *mens rea*.

- Recognise the way the courts have distinguished between crimes of specific and basic intent and illustrate this distinction by reference to *Beard, Majewski* and selected appropriate offences.

- Distinguish between voluntary and involuntary intoxication and illustrate the relevant principles by citation of appropriate case law, e.g. *Hardie, A-G's Ref (No.1) of 1975, Kingston.*

- Refer to the relationship of intoxication and other defences such as mistake, insanity and diminished responsibility by reference to relevant case law – *O'Grady, Jaggard v Dickinson, Gannon, O'Connor, Tandy, Egan.*

- Identify the 'dutch courage' principle by reference to *Gallagher.*

- Criticise liability that is based upon the foresight of a general risk rather than foreseeing the specific risk of committing the particular offence in question.

- Explain that the presumption of recklessness implicit in the *Majewski Rules* for crimes of basic intent seems to conflict with s.8 Criminal Justice Act 1967.

- Discuss the justification for separating the *actus reus* from the *mens rea* since the recklessness in becoming intoxicated precedes the commission of the offence.

- Consider the public policy reasons for adopting a pragmatic rather than a principled approach.

- Evaluate the inconsistencies that occur when there is no lesser offence of basic intent upon which to 'fallback', e.g. theft or the inchoate offences.

- Discuss the effect of the decision in *Kingston* which does not allow a defence of involuntary intoxication if the effect is merely to disinhibit the accused.

- Consider the Law Commission proposals and the need, or otherwise, for reform.

Question 2

- Define essential elements of the defences: the *M'Naghten rules* and s.2 Homicide Act 1957.

- Recognise diminished responsibility is a special and partial defence to a charge of murder only, but insanity is a general defence to all crimes.

- Provide examples of recognition of diminished responsibility – alcoholism, 'battered woman syndrome'.

- Identify that 'abnormality of mind' means what the jury would term 'abnormal' *Byrne,* and that it is a legal definition based upon adduced medical evidence.

- Identify that insanity is also a legal definition which has been broadened to cover the operation of the mind in all its aspects (*Sullivan, Hennessey, Burgess*).

- Recognise that insanity may be raised by the prosecution or judge as well as the defence.

- Refer to the relationship between insanity and automatism and the danger of diabetics, epileptics, etc., falling within the terms of the definition of insanity.

- Recognise the widened powers of disposition given to the court by the Criminal Procedure (Insanity and Unfitness to Plead) Act 1991 upon a finding of 'not guilty owing to insanity', but note that on a murder charge hospitalisation will ensue.

- Appreciate the relative frequency of pleas of diminished responsibility compared with the rarity of insanity pleas.

- Contrast the unavailability of insanity to the psychopath (as they know what they are doing but are seemingly unable to control their impulses), with the availability of a plea of diminished responsibility to a psychopath charged with murder (*Byrne*).

- Compare the need for medical evidence to establish either defence and the associated problems posed for jurors faced with technical psychiatric terminology.

- Suggest that the defences are effectively established or rebutted by medical experts rather than being decided upon by jurors; doctors should not be delivering opinions on legal or moral responsibility which are essentially jury issues.

- Criticise the antiquity and operation of the plea of insanity despite the mitigating effect of the 1991 Act.

- Evaluate the potential for jury confusion and misapplication owing to emotional considerations, sympathy or crude 'gut reaction' (e.g. Peter Sutcliffe, the 'Yorkshire Ripper'), where psychiatric evidence was unanimous in agreeing he was a paranoid schizophrenic yet he was convicted of murder.

- Consider proposals for reform, e.g. Butler Committee 1975 and Law Commission Draft Criminal Code.

Question 3

Students should refer to/consider the following offences/aspects:

- *the injury*: it seems the bleeding mouth must be at least actual bodily harm (s.47 Offences against Property Act); whether it amounts to a wound and the possibility of sections 18 and 20 is also something which ought to be considered (*Eisenhower*); a cut on the inside of the cheek has been held to satisfy the definition of a 'wound' (*Waltham*), appropriate definitions of the relevant offences should be provided.

- *damage to Gemma's glasses*: appropriate definition, s.1. Criminal Damage Act.

- *attempted assault on Wilf*: definition of an attempt/assault/battery.

- *mens rea and mistaken use of force in self-defence*: *Gladstone Williams:* where the accused mistakenly uses force in self-defence she is entitled to put forward the defence on the basis that she honestly believed he was entitled to use force, whether or not that belief would be considered honest; if force is unreasonable in the imagined circumstances, however, the defence may be lost (*Hughes*).

- *intoxication and self-defence*: according to *O'Grady* and *O'Connor*, where the mistaken belief has arisen out of voluntary intoxication, whether the accused is to be judged according to the facts as they actually were, or is the defence unavailable?

- *automatism*: some definition might be reasonably expected on the basis of *Bratty*. Self-induced automatism only provides a defence to crimes of specific intent and would be no defence to a s.47/s.20 charge. Does it even amount to automatism? (*Attorney-G's Ref [No.2 of 1992]*)

- *transferred malice*: a recognition of the problem of the unintended/unforeseen victim and the way the law deals with it by reference, for example, to *Latimer*.

- *the injury*: it seems as though Lucy has committed the *actus reus* for both sections 18 and 20 in that she has wounded Gemma by a direct application of force. Does she possess the necessary *mens rea*? Section 18 requires proof of an intention to cause grievous bodily harm. This is a possibility but seems unlikely on the facts and a s.47/s.20 offence will probably be appropriate.

- As crimes of basic intent, according to *Majewski/O'Grady,* therefore even an intoxicated belief inducing the mistaken use of force is no defence to a crime of basic intent and Lucy should be liable.

- automatism – even if Lucy is acting as an automaton, it is self-induced by the taking of a dangerous drug and is treated in the same way as voluntary intoxication within the *Majewski* rules *(Bailey)*. Therefore it is no defence to a basic intent crime. It follows that Lucy is probably guilty under s.47 and s.20. and guilty of the criminal damage. She may, of course, be able to deny the specific intent *re* the attempted assault on Wilf. If so, can the *transferred malice* concept survive as regards the injury to Gemma?

Question 4

- Distinguish between mistakes of law and fact; mistake of law generally no defence.

- Refer to the need to prove the relevance of mistake in negating *mens rea*.

- Identify a variety of situations in which mistake may be relevant, e.g. an honest mistaken belief as to the right of ownership in theft or as to the justified use of reasonable force in self-defence.

- Recognise the potential that mistake may well be linked with another defence, e.g. intoxication, duress, self-defence.

- Cite relevant cases to illustrate some of the above points, e.g. *Morgan, Tolson, Kimber, O'Grady, Beckford, Gladstone Williams, Jaggard v Dickinson, Gannon* (to name a few).

- Examine the relevance of mistake vis-à-vis *mens rea*, e.g. the mistaken victim where A shoots B wrongly believing B is a stag (and perhaps contrast a mistake of identity/transferred malice *(Latimer)*.

- Consider whether or not mistake should be recognised as a good defence if it is based upon an accused's honestly held belief or whether it ought to be subject to an objective test for reasonableness *(Morgan, Gladstone Williams)*.

- Analyse whether it is right to leave the jury to assess the honesty of the belief by reference to its credibility.

- Criticise the inconsistencies in the application of the defence such as the apparent objective assessment of the reasonableness of A's mistaken belief in duress *(Graham, Howe, Martin)*.

- Analyse mistakes induced by intoxication *(Majewski, Kingston, O'Grady, Jaggard v Dickinson, O'Connor, Gannon)*, and evaluate relevant public policy issues.

Question 5

- Define accurately the defences by reference to relevant cases.

- Realise that duress in any of its forms is a recognition that an accused may be entitled to be asked to be excused liability on the basis of their will being overborne in the face of an external threat as a result of which they felt compelled to commit the alleged offence.

- Comment on subjective/objective aspects of the defences (*Graham, Martin, Bowen, Emery*), the nature of the threat (*Valderrama Vega*), and the requirement of immediacy (*Hudson and Taylor*).

- Analyse the policy arguments for not allowing duress as a defence to murder, e.g. the anti-terrorism element of policy of Hailsham in *Howe*.

- Recognise the apparent denial of necessity as a defence until the emergence of duress of circumstance (*Dudley and Stephens, Buckoke, Conway, Willer, Martin, Pommell*).

- Appreciate duress denied if criminal associations voluntarily joined (*Fitzpatrick, Shepherd*).

- Evaluate the moral arguments that can be applied to duress, necessity and duress of circumstance concerning the degree of resistance to be expected from an individual under threat; is there hypocrisy in claiming this higher moral ground?

- Discuss the type of threat: ought it to be confined to self and immediate family? Why?

- Consider whether threats other than death or serious harm should be allowable?

- Comment on which characteristics (frailty, cowardice, submissiveness, low IQ) ought to be taken into account? (provocation, etc)

- Consider whether the proposals suggested by the Law Commission and the law as developed by recent cases are becoming more favourable to an accused in terms of the subjective element?

- Criticise the fact that it is still apparently available to a s.18 Offences against the Person Act 1861 grievous bodily harm charge.

Part 6 General Principles 2 (p. 305)

Participation

Question 1

- Ignore burglary issues, the question clearly asks for liability for the death.

- Identify the obvious principal offence of murder since the question says Del 'deliberately shoots Soames dead' (*Woollin*).

- Identify potential liability for participation in crime by secondary parties who 'aid, abet, counsel or procure' – s.8 Accessories and Abettors Act 1861.

- 'Aiding' involves giving assistance to a perpetrator to commit a crime (*NCB v Gamble*).

- The *mens rea* is the intention to assist the commission of the crime (*Bainbridge*).

- Refer to the difficulties associated with joint enterprise and common design (*Davies v DPP, Hui Chi-Ming, Pearman*).

- *Max's liability*:

- supplying of the gun would amount to the *actus reus* of participation by 'aiding' the commission of the offence.

- knowing Del was a violent criminal, did Max offer him a 'blank cheque'? (*Bainbridge DPP for N.I. v Maxwell*)

- if, when supplying the gun, Max realised there was a significant possibility of Stan using the gun with intention to kill or cause grievous bodily harm, could he be an accessory to murder? (*Chan Wing-Siu, Roberts*). Suppose he contemplated merely an accidental death?

- *Rodney's liability*:

- didn't he make it clear to Del he only agreed to the use of the gun to frighten?

- recognise Del has departed from the common design and evaluate its significance.

- did he realise that there was any possibility that Del might be lying to him about the gun being loaded with blanks? (*Chan Wing-Siu, Hui Chi-Ming*)

- were Del's actions, as a matter of fact, within the course of the joint enterprise?

- did Rodney contemplate the possibility of an 'accidental' killing by an unlawful and – dangerous act? (*Stewart and Schofield*)

- has Rodney eliminated the possibility of a killing at all? (*Pearman*)

- is there an apparent inconsistency, suggested by *Stewart and Schofield*, with the decision in *Wan and Chan* on liability for murder/manslaughter within a joint enterprise?

Question 2

- Identify the words as descriptive of the necessary conduct to be established in relation to accessorial liability and as such form the *actus reus* of participation.

- Emphasise the basic requirement that there must be a positive act of assistance/encouragement in some form in order to found liability.

- Recognise the traditional procedural practice of citing all four words in any charge.

- Refer to each of the words and give case examples to illustrate the courts' interpretation. This may include an analysis of the potential meaning of the four words:
  aiding: help or assistance to P before or at time of offence (*Bainbridge*).
  abetting: inciting, instigating, encouraging, probably at the scene (*Wilcox v Jeffery, Coney, Allen, Tuck v Robson, Clarkson*).
  counselling: advising, persuading, instructing, pressuring (*Calhaem*).
  procuring: the most obscure, probably means causing or producing a consequence by endeavour (*A-G's Ref No.1 of 1975*).

- Appreciate no necessity for a physical meeting as long as there is a meeting of minds.

- Recognise A may be convicted even where P is acquitted if there was a principal offence.

- Assess whether the *dicta* in *Howe* are valid suggesting that A may be convicted as an accessory to murder even though P is only convicted of manslaughter.

- Evaluate the Law Commission's proposals to attach liability to the act of assistance irrespective of whether P is convicted.

- Consider policy issues concerning the desirability of convicting of the organisers of crime.

Inchoate offences (incitement, conspiracy, attempt)

Question 3

- Refer to the Criminal Attempts Act 1981 so as to define the *actus reus* of the offence.

- Recognise importance of establishing at what point a criminal intention can be said to have progressed to the stage of an attempt.

- Cite relevant cases that provide principles applying the meaning of 'more than merely preparatory'; these may include *Widdowson, Gullefer Campbell* and *Jones*.

- Recognise that aspects of attempting the impossible may very well refer to the practical and theoretical absence of an *actus reus* of any sort unless defined by the accused's belief and refer to sections 1 (2) and (3) as well as *Haughton v Smith, Anderton v Ryan* and *Shivpuri*.

- Demonstrate an awareness of the Law Commission's report which preceded the Criminal Attempts Act and describe some of the questions considered by the Report, e.g. the desirability of striking a balance between the protection of the public from the social danger caused by the contemplation of crime and the individual freedom to think or even fantasize.

- Analyse the rationale of criminalising attempts.

- Discuss the proposition that a person ought not to be punished for merely contemplating the commission of offence.

- Consider, perhaps, some reference to 'proximity', 'equivocality' or 'last act' principles which may very well demonstrate the candidate's true understanding of the topic; older relevant cases discussed might include *Robinson, Stonehouse*.

- Observe that the decision in *Gullefer* reflects the wish expressed by the Law Commission that the point at which a course of conduct amounts to an offence is a matter of fact for the jury in each case using principles of common sense and that the older common law principles would not normally need to be considered in order for a jury to come to a conclusion about this.

- Explain that point at which the law intervenes to criminalize such thoughts is the point defined in the Act by the phrase in the question.

- Examine the difficulties in defining at what precise point if any an attempt can be said to have occurred, e.g. the problems in *Gullefer* and *Jones,* and consider how realistic it is to expect the ordinary juror to be able to determine this without some further guidance.

- Comment on whether it should still be permissible for a judge to make reference to the previous law in order to clarify matters for the jury?

- Discuss, for example, any possible alternatives, e.g. the US model of 'substantial steps... strongly corroborative of the actor's criminal purpose'.

- Analyse whether it should be necessary, e.g. in a case of attempted murder, that the accused need go as far as pointing a gun at his/her intended victim?

Question 4

- As in Question 3 above, but also consider the following:

- Identify the desirability of permitting the law to intervene at an early stage precisely to prevent any actual harm being done.

- Criticise the suggestion implicit in the quotation on the basis that the criminal law has always consisted of principles that seek to promote the prevention of crime and to deter those who would wish to engage in criminal activity in an organised or planned way.

- Appreciate the use of specific legislation in this context to promote societal objectives and regulate behaviour in sensitive areas like incitement to racial hatred, sex tourism or the use of common law offences of conspiracy to outrage public decency or corrupt public morality.

- Criticise the practical problems inherent in the operation and application of some of these offences.

- Evaluate the balance that is desirable between entrapment and inchoate offences.

B. ADDITIONAL QUESTIONS (pp. 309–315)

Question 1

(a) Considering any defence(s) which she may raise, discuss Amy's criminal liability arising out of her treatment of Ben and for the injuries which he suffered. (25 marks)

- Consider possible offences committed, in descending order of seriousness: first, causing GBH or wounding with intent to do GBH, s.18 OAPA. Consider *actus reus*: refer to cases such as *DPP v Smith* (1961) and *Saunders* (1985) on GBH; *Moriarty v Brookes* (1834) and *C v Eisenhower* (1984) on wounding.

- Consider *mens rea*: intent to do GBH to Ben. Intent may be direct (Amy desired Ben's injuries) or oblique (although she did not desire them, she foresaw that it was virtually certain that they would happen). This foresight would not equal intent but would be evidence from which a jury could 'find' that she did have it (*Woollin* [1998]).

- Consider defence: intoxication based on use of cannabis. S.18 OAPA is a 'specific intent' offence, so defence is available (*DPP v Majewski* [1977]).

- Consider next offence: inflicting GBH or wounding, s.20 OAPA. Consider *actus reus*: as above – no difference between causing and inflicting GBH [*Ireland* (1997)]. Consider *mens rea*: intention or subjective, *Cunningham* recklessness. Refer to cases (*Mowatt* (1968), *DPP v Parmenter* [1992]). Note that sufficient for prosecution to prove that Amy foresaw some injury to Ben when she pushed him.

- Consider defence: s.20 is a 'basic intent' offence so Amy cannot plead intoxication (*Majewski*). Jury should be directed to assume that Amy was sober, and assess what she would have foreseen in that condition (*Richardson and Irwin* [1999]).

- Consider next offence: assault occasioning actual bodily harm (ABH), s.47 OAPA. Consider *actus reus*: (*Donovan* [1934], *Chan Fook* [1994]). Consider *mens rea*: same as s.20 OAPA (*Roberts* [1972]; *Savage* [1992]). Consider defence: s.47 is also 'basic intent' same result as s.20 above.

- Consider also possible defence of consent. Note limitations: when the injuries suffered amount to at least ABH, consent available only in defined and limited circumstances (*Attorney-General's Reference* [*No.6 of 1980*] [1981], *Brown and Others* [1993]), one of which is rough play amongst children (*Jones and Others* [1987]). But apparent consent of a child may well be invalid (*Burrell v Harmer* [1967]).

(b) Considering any defence(s) which she may raise, discuss Claire's criminal liability for the murder of Derek. (25 marks)

- Define murder: the unlawful killing of a human being with malice aforethought.

- Consider *actus reus*: did Claire cause death? Consider causation in fact using 'but for' test (*White* [1910]). Conclude: Claire is the factual cause of death. Consider causation in law using 'significant contribution' test (*Cheshire* [1991]). Conclude: she is the legal cause of death too. Note also 'reasonable foreseeability' test (*Pagett* [1983], *Marjoram* [2000]) is satisfied: reasonably foreseeable that pushing someone onto a busy road may lead to their being run over and killed.

- Consider *mens rea*: 'malice aforethought', the intent to kill or do GBH. See discussion on intent above under part (a). Claire seems to have desired Derek's death/serious injury, so no reference to oblique intent required ('golden rule' in *Moloney* [1985]), unless Claire claims (for example) that she just wanted to frighten Derek.

- *NB* The question calls for students to consider 'Claire's criminal liability for the *murder* of Derek'. There is therefore no need to consider involuntary manslaughter. However, the facts clearly indicate possible defences of diminished responsibility (DR) and provocation. Both defences are regulated by the Homicide Act 1957, ss. 2 and 3.

- DR – consider elements of defence, particularly 'abnormality of mind'. Claire's 'very odd' behaviour suggests a form of post-traumatic stress disorder (PTSD), not unlike Battered Woman Syndrome (BWS) which is an abnormality of mind (*Ahluwalia* [1992], *Hobson* [1998]). Note role of jury is deciding whether a mental state is 'abnormal' and, if so, whether the impairment was 'substantial' (*Byrne* [1960]; *Lloyd* [1967]). Note also burden of proof on Claire. If defence succeeds Claire will be convicted of manslaughter.

- Provocation – if there is evidence of provocation by things said or done judge is obliged to direct the jury accordingly (*Rossiter* [1994]). Burden of proof on the prosecution to prove that Claire was *not* provoked or, if she was, that the reasonable woman would *not* have lost self-control. There is evidence that Claire was provoked by Derek. If defence succeeds Claire will be convicted of manslaughter.

- Subjective question: did Claire suffer a sudden and temporary loss of self-control? Consider cases involving delayed reactions and 'slow burn' (*Duffy* [1949], *Thornton [No.1]* [1992], *Ahluwalia* [1992], *Baille* [1995]).

- Objective question: reaction of reasonable woman sharing those of Claire's characteristics that affect the gravity of the provocation (*Camplin* [1979]), noting recent case law developments (*Dryden* [1995], *Humphreys* [1995], *Smith* [2000]).

(c) Discuss whether the defences to murder dealt with by the Homicide Act 1957 are in need of some clarification or reform. (25 marks)

Students could raise a number of points here (the following does *not* purport to be a definitive list of the points that could be addressed):

- The requirement that D's loss of self-control be 'sudden' for the success of the provocation defence remains very controversial;

- The situation when D relies on cumulative provocation and/or a 'slow burn' reaction to provocation has been clarified thanks to the cases of *Ahluwalia*, *Thornton* and *Humphreys* – but there has never been a definitive House of Lords case on this important point, which may be desirable;

- Whether a characteristic has to be some 'permanent feature of character' as required by *Newell* (1980) has been doubted by the House of Lords in *Morhall* (1995) – but that was *obiter*, so the position remains unclear;

- Whether the term 'abnormality of mind' should be replaced with 'mental disorder', as suggested by the Butler Committee and approved by the Law Commission;

- The relationship between DR and intoxication, particularly the possible hardship caused to alcoholics by the (arguably harsh) decisions in *Tandy* (1989) and *Inseal* (1992);

- Whether the burden of proof should remain on the defence in cases of DR;

- One issue that was in doubt has now been clarified by the House of Lords in *Smith* (2000) – the conflict in the authorities between the decision of the Privy Council in *Luc Thiet Thuan* (1997) and the Court of Appeal in *Campbell (No.2)* and *Parker* (both 1997).

Question 2

(a) Considering any defence(s) that he may raise, discuss Ian's criminal liability for the injury to John. (25 marks)
(If necessary, refer back to the answer plan to Question 1 above for definitions and appropriate case law.)

- Consider offences that may have been committed, in descending order of seriousness. Consider *actus reus* and *mens rea* of each.

- Consider defences: a 'few drinks' plus the powerblast drug raises intoxication. S.18 OAPA is 'specific intent' so intoxication is available; ss.20 and s.47 OAPA are both offences of 'basic intent' so which voluntary intoxication is no defence. But involuntary intoxication is available (*Kingston* [1995]). Ian's lack of knowledge of the powerblast drug may make his consumption of it involuntary (*Eatch* [1980]).

- Consider also consent. Note limitations on availability of defence, but one situation is contact games and sports. Refer to case law (*Billinghurst* [1978], *Cey* [1989]). Conclude: question of fact for a court to decide whether Ian had gone beyond what is acceptable in the 'sport' of arm-wrestling.

(b) Considering any defence(s) which Laura may raise, discuss her criminal liability for the death of Martin, and discuss the criminal liability of Karl arising out of his actions. (25 marks)

Laura's liability
NB unlike in question 1, students are invited to consider Laura's liability for the 'death' – not murder – of Martin. This clearly requires analysis of murder and involuntary manslaughter.

- Consider *actus reus* (common to both murder and manslaughter): has Laura caused Martin's death in fact (using 'but for' test) and in law (using 'significant contribution' test)? He may have had a weak heart or some other pre-existing condition but this would not break the chain of causation, as everyone must take their victim as they find them (*Martin* [1832], *Blaue* [1975]).

- Consider and discount *mens rea* of murder: 'malice aforethought'. On the facts there is very little evidence either that she desired Martin's death (or serious injury), or that she foresaw death or GBH as virtually certain (presumably there was no visible indication of his susceptibility to heart attack).

- Consider constructive manslaughter. (1) There must be an unlawful act. This means a criminal offence. Laura has committed battery against Martin – define battery (*Collins v Wilcox* [1984]). (2) The act must be dangerousness (*Church* [1965]). The *Church* test is objective, but if Martin was obviously frail this would be taken into account (*Dawson and Others* [1985], *Watson* [1989]).

- Laura's depression might suggest diminished responsibility (*Seers* [1984], *Ahluwalia* [1992]) – but DR is only a defence to murder and, given that Laura lacks malice aforethought, there is no need to pursue this possibility.

Karl's liability

- Laura's depression could be classed as either ABH (*Chan-Fook* [1994]) or GBH (*Burstow* [1997]), depending on its severity. Words (whether written or spoken) may constitute assault (*Ireland* [1997] – telephone calls; *Constanza* [1997] – threatening letters). Expert psychiatric evidence is required (*Morris* [1998]).

- Consider *actus reus*. Assault for s.47 OAPA requires apprehension of immediate, unlawful bodily harm, but note generosity of courts' approach to immediacy (*Smith* [1983], *Constanza*). To inflict GBH under s.20 simply means to cause it (*Ireland* [1997]).

- Consider Karl's *mens rea*. S.18 OAPA requires proof that Karl intended GBH, s.20 and s.47 satisfied by intention or *Cunningham*, subjective recklessness. Refer to relevant case law on s.20 (*Mowatt* [1968], *DPP v Parmenter* [1992]) and on s.47 (*Roberts* [1972], *Savage* [1992]).

(c) How satisfactory is the law on intoxicated defendants? (25 marks)

Students could raise a number of points here (the following does not purport to be a definitive list of the points that could be addressed):

- The lack of a completely clear definition of 'specific' and 'basic' intent and hence the blurring of the distinction between the two categories of offences;

- The clash of legal principle and policy inherent in *DPP v Majewski*, e.g. the apparent conflict between the rule in *Majewski* and s.8 of the Criminal Justice Act 1967;

- Whether a judge should be obliged to direct a jury on the defence even where it has not been relied upon by the defence but there is evidence of intoxication;

- The less than completely clear distinction between examples of voluntary and involuntary intoxication;

- The relationship between intoxication and other defences such as insanity, automatism, mistake and diminished responsibility;

- Whether an alternative offence should be introduced, e.g. 'dangerous intoxication'.

Question 3

(a) Discuss Stella's criminal liability arising out of the incidents described above. (25 marks)

- Consider making off without payment, s.3 Theft Act 1978 (when Stella leaves the restaurant without paying for her drinks). Define the offence and consider *actus reus*: does she 'make off' (contrast with *McDavitt* [1981]), without having paid as required or expected for goods supplied. Consider *mens rea*: dishonesty, knowledge that payment on the spot was required or expected, intent to avoid payment. Crucial issue is dishonesty: refer to *Ghosh* (1982) test. *NB* These events cannot amount to theft as, even assuming that she was dishonest in leaving without paying, by that point in time the property – the drinks – did not belong to another.

- Consider theft, s.1 Theft Act 1968 (when Stella uses her sister's store card). Define theft and consider *actus reus*: has she appropriated property belonging to the store? Note that an 'appropriation' may take place with another's consent (*Lawrence* [1972]; *Gomez* (1993), *Hinks* [2000]). (*NB* the case facts are very similar to *Gomez* itself, where D was convicted.) Consider *mens rea*: was Stella dishonest and did she intend to permanently deprive the store of the shoes? She could deny being dishonest on the basis that her sister would have consented to her using the card if she had known of the circumstances (s.2[1][b], Theft Act 1968). Otherwise dishonesty is tested using the *Ghosh* (1982) test.

- Consider, but discount, possibility of burglary, s.9, Theft Act 1968. Even if Stella does commit theft, she almost certainly did not enter the store 'as a trespasser', which is required for liability under either s.9(1)(a) or (b).

(b) Discuss Tina's criminal liability arising out of the incidents described above. (25 marks)

- Consider theft (when Tina decides to spend the £60). Consider *actus reus*: the purse and money are 'property' which 'belonged' to someone other than Tina. An 'appropriation' extends to the situation where D has come by property, without stealing it, but later assumes a right to it by 'dealing with it as owner'. Consider *mens rea*: intent to permanently deprive and dishonesty. Possibility of Tina claiming the owner cannot be traced by reasonable steps, therefore not dishonest, s.2(1)(c) Theft Act 1968. If this belief is genuine, not necessarily reasonable, then she is not dishonest – but the more unreasonable her belief, the less likely she will be believed (e.g. the purse is likely to have some form of identification in it). If so her state of mind would be examined using the *Ghosh* test, as above.

- Consider theft (when Tina is in the department store). Consider *actus reus*: she has appropriated (assumed rights of ownership, s.3 Theft Act 1968) property belonging to another. It is irrelevant that the store would have consented to her picking up underwear to examine it or try it on (*Gomez*). Consider *mens rea*: the dishonest intention to permanently deprive. None of the provisions in s.2(1) apply, leaving Tina again subject to the *Ghosh* test. Conclusion: appears guilty of theft. *NB* The fact she throws the underwear away and leaves the store does *not* mean it cannot be theft: all the elements of the offence are present. Students should *not* be distracted into considering attempted theft.

- Consider also robbery, s.8, Theft Act 1968. Consider *actus reus*: Tina must steal (i.e. commit theft, see above), and immediately before or at the time of doing so, and in order to do so, use force on any person. Note that an 'appropriation' may be continuous, hence she may still have been in the course of committing theft when she pushed over Vera (*Hale* [1978]; *Lockley* [1995]). Define 'force' and explain that it is for jury to decide (*Dawson and James* [1976], *Clouden* [1987]). Did Tina use force 'in order to' steal? On the facts it is difficult to say – was Vera blocking her escape from the changing area? It is irrelevant that the underwear did not belong to Vera, robbery is committed if force used on 'any person'.

- Consider possibility of burglary, s.9, Theft Act 1968. Consider *actus reus*: no doubt that she 'entered' the changing room. Given her plan to steal the underwear, did she enter the changing room 'as a trespasser'? Consider *Walkington* (1979) on 'part of a building'. Consider *mens rea* for trespass (*Collins* [1973]). Conclusion: if she entered the changing room, as a trespasser, intending to steal the underwear, she could be liable under s.9(1)(a) and also liable when she does steal the underwear under s.9(1)(b).

(c) To what extent should the claim that the defendant has made an honest, but not necessarily reasonable, mistake be a good defence in criminal law? (25 marks)

Students could raise a number of points here (the following does *not* purport to be a definitive list of the points that could be addressed):

• Refer to relevant case law on this point (*Morgan* [1976], *Williams* [1987], *Beckford* [1988]).

• Statute also supports the 'honest', as opposed to 'reasonable', approach: see s.5(3) Criminal Damage Act 1971; s.1(2) Sexual Offences (Amendment) Act 1976.

• Reference to 'honesty', as opposed to 'reasonableness', of a mistake is a subjective approach, and supports the general policy of the law on *mens rea* issues (especially intent and recklessness – at least those crimes where *Cunningham* provides the test). It focuses attention on what D believed, not what he should have believed. This may be seen as fair: those defendants who genuinely believe they are acting within the law do not deserve to be punished.

• But note important role played by reasonableness. The more unreasonable a belief the more likely that D will not be believed.

• Where offence is one of strict liability, then any mistake (genuine and/or reasonable) will not provide any defence.

• When D is intoxicated, they cannot plead mistake, for obvious reasons of public policy.

Question 4

(a) Considering any defence which he may raise, discuss David's criminal liability arising out of the incidents at the building society. (25 marks)

• Consider attempted robbery. Consider *actus reus*: has he done an act which is more than merely preparatory to the commission of the full offence (s.1, Criminal Attempts Act 1981)? Note various tests: had he embarked on the crime proper? (*Gullefer* [1990]); was he actually trying to commit the full offence? (*Geddes* [1996]). Contrast with *Campbell* (1991). Note that if David went beyond the preparatory state it was too late to withdraw – the attempt had been made. Consider *mens rea*: intention is essential (*Mohan* [1975]). But conditional intent suffices (*Attorney-General's Reference* [*Nos.*

1 and 2 of 1979] [1979]). Conclusion: David guilty, even though he only intended to go ahead if it was safe, if jury finds that he had gone beyond the preparatory stage.

- Consider burglary, s.9(1)(b), Theft Act 1968 (based on attempted theft). If David commits attempted robbery he also commits attempted theft (robbery includes theft). Thus he may be liable under s.9(1)(b). Consider *actus reus*: did he enter the building society as a trespasser? Refer to *Jones and Smith* (1976). Consider *mens rea*: did he know or suspect he was trespassing (*Collins* [1973]).

- Consider burglary, s.9(1)(b), Theft Act 1968 (based on inflicting GBH on Frances). Consider *actus reus*: as above, plus did he inflict GBH? To 'inflict' simply means to 'cause' (*Ireland* [1997]). Consider *mens rea*: as above on trespass. Is there any *mens rea* requirement as to the infliction of the GBH? S.9(1)(b) simply refers to 'he inflicts … on any person therein any grievous bodily harm' – there is no express requirement of *mens rea*. Court of Appeal in *Jenkins* (1983) decided no *mens rea* required – but the House of Lords reversed the decision on a different point. (*NB* he may not be guilty of inflicting GBH, under s.20 OAPA, because there the infliction must be 'malicious', which means intent or *Cunningham* recklessness, and it appears his collision with Frances was accidental.)

- Consider defence of duress by threats. Define the defence: general defence to most offences including robbery if D committed the alleged offence under threats of immediate death or serious violence to himself or other persons (note that David's children are threatened). Consider application of the defence to David: the *Graham* (1982) test must be satisfied. Even if it is, the defence may be denied on several grounds: (1) Edward gives him a week, so the threat is not immediate and/or David has time to seek police protection (*Gill* [1963]); (2) David voluntarily associated himself with Edward, a person with a reputation for violence (*Baker and Ward* [1999], *Heath* [2000]); (3) the threat lacked specific reference to one particular crime (*Cole* [1994]); (4) Edward's threat is too vague, that David's children would not 'be safe', and the threats must be of death or serious injury (*Hudson and Taylor* [1971]).

(b) Discuss David's criminal liability arising out of the incidents at the house of his friend, Gina. (25 marks)

- Consider burglary, s.9(1)(a), Theft Act 1968 (based on entering the bedroom with intent to steal). Consider *actus reus*: he enters 'part of a building' – the bedroom – as a 'trespasser'. His general permission to be in the house does not extend to entering private rooms, especially to look for things to steal. Consider *mens rea*: Did he know or suspect he was trespassing in the bedroom?

- Consider burglary, s.9(1)(b), Theft Act 1968 (based on theft). Consider *actus reus*: assuming he has entered the bedroom as a trespasser, he then takes jewellery. This is theft, s.1 Theft Act 1968, assuming all the elements are present: the dishonest appropriation (he assumes rights) of property (jewellery) belonging to another (Gina) with the intention of permanently depriving her of it. Consider *mens rea*: see above.

- Consider criminal damage, s.1(1), Criminal Damage Act 1971 (CDA). Consider *actus reus*: he 'forces open' the drawer in the bedroom, which presumably damages it; he also breaks the gas pipe in the kitchen, which clearly does damage it. Consider *mens rea*: this is intent (for the drawer) or objective *Caldwell* recklessness (for the pipe). He is reckless if he considered the risk of damaging the pipe or if he failed to consider the risk when it was in fact obvious to the ordinary prudent individual. If he thought about the risk and decided that the pipe would definitely support him (hence no risk of damage), then he would fall into the *Caldwell* lacuna, and therefore was not reckless (*Shimmen* [1986], *Reid* [1992]).

- Consider aggravated criminal damage, s.1(2), CDA. Consider *actus reus*: exactly the same as above – no requirement that life be endangered in fact (*Sangha* [1988]). Consider *mens rea*: intent or *Caldwell* recklessness as to whether life would be endangered by the damage: if there was an objectively obvious risk to life, which David either recognised or failed to recognise at all (in his haste to escape), then in either case he was reckless.

- Consider arson and aggravated arson, s.1(3), CDA. Consider *actus reus*: David does destroy Gina's house in an explosion, that is, by fire. Consider *mens rea*: was David *Caldwell* reckless as to whether Gina's house would have been destroyed by fire? Was he *Caldwell* reckless as to whether her life would have been endangered by fire? That is, did he either recognise those risks but carry on regardless or did he completely fail to consider the (objectively obvious) risks? If either is true then he was reckless.

(c) Discuss whether Caldwell (objective) recklessness is an appropriate state of mind on which to base criminal liability. (25 marks)

Students could raise a number of points here (the following does *not* purport to be a definitive list of the points that could be addressed):

- Explain why *Caldwell* objective recklessness was introduced in *Caldwell* (1982): to deny those defendants who were so intoxicated or enraged (for example) that they were prevented from foreseeing obvious risks a defence if charged with an offence requiring recklessness.

- Note that intoxicated defendants are already dealt with by the rules in *DPP v Majewski* (1977).

- Analyse Lord Diplock's reasons for introducing objective recklessness – recklessness is an ordinary English word; inadvertence is equally as blameworthy as advertence; objective recklessness will be easier for juries – and note the highly critical response by leading academic writers Professors Sir John Smith and Glanville Williams.

- Note initially enthusiastic reception by courts to *Caldwell* recklessness and application to other offences (*Lawrence* [1982], *Seymour* [1982], *Kong Cheuk Kwan* [1985]).

- Compare/contrast cases such as *Stephenson* (1979) and *Elliott v C* (1983)/*R (Stephen Malcolm)* (1984), and comment on whether the *Caldwell* test is too objective.

- Analyse 'lacuna' in *Caldwell* recklessness (*Shimmen* [1896], *Reid* [1992]).

- Note continued role of *Cunningham* subjective recklessness in non-fatal offences (*Savage, DPP v Parmenter* [1992]) and removal of *Caldwell* from manslaughter (*Adomako* [1995]).

Question 5

(a) Explain the elements of the offence of murder and, ignoring Alice's anxiety and depression and Ben's behaviour towards her, apply them to determine whether Alice could be guilty of murdering Ben. (10 marks)

- Prosecution must prove that Alice caused Ben's death with malice aforethought.

- Although Ben injected himself with heroin, Alice was under a duty of care as his wife to assist him and/or get help after she found him unconscious.

- As she omitted to do anything for an hour she may be liable for murder on the basis of her omission (*Gibbins and Proctor* [1918]).

- Malice aforethought means she must have intended his death or intended to do him grievous bodily harm (GBH) by leaving him for an hour.

- Intent could either be direct (she desired his death/GBH) or oblique (she foresaw death/GBH as virtually certain to occur, yet left him alone for an hour). In the case of direct intent she has malice aforethought; in the case of oblique intent it is then for the jury to 'find' that she had malice aforethought (*Woollin* [1998]).

- Students are told to ignore Alice's anxiety and depression – but not her drinking. She must be very drunk after having consumed over half a bottle of whisky so there is evidence of intoxication. As murder is a crime of specific intent (*DPP v Beard* [1920]) the intoxication could reduce her liability to that of involuntary manslaughter but would not absolve her altogether as her being drunk is evidence of recklessness and/or gross negligence (*Lipman* [1970]).

(b) Considering, especially, Alice's anxiety and depression and Ben's behaviour towards her, explain the elements of any defence(s) which Alice may raise to seek to reduce the crime to manslaughter and apply them to determine whether she would be successful in doing so. (10 marks)

- Defences of provocation and/or diminished responsibility will reduce liability for murder to (voluntary) manslaughter.

- Both offences defined in Homicide Act 1957.

- There must be evidence of provocation. This may be things done (Ben punches Alice) or things said (Ben calls Alice a 'drunken whore'). Defence must therefore be left to the jury (*Doughty* [1968]) – prosecution must disprove it beyond reasonable doubt.

- The fact she may have provoked Ben (by drinking a bottle of whisky in front of him) into provoking her is no reason to deny her the defence. If there is evidence it *must* be left to the jury to decide.

- Was it possible that Alice was provoked to suddenly and temporarily lose her self-control? Although the fact she damages the television/mirror/furniture is evidence of a loss of self-control, the crucial issue is whether she was 'not master of her mind' (*Duffy* [1949]) at the time when she decided to leave Ben unconscious. This point is 'about 10 minutes' after the provoking things done/said – has she had an opportunity to cool off? Especially relevant is the fact she was able to make and drink coffee in the meantime. Nevertheless this is a question of fact for the jury (*Baille* [1995]) although the longer the time delay the weaker the defence (*Ahluwalia* [1992]).

- All of the provoking events (Ben's 'unpredictable behaviour') over the past five years are relevant as cumulative provocation in determining whether she may have lost self-control (*Humphreys* [1995]).

- The fact that she arms herself with a knife suggests a desire for revenge, not a sudden loss of self-control (*Ibrams and Gregory* [1981], *Thornton* [No.1] [1992]).

- Might the reasonable woman have lost self-control and done as Alice did? Alice's mental characteristics of being 'anxious, depressed' may be relevant (*Smith* [2000]). Her being the victim of sustained domestic violence suggests battered woman syndrome (*Ahluwalia, Thornton* [No.2] [1996]).

The fact that some of her characteristics are the long-term products of her alcoholism does not prevent her from relying upon them: characteristics may be self-induced (*Morhall* [1996]). But the fact that she is 'short-tempered' is irrelevant (*Camplin* [1978]) as is the fact that she is almost certainly very drunk after drinking so much whisky (*Newell* [1980]). Finally the fact that she is specifically provoked about being a 'drunken whore' means that both her alcoholism and her life as a prostitute are potentially relevant as characteristics (*Morhall*).

- Diminished responsibility must be proven by the defence on the balance of probabilities.

- Alice must show that was suffering an abnormality of mind (*Byrne* [1960] test).

- Depression is such an abnormality (*Seers* [1984], *Ahluwalia*).

- Alcoholism is not enough of its own, although it can be if there is proof of brain damage and/or drinking becomes involuntary (*Tandy* [1989], *Inseal* [1992]).

- Although the abnormality must arise from a specified cause, depression/alcoholism are both 'diseases'.

- Whether Alice's responsibility was 'substantially' impaired is a question for the jury alone (*Lloyd* [1976]).

(c) Explain the elements of unlawful act manslaughter and gross negligence manslaughter and consider whether, if a murder charge were to fail, Alice could be guilty of either. (10 marks)

- Constructive manslaughter requires proof of an unlawful and dangerous act that causes death. An unlawful act means a criminal offence, not a civil wrong. Dangerous means subjecting another person to the risk of some (not necessarily serious) harm (*Church* [1965] test). Although Alice causes a considerable amount of criminal damage (a criminal offence), none of this has any effect on Ben, and so is not dangerous.

- Entering a room armed with a knife may have been an assault had Ben been awake but as he is unconscious he could not have apprehended immediate violence, hence no criminal offence committed (*Lamb* [1967]). Constructive manslaughter requires a positive act, not a mere omission, so Alice leaving Ben alone cannot form the basis of this crime either (*Lowe* [1973]).

- Gross negligence manslaughter requires a breach of a duty of care which causes death and that is so 'gross' that a jury deems it a criminal offence (*Bateman* [1925], *Adomako* [1995]). Alice clearly owed Ben a duty of care as his wife. Leaving him unconscious for an hour suggests a breach of duty (this is a question for the jury). Whether or not it was a 'gross' breach of duty is purely for the jury. The fact that Alice was so drunk may strengthen prosecution case. Gross negligence manslaughter may be incurred for an omission (*Adomako*).

- As a general point regarding involuntary manslaughter, Alice's obvious intoxication from drinking whisky does not provide a defence as all forms of involuntary manslaughter are classed as 'basic intent' (*Majewski*, *Lipman*); unless she argued that her alcoholism has rendered her drinking involuntary, in which case it might provide a defence but only if it prevents the prosecution in proving that she had the relevant *mens rea* (*Kingston*).

(d) Alice might have difficulty in being able to pay for legal advice and representation. Explain what statutory provision is made to assist accused persons in her position. (10 marks)

- If Alice has little money then she can apply for Legal Aid, under the Legal Advice and Assistance Scheme, to cover the cost of advice from a solicitor before any appearance in court.

- Alice may also be entitled to Legal Aid to cover the costs of legal representation by one or two barristers in the Crown court, expert reports, etc. Legal Aid is granted on satisfaction of two tests: (a) the means test (i.e. whether Alice's financial resources are sufficiently small); (b) the merits test.

- The merits test is based on criteria set out in s.21 of the Legal Aid Act 1988. Those relevant to Alice's case include: the likelihood of her facing a prison sentence, whether she would suffer loss of livelihood and/or serious damage to their reputation; whether the case involved a 'substantial' question of law; the possibility that she may be unable to understand the proceedings; the likelihood of expert cross-examination of witnesses being required.

(e) In answering parts (a) – (c) above, you have discussed rules of law concerning the offences of murder and manslaughter and related defences. Select either the offences or the defences and consider what criticisms may be made of the rules and what improvements might be suggested. (10 marks)

- *Of murder:* difficulty explaining/applying oblique intent, even after *Woollin*; imposition of liability for an omission may be seen as unfair.

- *Of provocation:* continued insistence on 'sudden and temporary loss of self-control'; uncertainty about meaning of/difficulty in applying characteristics to reasonable person; artificiality in asking how the hypothetical reasonable person would have reacted.

- *Of diminished responsibility:* determination of 'abnormality' and 'substantial' impairment both left to jury to decide, with unpredictable/inconsistent results; refusal of courts to recognise alcoholism as a 'disease' *per se* and insistence on further requirements may be seen as unfair to alcoholics.

- *Of constructive manslaughter:* imposition of constructive liability may be seen as unfair as defendant is convicted of homicide when the fatal consequences are neither intended nor foreseen, and may even be utterly accidental.

- *Of gross negligence manslaughter:* vagueness/uncertainty in allowing jury to determine guilt based on what is 'gross'; uncertainty even following *Adomako* as to exact terms of the offence; breach of duty of care is a civil concept not a criminal one.

Question 6

(a) Taking account of any possible defences which Andy might raise, discuss his liability for the murder of Betty (15 marks)

- To be guilty of murder, it must be proved beyond reasonable doubt that Andy caused Betty's death, and did so with malice aforethought.

- Andy caused Betty to die as a matter of fact, applying the 'but for' test, as she would not have died had he not thrown the ball that killed her dog (*White* [1910]). Andy may argue that he did not kill her as a matter of law; he may argue that the chain of causation was broken by Betty's heart attack. However, this would be met with the 'thin skull rule' – the proposition that one must take one's victims as one finds them, physical defects and all (*Blaue* [1975]).

- He might also argue that Betty's death was unforeseeable. This is a question of fact for the jury – although they will be told that Andy's act(s) need not be the main cause of death, it is sufficient if they make a more-than-trifling contribution to it (*Pagett* [1983], *Mellor* [1996]).

- Malice aforethought means he must have intended to kill or do grievous bodily harm (GBH) to the owner of the shy. Intent could either be direct (Andy desired his death/GBH) or oblique (he foresaw death/GBH as virtually certain to occur). In the case of direct intent being proven then he has malice aforethought; in the case of oblique intent it is then for the jury to 'find' that he had malice aforethought (*Woollin* [1998]).

- If intent is established, then transferred malice applies to transfer his *mens rea* from the shy-owner to Betty (*Latimer* [1886]).

- Andy has been drinking all day, so he may plead voluntary intoxication. Murder is a specific intent crime, so the defence is available (*DPP v Beard* [1920]) but will only inevitably lead to his conviction of manslaughter (a basic intent offence (*Lipman* [1970]).

(b) Taking account of any possible defences which Colin might raise, consider whether he might be guilty of murder or manslaughter in connection with Dave's death. (15 marks)

- Colin has caused Dave's death as a matter of fact, applying the 'but for' test (*White*). He has also caused his death in law.

- He may plead insanity, on the basis of his paranoid delusions. The *M'Naghten* Rules state that Colin has a defence if he was suffering a 'defect of reason' caused by a 'disease of the mind'. We know he suffers paranoid delusions. This defect must prevent him from knowing the 'nature and quality of his act' or, if he did, that he did not know it was wrong. 'Wrong' means not appreciating the act was illegal (*Windle* [1952]). If Colin did believe he had been ordered to kill a spy then he would not believe he was breaking the criminal law and thus the defence would be made out. If successful, this would lead to the 'special verdict' of not guilty by reason of insanity followed by indefinite detention in a special hospital.

- He could also plead diminished responsibility, s.2 Homicide Act 1957. His paranoid delusions suggest an 'abnormality of mind', induced presumably by disease or some other inherent cause. It is then for the jury to decide whether the mental responsibility impairment was 'substantial'.

- He may also plead non-insane automatism, on the basis of the noise, music and flashing lights being external factors that induced a trance-like state. This would be non-insane automatism (*Quick* [1973]), leading to a complete acquittal, unless the judge ruled that the true cause of the trance-like state was Andy's paranoia, i.e. an internal factor suggesting insanity (*Sullivan* [1984], *Hennessy* [1989], *Burgess* [1991]).

(c) In examining (a) and (b) above, you have considered various offences and defences. Discuss who bears the burden of proof in those offences and defences, and what standard of proof is required. (5 marks)

- *Murder*: Burden of proof on the *prosecution* to establish all elements beyond reasonable doubt.

- *Insanity*: For the *defence* to prove all the elements of the *M'Naghten* Rules, on a balance of probabilities.

- *Diminished responsibility*: For the *defence* to prove all the elements in s.2, on a balance of probabilities.

- *Automatism*: For the defence to provide evidence making the defence a 'live' issue, thereafter for the *prosecution* to disprove it beyond reasonable doubt.

(d) Being careful to give your reasons, explain what changes you would propose to the current law on unlawful homicide. (15 marks)

- Clarify oblique intent. Reason: still not free from all doubt even after *Woollin*. Serious crimes such as murder should be very clearly defined.

- Abolish constructive manslaughter. Reason: 'constructive' crime imposes liability on defendants for consequences that they did not foresee; arguably this is unfair: e.g. D1 punches V1, who falls to the ground and suffers minor bruising; D1 liable for s.47 ABH (at worst). Maximum sentence (if tried in Crown Court) 5 years. D2 punches V2 who falls to the ground but lands awkwardly, breaks his neck and dies. D2 is liable for manslaughter, maximum sentence life imprisonment. Constructive murder was abolished in 1957 by s.1 Homicide Act; arguably constructive manslaughter should likewise be removed from the criminal law.

- Clarify some of the ambiguities with gross negligence manslaughter. Reason: certain issues left unresolved following *Adomako*. Serious crimes such as manslaughter should be very clearly defined.

- Clarify whether subjective (*Cunningham*) reckless manslaughter exists. Reason: serious crimes such as manslaughter should be very clearly defined.

Question 7

(a) Taking into account any defences which each may be able to plead, discuss the liability of Gerry and Henry in connection with the injuries suffered by each (15 marks)

- Henry suffers a 'long deep cut to his cheek'. This is clearly a wound, suggesting malicious wounding, s.20 OAPA. Wounding requires a break in the continuity of the skin, this is obvious on the given facts.

- Was Gerry 'malicious'? This means intent or subjective (*Cunningham*) recklessness as to the causing of some injury, not necessarily the harm that was caused (namely the wound) (*Mowatt* [1968], *Savage* [1992]). This is a question for the jury/magistrates but given the circumstances Gerry may well argue that he did not foresee any injury to Henry.

- Alternatively, Gerry may plead duress of circumstances. This is a plea based on his reaction being appropriate in the emergency situation. The jury must apply the test established in cases such as *Willer* (1986), *Conway* (1988) and *Martin* (1989): did he honestly believe that he was in danger, and would the reasonable man have responded to the duress in the same circumstances?

- Gerry dislocated his knee. This could (depending on the seriousness) amount to grievous bodily harm, s.20 OAPA, or actual bodily harm, s.47 OAPA. This requires some interference with his health and comfort, which is apparent on the facts. The question is whether Henry was reckless. The *mens rea* for s.47 ABH is either intent or *Cunningham* subjective recklessness (*Venna* [1976]). But Henry need only have foreseen the causing of some harm, not necessarily that which was in fact caused (*Roberts* [1972], *DPP v Parmenter* [1992]).

- Both boys could plead consent, on the basis that what happened was all part of 'rough horseplay', which has been accepted as a defence to even serious assaults as on the present facts (*Jones and Others* [1986], *Aitken and Others* [1992]).

(b) Taking into account any defence(s) which she may be able to plead, discuss Ellen's liability arising out of the telephone call to Frances and the injury to Ian (15 marks)

- Ellen's phone call could be treated as an assault, perhaps even assault occasioning ABH. Since *Burstow*, *Ireland* and *Constanza* (all 1997) it is possible to commit assault by words alone, including telephone calls, provided that the victim is placed in fear of immediate harm. This is satisfied if the victim does not know what the caller is going to do next (*Constanza*). Since *Chan-Fook* (1994) it is possible to be liable for s.47 ABH even where the only injuries incurred are psychological, although there should be psychiatric evidence (*Morris* [1998]). Ellen must have the *mens rea*, either intent or *Cunningham* subjective recklessness.

- Regarding Ian's fingers, Ellen commits s.47 ABH at least, possibly s.20 GBH and probably s.20 wounding. The *actus reus* and *mens rea* elements have been discussed. If she did not realise Ian's hand was in the way of the door then she would not have *mens rea* and would be acquitted.

- Even if she knew his hand was in the way she could plead self-defence. The fact that she was mistaken is no bar to the defence, the crucial element is that she genuinely thought Ian was going to punch her (*DPP v Morgan* [1976], *Williams* [1987]), and that she genuinely believe the amount of force used was reasonable in the circumstances as she believed them to be (*Scarlett* [1994], *Owino* [1996]).

(c) Explain what factors would be considered by the Crown Prosecution Service in determining whether, and for which offence(s), Ellen might be prosecuted. Consider how she could obtain legal advice and representation if she had little money. (10 marks)

- According to the *Code for Crown Prosecutors*, there are two key tests in deciding whether to pursue a prosecution: (a) the evidential test, (b) the public interest test.

  (a) the evidential test: the CPS must be satisfied that the evidence in the case provides 'a realistic prospect of conviction', which means, can it be used in court and is it reliable? Would a jury or bench of magistrates be more likely than not to convict? If the case fails the evidential test, then the prosecution must be dropped. But if it passes the test, the CPS must then look at the public interest test.

  (b) the public interest test: the CPS must consider various factors, which come in two categories – those in favour of prosecution (13 factors) and those against (8 factors). The *Code* states that in cases of 'any seriousness' a prosecution will 'usually' proceed unless the factors against 'clearly outweigh' those in favour.

- In Ellen's case, those factors in favour of prosecution are: (2) violence was threatened (against Frances and her family); (6) the offence (against Frances) was pre-meditated; (8) the victim was put in fear (Frances) or suffered personal attack (Ian). One factor against prosecution is: (2) the offence (against Ian) was committed as a result of a mistake or misunderstanding. Other factors may be present of which we are unaware, e.g. another factor against prosecution could be (7) the accused has already made reparation or paid compensation – but defendants must not avoid prosecution simply because they can pay compensation.

- In deciding for which offence to prosecute, reference would be made to the *Charging Standards* for assault, introduced in 1994.

- If Ellen has little money then she can apply for Legal Aid, which will cover the costs of legal representation in court (magistrates or Crown court, as the case may be). Legal Aid is granted on satisfaction of two tests: (a) the means test (i.e. whether Ellen's financial resources are sufficiently small); (b) the merits test.

- The merits test is based on criteria set out in s.21 of the *Legal Aid Act 1988*, including whether D, if convicted, is likely to face a prison sentence, and whether they would suffer loss of livelihood and/or serious damage to their reputation.

(d) If Ellen, Gerry and Henry were to be convicted of any offence(s), discuss what aims might be pursued in sentencing them and suggest what sentence(s) might be appropriate. (10 marks)

- The main aims pursued in sentencing are: (a) retribution (the taking of revenge, by the victim and society in general); (b) deterrence (preventing the commission of future crimes by people generally, not just the defendant); (c) rehabilitation (reformation of the offender themselves, so as to reduce the likelihood of them re-offending); and (d) public protection (while the accused is in prison they cannot pose a threat to the general public).

- Note the maximum custodial sentences for wounding and ABH, the most likely offences committed by the three accused, are 5 years' imprisonment if tried in the Crown Court; 6 months if tried in the magistrates' court. However, the *Criminal Justice Act 1991* (CJA) requires a judge to start with a presumption that the sentence will be a fine. Community sentences (e.g. probation orders) are also available.

- It will be relevant whether any of them have previous criminal convictions.

- Where an offence of violence is involved, the CJA requires a court to take into account both the 'just deserts' policy set out in the 1990 *Crime, Justice & Protecting the Public White Paper*, and public protection. A custodial sentence may be imposed to protect the public from 'serious harm'.

- Judges typically apply a two-stage tariff system: (1) what sentence is generally appropriate for the offence; (2) whether the sentence should be modified by the presence of various factors, including the age of the accused, previous good character, presence of provocation. It is obviously significant that both Gerry and Henry are only 15.

Question 8

(a) Discuss the criminal liability of Adam and Ben for the manslaughter of Clare (15 marks)

- Ben clearly did not have malice aforethought for Clare's murder, hence manslaughter is the appropriate charge.

- Has he caused her death as a matter of fact, applying the 'but for' test? Is he a legal cause also? He may argue that her stepping back into the road is her own voluntary act thereby breaking the chain of causation. This is answered by the jury using the 'daftness' test (*Roberts* [1972]): was Clare's reaction unreasonable? Frightening the victim into jumping or running away in order to escape with the end result of injuries sustained in the escape bid did not break the chain of causation in *Roberts, Williams and Davies* (1992), *Corbett* (1996) and *Marjoram* (2000).

- Assuming that he is both the factual and legal cause of death, consider what form of manslaughter charge is most appropriate. Constructive manslaughter requires proof of an unlawful, dangerous act. In frightening Clare he may have committed the *actus reus* of assault, which is a crime.

- Ben could argue that he had no *mens rea*, which is intent or Cunningham subjective recklessness. He would use his intoxication to support this argument. Normally intoxication is no defence to a crime such as assault, because it is basic intent (*DPP v Majewski* [1977]), but Ben's intoxication may be deemed involuntary, in which case it would provide a defence (*Kingston* [1995]). Although consuming one alcoholic drink that has been spiked with another alcoholic drink is deemed to be voluntary (*Allen* [1988]), this approach does not hold true when the drink is spiked with a different form of intoxicant altogether (*Eatch* [1980]).

- Gross negligence manslaughter may be charged on the basis that he owed Clare a general duty of care, he breached this duty in a way that a jury may deem it to be gross enough to amount to a crime (*Adomako* [1995]). Again, while voluntary intoxication would be no defence no such a charge (*Lipman* [1970]), involuntary intoxication could be a defence leading, if successful, to a complete acquittal.

- Although Ben did not directly cause Clare's death, he may be held liable for manslaughter on the basis that he procured the offence (*Attorney-General's Reference [No.1 of 1975]* [1975]). It would be no defence to such a charge against Adam that Ben might have a defence of involuntary intoxication (*Bourne* [1952], *Cogan and Leak* [1976]). Although a secondary party, he is liable to be tried and punished as if he were the principal (s.8, Accessories and Abettors Act 1861).

(b) Discuss Daniel's criminal liability for Elaine's death (15 marks)

- Daniel has clearly caused Elaine's death in fact and law.

- Although he did not intend to cause her any harm, he may be found to have malice aforethought under transferred malice principles if it can be proven that he intended to kill or cause grievous bodily harm (GBH) to Adam. Intent may be direct (Daniel wanted to kill/do GBH to Adam) or oblique (he foresaw that in thrusting a knife at Adam he was virtually certain to kill him or cause him really serious injury). In the former case, malice aforethought is established; in the latter case foresight of consequence is only evidence of malice aforethought and the jury should be left to 'find' that he had the intent (*Woollin* [1998]).

- Possible defence of provocation, s.3, Homicide Act 1957, which would reduce murder to voluntary manslaughter. There is evidence of provocation by 'things done' (his girlfriend suffering a violent death; Adam making flying gestures, giggling and punching him). It is no bar to the defence that Daniel may have been provoked by Adam but actually killed Elaine (*Davies* [1975]). Did Daniel lose his self-control? It must have been a sudden and temporary loss (*Duffy*). Although he armed himself, which may suggest an element of control (*Thornton [No.1]*) there have been cases where defendants armed themselves in advance but were nevertheless allowed the defence (*Pearson*).

- Might the reasonable man have lost self-control and done as Daniel did? This is a jury question. Characteristics of the defendant may be given to the reasonable man but we know little about Daniel other than the fact that he has just witnessed his girlfriend's violent death. Is this sufficient for a characteristic? *Newell* decided that characteristics need a degree of permanence; *Morhall* cast doubt on that.

- Another possible defence is self-defence, which would lead to a complete acquittal. Daniel was certainly subject to a violent assault so he is entitled to use (no more than) reasonable force to protect himself (*Palmer* [1971], *Whyte* [1987]). There is no obligation on him to retreat (*Bird* [1985]). Responding to punches with punches of his own would appear reasonable, but his use of a knife may not. The jury have to decide, although they must place themselves in the circumstances as Daniel perceived them to be (*Scarlett*, *Owino*).

(c) Any trials for homicide would be before a jury. Explain and evaluate the role of the jury in criminal trials. (10 marks)

Explanation
- Essentially the jury's task is to determine questions of fact. All questions of law are dealt with by the judge.

- The role of the jury is to listen to the evidence presented by the prosecution and defence and decide whether the prosecution has proved its case (including disproving any defences – other than insanity and diminished responsibility – raised by the defence) beyond reasonable doubt.

- If so, the jury should convict by returning a guilty verdict. It is then up to the judge to decide on an appropriate sentence. The jury has no part to play in the sentencing process (unlike in civil trials, e.g. for defamation, where the jury makes awards for compensation).

- If the prosecution has not proved its case beyond reasonable doubt then the jury should return a not guilty verdict.

Evaluation

This question offers students a great deal of flexibility; academics have written entire books about the role of the jury. The following, therefore, is an indication of some of the points that students could make about jury trials in the Crown Court.

- A major strength of the jury trial is that it involves the public in the criminal trial process. In *Watson* (1988) Lord Lane CJ said that each juror was under a duty to act: 'not only as individuals but collectively. That is the strength of the jury system. Each of you takes into the jury box with you your individual experience and wisdom. Your task is to pool that experience and wisdom. You do that by giving your views and listening to the views of others.'

- It has been pointed out that the importance of juries is more symbolic. Only about 2 per cent of criminal cases that go to trial are heard by juries.

- Juries can acquit, despite the evidence, purely on grounds of conscience (*Ponting* [1985], *Kronlid and Others* [1996]). This may be seen as valuable in that it prevents undeserving convictions; but it could be seen as dangerous in that it disguises what may be unfair laws that would otherwise come to the attention of Parliament.

- Jury trials are much more expensive than trial by magistrates. An uncontested case costs about five times more; a contested one about eight times more. Jury trials are also much lengthier than trial by magistrates, which can lead to defendants spending months on remand and can also lead to witnesses' recollection of the events getting weaker.

- Random selection of jurors produces people who lack the intellectual capacity, education, physical stamina, etc., to keep up with many trials, especially complex fraud cases.

- The jury has to hear and, sometimes, see very graphic and potentially distressing evidence. After the trial of *Rosemary West* (1995), some jury members were offered professional counselling.

- Jury 'nobbling' occurs when a jury verdict (whether guilty or not guilty) is 'tainted' by doubt that the jury was in some way interfered with, threatened, blackmailed or bribed into their decision. This problem led to the suspension of jury trials for terrorist offences in Northern Ireland in 1973. It has caused problems in England too, although the Criminal Procedure and Investigation Act 1996 allows for new prosecutions where 'tainted acquittals' are produced.

(d) Discuss the extent to which the rules of law you have explained and applied in answering parts (a) and (b) above reveal evidence of the importance of establishing fault in criminal liability (10 marks)

Many points could be made here! The following is a suggested list:

- Murder is only established on proof of intent, thus indicating its status as the most serious of homicide offences.

- Unlawful killings that are not intended can only be manslaughter, a lesser crime.

- The law recognises partial and general defences to reflect the fact that people often find themselves in very difficult and/or dangerous circumstances, and as a result do things that they would not otherwise do.

- However, these defences are all subject to fairly stringent qualifications. Thus, provocation and self-defence (as well as duress) all make reference to what was 'reasonable'. The defendant is allowed to avoid liability (wholly or partially) depending on whether he acted reasonably in difficult circumstances.

- Provocation (like diminished responsibility) is only a partial defence, and not a complete defence, to reflect the fact that the defendant deserves some level of punishment (he has, after all, killed another human, albeit being during a loss of self-control).

- Self-defence, on the other hand, is a complete defence (like duress), to reflect the fact that the defendant only did what was appropriate in the circumstances, by using reasonable force to defend his own personal safety or that of others.

- Voluntary intoxication is a *very* limited defence, to crimes of specific intent only, to reflect that fact that the defendant was himself responsible for getting intoxicated in the first place. But involuntary intoxication is much wider, possibly providing a defence to basic intent offences, to reflect the fact that the defendant was not at fault in becoming intoxicated.

C. SOURCE-BASED QUESTIONS: OCR CRIMINAL LAW SPECIAL STUDY (pp. 339–340)

Question 1

- State the purpose of the Law Commission (s3 Law Commission Act 1965), giving details of its rôle (consultation, report, draft bills, criminal code) and discuss its effectiveness.

- Give examples of its work where legislation has been created, for example the Theft Act 1968, Criminal Damage Act 1981, Criminal Attempts Act 1981.

- Consider the lack of any member of the Government having direct responsibility for the implementation of its proposals leading to slowness in implementation of, e.g., the Draft Criminal Code, and conclude that implementation depends upon political will and available Parliamentary time.

Question 2

- State Lord Mackay's definition of gross negligence manslaughter in *Adomako*.

- Refer to other relevant cases, e.g. *Bateman; Andrews.*

- Mention the Court of Appeal decision in *Prentice, Holloway* and *Adomako.*

- Develop the various aspects of the definition and discuss the concept of recklessness previously applied in *Seymour.*

- Recognise that the test for gross negligence is potentially broader than that for recklessness and is clearly designed to cover omissions and is not limited to experts such as doctors or electricians; and comment on the 'circularity' of the definition which requires the jury to decide whether the conduct of the defendant is so 'bad' as to amount to a criminal offence.

Question 3

- Make some statement by way of definition, e.g. where an accused causes a victim's death by an unlawful and dangerous act but without malice aforethought or intention to kill or do serious harm; define the meaning of constructive (built out of liability for another act).

- Define the meaning of dangerous, i.e. such that any sober and reasonable person would regard as likely to cause some harm to the victim, albeit not necessarily serious harm (*Church*).

- Criticise the artificiality and potential unfairness that may be caused by 'constructing' liability for a more serious crime out of another less serious one.

- Consider whether and in what circumstances liability ought to be incurred as a result of causing emotional shock/psychiatric injury, e.g. a heart attack (*Dawson; Watson*).

Question 4

- Give a broad definition of manslaughter by reference to the *actus reus* of causing a death in a criminal sense but without malice aforethought, and identify the *actus reus* of homicide.

- Identify potential charges of constructive or gross negligence manslaughter, defining them and citing relevant cases, e.g. *Church; Newbury and Jones; Bateman; Andrews; Adomako.*

- Analyse liability for constructive manslaughter by reference to an unlawful act, potentially an assault.

- Conclude that Imran's consent would negative an assault (*Lamb*).

- Analyse liability for gross negligence manslaughter by applying *Adomako*.

- Apply the Law Commission's proposals recognising there could no longer be any liability in any event on the basis of constructive manslaughter.

- Consider whether David would be liable under the Law Commission's definition of reckless manslaughter and conclude that he may not be liable.

- Consider whether David would be liable under the Law Commission's definition of killing by gross carelessness.

Glossary

ABH

Actual Bodily Harm. The offence of assault occasioning actual bodily harm is found in s.47 of OAPA.

Actus reus

Latin expression, meaning all the elements of a criminal offence not including the *mens rea*. Depending on the particular crime, this could include the defendant's conduct (e.g. in theft, D must appropriate property), and/or the consequences of D's act (e.g. in murder and manslaughter, D must cause the death of another human being), and/or the circumstances at the time (e.g. in theft, the property must belong to someone else)

Aiding and abetting

To assist in a criminal offence. Aiding refers to providing help at any time (e.g. supplying equipment, acting as lookout, driving a getaway car); abetting refers to encouragement provided at the time of the offence

Assault

To cause another person to believe that they are about to suffer immediate bodily contact

Attorney-General's Reference

A case will be referred to the Court of Appeal (Criminal Division) by the Attorney-General (the government's main legal advisor) when he believes that a Crown Court judge misapplied the law resulting in an acquittal. The acquittal may not be reversed but it gives the judges of the Court of Appeal an opportunity to correct any mistakes for the benefit of Crown Court judges in future cases.

Basic Intent Offence

Describes any one of the group of criminal offences (e.g. manslaughter, assault) to which intoxication is not a defence.

Battery	The application of unlawful force to another person
Butler Committee	A Committee set up in the 1970s to report on mentally abnormal offenders.
BWS	Battered Woman Syndrome. A recognised (since 1994) mental disease, affecting victims of sustained domestic abuse (physical and psychological). Relevance in criminal law terms as (a) an abnormality of mind for the purposes of diminished responsibility; (b) a characteristic for the purposes of the objective question in provocation.
CJA	Criminal Justice Act.
Caldwell recklessness	See: Objective Recklessness
Causation/chain of causation	The link between a defendant's conduct and a consequence. Most often discussed in murder/manslaughter cases, where the issue is whether D caused the victim's death
Consent	General defence, whereby the victim expressly or impliedly (that is, by conduct) agrees to the risk of injury
Counselling	Encouraging someone to commit a criminal offence
Court for Crown Cases Reserved	A forerunner of the Court of Appeal, this court no longer exists.
Court of Criminal Appeal /Court of Appeal (Criminal Division)	Prior to 1967 there were two English appeal courts, the Court of Appeal (which dealt with civil matters) and the Court of Criminal Appeal. In 1967 the two courts were amalgamated into the modern Court of Appeal, albeit divided into the Civil Division and Criminal Division.
Criminal Code Bill (1989)	The Law Commission's proposal to place all of English criminal law (general principles, offences and defences) into one legislative document. The Bill is attached to the end of the Commission's Report, A Criminal Code

for England and Wales (Law Commission Report No.177). Although similar reforms have taken place in Canada and New Zealand, in England the Code Bill remains in draft form, with no legal status. This is mainly due to the lack of political will necessary to push such a major reform through Parliament.

Criminal Law Bill (1993)   The Law Commission's less ambitious proposal to place the non-fatal offences and certain general defences on a statutory basis. It was attached to the end of the Commission's Report Legislating the Criminal Code: Offences Against the Person and General Principles (Law Commission Report No.218). This Bill also remains in draft form, with no legal status.

Criminal Law Revision Committee (CLRC)   An English law reform body, comprising mainly judges and leading academics, specialising in criminal law. Not to be confused with the Criminal Cases Review Commission (CCRC), established in 1995.

Cunningham recklessness   See: Subjective Recklessness

Defendant   A person charged with a criminal offence (the accused)

Divisional Court   The Divisional Court of the Queen's Bench Division of the High Court hears appeals from magistrates' courts brought by either the Crown (appealing against acquittals) or the defence (appealing against convictions). These appeals are known as 'appeals by way of case stated' and involving questions on points of law only.

DPP   The Director of Public Prosecutions is the head of the Crown Prosecution Service.

Duty of care   A legal responsibility placed upon the defendant to act in a particular set of circumstances

GBH   Grievous Bodily Harm. The offence of inflicting grievous bodily harm is found in s.20

of OAPA, and that of causing grievous bodily harm with intent is found in s.18 OAPA.

Ghosh test
The test for establishing dishonesty in crimes such as theft, making off, obtaining property or obtaining services by deception.

Intention
One type of *mens rea*. Comes in two forms: direct intent (meaning desire) and oblique intent (meaning the situation where D foresees a consequence as virtually certain to occur, whether s/he desires it or not).

Joint enterprise
The situation where two or more persons embark upon a criminal operation (typically burglary) together.

Law Commission
An English law reform body, established in 1965, whose job it is to review all aspects of law (not just criminal law) and, where it feels that reform is required, produce reports, including draft legislation. For the purposes of this book, its most interesting reports are *A Criminal Code for England and Wales* in 1989 (Law Commission Report No.177), which included the draft Criminal Code Bill, and *Legislating the Criminal Code: Offences Against the Person and General Principles* in 1993 (Law Commission Report No. 218), which included the draft Criminal Law Bill.

M'Naghten Rules
A set of 'rules' established by the judges of the House of Lords in 1843 to deal with cases where a defendant pleads not guilty by reason of insanity. Although technically not of the same legal status as a judicial decision, they have been regarded as legally binding for over 150 years.

Majewski Rules
The legal principles covering the intoxication defence.

Manslaughter
The unlawful, but unintentional, killing of another human being.

Mens rea
The mental element of any criminal offence. Includes intention, recklessness, dishonesty,

gross negligence. Most offences satisfied with one of these but some require two (e.g. theft requires a dishonest intention) while others require none at all (crimes of strict liability).

Model Penal Code

This is literally a 'model' for a comprehensive, criminal code, produced by the American Law Institute. It contains statements of general principles, definitions of offences and defences. The 50 US states are free to choose whether to adopt all or some of the Code into legislation as they feel appropriate.

Murder

The unlawful, and intentional, killing of another human being

Novus actus

Latin expression, dealing with causation, and referring to any external and independent event, sufficient to break the chain of causation that would otherwise exist connecting D's conduct with a particular consequence

Obiter

Statements made by judges in court that are 'by the way'. They do not form part of the ratio, and are not therefore legally binding, but may be highly persuasive, on judges deciding future cases.

Objective recklessness

The form of recklessness where the defendant may be convicted on proof that he failed to give thought to a risk of some prohibited consequence occurring, when that risk was in fact obvious to the ordinary prudent individual, then went ahead and took that risk. Applies to criminal damage and arson.

Oblique intent

A state of mind where D appreciates that his conduct is virtually certain to lead to a particular conclusion (whether or not that conclusion was desired)

OAPA 1861

The Offences Against the Person Act 1861.

Privy Council

The final appeal court for those Commonwealth countries that wish to use it. Over time, many of the larger Commonwealth countries (including Australia, Canada and

South Africa) have dropped the Privy Council, but it is still used by New Zealand and Singapore, among others. Its decisions are not binding but, because the Court comprises the same judges as the House of Lords, are highly persuasive on English courts.

Procuring

To take steps to enable someone else to commit a criminal offence.

Ratio

The legally binding part of any court judgment.

Recklessness

One type of *mens rea*. Comes in two forms, subjective recklessness (also known as Cunningham recklessness) which requires D to have foreseen a consequence) and objective recklessness (also known as Caldwell recklessness) which requires D to have failed to consider an obvious risk).

Specific intent offence

Describes any one of the group of criminal offences (e.g. murder, theft) to which intoxication is a defence.

Strict liability

Describes all offences where D may be convicted on proof of *actus reus* alone – *mens rea* not required

Subjective recklessness

The form of recklessness which means that the defendant can only be convicted on proof that he foresaw the risk of some prohibited consequence occurring, but went ahead and took that risk anyway. Applies to non-fatal offences against the person and (probably) manslaughter.

Index